Library of Congress Cataloging in Publication Data

Blackburn, Norma Davis.
   Legal secretaryship.

   Includes index.
   1. Legal secretaries—United States—Handbooks,
manuals, etc. I. Title.
KF319.B53 1981   651'.934   80-25691
ISBN 0-13-528927-0

*Editorial/production supervision
and interior design by Natalie Krivanek.
Manufacturing buyer: Gordon Osbourne*

Printed in the United States of America

10 9 8 7 6 5 4 3 2 1

Prentice-Hall International, Inc., *London*
Prentice-Hall of Australia Pty. Limited, *Sydney*
Prentice-Hall of Canada, Ltd., *Toronto*
Prentice-Hall of India Private Limited, *New Delhi*
Prentice-Hall of Japan, Inc., *Tokyo*
Prentice-Hall of Southeast Asia Pte. Ltd., *Singapore*
Whitehall Books Limited, *Wellington, New Zealand*

second edition

Legal
Secretaryshi

NORMA DAVIS BLACKBURN

Prentice-Hall, Inc., *Englewood Cliffs, New Jersey* 0763

Dedicated to
my son
Richard Lindsay Blackburn

and to
my mother
Madge Marie Davis

Contents

PART THREE

PART FOUR

Preface

When I wrote the original edition of *Legal Secretaryship* I tried to cover aspects of procedural law in such a manner that the text could be successfully used in all fifty of the United States. I also tried to create a book that would help ensure a useful, worthwhile course in legal secretaryship.

My success in achieving these two goals has been demonstrated by the adoption of the book in colleges and universities throughout the United States and by the comments I have received from instructors of legal secretaryship, who have indicated that the book has contributed to the success of their courses.

The dynamics of the law, the technological advancements in office machines, procedures, and the dramatic growth in size, scope, and responsibility of the law office have made the updating of *Legal Secretaryship* mandatory.

The basic concepts presented and discussed in the first edition remain the same: For success in a law office, a legal secretary must have good working knowledge of legal language, must be able to maintain public relations, and must understand legal procedure as it applies to the special kind of law practiced by a particular firm.

New and, I believe, helpful changes in the text include:

— updating of the content, including revised forms.

— removal of sexist language. Male students are not excluded by word or implication. There are many male legal secretaries, and their numbers are increasing.

— reference to divorce and dissolution procedure. Dissolution was so new in 1971 that even a reference to it would have been premature.

— symbol change in letter writing. Copy machines today are so utilized that a distinction must be made between carbon copies (cc) and copies (c or copy), between blind carbon copies (bcc) and blind copies (bc).

— suggestions for special assignments given at the end of each chapter. These are designed to involve the student in discovering and adapting local and state legal procedure, style, and wording to course work.

In many of the samples of legal writing and legal documents included in this book, I have used fictitious names for individuals and companies. If any of these bear any similarity to names of actual persons or companies, the resemblance is purely coincidental.

To the American Bar Association for permission to include excerpts from the Model Code of Professional Responsibility, as amended February, 1979;

To the National Association of Legal Secretaries for permission to reprint the Code of Ethics of that association;

To the attorneys, businesspersons, and government officials who granted permission to use quotations, forms, or sketches;

To all of you — my thanks and grateful appreciation.

Norma Davis Blackburn

PART ONE

Part One is designed to acquaint you with legal rhetoric and typing style;

To illustrate the importance of the use of good public relations techniques;

To introduce the attorney, the legal secretary, and the law office;

To enumerate some of the many outside services and agencies that are essential to law office performance;

To present the form and style of client documents, including wills and leases;

To discuss legal correspondence.

1.

Legal Vocabulary and Rhetoric

IT IS HEREBY STIPULATED by and between the parties hereto,
through their respective attorneys of record. . . .
  AND FOR A SEPARATE AND DISTINCT AFFIRMATIVE
DEFENSE TO SAID COMPLAINT, defendant alleges:

In any business or profession, in any area of interest, in sports, in space, in education, skill in vocabulary is essential if one is to succeed in and enjoy a chosen pursuit.

The golfer uses and understands such terms as *birdie, eagle, slice,* and *nineteenth hole.* A stranger to golf would be lost in the special language easily understood by devotees of the sport.

The engineers and scientists engaged in the space program use such words as *telemetry, comsat,* and *glitch* with ease. Communication would not be easy among space specialists without a ready understanding of all of the terms necessary to that program.

In law the same situation exists. The legal secretary with little or no understanding of the legal phrases, words, and statements that are peculiarly legal is truly handicapped. How can one be expected to recognize whether dictation is complete if *here and above* is heard when, in fact, the word is *hereinabove?* How can one be expected to understand the dictation if the word should have been *corespondent* (a third party in a divorce matter) when what was heard is *correspondent* (one who writes or receives letters)? The words *depositary* and *depository* may not be a part of a secretary's vocabulary. How then could the individual know that *depositary* is the person who receives a deposit and that *depository* is where the deposit is placed? With no knowledge of the Latin language and no experience in the use of Latin terms, how could one know that *Henry Smith et ux* means *Henry Smith and wife?*

Legal terminology is not something to be studied solely by word lists. Rather, words, phrases, and clauses must be studied in context, for legal rhetoric is the English language used in a particular manner to achieve a precise meaning.

PREVIEW OF LEGAL TERMINOLOGY

In anticipation of our later study of completed court and client documents, legal terminology will be previewed here in the following order:

- Compound words
- Latin words and phrases
- Words peculiarly legal
- Words with special legal meaning
- Words in series
- Introductory phrases and words
- Sentence length and "that" clauses

Compound Words

Compound words are words containing combinations of words. Some compound words recognized and used by all of us are these: *moonrise, nighttime, daylight, weekend, football, commonplace.* Legal papers are filled with such compound words as *hereinabove, wherefore,* and *whomsoever,* which permit exact reference with a minimal use of words.

"The compound words *hereinabove* mentioned . . ." can mean nothing more nor less than those compound words, *moonrise, nighttime, daylight, weekend, football, commonplace, hereinabove, wherefore,* and *whomsoever,* which are used in the paragraph preceding the one you are now reading.

In the following paragraph taken from a court document filed in the Circuit Court of the First Circuit, State of Hawaii, observe the special meaning of the compound word *hereinafter*.

> That on or about the 12th day of April, 19__, on Puuloa Road, defendant so negligently and carelessly operated his motor vehicle so as to cause it to crash into and collide with plaintiff's motor vehicle, causing serious injuries to plaintiff as more specifically hereinafter set forth.

"As more specifically *hereinafter* set forth" is an economical way of saying "as more specifically set forth *later in this document.*"

The following statement was taken from an original petition filed in the Judicial District Court of Dallas County, Texas:

> A true and correct copy of said note is attached hereto and made a part hereof for all purposes....

Hereto can mean nothing more nor less than *to this document. Hereof* can mean only *of this document.*

The following statement was taken from a complaint filed in a court in New York State:

> Said accident and the injuries and damage suffered by plaintiff as a result thereof were caused solely by the negligence of the defendant and without any negligence of the plaintiff contributing thereto in any manner.

Thereof can only mean *of the accident* and *thereto* can only mean *to the accident.*

Following are other examples of the use of the very special compound words used in legal papers:

> ...and charges made by lessees or by anyone on behalf of lessees or by or on behalf of any subtenant, concessionaire or other persons for the rendition of any service of any kind whatsoever to the lessees' customers....

> That each and all of the above and foregoing acts of defendant, both of omission and commission, were negligent and constituted negligence.

> ...that plaintiff have judgment against defendants, jointly and severally,

for damages in the sum of One Hundred Fifty Thousand Dollars ($150,000.00),
with interest thereon at the rate of six per cent (6%) per annum....

By reason thereof, plaintiff has been unable to execute the sale of the
business and the lease heretofore referenced, has been unable to receive
income therefrom and has been unable to operate the business on said
premises, all to its damage in the total sum of Twenty-Five Thousand
Dollars ($25,000.00).

As a result of the aforesaid negligence of the defendant, the plaintiff was
obliged to expend large sums of money for medical and surgical care, hospital
care and medicines and will be obliged in the future to expend money for such
purpose.

Thereafter plaintiff sold all of its right, title and interest in said lease
and in the business thereon conducted to XYZ CORPORATION.

Among other compound words regularly used in legal papers
are: *hereafter, inasmuch as, notwithstanding, undersigned, whereas,
hereby, insofar as, thenceforth, wheresoever,* and *whereof.*

Latin Words and Phrases

Latin was the language of the Roman Empire and was spread
over Europe by Roman soldiers and merchants. Whereas Greek was
the language of the arts, Latin was the language of government and
law.

Latin has contributed much to the richness of the English language. Particularly is its influence noted in the language of the law,
where Latin words, unchanged in either original meaning or spelling,
are regularly used.

Latin words and phrases are included in the following excerpts
from legal documents that have been filed in various courts throughout the nation:

...said judgment was entered under Rule 20 of the civil rules of this court
as in the case of a judgment by default on a verified, liquidated ex contractu
claim, whereas the action against the defendant herein is actually based on
an unverified claim for unliquidated damages in an action ex delicto, and
therefore....

ex contractu, **from the contract**
ex delicto, **from the crime**

That this is an action in personam in which the defendant was not served with summons according to law.

in personam, **directed against a specific person**

That the court order defendant to pay plaintiff a reasonable weekly sum as alimony pendente lite.

pendente lite (pen-DEN-tē LĪ-tē), **pending litigation; during the suit**

I give, devise and bequeath equally per stirpes to my brother, JOHN SMITH, or his issue, and my sister, MAUDE SMITH, or her issue....

per stirpes (per STIR-pēs), **by representation; distribution of an estate where heirs divide an inheritance that would have gone to one now deceased**

... and that JOHN SMITH, her father, has been duly and regularly appointed and is now the qualified and acting guardian ad litem of MAY SMITH, a minor.

ad litem (ad LĪT-em), **for the suit; for that lawsuit only**

The plaintiff is now and has been for a period of twelve months at the time of exhibiting this petition an actual bona fide resident of this state....

bona fide (BO-ni FĪ-dē), **in good faith; openly; without fraud**

It appearing to the court that the minute order of July 17, 19__, Department South G, does not properly reflect the order of the Court, it is therefore ordered that the minute order of July 17, 19__, Department South G, be corrected nunc pro tunc as of that date by vacating said minute order and entering the following minute order:

Defendant's OSC [Order to Show Cause] re modification of the interlocutory judgment, continued from July 20, 19__, comes on for hearing. A pro tem stipulation is executed this date. Parties are sworn and testify.

The interlocutory judgment of divorce is granted in the following partic-

ulars:

Defendant is granted the right....

nunc pro tunc, now for then
pro tem, a short form of *pro tempore* (prō TEM-pō-rē), meaning for the
    time; temporarily

In the example above, the minute order of July 17, 19—, was an-
nulled or set aside and was replaced by another order correcting it.
The second order was effective as though it had been written on
July 17, 19—; thus, it was written *now for then*, or *nunc pro tunc.*

I served the foregoing subpena duces tecum by showing the original thereof

to each of the following named persons and delivering a copy thereof....

subpena duces tecum also spelled *subpoena duces tecum* (su-PĒ-na DU-sēs
                     TĒ-kim), Latin for "under penalty you shall bring
                     with you"; a form commanding the one served to
                     appear in court with certain items

Latin Words and Shorthand Symbols

Legal language is replete with Latin words and phrases. It follows
that both the newest legal trainee and the most experienced legal
secretary will encounter them in dictation. As with any unfamiliar
word, the legal secretary should write exact shorthand symbols for
the sounds of the Latin words. Both the spelling and meaning of
Latin words and phrases used in law may be found in the legal dictionary, which is a proper and necessary reference book for a law
office. If the legal secretary is unable to locate the dictated word in
the dictionary, the assistance of the attorney should be sought.

Words Peculiarly Legal

Some words and phrases are common only to law. They serve a
special use and permit exact communication to all who are a part
of the profession. A sampling of these words follows:
From a complaint for damages:

Plaintiff complains of defendant and for cause of action alleges:

plaintiff, party bringing or beginning the lawsuit

defendant, party against whom the suit is brought
cause of action, facts or conditions upon which a lawsuit is based

From a complaint for divorce:

That plaintiff has been required to employ an attorney to represent her in
this action, and she does not have sufficient means or funds therefor....

therefor, for it (note the spelling)

From an answer:

In answer to the allegations incorporated by reference in paragraph I,
defendant incorporates herein by reference paragraphs I and II of its answer
to the alleged First Cause of Action, realleging each and every denial
therein contained.

allegations, assertions or statements made in a pleading
incorporates herein by reference, includes by mentioning

From an answer to complaint:

...this defendant prays that plaintiff take nothing by his action; that
defendant be awarded its costs of suit; and for such other relief as the
court deems proper.

take nothing by his action, receive no benefit as a result of the proceeding
deems, considers; determines

From a demurrer to complaint:

Defendant demurs to plaintiff's complaint as follows:

demurrer (noun), a pleading questioning that the pleading of the other side
states facts of sufficient legal consequence to require
further answer or proceeding
demur (verb), to question the sufficiency of the law in a pleading or set of
facts alleged or asserted

From a power of attorney:

To ask, collect and receive rents, profits, incomes or issues of any and all
of such lands, tenements and hereditaments, or of any part thereof....

tenements,   anything that may be held or possessed
hereditaments (her-e-DIT-a-ments),   things that may be inherited

From a power of attorney:

To sell, mortgage or hypothecate any and all shares of stock, bonds or other

securities now or hereafter belonging to me, and to make, execute and deliver

an assignment or assignments of same either absolutely or....

hypothecate,   to pledge a thing without actually delivering possession of it
of same,   of the same (referring here to "shares of stock, bonds or other
       securities")

These special legal words and many others will gradually become
a part of the legal secretary's working vocabulary.

Words with Special Legal Meaning

Many words and phrases regularly used in the American and
English languages have very special meanings when used in legal
rhetoric. We all have *complaints* of one kind or another about the
way we are treated or the way we feel. But in law a *complaint* is
the title of a legal document. *Will* is a word we use regularly in our
daily conversation. In law, a *will* is a legal document by which one
may arrange for disposal of property after death. *Pleading*, too, is
frequently used by most of us. In law, a *pleading* is a court document
that either presents or answers contentions in a legal matter.

Following are excerpts from various legal documents. Observe
the use of the italicized, defined words that follow the excerpts.

From an answer:

...and in response to the complaint filed against them, would make known

to the court and jury as follows:

complaint,   the first pleading filed in a civil suit

From a verification attached to an answer:

I have read the foregoing answer and know its contents. The same is true

of my own knowledge except as to those matters which are therein....

answer,   a legal document that answers the allegations of the complaint or
       first petition

Legal Vocabulary or

From a petition for sale of securities:

...that notice of sale be dispensed be proper in the premises.

premises, that which precedes;

Also from a petition for sale

Article Tenth of decedent's will give the power to sell all or any of the assets of decedent's estate, without notice, upon such terms and at such prices and in such manner as she deems advisable.

will, a legal document by which one disposes of property after death

From a petition for probate of will:

Comes now your petitioner and makes application for the probate of a certain instrument in writing, dated August 26, 19__, alleged to be the last will and testament of said MARY ALICE SMITH, deceased.

instrument, a written document

From an answer to complaint for damages:

Defendants pray that plaintiff take nothing by reason of this suit, that the defendant be discharged, and that they go hence with their costs without day, and for all such other and further relief, both general and special, at law and in equity, to which they may show themselves justly entitled, for which they will in duty bound forever pray.

pray, ask; seek relief
without day, no time is fixed for a subsequent meeting

From a lease agreement:

...the lessor and lessee have executed these presents the day and year first above written.

executed, completed; made (a contract is executed when it is signed, sealed, and delivered) *presents*,   the present document or instrument

From a plaintiff's original petition:

...and that upon final hearing hereof, the plaintiff do have and recover judgment against the defendant in the sum of Three Thousand Eight Dollars ($3,008.00), together with....

judgment (note spelling),   official decision of the court

From a petition for probate of will:

...that at the time of his death, said WILLIAM HENRY JONES was seized and possessed of real and personal property of an estimated value of....

seized,   owned; possessed

From a complaint for divorce:

That plaintiff has been required to employ counsel to represent her in this action, and she does not have sufficient means or funds therefor, and defendant is able to pay a reasonable sum for plaintiff's attorney's fees and costs herein.

counsel,   attorney
action,   court proceeding

Words in Series

Words in series —all similar in meaning, but each different from the other in its fine or precise meaning—are regularly used in legal documents to close possible legal loopholes and to assure complete and exact meaning of the statement.

Punctuation

Punctuation used in business documents and that used in legal documents differ in some respects. However, the goal of both systems of punctuation is to assure clear communication.

A series of words in business writing usually includes a comma before the final *and* or *or* in the series. Example: *Reports, letters, and manuscripts were carelessly strewn across the table.*

Series of words in legal documents usually omit the comma before the final *and* or *or* in a series. Example: *Reports, letters and manuscripts were carelessly. . . .*

Other examples of the use of this style of punctuation in legal writing are given in this chapter. Most law offices use this usual, distinctive legal style in punctuating words or phrases in a series. Some offices, however, have begun using the business style of punctuating series of words.

NOTE: For clarity, in the event a legal question should arise over the exact meaning of a written statement, it is important that one style or the other always be used by a law firm. If the comma is preferred before the final *and* or *or* in a series, it should *always* be used; if not, it should *never* be used. Consistency in punctuation style will protect the legal secretary and will remove that moment of question regarding whether or not to add the comma.

The following examples of words and phrases in series are offered for three reasons:

1. To show the omission of the comma before the final *and* or *or* in a series
2. To acquaint you with legal terminology
3. To challenge you to observe the spelling of the words and to study the meaning of the statements

The excerpts are from legal documents titled as indicated:
From a cross-complaint:

That cross-complainant and cross-defendant be enjoined and restrained from molesting, injuring, striking, harassing or committing any acts of violence against the person of the other.

From an interlocutory decree of divorce:

That the care, custody and control of the minor child of the parties hereto be awarded to the plaintiff with reasonable rights of visitation granted to the defendant.

From an answer to complaint:

Comes now the defendant and admits, denies and alleges as follows, to wit:

From a notice of appeal:

...and that a reporter's transcript of the testimony offered or taken; evidence offered or received; and all rulings, acts or statements of the court and all objections or exceptions of counsel and all matters to which the same relate be made up and prepared.

From a judgment:

The said XYZ CORPORATION, a corporation, be, and it is hereby, excluded from any and all offices, franchises or corporate rights in the state of....

From plaintiff's original petition:

...that the court forthwith issue its temporary restraining order, without notice, restraining the defendant from selling, disposing of, encumbering or secreting the property of plaintiff and defendant.

From a last will and testament:

I direct that all legacy, succession, inheritance, transfer and estate taxes, levied or assessed upon or with respect to any property which is included as part of my gross estate for the purpose of any such tax, shall be paid by my executor out of my estate as an expense of administration.

From a last will and testament:

All the rest, residue and remainder of my estate, both real and personal, of whatsoever kind and character and wheresoever situated, I hereby give, devise and bequeath to my husband....

From a petition for change of name:

Your petitioner represents that he is not indebted to anyone at this time and that he is not changing his name for the purpose of cheating, delaying or defrauding his creditors or anyone.

From the minutes of the first stockholders' meeting of a new corporation:

Upon motion duly made, seconded and unanimously passed, the designation of the directors in the Articles of Incorporation to serve for the ensuing year and until their successors are duly elected was ratified, approved and confirmed.

Introductory Phrases and Words

In law, visible recognition of introductory, closing, or special paragraphs in legal documents is accomplished by typing the introductory few words of such paragraphs in all caps. Some such phrases follow:

WITNESS:

That for and in consideration of the sum of Ten Dollars ($10.00) cash in hand paid, and other good and valuable consideration, receipt of which is hereby acknowledged, the parties of the first part hereto do hereby grant, bargain, sell and convey to the party of the second part....

COMES NOW plaintiff, MARY JANE SMITH, and complains of defendant as follows:

FOR VALUABLE CONSIDERATION, plaintiff has transferred and assigned unto defendant corporation and its assigns that certain judgment....

YOU AND EACH OF YOU WILL EACH TAKE NOTICE that defendant hereby appeals to the....

NOTICE IS HEREBY GIVEN that on....

FURTHER NOTICE IS HEREBY GIVEN that said defendant....

THIS AGREEMENT, made and entered into this 30th day of May, 19__, by and between....

WHEREFORE, this defendant prays that plaintiff take nothing by his action; that defendant be awarded its costs of suit; and for such other relief as the court deems proper.

IT IS HEREBY STIPULATED by and between the parties hereto and their respective counsel that the Office of the Court Trustee shall suspend enforcement proceedings relative to the payment of child support payments as ordered herein.

IT IS FURTHER HEREBY STIPULATED by and between the parties hereto and their respective counsel that plaintiff may at any time cause enforcement proceedings to be initiated and....

YOU ARE HEREBY ORDERED to appear before the judge presiding in the above entitled proceeding in the Judiciary Building, Honolulu, Hawaii....

YOU ARE FURTHER ORDERED to bring with you such payroll statements, tax returns or other records under your control reasonably necessary to verify your income, expenses, assets and liabilities.

IT IS HEREBY ORDERED, ADJUDGED AND DECREED that the findings and recommendations of the referee be and they are hereby confirmed and adopted as the adjudication of the court; and, pursuant to said findings and recommendations....

IT IS HEREBY FURTHER ORDERED, ADJUDGED AND DECREED as follows:

KNOW ALL MEN BY THESE PRESENTS:

TO WHOM IT MAY CONCERN:

IN WITNESS WHEREOF, the above bounden principals and surety have hereunto set their hands and seals this 23rd day of November, 19__.

WHEREAS, the above named plaintiffs have commenced the above entitled action in the....

NOW, THEREFORE, the condition of this obligation is such that if the above named principals shall pay all costs that may be adjudged or awarded against them in said action....

This distinctive use of all caps for these and other introductory words and phrases is good legal style.

Sentence Length and "That" Clauses

In law, it is the rule rather than the exception to use very long sentences and "that" clauses. As we move from legal document to legal document in this volume, it will become apparent that sentences and clauses may be any length — from less than one line to half a page or more in length. No matter the length, however, the statements will always make good sense. To be certain that the transcription is correct, the legal secretary must understand

- The meaning to be communicated
- Punctuation principles
- Spelling

The first of the legal rhetoric paragraphs that follow consists of several short sentences. The second paragraph is one very long "that" clause.

It is true that an automobile collision occurred at the approximate time and place stated in the complaint, involving the parties named in this suit. The charges against defendant are denied as false. The allegations of the complaint are generally denied, and defendant asks that plaintiff be required to make strict proof by a preponderance of credible evidence as required by law.

That the Honorable Commissioner heretofore, namely on or about June 1, 19__, granted his permit to applicant authorizing the issuance and sale of securities; that said permit is due to expire on May 31, 19__; that said permit authorized the issuance and sale of applicant's unsecured seven per cent (7%) per annum notes of an aggregate principal amount of not to exceed Five Hundred Thousand Dollars ($500,000.00) at the principal value thereof; that applicant has issued and sold, pursuant to the terms of said permit, its unsecured seven per cent (7%) per annum notes only of an aggregate principal and not to exceed Three Hundred Fifty Thousand Dollars ($350,000.00); that applicant desires to sell and issue the remaining One Hundred Fifty Thousand Dollars ($150,000.00) of said notes and apply the proceeds received from the sale thereof for the uses and purposes recited in the original application of applicant filed with the Commissioner of Corporations; that said notes to be sold will be in the same form and bear the same maturity dates as set forth in the original application and will be sold in the same manner.

Observe the use of semicolons between the "that" clauses. Without the "thats" each clause would be a complete sentence. The "thats" and the semicolons bind the several statements together.

> It appearing to the satisfaction of the Court that due notice of
> the time and place of said hearing has been given in the manner and for the
> time required by law and no person appearing to except to or contest said
> account; and it appearing that no special notice has been requested, the
> court, after hearing the evidence, finds that all of the statements in the
> said Account, Report and Petition are true and correct; that said conservator
> has in her hands belonging to said estate as of October 15, 19__, assets
> consisting of cash in the total sum of $8,322.45; that said conservator
> should be allowed the sum of $250.00 for her services as conservator; that
> she should be allowed reimbursement to herself for the sum of $145.53 as and
> for costs of administration advanced by her from her personal account; that
> HENRY SMITH, attorney for said conservator, should be allowed the sum of
> $300.00 for services rendered to the conservator in these conservatorship
> proceedings; that he should be reimbursed for his costs of administration
> expended by him in the sum of $14.15; and good cause appearing therefor....

In the above excerpt from a court order, figures alone — not words and figures — are used for the money amounts. This is accepted style in many areas of the country.

In the following excerpt from an answer, money amounts are written in both words and figures. Make note of the typing style used.

> Answering paragraph VII, these answering defendants allege that
> Five Thousand Dollars ($5,000.00) was paid by them on February 20, 19__;
> that at the time of making such payment they requested of plaintiff's
> collecting agent, ABC BANK AND TRUST COMPANY, that they be allowed to prepay
> interest to May 1, 19__, and to postpone payment of the balance of Eight
> Thousand Dollars ($8,000.00) principal installment due February 1, 19__,
> until May 1, 19__; that these defendants did not receive any reply to such
> request and did not receive any demand, either from the plaintiff or from
> plaintiff's collecting agent, for the balance of the installment of
> principal which became due and payable on February 1, 19__; and that, based

on plaintiff's failure to respond to defendants' request for modification
and based on plaintiff's failure to demand payment of the balance of
principal installment due on February 1, 19__, these defendants reasonably
assumed that their request for modification had been granted.

Understanding Legal Rhetoric

It is the legal secretary's responsibility to understand what is to
be communicated in the documents that are prepared. Correct communication can be accomplished only if the secretary spells the
legal words and phrases correctly, understands their meanings, and
punctuates correctly so as to express the meaning intended by the
dictator.

Legal rhetoric is complicated. It is so complicated that unless
the secretary understands the contents, a word, phrase, line, or
several lines might inadvertently be omitted. The omission might not
be discovered until some time later when a lawsuit resulted from
such carelessness.

Learning Legal Language

Learning legal language is a matter of reading, rereading, and
working with legal documents. It is possible to copy, with no understanding, page after page of legal jargon. It is also possible to copy
those pages with care and attention. The latter method will help to
imprint terms and spelling on the "computer tapes" we call our
memories.

In this volume, the study of legal language will be approached
through the legal documents themselves rather than by word and
phrase lists. When the terms have begun to take on a friendly appearance, you will know you are beginning to think like a legal secretary!

Helping Yourself to Good Spelling

Helping yourself to good spelling is a matter of personal application and training. As you copy legal rhetoric, look intently at the
copy. See the spelling. See the two r's in *demurrer*. See that *counsel*
means attorney, and spell it ever after with an *sel*. The other *council*
means a body of people — city coun*cil*.

Use mnemonics: *Principal* — he's your pal. *Defendant* — he's an
ant. (Ridiculous, but the more ridiculous the mnemonic, the greater
the help sometimes.) *Decedent* — all *e*'s. *Therefor* — *for* it. With this

word you must study the meaning of the entire sentence before typing the word; *therefor* and *therefore* are not synonymous.

SUMMARY

Learning the vocabulary of the law is perhaps the most difficult and the most vital task of the legal secretary. For study purposes, legal terminology has been grouped as follows:

Compound words are those words peculiar to law that are composed of two or more words. Examples follow:

whomsoever	*hereinbefore*
therein	*hereto*
heretofore	*thenceforth*

Latin words and phrases are abundant in the language of the law. Examples follow:

in personam	*subpena duces tecum*
pendente lite	*ad litem*
nunc pro tunc	*per stirpes*

Words peculiarly legal are those words used in law and only in law, as *right tackle* is used only in football and as *shortstop* is used only in baseball. Some such legal words follow:

plaintiff	*defendant*
demur	*demurrer*
hypothecate	

Words with special legal meaning may also be commonplace words in our everyday language. Examples follow:

complaint	*answer*
will	*instrument*
executed	*presents*

Words in series are punctuated without a comma before the final *and* in the series. An example of this punctuation follows:

all of the *rest, residue and remainder* of my property. . . .

Introductory phrases and words of certain legal paragraphs are typed in all caps. This style of typing is distinctively legal. Some such phrases follow:

IN WITNESS WHEREOF	WHEREFORE
WHEREAS	NOW, THEREFORE

Sentence length varies greatly in legal documents, and correct legal style includes short and long sentences and "that" clauses. No matter the length, however, all statements must communicate a specific and complete meaning.

SUGGESTED SPECIAL ASSIGNMENTS

These special assignments are exercises in straight copy typing and in proofreading — two basic skills of a successful legal secretary.

1. Select any of several legal statements, paragraphs, or sentences included in Chapter 1 that together will total two typewritten pages. Prepare one copy using one-inch (top, bottom, left, and right) margins and one-inch paragraph indentions. Double space. Proofread for accuracy in spelling, style, and punctuation. In pencil, underscore the following:

   a. compound words
   b. Latin words and phrases
   c. words in series
   d. words and phrases typed in ALL CAPS

2. Type two pages of a legal document you may have found in a legal typing book, a form file in a law library, a law office, your personal papers, or Part Four of this textbook. Use the typing style suggested in problem 1. Underscore items *a* through *d* above.

2

Public
Relations

Businesses large and small, government agencies, colleges, universities, and school districts have public relations departments. Public relations directors are the professionals who are responsible for creating and maintaining desirable public images for their institutions. The new employees who spend days or weeks assigned to an employee training program are learning, among other things, how they fit into the company's public relations picture.

In law and in the law office, image building and public relations are the responsibility of all the office employees. There is no public relations department per se. Each employee of the law firm shares in building the public relations, good or bad, of the firm.

DEFINITION

Public relations is the effort made by business, the professions, industry, and government institutions to create and establish the understanding and the goodwill of the public. Public relations is simply relations with the public. It includes human relations, for in our concept the relationship existing between individuals is an inseparable part of public relations for the legal secretary.

Public relations has come to mean the creation and maintenance of goodwill between an individual and the many publics or between a firm or agency and its publics. Think of this a moment before you read on.

PUBLICS OF THE LEGAL SECRETARY

Who are the publics of the legal secretary? Which groups of people will be contacted? Consider these:

- The office staff, including the attorneys
- Clients
- Other attorneys
- Other legal secretaries
- Court personnel
- Local legal newspaper editors and employees
- Law librarian and library staff
- Bank personnel
- Insurance company personnel
- and the many others who are a part of, doing business with, or representing the law firm

The legal secretary represents the attorney and the firm to all of these publics, whether in person, by phone, or by letter. A courteous, friendly, reserved, businesslike, and helpful posture must be evident at all times. At no time does the legal secretary have the right to be tired, cross, impatient, or otherwise negative in the role of public relations representative of the firm.

The Office Staff

The legal secretary must share the responsibility for establishing and maintaining a pleasant, businesslike office atmosphere. After all, each full-time employee spends at least eight hours a day, five days a week, in the law office. An employee who is unhappy, finds time passes slowly, or is dissatisfied with the work or surroundings does not belong in that office. Employees are hired to enhance, not harm, the office atmosphere.

If one is not able to respect, enjoy, and appreciate fellow workers, another kind of employment or at least another place of employment should be sought. The law office must be a pleasant place in which to work.

Personality Differences

Personality differences sometimes arise, and for no apparent reason. Don't tolerate the situation. Take the first step toward removing the unpleasant feeling. Everyone in this world has some good qualities, even an individual you think you dislike. Search for those qualities and mention them in a casual but complimentary manner to the person concerned and to others in the office. No one can resist sincere and well-meant compliments.

Perhaps you can change the feeling of hidden animosity to one of friendship or at least comfortable tolerance. If you can bring about such a change — whatever the effort — you have grown ten feet tall!

Attitudes and dispositions are contagious. By your attitude you may work your way to one of the coveted positions in the office. If people trust you and enjoy your company, you are on your way to success as a secretary and as a person.

Complainers

Complainers are loners and lonesome. Among my acquaintances is a lady in her mid-forties. She wants company, encourages acquaintances to call on her, yet people shy away. She complains. She complains about her job, about her employer, about the cost of living, even about the weather! Her personal public or human relations techniques are near zero and would, no doubt, be the same in an office situation.

People flock around happy people and happy people flock together.

Personal and Office Problems

An office is not the place for family or personal problems. Keep them at home. And keep office problems at the office. The professional secretary is able to accomplish this very real separation of office and home life responsibilities, whereas the less successful secretary is able neither to recognize nor maintain the separation.

Of course, a secretary should not become isolated. To the contrary, there should be just enough talk about personal affairs to make small conversation — not enough to create a gossiping situation, and not enough to arouse envy or pity among fellow employees. Coffee breaks, lunch hours, and after-hours gatherings are the proper times for friendly discussions of interesting nonoffice subjects.

There is never a time outside the office when office topics should be discussed. Everything the legal secretary hears in the law office is confidential.

When prying neighbors, friends, and relatives inquire about an interesting newspaper item concerning the firm or any member, change the subject. You will gain the respect of even those who are prying. What is more, you will lend importance to your position. By your attitude and actions you have indicated that your work is important and confidential — and no one is in a position to contradict you.

Sharing Good News

Really good news must be broken gently. Why? We human beings are all subject to that ugly emotion — jealousy. The secretary (or anyone) who happily and proudly talks of advantages, special privileges, personal accomplishments, or brags of the attainments of spouse, children, family, or friends is behaving in poor taste. Of course the braggart is happy. But there may be those who are envious, who will do what they can, in a small way, to lessen the braggart's joy.

The watchful legal secretary will casually mention good news, but detailed discussion and bragging are not good PR techniques in an office.

Misfortune and Sorrow

Serious personal problems should be taken directly to the attorney if they in any way affect office work or decorum. If misfortune or sorrow have arisen, it is only fair to inform the attorney. Perhaps helpful advice will be given. At least the temporary personality change will be understood and overlooked.

Small, everyday personal problems that regularly arise in the lives of all of us must be left at home and solved personally.

Treading the Line

The employee who can tread a fine line — communicating with all employees, yet not violating the policy of the separation of home and office — will enjoy office life and will be a stabilizing influence in the office. More and more friendships will be extended. Office hours will be anticipated with pleasure, and professionalism will be a natural development.

Clients

Have you really thought about the clients and just how important the client public is? Without clients there would be no law office. Without a law office there would be no need for legal secretaries. A law office cannot afford a secretary who offends even one client. No matter how efficient, no matter the production rate, the legal secretary who offends clients is expendable.

The legal secretary is not authorized to give legal advice. Yet there are many PR techniques that may be used to assure a pleasant relationship between the law office and the client public. Some of these are

- Anything that can be done to make the clients feel at ease
- Anything, within the guidelines, that can be done to keep clients informed
- Anything that can be done to avoid unnecessary time delays in the preparation of legal papers, letters, and steps of legal procedure

It is important to remember that too much conversation and attention are more offensive than too little. Try to strike the happy medium.

Public relations techniques for creating and maintaining the goodwill of the client public are discussed throughout this volume. As you read each one, you may think of other or better ways to handle the situations. We're all individuals. A public relations technique usable for one legal secretary could be clumsy or useless for another. The legal secretary who is sensitive to and aware of another's "feelings" is the legal secretary who will search for and use the most varied and adequate PR techniques.

Other Publics

In dealing with the many other publics, the legal secretary must remember that each contact made with those publics should pave the way for later and even easier and more satisfactory contacts with them.

Respect, concern, and cordiality are pleasant qualities. Pomposity, brusqueness, irritability are ugly. All can be transmitted by telephone, letters, or personal appearance — and the receiver seldom forgets. Which qualities are part of your personality? Tact, caution, and pleasantries elicit information and favors from even sullen. unwilling publics.

During telephone calls, forget your own emotional state. Put a smile on your face, turn the corners of your mouth up, and the voice reaching the other end of the line will be pleasant. Anyone asking for or receiving information from a pleasant voice is affected positively. Be the one everyone is happy to talk with.

The first, last, and most important PR telephone technique is having at your fingertips and at the tip of your tongue the exact and complete data you wish to give or request. Neither business people nor attorneys have time for a secretary who stumbles and stutters and perhaps even has to make a second call because of failure to furnish complete information the first time. Notes for easy reference are invaluable.

PUBLIC RELATIONS TOOLS

Three public relations tools of sufficient importance to warrant special discussion are

1. Using proper names
2. Communicating — keeping others informed
3. Maintaining confidences

Using Proper Names

Do you like the sound of your own name? Of course. To me and to you the sound of our own names is the sweetest sound in the world. Isn't this enough to tell you that an excellent way to make friends for yourself, your attorney, and your firm is to remember names and to use them?

Using a name too frequently in a short conversation can be a source of annoyance. However, a client will appreciate a pleasant "Hello, Mrs. Client, may I help you?" Or, "Good afternoon, Mr. Client. Mr. Attorney is on the phone and will be with you in a moment."

Mnemonics (pronounced na-MON-iks), from a Greek word meaning "to remember," includes any trick or technique useful for improving memory. Mnemonics may be used to help in remembering dates, facts, names.

Tying a string around a finger as a reminder of some unfinished task is an old but useful mnemonic. Music teachers long ago composed the sentence, *"Every good boy does fine,"* to help students remember that the five lines on a music staff are E, G, B, D, F; and F, A, C, E are the letters by which the spaces of the staff are known.

Any gimmick, any trick that recalls a client's name is valuable. Mnemonics don't have to make sense. In fact, sometimes the sillier the association, the better the mnemonic.

I recall meeting a Mrs. Corroton. Somehow the lady reminded me of a corridor (she really wasn't that big!), and I had no problem calling her by name when she walked through the office door.

Mr. Flowers looked nothing like a flower, of course, but I pictured him carrying a huge bouquet of flowers to his wife each evening. It made a pretty picture. And I was thereafter able to call him by name.

C. Brown reminded me of a boy I had known long ago. His name was Browning. But it helped me remember Client Brown's name.

Repeating a name following an introduction may be helpful in later recalling the name. Using a name two or three times during conversation often permanently imprints the name on the memory.

Jotting a name on a notepad on the desk when a new client enters the office is a helpful name-recalling technique. Later, when the legal secretary accompanies the client to the attorney's office, the introduction of the client and the attorney will be made, using both names: "Mrs. Client, this is Mr. Attorney," or "Mr. Client, Mr. Attorney." The reverse order is satisfactory if both the attorney and the client are gentlemen.

The important thing to remember in making introductions any time, in or out of the office, is to *make* them.

The wise and well-mannered legal secretary will accompany the client to the attorney's office, even a client of long standing, and mention both names as the client moves over to take a chair in the attorney's office. The simple act of introducing the client helps the attorney with the client's name. However, if the attorney has an unusual ability for remembering names, or has already recognized the client, jumped up from the chair, and even started to call the visitor by name, the introduction is obviously unnecessary.

Remembering and using names is a little thing in an office where solving major problems is the real reason for existence, but it is an extremely valuable asset that will greatly increase the stature of the legal secretary.

Communicating

Communication is the process of interchanging comments, instructions, thoughts, and ideas, whether spoken or written. Communication is not complete if it is one-sided. *The interpretation by the receiver is as important as the message of the sender.*

The most severe criticism of communication in an office situation is its absence.

My family and I once stood in line —and some line it was, too. Disneyland had opened, and this line led to the highly touted Matterhorn fun ride. The line moved slowly but steadily. Then it stopped. We, and hundreds of others, stood in place several minutes. The heated attitudes had nothing to do with the warm weather. But Disneyland has an excellent public relations department. It knows the importance of communication.

Nice-looking young people in striped coats and straw hats soon appeared and explained:

"There has been a mechanical breakdown which will be repaired shortly. Please wait a few minutes. The problem will be corrected and the lines will begin moving."

Over and over again they repeated this information as they walked along the lines. Now we were informed. Faces again wore smiles and conversations resumed the normal, happy tones of people on vacation.

Communication and Clients
(Keeping Clients Informed)

Attorneys are almost always busy with dictation, research, clients; or they are on the telephone, at court, or on an errand. It is the legal secretary who must use public relations techniques to make the client's waiting period agreeable.

When a client enters the office, the legal secretary has a choice. The client may be simply greeted: "Good morning, Mrs. Client, Mr. Attorney is busy (or in conference), but he will see you in a few minutes."

Of course this is acceptable. The client will wait.

But another choice is that of *communicating* some information.

"Good morning, Mrs. Client. Mr. Attorney is *on the phone* for a few minutes. I don't think he will be too long. Would you like to read a magazine?" Or,

"Good morning, Mr. Client, Mrs. Attorney is *with another client*. She shouldn't be too long."

Now the client has some "inside" information. He now knows what the attorney is *really* doing. The legal secretary has communicated with the client. He won't mind waiting.

If the waiting period becomes overlong, reassurance by the secretary, "I'm sure Mrs. Attorney won't be much longer," tells the client that he has not been forgotten.

Informed people are almost always pleasant people. Those few exceptions—the unpleasant people—may tax the patience and understanding of the legal secretary. But it is important that patience and understanding are evident.

Incoming Letters and Telephone Calls

Incoming letters and telephone calls that require the attorney's attention should be a main concern of the legal secretary. It is not enough to place the telephone message or the letter on the attorney's desk and forget it. It is essential that an attempt is made to get and send answers.

Attorneys are involved in so many matters, both in and out of the office, that it is not unusual for phone calls to go unreturned and letters to go unanswered, sometimes for several days. This delay is, in part, the fault of the secretary. The conscientious legal secretary will assume responsibility for returning calls to clients *after* the attorney has provided the necessary information and authorization. A legal secretary may not disseminate certain information, but with instructions from the attorney there is a great deal of information that can be transmitted to clients.

Paragraph 6 of Canon 3 of the American Bar Association's Model Code of Professional Responsibility states:

> EC [Ethical Considerations] 3-6. A lawyer often delegates tasks to clerks, secretaries, and other lay persons. Such delegation is proper if the lawyer maintains a direct relationship with his client, supervises the delegated work, and has complete professional responsibility for the work product. This delegation enables a lawyer to render legal service more economically and efficiently.[1]

If the legal secretary, with the attorney's instructions and approval, is able to return a phone call simply stating, "Miss Attorney asked me to let you know that she has no new information, but that she will keep you informed of any developments," a client will have been pacified. The PR value of such calls is inestimable. If the client insists upon speaking to the attorney, this information should be relayed to the attorney.

Routine replies to letters might be prepared by the legal secretary for the attorney's signature. Both the incoming letter and reply should be placed on the attorney's desk. If the reply is approved, the letter will be signed. If not, the secretary will be called in for dictation. In either event, a client will have been served.

---

[1] Excerpted from the *Model Code of Professional Responsibility*, as amended February, 1979, ©, American Bar Association.

When routine letters are answered by the secretary, a note to that effect should be attached by paper clip to the letter before it is placed on the attorney's desk. This informs the attorney that the outgoing letter should be checked more than casually and that the incoming letter should be read. It also tells the attorney that a competent, thoughtful secretary was at work.

Every incoming call or letter requiring an answer deserves an answer. Each has taken the time of the caller or correspondent, and it is a matter of courtesy that it be answered. The legal secretary should assume the responsibility for seeing that the telephone call is returned and the letter answered as soon as possible.

Letters Received in Absence of the Attorney

When letters are received in the office during the attorney's absence from the city, a *short* letter should be typed for the legal secretary's signature informing the writer of that fact. The file copy will be attached to the original incoming letter, turned under the incoming letter so the attorney will immediately recognize that the letter has not been fully answered. The letter and its "in absence" reply will remain on the attorney's desk for later action.

NOTE: If the attorney is averse to constant reminders and to the secretary's answering mail in this manner, such instructions must be followed. After all, it is the attorney's office.

Office Communication

Communication in the office is the backbone of good office management, and the legal secretary is part of office management.

A telephone message cancels a court appearance. That message must be communicated to the attorney concerned, otherwise no real communication has taken place.

Employees are wondering if a certain day will be an office holiday. The moment the decision is made, it should be communicated to all employees. With doubt and uncertainty resolved, employees will resume their normal office attitudes.

Compliments.   Pass on to the ones concerned any kind or complimentary statements you hear. They'll glow. And it's always fun to be a part of such situations. You are now involving yourself in public relations for yourself personally as well as for yourself as a legal secretary.

Gossip and rumors.   Someone is always willing to dabble in malicious gossip. The professional legal secretary will avoid it. Someone is always eager to pass along a gibe or an uncomplimentary remark. The professional legal secretary will fail to hear and will not repeat such statements.

Communication to confirm or deny rumors should be swift. Passing rumors back and forth consumes valuable office hours, and time is money.

General office information to pass to clients. The PR-minded secretary must be highly selective in the information given to clients. That the attorney is on a long-distance telephone call is good information to give a waiting client. But *who* is at the other end of the line is confidential information. That the attorney is in court and will or will not return shortly is good information to pass along. The name of the case or other identifying information is confidential.

General information for office personnel. Information should be given to all employees in the office who would find it valuable and useful. Such information includes

- Changes in court procedure
- Changes in legal procedural requirements
- Additions and deletions to the list of service agencies used by the law firm
- General office information, including personnel changes and promotions, approved holidays, luncheon scheduling, changes in office hours, vacation schedules, special directives concerning workload, and changes in time-keeping and record-keeping procedures
- Client information of interest to the attorneys and secretaries concerned

Maintaining Confidences

The work of the legal secretary is confidential in nature. Paragraph EC 4-2 of Canon 4, "A Lawyer Should Preserve the Confidences and Secrets of a Client," of the American Bar Association's Model Code of Professional Responsibility states:

EC 4-2 The obligation to protect confidences and secrets obviously does not preclude a lawyer from revealing information when his client consents after full disclosure, when necessary to perform his professional employment, when permitted by a Disciplinary Rule, or when required by law. Unless the client otherwise directs, a lawyer may disclose the affairs of his client to partners or associates of his firm. It is a matter of common knowledge that the normal operation of a law office exposes confidential professional information to non-lawyer employees of the office, particularly secretaries and those having access to the files; and this obligates a lawyer to exercise care in selecting and training his employees so that the sanctity of all confidences and secrets of his clients may be preserved. If the obligation extends to two or more clients as to the same information, a lawyer should obtain the permission of all before revealing the information. A lawyer must always be sensitive to the rights and wishes of his client and act scrupulously in the making of decisions which may involve the disclosure of information obtained in his professional relationship. Thus, in the absence of consent of his client after full disclosure, a lawyer should not associate another lawyer in the handling of a matter; nor should he, in the absence of consent, seek counsel from another lawyer if there is a reasonable possibility that the identity of the client or his confidences or secrets would be revealed to such lawyer. Both social amenities and professional duty should cause a lawyer to shun indiscreet conversations concerning his clients.[2]

Paragraph EC 4-5 of Canon 4 of the ABA's Model Code of Professional Responsibility discusses misuse of information acquired from a client:

> EC 4-5 A lawyer should not use information acquired in the course of the representation of a client to the disadvantage of the client and a lawyer should not use, except with the consent of his client after full disclosure, such information for his own purposes. Likewise, a lawyer should be diligent in his efforts to prevent the misuse of such information by his employees and associates. Care should be exercised by a lawyer to prevent the disclosure of the confidences and secrets of one client to another, and no employment should be accepted that might require such disclosure.[3]

Although included in the ABA's Model Code of Professional Responsibility reproduced in Part Four of this volume, these paragraphs are given here in their entirety especially to inform the legal secretary of the extreme confidentiality of law office information.

Privileged Information

Everything a legal secretary hears in a law office is privileged information. (Is the information for public consumption? Is the information available to the legal secretary only because of employment in that office?) Privileged information is secret or confidential information.

SUMMARY

Public relations is the building of goodwill. It is vital to personal and business success. In business, public relations departments and public relations directors are the image builders. In law and in the law office, public relations is the responsibility of all employees.

Some of the publics—that is, some of the groups—the legal

---

[2] Excerpted from the *Model Code of Professional Responsibility*, as amended February, 1979, ©, American Bar Association.
[3] Ibid.

secretary will contact are: the office staff (including the attorneys), clients, other attorneys, other legal secretaries, court personnel, local legal newspaper editors and employees, law librarian and staff, bank personnel, and insurance company personnel.

Three PR tools which will be useful to the legal secretary in developing goodwill are: using proper names, keeping others informed (communicating), and maintaining confidences.

The legal secretary must single out and develop the public relations techniques that can be used most effectively. What is useful for one may not work equally well for another.

SUGGESTED SPECIAL ASSIGNMENTS

1. List and describe ten public relations techniques you believe would be most useful to you as a legal secretary. (Refer to textbooks, periodicals, and corporate or business publications.)

2. Describe an experience, pleasant or unpleasant, that you have had recently in a business or professional office. Whether pleasant or unpleasant, how could you have improved the situation?

3

The Law Office,
the Attorney,
the Legal Secretary

Law office personnel may include messengers, receptionists, legal stenographers and trainees, legal secretaries, paralegals or attorney assistants, law clerks, researchers, associates, and members of the firm. Discussion in this chapter will be limited to the office, the attorney, and the legal secretary.

THE LAW OFFICE

Where but in a law office can be found the problems of birth, life, and death and the myriad problems each generates?

Where but in a law office is an adoption handled one moment, a divorce the next, then a lease involving a modest monthly rental or one running into five or six figures? Where, on the one hand, do two people very new at business begin a partnership, and, on the other hand, experienced or more worldly-wise folk take the first steps in forming a corporation that may one day be not only sizable but of real importance to the economy? Where else can be solved the problems, legal and personal, resulting from the death of a family member or close friend?

The law office, formidable to those unaware of its real reason for being, exists because people do have problems. It continues to exist because those working within its walls are dedicated to relieving those problems.

Specialization and General Practice

Law firms may specialize in various branches of the law. Many firms handle personal injury and property damage suits exclusively. Others handle probate matters, including adoptions and guardianships. Others specialize in constitutional law, tax law, administrative law, patent law, environmental law, civil rights, or any of the many other special areas of law.

Some attorneys are in general practice and handle a great variety of legal problems.

Size

Law offices come in every size. There is the one-attorney law office; the one-attorney, one-secretary law office; the two-attorney, one-secretary law office; the one-attorney, two- or three-secretary office; the law office or firm that houses many attorneys, secretaries, stenographers, receptionists, and researchers, with total personnel well into the hundreds.

The legal secretary in a one-secretary, one-attorney office of general practice will find the day filled with a wider variety of office duties than will the secretary to an attorney who is a specialist in a large law firm.

One-Secretary Law Office

The lone secretary in a small office can rarely be absent. When the attorney is out of town or in court, the office will remain closed if the secretary is not in attendance. The secretary will help in the search for a temporary replacement during annual vacations, sick leaves, or other periods of absence. The legal secretary is not only secretary but receptionist, mail clerk, typist, messenger, part-time custodian, and all-around assistant.

If the office is one of general practice, the legal secretary will be working with and learning law and legal procedure for many kinds of legal matters. This is one of the fringe benefits of employment in a law office of general practice. Because of the many kinds of law practiced, work will be varied and interesting. A legal secretary in this office can become almost indispensable.

Large Law Firm

The secretary in a large law firm, on the other hand, is often a specialist in one area of law. This secretary will know all there is to know about the work of one attorney, who is a specialist. The absence of a secretary in a large office is covered by another secretary. Vacations are scheduled on a rotation basis.

The office manager has the responsibility for arranging for a temporary replacement or a substitute for a secretary who is absent from the office.

The wide differences between the very large and the very small office situations should be studied. Perhaps both kinds of offices should be visited so that comparisons could be made. Personality and personal preference will determine the kind of office best suited for each prospective legal secretary.

Appearance of the Office

Law offices are as different as the attorneys who preside in them, yet they fall into a single mold: conservative, handsome, neat.

The attorney with a light practice will have a small, modest office with limited facilities. As the practice grows, the office will increase in size — both in physical size and in the number of employees — and will take on a more affluent appearance. Clients are drawn to plush, thickly carpeted offices because they are attracted by this appearance of success. Most attorneys, therefore, are sensitive to the decor of their offices.

The law office should appear neat, orderly, and attractive. If the windows have shades, they should be kept lowered or all raised to equal heights. No file or desk drawers should be left partially opened. If a paper falls to the floor, it should be picked up. Magazines in the reception room should be arranged neatly.

It is an excellent public relations tool to provide *current* reading material for waiting clients. If a cover is torn, the magazine should be removed. Ashtrays should be emptied during the day. Cold ashes are offensive to both sight and smell. If smoking is not desired in the reception area or in the offices, ashtrays should not be available and a positive-sounding sign, small and in good taste, should announce the "no smoking" policy.

Other small housekeeping jobs are left to the good judgment of the legal secretary, who must strive to maintain a pleasant, business-like atmosphere in the reception room and all offices in the suite.

THE ATTORNEY

In America, attorneys are also sometimes referred to as lawyers, attorneys at law, counselors, and counselors at law.

In England, the lawyer who conducts the trial is called a barrister. (*Barrister* originated with the word *bar*, which comes from *bar of justice*.) Other practitioners are called attorneys or solicitors; the difference between the two titles is a technical one.

The word *attorney* and the less formal *lawyer* are the commonly used terms to identify the practitioners of the legal profession in both countries. The attorney heads the business. Whether the attorney is alone in a firm or is one partner among many, it is the attorney who sets the pace in the office.

Education

Attorneys have usually had excellent formal educations consisting of at least six years of college or university, including law school. They have also passed the state bar examination, which is a comprehensive test administered by each state to cover its law. This examination must be successfully passed before an aspiring attorney may be licensed to practice in the state.

Characteristics

Law school trains attorneys to note facts and select them from among much extraneous material. If at times these professionals appear preoccupied, perhaps it is because they are deep in thought on new or difficult legal matters. By training they are deep thinkers, direct in conversation, analytical, and close-mouthed. They are also friendly and sociable.

Specialization and General Practice

Attorneys may specialize in particular phases of law or they may be in general practice. Attorneys specializing in patent law, for instance, may refer clients to other specialists if those clients bring in legal problems outside patent law.

Attorneys in general practice, on the other hand, handle a variety of legal problems, which could very well include domestic relations, probate, collections, breach of contract suits, and other legal matters. If warranted, these attorneys refer clients to specialists for those legal problems clearly out of their domain.

Code of Professional Responsibility of the American Bar Association

The code of conduct adhered to by members of the American Bar Association, the attorneys' professional organization, is contained in the Model Code of Professional Responsibility of the American Bar Association, reproduced in part in Part Four.

Read the Code. It will help you understand the duties, responsibilities, and attitudes of attorneys. In addition, you will be reading and working with legal terminology.

Building a Clientele

Attorneys are gregarious, social people. They attend church. They join service clubs. They seek and accept speaking engagements. They are quick to introduce and happy to be introduced. Their names and accomplishments are spread by word of mouth, by clients, friends, relatives, and associates. Acquaintances and friends may become clients; their acquaintances and friends may likewise become clients.

Conservative forms of advertising in the various media are used in the profession. However, the vast majority of the law firms do not advertise. (See EC 2-8, EC 2-9, and EC 2-10 in Appendix A.)

A legal secretary is a part of the public relations effort to build the clientele. If a client is impressed with the courtesy, ability, and understanding of the legal secretary, this professional is an asset to the attorney and to the firm.

A longtime client could be offended by the poor manners or abrupt attitude of a legal secretary and remove the account from the firm. An attorney cannot afford to let this happen. There would be no choice but to replace the unthinking secretary with one more sensitive to the use and value of good public relations techniques.

THE LEGAL SECRETARY

In the law office, the legal secretary is second in importance only to the attorney. The professional, capable legal secretary is all but indispensable. Of course, not every legal secretary fits this description.

Those who do, however, find their services in demand and their capabilities respected. It is they who have placed legal secretaryship at the top of the secretarial ladder.

Title

The aspiring legal secretary may begin working in a law office as a clerk, receptionist, legal secretarial trainee, or stenographer. However, a great deal of actual work experience in a law office is necessary before this office employee can be called a legal secretary.

Because titles are important to all of us, even the newest, least-trained employee in a law office usually assumes the title of "legal secretary." But the *real* legal secretary is one who has training, understanding, and experience in the profession.

Characteristics

The legal secretary must have the personality, ability, and skills of the business office secretary, as well as a liking for and an understanding of the law. In addition, this professional must have the ability to respect the confidentiality of the position and the requirements concerning dissemination of legal advice.

The legal secretary must be able to control the impulse to repeat information. Anything heard or overheard in the law office is confidential. Reporting newsy items to parents, close friends, or other legal secretaries is a breach of confidence and could result in a client's loss of money, prestige, or reputation. This, in turn, would reflect upon the secretary, the attorney, and the law office. It might also result in a lawsuit.

The legal secretary must control the inclination to offer legal advice. At no time may the legal secretary give legal advice. The attorney is licensed to do that. Lawsuits result from incorrect or inadequate legal advice given by persons other than attorneys. One untrained in the law frequently fails to consider all the facts and all the ramifications of the law. The advice may be worthless, or even harmful.

The attorney gives legal advice. The legal secretary gives only such information as is specified by the attorney.

Education and Experience

The successful legal secretary will usually have completed high school and at least two years of college or specialized training in business college. An educated person fits easily into the law firm atmosphere created by the very well-educated attorney who offices there.

The secretary with a four-year college education is even better equipped to converse with the attorneys, clients, and others who compose the law office publics.

Prior business office experience gives a prospective legal secretary firsthand knowledge of office procedures, occurrences, and situations that will be of value in the law office. As a matter of fact, an applicant for a legal secretarial position should have either business secretarial experience, specialized training in a business college, or two or more years of specialized college education; otherwise, preparation has not been adequate. One with minimum skills and education is entitled to and will receive only a minimum salary.

Skills

The professional legal secretary must possess and be proficient in all the secretarial skills, some of which are

- Educated use of the American-English language
- Typing excellence
- Speed in machine or manual shorthand (Required in many offices)
- Training on word processing equipment
- Transcription excellence
- Familiarity with special office machines

Educated use of the American-English language.   This skill is a basic requirement of the successful legal secretary, who must be proficient in spelling, punctuation, and usage. College evening and extension courses offer both interesting and valuable study of the language. It is not possible to take too many English courses. Each adds to the legal secretary's vocabulary and improves understanding of both language and grammar principles.

Linguistics courses that study the language as it is used today are both interesting and informative.

Typing excellence.   The legal secretary is expected to be an excellent typist. Sixty words a minutes is average. A *good* legal secretary types at least 70 or 80 words a minute. Practice increases speed, and accuracy improves as speed climbs. A speed of 50 to 60 words a minute is not enough in this business where a legal document of ten or twenty pages must be produced accurately by a specified time, sometimes immediately.

Typing skill is the one secretarial skill visible and audible to everyone—the attorney, fellow employees, and clients. Make this a skill at which you excel. You will be working on your own public relations. Automatic typewriters play back (type) at rates beginning at about 180 words a minute. However, the *initial* input (typing) is made by the typist. Excellence in typing speed and accuracy is a much sought-after skill.

Speed in machine or manual shorthand. This skill is required of many legal secretaries. Dictation may be given by the attorney or, occasionally, by clients in the office. It may also be given over the telephone, local or long distance. The legal secretary will find that a speed of 120 words a minute is usually adequate. However, the ability to take short spurts at 140 words a minute and up is desirable. It is this kind of skill that earns a secretary the respect of the attorney, which is, in turn, translated into salary increases.

NOTE: It must be obvious that not all legal secretaries type 70 words a minute or take shorthand at 120 words a minute. A shorthand speed of 80 to 100 words a minute and a typing speed of 55 to 65 words a minute will qualify an applicant for the job. However, the sharper the skills the higher the salary that the secretary can demand. The confidence gained by having superb skills is worth all the work and effort required to attain them.

Pressure is ever present in a law office. Perhaps that is why it is such an interesting place to be. Clients who have waited a lifetime to decide to make wills frequently request that they be made immediately because, "We're leaving town this afternoon." What a chance to build good public relations by producing flawless documents — and quickly!

Many attorneys prefer direct dictation, because it is faster if the secretary is able to take fast dictation, and because they are able to check the secretary's reaction to the content during dictation. Two heads are better than one in recognizing brusqueness, insincerity, or incompleteness of thought.

Training on word processing equipment. This is a basic requirement for employment in many law offices.

Word processing is a term used to describe the following office procedure:

a. Dictator, using dictating equipment, records legal documents or correspondence on a cassette tape.

b. The tape is transcribed by a typist who operates an automatic typewriter. A typed copy is produced. At the same time the material is held "in memory" for later recall. The "memory" may be an integral part of the automatic typewriter. Or the "memory" may be a recording card or tape, which may be removed from the typewriter and filed for later use.

c. The typed copy is sent to the dictator for perusal and editing.

d. The edited copy is returned to the typist.

e. The typist produces the final copy by using a combination of the material in memory (typed out automatically at 180 or more words a minute), plus manual insertion or deletion of words as shown in the edited draft.

f. The final copy is sent to the dictator for signature or other use.

Most law offices have word processing equipment. The equipment may be a memory typewriter that retains in memory a limited amount of dictation. Or the equipment may be highly sophisticated with viewing screens, special editing features, and almost limitless memory capability.

A prospective legal secretary should become familiar with the principles of word processing. Some skill on an automatic typewriter will prepare the secretary for possible later use of sophisticated word processing equipment.

Dictating equipment permits the attorney to dictate after regular office hours, at home, or while on business trips. The efficiency of dictating equipment is undeniable when it is properly used by both the dictator and the transcriber.

Transcription excellence.   The legal secretary must be able to type at a very rapid rate, be able to write shorthand at extraordinary speeds, and be able to transcribe machine dictation efficiently. But these skills are valuable only if they produce usable, accurate legal documents and letters.

Papers emanating from a law office must be neat, smudge-free, and accurate. They must be accurate to eliminate misunderstanding, delay, or a possible lawsuit.

Familiarity with special office machines.   This may be the special skill that qualifies an applicant over others for a position in a law office — or an employee for advancement to a coveted position. Knowledge of or at least a brushing acquaintance with the following machines is advisable:

- Word processing equipment
- Any of the several automatic typewriters
- Copying machines
- Dictating equipment

An office machines company or a local college or business college may provide an opportunity for an interested secretary to observe and perhaps briefly use this special equipment.

In-Service Training

In-service training is engaged in while one is fully employed. It is invaluable. The progressive, alert legal secretary, aware of the dramatic changes in office techniques, machines, and skill requirements, has two choices: either ignore them or enroll in classes at a local college or adult school.

Electronic data processing systems and computers are an integral part of our society. The legal secretary who knows something about this special science will better understand why and how it is used in law.

Speech courses will give the legal secretary poise and self-assurance. English and linguistics courses will renew and develop interest in correct grammar usage. Business law courses will have a two-fold result: increase the secretary's legal vocabulary and broaden the knowledge of law. Secretarial courses will sharpen skills. Art, music, and foreign language courses may arouse a special interest that will lead to enjoyable hours of recreation.

Seminars and workshops in legal secretaryship are available in many cities. These are an excellent form of in-service training for the professional legal secretary.

Some local legal secretaries' associations offer special in-service training courses leading to qualification for the Professional Legal Secretary certification test. These courses, together with selected college courses, could lead to that special title, Professional Legal Secretary.

In-service training may be both helpful and interesting to those ambitious many who are legal secretaries. Some may enroll in law courses, with the ultimate goal of practicing law themselves.

Legal Secretaries Associations

In 1929 in Long Beach, California, a group of legal secretaries founded the California Legal Secretaries Association. From this modest beginning of the professional organization for legal secretaries have come many state associations, local associations, and the National Association of Legal Secretaries (International).

Members of the various branches have established for members' use and protection credit unions, group health and accident insurance programs, and employment and other services.

NALS and all branches of the organization are active and alert to the needs of their members. Through this association has come a code of ethics that guides the professional legal secretary.

Members of the National Association of Legal Secretaries (International) are bound by the objectives of this association and the standards of conduct required of the legal profession.

Every member shall:

Encourage respect for the law and the administration of justice;

Observe rules governing privileged communications and confidential information;

Promote and exemplify high standards of loyalty, cooperation, and courtesy;

Perform all duties of the profession with integrity and competence; and

Pursue a high order of professional attainment.[1]

Professional Legal Secretary Certification

The National Association of Legal Secretaries (International) has developed a program and test leading to certification as a Professional Legal Secretary.

To qualify to take the test, one must have worked in a law office for five years or more and have become an expert in all phases of legal secretaryship. The test is comprehensive and demanding. Relatively few legal secretaries have felt themselves qualified to take the test.

Legal Assistant or Paralegal

The title of legal assistant or paralegal is given to those who have achieved knowledge and skill in a particular area of law. For example, one who is able to handle the procedural aspects of a probate matter from its inception to its conclusion could very well be considered a legal assistant. Whether the title is conferred is the decision of the attorney. Court appearances, decisions regarding substantive law, conferences with beneficiaries and other interested parties concerning questions of law are all handled by the attorney.

Legal assistants are drawn from among nonlawyers who have received special training and education that would enable them to discharge a higher level of responsibility than many legal secretaries assume. This relieves the load of the attorneys; the pay should, therefore, be commensurate with the added responsibility.

Duties and responsibilities of legal assistants vary considerably,

---

[1] Code of Ethics of the National Association of Legal Secretaries. Reprinted by permission.

depending upon the size and practice of the law firm. Many offices have developed systems for utilizing this high level of delegation of responsibility and have attracted law school graduates as legal assistants.

Colleges and universities in many states offer courses that lead to a degree for the legal assistant. State certification of legal assistants, where that is possible, serves to identify this position and separate it from that of legal secretary.

Duties of Legal Secretaries

Legal secretaries are responsible for everything not specifically assigned to others. They are many things to many people.

To their attorneys they are secretaries, confidantes, sounding boards, and right arms.

To clients they are their friends, their assistants, their confidantes, and their sounding boards.

To associates in the business of law, they are informants, solicitors of information, authorities, and producers.

From the opening of the office door in the morning until its closing in late afternoon, secretaries are busy. It is indeed a rare law office where the legal secretary is bored from lack or variety of work. Among the duties of these career professionals are these:

- Greeting, helping, and discreetly comforting clients
- Answering the phone and taking and delivering messages
- Placing and making telephone calls
- Taking and transcribing letters, memos, court and client documents
- Searching files
- Filing incoming and copies of outgoing papers
- Composing and writing brief letters and memos
- Preparing court and client documents by expertly using form files, facts, experience, and by following instructions
- Reminding attorneys of appointments and helping them to punctuality (sometimes called "bullying" or "henpecking," but always appreciated)
- Running errands
- Maintaining their desks and their attorneys' desks in neat and orderly fashion
- Ordering supplies
- Keeping legal periodicals and supplements filed
- Maintaining lists of frequently called telephone numbers
- Opening new files and closing and transferring completed files

- Addressing the firms' Christmas cards from carefully maintained Christmas card lists.
- Beginning and maintaining office scrapbooks, if warranted
- . . . and much, much more

One sure sign of accomplished legal secretaries is their ability to obtain information.

For information on:	*The secretary would refer to:*
court cases	court clerk's office
real property	recorder's office or a real estate office
miscellaneous matters	public library
law firms and attorneys	Martindale-Hubbell Law Directory
Social Security matters	local Social Security office
tax matters	tax office or the law office accounting firm
stocks and bonds	an investment company or stockbroker's office
mailing problems	U.S. Postal Service
banking	firm's bank
publication of notices	local legal newspaper
addresses	phone company or city directory

As incomplete as this list is, it still provides some clues as to sources of information. The longer the list of outside sources of information, with names, addresses, and telephone numbers carefully recorded, the more efficient the legal secretary. (See Chapter 4.)

SUMMARY

Law offices come in all sizes — small, large, and in-between. They exist to help those who are in legal difficulties. Conservative, handsome, and neat best describe the appearance of the average law office.

Attorneys and legal secretaries work together to solve the problems of the clients — the attorney doing the research and actual problem solving; the legal secretary producing the paper work and providing miscellaneous information and assistance.

Attorneys are well educated, factual, social, and deeply aware of public relations. Professional legal secretaries have above-average ability and skills. They use the American-English language well and spell and punctuate it correctly. Their function is to help attorneys, to help clients, and to run smooth offices. They are jacks-of-all trades — and masters, too. Their attitude toward public relations is above reproach.

SUGGESTED SPECIAL ASSIGNMENTS

1. Visit a law firm of your choosing — a large firm if you are interested in employment in such a firm, a small firm if your employment interests are with a small firm. Write a two-page, double-spaced summary of your impressions of the office, the office staff, the equipment, the furnishings, and the attorney (if you meet one).

2. Interview a legal secretary. Write a two-page, double-spaced summary of your experience.

4

Extraoffice Information and Assistance

A law office is not self-sufficient. Rather, it is dependent upon a great variety of outside sources for information, assistance, and materials vital to its existence. These outside sources are used frequently by the legal secretary in meeting daily office demands. Sources of extraoffice information and assistance are found both in the government and in the business community.

GOVERNMENT AGENCIES

Government agencies, including federal, state, county, and local government, are important sources of information for the law office. These agencies exist to provide special services or to perform specific functions. The legal secretary must be familiar with those agencies important to the particular law firm. Many are discussed in this chapter.

BUSINESS FIRMS

Business firms are listed in profusion in the Yellow Pages of the telephone directory. It is neither the legal secretary's responsibility nor right to choose one from among the many firms that provide similar services. The attorney will and does select the individual or the company that will perform the service. The choice will depend on any of the following factors:

- Proximity of location (same building)
- Church associate
- Service club associate
- College chum or longtime friend
- Excellence of reputation
- Outstanding efficiency and attention to detail

A business firm with an excellent reputation and offering outstanding efficiency and attention to detail will find its services in regular demand.

SOURCES OF INFORMATION AND ASSISTANCE

The legal secretary must maintain a complete and up-to-date list of all sources of information and assistance regularly used by the firm. The list should be available to everyone in the office including the attorney. A duplicate list should be available at the attorney's desk.

Listed alphabetically here are some, but by no means all, sources of information and assistance, together with some of the services they offer a law office.

- Accounting firms
- Bail bond agents (bail agents)
- Banks
- Court clerk's office
- Department of vital statistics or health department
- Insurance companies
- Internal Revenue Service
- Law library
- Legal newspapers
- Messenger service
- Office sales representatives
- Private investigative agencies

- Process servers
- Public library
- Records or recorder's office
- Stockbrokers or investment counselors
- Title and abstract companies
- Trust companies and departments

Accounting Firms

Law offices frequently use the services of accounting firms to handle law office accounts, to prepare state and federal tax returns, to prepare financial statements, to handle tax aspects of some legal matters, and to take over and solve other accounting problems.

If the legal secretary has an accounting problem or a question relating to the firm's accounts, the accounting firm should be referred to for help and advice.

Bail Bond Agents (Bail Agents)

An individual accused of a crime will be taken into custody. After bail has been set by the court, a bail agent may provide the release necessary to free the accused (defendant) from custody.

An accused person has the right to make certain telephone calls. One call may be used to contact a bail agent direct or to call an attorney. An attorney who is called will in turn telephone a bail agent, who will arrange for the bond necessary to release the accused from custody. The bond guarantees that the individual will appear in court at all times and places designated.

The bail agent acts in the capacity of liaison between the court and the accused and between the attorney and the accused. In addition, the bail agent assumes responsibility for the defendant's appearance when it is required.

The bond premium covers the bond for a year or until the case is closed, whichever is earlier. If the bond is required beyond a year, a renewal fee is charged.

Banks

Banks offer a great variety of services, all available to the law firm, the attorneys, the office personnel, and the clients. Some of these services are

- Checking accounts
- Savings accounts

- Safe deposit boxes (NOTE: They are not "safety" deposit boxes.)
- Trust departments (discussed later as a major listing in this chapter)
- Loan departments
- Miscellaneous publications, including the city directory, telephone directory, directory of business firms, and bankers' directory; and miscellaneous materials that an inquiring legal secretary may find useful.

The legal secretary may be called upon to visit the firm's bank in order to conduct business in any of its many departments. Perhaps an elderly or uncertain client should be escorted to the bank and helped in opening a new account or in transferring funds from one account to another. A client may wish to be introduced to a bank officer, who, in turn, will explain or provide a necessary service for the client.

The legal secretary whose duty it is to conduct law office business with a bank should become familiar with its various departments and all of its services. The self-assurance that results from knowing all of the services of the bank will further increase the confidence and prestige of the legal secretary.

Court Clerk's Office

Each court of law has its own clerk's office, which receives and files all documents to be used in that court. The personnel are government employees. If the court is a federal court, the employees are under federal civil service. If the court is a state court, the employees are usually under state civil service.

All the employees in these offices, including the stenographers and secretaries, have successfully completed the civil service tests qualifying them for their particular positions.

The clerk's office is physically separate from the courtroom it serves. The legal secretary whose duty it is to file legal documents with the clerk of the municipal court, for example, would find the clerk's office for that court located near the municipal courtrooms.

The legal secretary's first visit to the court clerk's office might be accompanied by feelings of uncertainty occasioned only by inexperience. If a candid explanation is made that this is the first visit to a clerk's office, the deputy clerk will be inclined to offer extra information and assistance. The novice legal secretary should observe carefully and learn everything possible during the first visit. The second and succeeding visits will then be pleasant and welcome breaks in the day.

It is important for a cordial relationship to exist between law office personnel and court clerk personnel. On the rare occasions, and they should be as rare as possible, when the law office must request special information or attention of court clerk personnel, a friendly relationship will assure prompt action in the clerk's office.

One court clerk includes in his remarks to various groups of legal secretaries that those in the clerk's office wish to be of all possible help to the law offices. However, he goes on to say, they would like that help reciprocated.

An extreme example he uses is that one legal secretary may call the clerk's office several times in a week requesting identical information. This can lead only to the conclusion that the legal secretary did not make a proper notation at the time of the first or succeeding calls. He suggests that legal secretaries can ease the rush and pressure of the clerk's office by

- Following directives issued by the clerk's office
- Making proper notations of needed information the first time it is available
- Following the rules of the court
- Using court forms whenever they are available

The professional legal secretary will observe the requirements of the clerk's office and help to build and maintain a good relationship between the two offices.

Department of Vital Statistics or Health Department

Birth certificates, death certificates, and marriage certificates may be available from the department of vital statistics, health department, or the records office. It varies from state to state.

Certified copies of these legal papers are required during the course of various legal matters. *A certified copy of a legal paper is one that has been signed and certified as a true copy by the one who holds the original document.*

The department will furnish certified copies of birth, marriage, and death certificates upon request and upon payment of a nominal fee. Certified copies may be requested in person, by telephone, or by mail. There is frequently a waiting period of several days.

Three of the many uses for certified copies of birth, marriage, or death certificates are

1. A life insurance company may require a certified copy of a decedent's death certificate before the proceeds of a life insurance policy will be paid to the beneficiaries.

2. Birth certificates are a necessary part of adoption proceedings.
3. A certified copy of a marriage certificate may be required if there is a question concerning ownership of property in a community property state.

The legal secretary is usually responsible for obtaining copies of the certificates. Sometimes this requires a phone call and a visit to the department to pay for and pick up the certificate. Sometimes it requires a short letter requesting that the certificate be forwarded. It always requires the preparation of a law firm check made payable to the department for the exact amount of the charge.

Insurance Companies

The legal secretary will soon discover the importance of insurance services to the law firm.

Fidelity bonds are written by some insurance companies. They are *good-faith* bonds. It is the law's way of protecting those who put their faith (money or valuable property) in the hands of others. If an administrator absconded with funds belonging to an estate, the fidelity bond would assure reimbursement to those who were to share the estate property. If an employee absconded with company funds, the fidelity bond would assure that the company would recover its money.

Such a bond is required by law before an administrator can act in an estate matter. The bond will be written for the amount of the estate's disposable assets and is not usually written to cover real estate holdings.

A notary public is bonded by a fidelity bond. Many employees, in or out of law offices, who may have access to large sums of money or articles of great value are covered by fidelity bonds.

The bond premiums for the bond required of an administrator of an estate are paid out of estate funds. Bond premiums covering employees in and out of law offices are usually paid from company funds.

Other insurance services that may be required by attorneys, employees, or clients are

- Income protection insurance for attorneys and other employees
- Life and health insurance
- Professional liability insurance
- Property and casualty insurance

A client may seek legal assistance in an effort to borrow money on an insurance policy, to collect the money due the beneficiary upon the death of an insured policyholder, or to have a fidelity bond written.

In each of these instances and countless others, the attorney, and often the legal secretary, will be working very closely with one or another insurance company.

Internal Revenue Service

The Internal Revenue Service is an agency of the federal government. Although the legal secretary may work with the office accounting firm, through the attorney, in the preparation of federal and state tax returns, it may be convenient or necessary to call the Internal Revenue Service for special assistance and information.

The IRS agents assigned to audit tax returns may be working with both the attorney and the legal secretary in connection with various federal income and estate tax returns.

Law Library

Many law offices boast rather extensive law libraries, and law school libraries are frequently quite large. However, the county and state law libraries, supported in part by a portion of the court filing fees, are the libraries that contain the vast number of law books necessary for the attorney to conduct legal research. There is a reciprocal service among law libraries: law books not found in one law library may be obtained on loan from another for a stated period of time. Thus attorneys have access to all law books.

Facilities of the law library are available to attorneys and to the secretaries acting as agents for the attorneys. Nonlawyers may use the law library facilities but usually may not borrow books.

Attorneys may require information from law books and periodicals that are not available in their own office libraries, and they may spend a good deal of time at the law library researching legal problems.

Not infrequently, a legal secretary will act as a messenger between the law library and the office, borrowing and returning law books for the attorney.

As an accommodation to the attorneys, most law libraries have installed copy machines that will produce photocopies of any desired material.

Legal Newspapers

In many smaller towns legal notices are printed in the local newspaper. In cities of any size, however, legal newspapers provide a relatively inexpensive means of publishing the legal notices that, by law, must be published in a newspaper of general circulation. Some notices that require legal publication are

- Notice re change of name
- Notice of probate of will
- Notice that a new business is coming into existence
- Notice of sale of real estate in a probate matter

Many notices require a series of publications. When the required publication has been completed, an affidavit to that effect must be prepared and filed with the court. When authorized to act as publisher in a particular legal matter, many legal newspapers assume the responsibility for preparing and filing the affidavit of publication as soon as publication has been completed. This relieves the law office of this detail.

Legal newspaper personnel are extremely efficient. However, the responsibility for the publication and the filing of the affidavit of publication still rests with the law office. Therefore the legal secretary must check the office copies of the paper to assure that the legal notices are being published. Law office records must also be checked to make certain that the affidavit has been filed with the court.

Legal secretaries regularly talk with representatives of the legal newspaper regarding publication of notices, billing, and various other items of business. A cordial relationship makes the calls pleasant to anticipate.

Messenger Service

Legal papers must be delivered to the courthouse or picked up from the courthouse and delivered to the law office. Registered mail must be taken to the post office. Papers must be delivered to various businesses and to other law offices.

Any and all of these deliveries may be made by office personnel. However, particularly in large cities where distance may create a very real time factor, law offices may make use of attorney messenger services.

Some offices subscribe to a regular pickup service. Others use the service only occasionally. Legal messenger service may prove exceptionally valuable to the law office and, of course, to the legal secretary. Distance, frequency of pickups and delivery, and other factors determine the service charge.

Office Sales Representatives

Representatives of various publishing houses regularly call upon attorneys. These sales representatives are able to discuss with authority the latest law books and legal periodicals. The legal secretary will announce their presence to the attorney. If time permits, the attorney will visit with the sales reps, sometimes leaving a client for a brief time. The attorney is able to maintain an up-to-date law office library by utilizing the services of these salespeople.

The office manager or legal secretary responsible for office supplies will find the advice of the office supply and equipment salespeople helpful. It is they who are selling the newest in stationery, copyholders, dictating equipment, typewriters, copy machines, and other supplies and equipment.

Although a great deal of office time cannot be spent with the salespeople, the office manager or secretary who does not take advantage of their specialized knowledge is being shortchanged. The employer and fellow employees are being shortchanged as well.

Private Investigative Agencies

Licensed private investigators provide a very special service. They may be asked to locate individuals, information, or materials. Some investigative agencies also act as process servers.

If a defendant or witness is evading service, rather extensive investigation may be required before service of summons or subpoena can be made.

In divorce cases, one party or the other may hire the services of an investigative agency. This action may or may not be the result of an attorney's advice. However, if an investigation is necessary in any legal matter, the legal secretary may be instructed by the attorney to telephone the investigative agency. The investigator will receive instructions from the attorney.

Process Servers

In the first divorce case I worked with, I learned a legal secretary might very well be the one to call a process server for service of summons on a defendant. It was at that time that I found a process server's life is not all a bed of roses. It required two nights and a day of almost continuous surveillance of the defendant's apartment building before service could be made upon him. The defendant was obviously avoiding the lawsuit as long as possible!

Process servers are called upon to serve *defendants* with *summonses* in personal injury and property damage suits, breach of contract suits, and any civil suits requiring such service.

Subpoenas must be served on *witnesses* if there is a question as to whether they will voluntarily appear in court to testify at a trial. Service of a subpoena upon such witnesses assures their appearance; if they are not in court at the time specified in the subpoena, they may be found in contempt of court, which is a criminal charge.

Service of a *subpoena duces tecum* assures that the one served will appear in court and bring certain specified documents or other material.

When a copy of the summons has been handed the defendant or a copy of a subpoena has been handed a witness, the process server completes, dates, and signs the affidavit of service (a statement certifying that the document was served upon the named party) and returns the original summons or subpoena to the law office. Some process servers act as a messenger service for law firms by taking summonses (sometimes complaints, also) to the court clerk's office for filing. An additional charge is made for this extra service.

The attorney, or the secretary if so instructed, provides the process server with all available information that will be helpful in locating the party to be served. The quicker and easier the service, the smaller the charge for the service.

Public Library

The legal secretary who makes use of the services offered by the public library may eliminate many nagging minor problems that arise in connection with law office work. Some information is available by telephone, some requires a personal visit to the library.

When back issues of newspapers and magazines must be referred to, they may be found in the periodical section of the local library.

Although correct forms of address are available in the back portion of most good desk dictionaries, not all the forms of address that the legal secretary may be called upon to use will appear there. The librarian will be able to furnish unusual addresses or special forms of address.

Names and addresses of prominent persons, encyclopedic information, spellings and correct pronunciations of foreign or unusual words, and a great deal of other miscellaneous information may be obtained from the information department of the public library.

The inquiring legal secretary may discover other special services available at the local public library.

Records or Recorder's Office

The Statute of Frauds, adopted by most of the states, provides that certain kinds of contracts must be in writing. Included are those contracts that transfer title to real property (real estate). It is not usually sufficient for such contracts to be signed and delivered; they must also be recorded in the official records of the county in which the real property is located.

The records or recorder's office is the official depository for such documents. The recordation service is not free; the charge varies with the location. The fee will be advanced by the law office, and the client will be billed later.

Upon receipt of a document at the records office, identifying information is stamped on it. This includes the time and date of arrival, where the document is officially recorded, and the number assigned to that document. The information permits immediate identification of the document if copies are later required. Most records offices microfilm all recorded documents.

Recordation

A document may be recorded at the records office by sending it to that office with a letter of transmittal requesting recordation, together with a check to cover the recorder's fees. The shorter the transmittal letter the better. It must include only the following:

- The name of the document to be recorded, its date, and such other information as is necessary to identify it
- A request that the recorded document be returned to the law office (or client if so desired)
- Reference to the check enclosed to cover recordation costs

To avoid unnecessary communications, a check marked "Not over $—" may be enclosed. The records office, if asked to fill in the amount of the recordation costs, will do so. Such a check is shown in Figure 4-1.

A suggested transmittal letter follows:

```
Records Office
Blank County Court House
Address
City, State  Zip Code
```

Gentlemen:

Please record the enclosed deed dated February 10, 19__, between Nabor West and Jack Brown Smith and return the recorded instrument to this office.

Also enclosed is our check No. ___ marked "Not over $10.00." Please fill the check in for the amount of the recordation fee.

Sincerely yours,

BLANK AND BLANK

By_____
Henry L. Blank

```
abc
enclosure
REGISTERED—RRR
```

DISCUSSION

1. The word *enclosure* may be used for one or several enclosures. The enclosure notation is to remind the legal secretary that something is to be enclosed before the letter is sealed and mailed. The careful secretary will briefly itemize all of the enclosures on the yellow office copy if that information is not included in the body of the letter.

2. Valuable documents difficult or impossible to replace are sent by registered or certified mail. Such mail must be taken to the post office. Registration or certification assures that a letter will be given special care and attention from its mailing station to its destination. Mail delivery services other than the U.S. Postal Service are also available.

3. *RRR* is an alphabet abbreviation for *return receipt requested.* This refers to a special service of the U.S. Postal Service. For a small fee a signature card, addressed to the law office, is attached to the envelope. When the envelope and its attached card reach the destination, the addressee or agent must sign the card before the letter will be delivered. The card is then returned to the law office. It serves as physical evidence of the delivery of the letter to the addressee.

Certified and certified RRR mail is similar in service to registered and registered RRR mail with one exception: the contents of a certified envelope are insurable for a limited value.

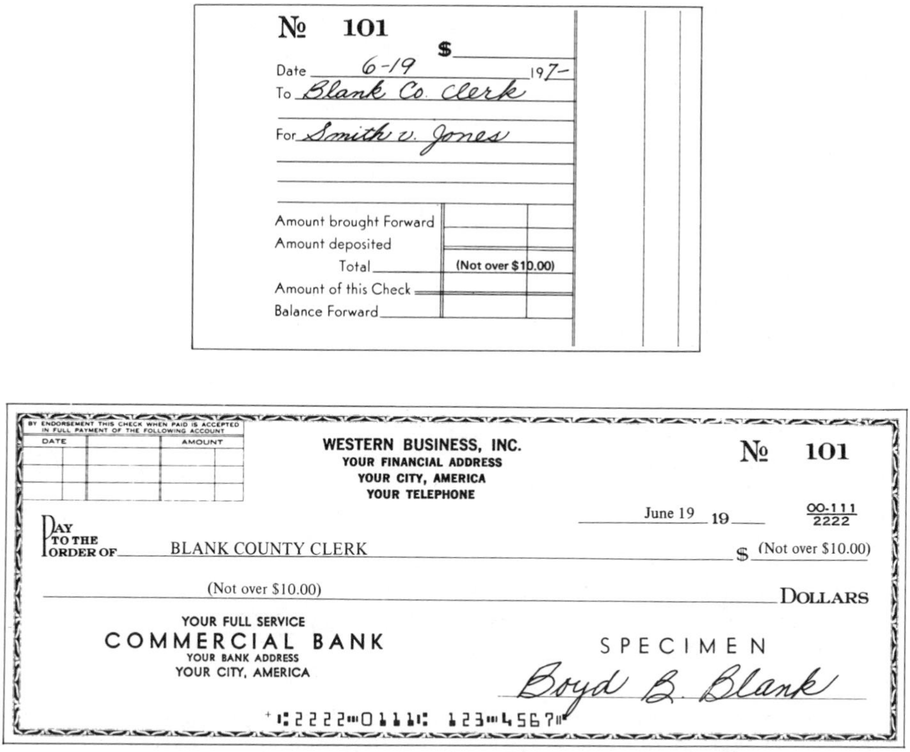

No 101

$

Date _____6-19_____ 197-

To ___Blank Co. Clerk___

For ___Smith v. Jones___

Amount brought Forward		
Amount deposited		
Total_____	(Not over $10.00)	
Amount of this Check ___		
Balance Forward_____		

BY ENDORSEMENT THIS CHECK WHEN PAID IS ACCEPTED IN FULL PAYMENT OF THE FOLLOWING ACCOUNT		
DATE	AMOUNT	

WESTERN BUSINESS, INC.
YOUR FINANCIAL ADDRESS
YOUR CITY, AMERICA
YOUR TELEPHONE

No **101**

_____June 19__ 19____ $\frac{OO-111}{2222}$

PAY
TO THE
ORDER OF_____ BLANK COUNTY CLERK _____ $ (Not over $10.00)

(Not over $10.00)   DOLLARS

YOUR FULL SERVICE
COMMERCIAL BANK
YOUR BANK ADDRESS
YOUR CITY, AMERICA

SPECIMEN

Boyd B. Blank

⑈2222⑈0111⑈ 123⑈4567⑈

FIGURE 4-1   Check stub and signed check marked "Not over $10.00."

SOURCE: Ritter Division of Litton Industries, Los Angeles, California. Printed by permission

Return Notation on Document

On the document to be recorded—preferably on the back of the legal cover if attached, or on the reverse of the document if it is a form, or on the face of the instrument if it is a typed paper with no legal cover—should be typed this information

> When recorded return to:
> Law Office
> Address
> City, State ZIP code

When the document has been returned to the law office, the legal secretary should immediately conform the office copy to show the complete recordation information, including time, date, document number, and book and page of recordation. The legal instrument is then ready for transmittal to its ultimate destination — usually the client.

Documents Usually Recorded

Some of the papers recorded with the records office are

- Deeds
- Judgments
- Mortgages
- Contracts
- Liens
- Federal tax liens
- Birth certificates
- Death certificates
- Marriage licenses
- Separation reports of servicemen
- Certificates of armed services discharge
- Final decrees of divorce or marriage dissolution
- Decrees of distribution in estate matters

Once recorded, these papers are all matters of public record. For a fee, copies of recorded instruments may be obtained by anyone requesting them, including, of course, law firms.

Stockbrokers or Investment Counselors

Very early in my career as a legal secretary, I was typing an estate inventory that consisted almost entirely of common stocks. (Later I learned that the value of the stock at date of death of the owner was in the neighborhood of a quarter of a million dollars.) At that time I knew nothing more about common stocks than that they existed. I had before me an estate inventory showing that the decedent had owned shares of common stock in over thirty different companies. Further, in view of the relatively low cash balances in the checking and savings accounts, it was obvious that some of the stocks would have to be sold to pay estate expenses and provide money for the specific money bequests.

The attorney carefully explained the procedure that would be followed in handling these investments. The able and cooperative assistance of a stockbroker was a major ingredient of the procedure. With the broker's help, no problems were experienced in either selling stocks or transferring the remaining stocks to the residuary legatee.

Title and Abstract Companies

Title and abstract companies are in the business of searching, examining, and insuring titles to real property.

If a legal matter involves real property, the services of a title or abstract company may be required. The company searches records of the county records office to ascertain the chain of title to the real property located in that county. It examines the title and uncovers "clouds," which are flaws to clear title. *Fee simple* is the legal term used to signify clear or absolute title or ownership to real property. (Liens, which are charges or encumbrances against real property, are among the clouds that may be discovered.)

The company insures title to real property. Unlike other insurance, which extends from the policy date into the future, title insurance extends from the policy date into the past. It insures that no previous, undiscovered owner or lienholder can declare an interest in and to the real property.

Those law firms that handle complex real estate transactions or the transfer of real property by sale or inheritance will frequently require the services of title or abstract companies.

Trust Companies and Trust Departments

An elderly lady called at the law office one day. She had no near relatives, had inherited a good deal of money, and wished to make her will leaving all her property to her alma mater. She wondered about naming a bank or trust company rather than a friend to act as executor.

I learned then that corporations sometimes are named executors because of their longevity (a corporation does not die), impersonality, and experience in such capacity. Later, I learned also that corporate executors are experienced in selling property and in making estate accountings. Further, they are always available for signatures and assistance when required.

Trust departments also act as

- Administrators
- Administrators with will annexed
- Conservators
- Guardians

- Investment management agencies
- Life insurance trustees
- Trustees in *living* trusts (a living trust is one that functions while the trustor is still alive)
- Trustees in testamentary trusts (a testamentary trust is created by a will when it is probated)

SUMMARY

A law office is not sufficient unto itself. It relies upon many outside sources for information and assistance. These outside sources available to law firms are a necessary part of legal machinery. The legal secretary must rely on them for special information and assistance.

The law office that uses good public relations techniques in all its associations with service agencies will find information and assistance readily given.

It is the legal secretary's responsibility to maintain a pleasant relationship with each source of extraoffice information and assistance and to reciprocate favors whenever legally possible.

SUGGESTED SPECIAL ASSIGNMENTS

1. Visit your local records or recorder's office. If possible, obtain a copy of the stamped information used to record documents. Write a one-page, single-spaced paper describing your experience. Attach a copy of the stamped information or state the data included on the stamp.

2. Interview a process server or a bail bond agent. Write a one-page, single-spaced report of your interview. Include a description of the services performed by the individual or office.

3. Visit a trust company or a trust department of a bank. Write a one-page, single-spaced report of your experience. Include a discussion of the services offered by the institution.

5

Client
Documents

The legal secretary's day is filled with legal documents. Some are for the use of the client; these will be referred to as client documents. Some are for the use of the courts; these will be referred to as court documents. (Court documents are discussed in Chapter 11.)

Client documents are those legal papers prepared primarily for the use of the client. Originals and necessary extra copies of client documents, when completed, are given to the client. (Copies of anything and everything originating in a law office are retained in the law office files.)

Included among client documents are wills, leases, powers of attorney, agreements, contracts, transfers of title to property, resolutions, and many others.

APPEARANCE OF CLIENT DOCUMENTS

Pica or equivalent type is used in the preparation of all legal documents. Client documents follow a particular pattern in their preparation, appearance, and mechanical details; and they must be accurate, complete, neat, and attractive.

The attorney is responsible for the substantive contents of the documents and is also responsible for the accuracy of the completed product. However, the legal secretary is responsible for the appearance and also for spelling, punctuation, and other mechanical details.

Paper

Good quality, plain, erasable legal paper (8½ by 13 inches) is used in most jurisdictions. From the secretary's point of view the long paper is practical for many reasons. The extra length permits more typing to the page, thus fewer pages need be handled when the completed document is assembled. Fewer pages need be inserted into the typewriter or into the copying machine, saving time. Closing paragraphs, date lines, and necessary signature and title lines sometimes require considerable space; with planning, legal-size paper usually permits all the data to be included on one page.

The lengthy descriptive clauses included for the client's protection result in long, wordy documents. Such documents typed on legal-size paper are less bulky than the same documents would be if they were prepared on letter-size paper. Nevertheless, there are some who advocate the use of letter-size paper for all legal documents; and some jurisdictions have adopted the use of letter-size paper.

In microfilming court documents and various legal instruments for permanent records, two exposures or shots are necessary to record a sheet of 8½- by 13-inch paper. Only one exposure is required to record a sheet of 8½- by 11-inch paper. This could be a major consideration in determining whether a jurisdiction will adopt letter-size paper for court use.

If the change should be adopted in your jurisdiction, be among the first to learn of it. Be prepared for the change. Do not be caught with a large supply of legal-size paper and with a negligible supply of the new, short length. The change may never come to pass in your area — but be aware that there is the possibility that in your state letter-size paper may be required for all legal documents.

Law Office Heading

Just as a firm's stationery carries a letterhead identifying the firm and furnishing the address and telephone number, so also is the firm's legal paper identified. The heading is small, complete (including firm name, address, ZIP code, and telephone number), and usually located in the margin area near the upper or lower left-hand corner of the paper.

The heading immediately identifies the law office that prepared the document. Thus, the firm's name is introduced to any who see the legal instrument. Offices using plain, unidentified paper are perhaps overlooking an inexpensive but very valuable public relations tool.

Copies

Bond paper is used for the original, white onionskin for carbon copies, and colored (usually yellow) lightweight paper for the office file copy. Except for the single exception cited in the note below, *all* carbon copies are typed on lightweight paper. As with so many rules that guide the thinking secretary, this, too, is practical. The lighter the weight of the paper used for carbon copies, the greater the number of legible copies that may be produced at one time.

Only the first page of the original and white carbon copies of the client document need carry the office heading. The stationery required for client documents, therefore, would be as follows:

- Bond — with printed heading
- Bond — plain
- Onionskin — with printed heading
- Onionskin — plain
- Yellow — lightweight, plain

Carbon copies must be legible and neat. The same care used in correcting the original should be used in making corrections on the carbon copies. This applies as well to the office file copy.

NOTE: Two or more *executed* (signed) copies of some client documents are required. Bond paper is used for all copies that are to be signed, for three very sensible reasons: First, it is easier to write a signature on bond than on lightweight paper; second, bond paper resists wear and tear better than lightweight paper (legal documents are frequently referred to, and some must withstand a great deal of handling); third, executed documents are valuable, and bond paper "looks" more important than lightweight onionskin.

Photocopies

Photocopying machines are an important part of law office equipment. Prior to the introduction of copying machines to the law office, a heavy part of the stenographic work included straight copy typing. Original wills ready for the probate court, contracts and leases and agreements under consideration for possible litigation, enclosures or attachments for letters and court documents — all had to be typed by office personnel. The copying machines have almost entirely eliminated this tiresome task.

Not only are these documents photocopied, but photocopies are often used in lieu of carbon copies for the legal papers originally prepared in the law office. If an office copy machine is available and office policy permits the use of photocopies in place of carbon copies, the secretary has three choices:

1. The copying machine and its timesaving features may be ignored.
2. An original and an office file copy may be typed and all other copies made on the copying machine.
3. Only the original may be typed and all other copies, including the office file copy, may be made on the copier.

File Copies

If the file copies of all correspondence and documents are typed (second choice above) on yellow or other colored paper, searching the files for material emanating from the office is greatly facilitated. The color identifies the office-prepared papers. Incoming papers are immediately recognized by their white color.

Some offices have found that this distinct filing-finding advantage is outweighed by the time saved by the secretary who originally typed the document. No doubt about it, it is faster to make one original than it is to make even an original and one copy.

ONE-PARTY CLIENT DOCUMENTS

One-party client documents are those legal instruments prepared for the sole use of the client. A will is an example of a one-party client document. A power of attorney is also a one-party document. A minimum of two copies are prepared. The original is for the client's use; the copy is for the law office files.

However, since the executed original is a valuable legal instrument, it is usually deposited in a safe, not a readily accessible place, for safekeeping. Preparing an extra copy of the document and delivering it to the client for ready reference is a public relations gesture practiced by most law firms.

Therefore, for all practical purposes, the *minimum* number of copies prepared of one-party client documents is *three:* the original (signed by and delivered to the client), the client's reference copy (on lightweight paper if carbon copies are made), and the office file copy.

TWO-PARTY CLIENT DOCUMENTS

Two-party client documents are for the use of the client and another party. A written contract between two parties—for example, one party to have a house painted and the other party to paint it—is an example of a two-party client document. Minimum copies prepared are three: one dated and executed copy for the client, one dated and executed copy for the second party to the document, and one office file copy.

Here again, it is common practice to make an extra reference copy for the client. The original executed contract or agreement will be deposited in a safe place; the extra copy may be kept in a handy place for ready reference.

Thus, for all practical purposes, the *minimum* number of copies prepared of two-party client documents is *four:* the original executed copy on bond paper for the client; the bond second copy, also executed, for the second party to the document; the client's reference copy on white onionskin (if a *carbon* copy is made); and the law office file copy.

MULTIPARTY CLIENT DOCUMENTS

Multiparty client documents are for the use of a client or clients and other party or parties. One example of a multiparty client document is a lease drawn up between two or more owners of a piece of real property and one or more parties desiring to build on the property. Several copies of multiparty documents may be required. Each party to the agreement will receive an executed copy of the document, and all the executed copies will be signed by all parties to the agreement.

If any or all other parties to an agreement are represented by attorneys, unsigned but conformed (see page 79) copies are prepared for their use. These copies, if typed, are prepared on onionskin paper. If they are made on a copying machine, the copies are conformed prior to delivery to the attorneys.

STYLE

Standard manuscript style is used in the preparation of most client documents, because it is both attractive and easy to read.

Margins

The margins of client documents are wide enough to produce an attractive instrument and narrow enough to permit as much typing on the page as possible. Standard margins are

left margin: one inch
right margin: one inch, more or less (Overall appearance of right margin should be slightly narrower than the left margin.)
top margin: first page, two inches; following pages, one and one-half inches
bottom margin: one inch

The wide top margin is necessary to permit the use of legal backs, sometimes called blue backs, which are discussed later in this chapter. The wide top margin is necessary, also, since the top inch will be covered by the fasteners used to secure legal papers in file folders.

Spacing

Client documents are usually double spaced. This permits easy reading of long and involved statements and also permits quick identification of sections or conditions under discussion. However, to avoid exceptional bulkiness, very long documents are sometimes single spaced. Long and involved trust provisions of a will and the many specific conditions of some leases are examples of material that would be single spaced.

A study of the law office files will reveal other exceptions to the rule of double-spacing client documents. When there is doubt, however, double spacing should be used.

Paragraph Indentions

Paragraph indentions are one inch on all double-spaced legal documents. The one-inch indention is large enough to permit ready identification of paragraphs; the one-half-inch indention sometimes used in double-spaced work blends into the left margin.

The legal secretary who learns to set tab stops for paragraph indentions and columnar typing by guesstimating rather than by laboriously counting spaces will save precious seconds. It is a skill that requires very little practice — but any time spent learning to judge good placement accurately and quickly is time well spent.

Pagination

Page numbers are centered one-half inch from the bottom of the page. The first page is usually *un*numbered. It is obviously page one for it carries the title and is on top. However, whether or not page one is numbered is really unimportant. If you prefer to have it numbered, number it.

Numbering on all succeeding pages may be *2, 3, 4,* or *two, three, four,* or *Page 2, Page 3, Page 4.* All are acceptable. However, the first given is most commonly used because it requires less time, less typing, and fewer chances for typing errors. (Any underscoring, capitalizing, or words that are unnecessary should be eliminated. The result: fewer opportunities for type errors.)

A quick check through an office file drawer will disclose the numbering style used by that office. The wise legal secretary will follow the style currently used. As the secretary gains experience and status in the office, more efficient or personal style changes may be introduced.

CAUTION: The same numbering style must be used throughout a document.

Titles

The title begins two inches from the top edge of the first page, is typed in all caps, and is centered. It is double spaced if it is too long for one line. A triple space separates the title from the body. A title written in all caps is *not* underscored. The caps call sufficient attention to it; the underscoring gives chance for error and adds nothing to the appearance.

PRENUPTIAL AGREEMENT   LAST WILL AND TESTAMENT

OF

JOHN HENRY JONES

Subtitles

Subtitles are typed in lowercase with the first letter of the title and all main words capitalized. Only the articles, *a, an, the;* conjunctions; and small prepositions such as *in, on, of,* and *for* are not capitalized. Prepositions containing seven or more letters are capitalized, i.e., *beneath, through, between.*

Continuation Sheets

The first line of a continuation sheet (pages 2, 3, and so on) begins one and one-half inches from the top of the paper. No introductory information is used.

Signature Lines

Signature lines should be 2½ to 3 inches in length and two double spaces apart. This will provide ample room for signatures of all lengths and for very large handwriting. It is annoying to be given an inch-long line for a three- or four-name signature.

The name, exactly as it is to be signed, should be typed in all caps and centered *immediately below* the signature line. This is a public relations gesture, since one person may use, at various times, many signatures — that is, *Ada Jessica Williamson Browning, Ada Jessica Browning, Ada J. W. Browning, Ada Williamson Browning,* or even *Ada Browning* — and the typed signature will immediately alert the signer to the correct signature for that document.

Legal Backs or Covers

The original of a client document is stapled into a legal cover, which is a 9- by 15-inch sheet of extra-weight colored paper. The shorter 9- by 13-inch backs are used in those jurisdictions accepting letter-size paper for legal documents. Legal backs come in a wide assortment of colors, with blue or grey the most popular. Blue covers are so commonly used that legal backs are frequently referred to as "blue backs," whatever their color.

The 9- by 15-inch cover is turned down one inch at the top. The shorter cover is turned down one-half inch. The document that is to be executed is carefully inserted into the fold and centered so the cover frames the document. The document is then stapled in two places: one inch from either margin and one-eighth inch from the bottom edge of the fold of the cover. (See Figure 5-1).

The cover serves two purposes: protection and identification.

Protection results because the cover completely encloses the document when it is properly folded (See Figure 5-2). The heavy weight of the legal backs helps to prevent tearing, spindling, and the

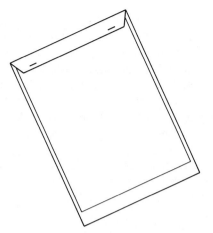

FIGURE 5-1   Legal document in cover

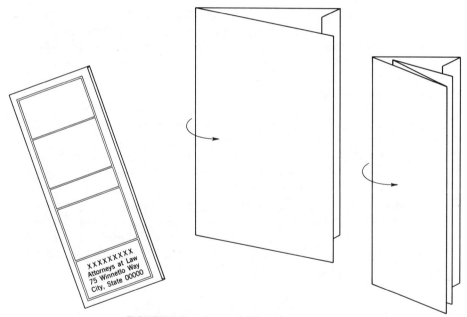

XXXXXXXXX
Attorneys at Law
75 Winnetio Way
City, State 00000

FIGURE 5-2   Correct folding of legal back

regular wear and tear resulting from the handling sometimes given legal instruments.

Identification results because a legal back is wider than most paper, making the document prominent among other papers. Some law offices consistently use a legal back of one color for the original, executed copy given to the client and a back of another color for the extra reference copy, also given to the client.

To fully identify the contents, the following information should be typed on the outside of the second fold of the legal back: title and date of the document; names of parties to the agreement (or testator, if a will); and law firm's name, address, and telephone number. In some areas, this information is referred to as the *endorsement*.

When the folded document is filed among the client's other personal papers, both its size and the information typed by the legal secretary will permit quick and easy identification of the instrument.

A legal-size document is folded as shown in Figure 5–2. A letter-size document is folded in thirds; the endorsement is placed on the center fold of the legal back.

Placement and Space Adjustment

Pace the typing to avoid having the body of the document end on the last line or two of a page, with no space remaining for signature lines. Signature lines may *not* fall on a page by themselves (unless numerous signatures requiring more than a page are a part of a document). At least one line of copy in addition to the date line, and preferably more, must be on the signature page.

If, near the end of the document, it appears that there will be insufficient space on the page for the signature lines, determine which of the two following techniques should be used:

Stretching. Shorten the length of each of the last several lines of typing. Leave extra space between the lines. Allow a bottom margin of 1½ inches. This may s-t-r-e-t-c-h the copy to permit continuation of at least one line and possibly two for the signature page.

Shortening. Make lines longer (even a quarter-inch right margin). Leave slightly less than a double space between each of the last several lines of the body. Triple space or even double space signature lines in this spacing situation.

Proper Names

In most jurisdictions, proper names are typed in all caps to permit easy reference and identification. Not only names of the main parties to the legal instrument are typed this way, but also the names of other individuals, businesses, agencies, and institutions named in the legal document.

This style is used in legal documents but is not carried over into legal correspondence.

Introductory Phrases

Legal typing is characterized by its regular use of all caps for some introductory words and phrases to emphasize new sections of a legal document. The particular introductory words and phrases to be typed in all caps are not chosen at random. Practice over the decades has made the capitalizing of certain words and phrases standard. The legal secretary must observe the style used in the office and on printed forms, and thus learn which phrases are always typed in all caps and which are not. Style varies from state to state, and the traveling legal secretary must respect the style used in the state of current employment.

Hyphenation

Hyphenation of words at the end of a line should be avoided whenever possible, and the last word on a page should *never* be hyphenated. If it is necessary to divide a word, the dictionary should be consulted. An incorrectly hyphenated word is a misspelled word. In law, misspelling is intolerable.

A proper name should never be hyphenated to carry a part of the name to a continuation line. It is even preferable not to split a name, but rather to write the full name on one line, although this is not always possible.

Number and Money Amounts

Numbers of legal significance are usually written in words followed by figures in parentheses:

fifty (50) carloads
six (6) months

It would be awkward to use both words and figures in such an instance as *six-month period*, because of the hyphen. Common sense resolves the problem: eliminate the (6).

Money amounts are written in words followed by figures in parentheses:

Two Thousand Five Hundred Dollars ($2,500.00)
Nine Hundred Twenty-Three and 45/100 Dollars ($923.45)

Words for the money sums are capitalized (not all caps), to make them stand out on the typewritten page.

It is never good practice to make a correction in anything as important as a number, name, or sum of money. However, the double writing of numbers in both figures and words permits positive identification of the correct amount, and probably no legal question would be raised if either a single digit or a single letter in one of the words were erased or otherwise corrected.

There is a trend in legal typing to type numbers and sums of money only once, in figures, that is, *50, 6, $25.00, $923.45.* If this style is acceptable in a law office, it eliminates entirely the right of the legal secretary to correct numbers. A correction in a number would give rise to a legal question as to the time of the correction — was it before or following execution of the document?

The legal secretary must exercise great care in the typing of numbers. If a typing error occurs, there is no choice but to begin the document again. An erasure or alteration could be the basis for later litigation.

In business, sums of money are written in figures (unless the sum begins a sentence). Dollar-and-cents amounts are written: *$5.05, $55.67, $678.09, $25,368.70.* Even-dollar amounts are written: *$5, $55, $678, $25,368.*

In law, the dollar-and-cents amounts are written as in business. However, the even-dollar amounts are written to show that there are, in fact, no cents: *$5.00, $55.00, $678.00, $25.368.00.* This style illustrates very well the exactness of legal typing.

Apostrophe

My husband's nieces means *the nieces of my husband. My husbands' nieces* means that I have more than one husband with nieces!

A legal secretary must recognize the correct use of the possessive case — when and when not to use an apostrophe, and its correct placement when used.

An apostrophe means something has been omitted. It may be one or more letters or one or more words. Consider these contractions: *won't* for *will not, it's* for *it is.* And consider these possessives: *testator's last will and testament* means *last will and testament of the testator, six months' period* means *a period of six months.*

In other words, the use of the apostrophe indicates an economy in the use of words: In contractions, the apostrophe makes one word out of two; in the possessive case, the apostrophe replaces one or two words of a prepositional phrase.

clients' documents means *documents for the clients*

client's documents means *documents for the client*
lawyers' offices means *offices of the lawyers*
lawyer's offices means *offices of the lawyer*
attorney's fees means *fees for the attorney*
attorneys' fees means *fees for the attorneys*

Converting what is believed to be the possessive case into a prepositional phrase will clarify whether the apostrophe precedes or follows the letter *s*.

Most desk dictionaries contain a section on the correct use of the apostrophe, as does any secretary's reference manual.

Misuse of the apostrophe is a spelling error; but more than that, it could be the basis for misunderstanding and possible litigation. Learning the correct use of the possessive case is like learning to drive a car: difficult at first but never forgotten once you get the hang of it!

Stapling

Legal documents that are enclosed in legal backs are stapled in two places, near the lower edge of the top fold of the cover and one inch from either margin.

Legal documents that are not enclosed in legal backs, whether they are originals, carbon copies, or office copies, are stapled in two places, one inch from either margin, one-quarter inch from the top of the page. (See Figure 5–3.)

This manner of stapling secures the pages, yet permits use of the two-hole punch described below. Careless stapling could place staples in the punch area and cause a "punching" problem.

Two-Hole Punch and Acco Fasteners

A two-hole punch (see Figure 5–4) is a basic piece of the legal secretary's desk equipment. The two punches are permanently set

Legal document in cover

Multipage legal document

FIGURE 5-3   Correct stapling of legal documents

FIGURE 5-4   Two-hole punch

SOURCE: Master Products Manufacturing, Los Angeles, California. Printed by permission

2¾ inches apart. All papers to be filed are punched at the center top with the two-hole punch and filed chronologically in the appropriate file folder.

All legal papers, even memos and telephone messages, are carefully filed in a folder. They are securely fastened to the top edge of the file folder by Acco fasteners, which are two-pronged metal or plastic fasteners. (See Figure 5–5.)

Many law offices use file folders that have two-pronged fasteners already attached.

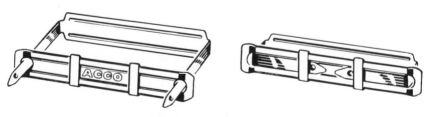

FIGURE 5-5   Acco fastener

SOURCE: Acco Division, Gary Industries, Inc., Chicago, Illinois. Printed by permission.

PUBLIC RELATIONS AND CLIENT DOCUMENTS

A client pays $$$$$ for a client document. It is the legal secretary's responsibility to make the document look as though it is worth the fee.

The content is the attorney's responsibility and is the result of years of study, years of training, and hours and hours of research. The document should show off the content to best advantage.

ACCURACY AND PROOFREADING

It can go almost without saying that accuracy is all-important to law. Many lawsuits result from inaccuracies of one kind or another. Some lawsuits result from careless typing and copying errors. Everything typed by the legal secretary must be carefully proofread. If a document is complicated or contains real property descriptions, it is sometimes wise to proofread all or portions of it more than once.

Accuracy is the hallmark of the successful legal secretary. Inaccuracy could very well lead to unemployment.

CONFORMING COPIES

When the original document has been completely executed, all copies are conformed; that is, the typewriter is used to reproduce all signatures, dates, and any corrections or additions contained on the original. The carbon copies, including the office file copy, will then be, in every respect, exact copies of the executed original.

NOTE: If a secretary were to conform copies by pen or pencil, the copies could be mistaken for executed copies. Therefore, it is imperative that copies be conformed on the typewriter. In an emergency situation where a typewriter is not available, pen or pencil printing could be substituted.

If a photocopying machine is available, conformed copies may be obtained by running a *conformed* copy of the document through the photocopier.

SUMMARY

Client documents are primarily for the use of the client. They may be one-party, two-party, or multiparty documents.

All client documents should be neatly and accurately typed and carefully proofread. Care in form and style should be used. Careless corrections, misspelled words, sloppy margins, and inattention to detail mar the appearance and lower the intrinsic value of the document.

If the legal secretary is aware of good public relations as the client documents are typed, the secretary, the attorney, and the office will benefit.

See Appendix B for completed client documents.

SUGGESTED SPECIAL ASSIGNMENTS

1. Visit a court clerk's office and learn whether 8½ by 11- or 8½ by 13-inch paper is used for legal documents in your area. If the standard legal size of 8½ by 13 is used, inquire if there is any likelihood that letter-size paper will be used in the foreseeable future. Write a brief paper stating your findings.

2. From a law office, a family member, a friend, or your own personal files, obtain a copy of a client document. Make photocopies of the first and signature pages. Use a permanent marker pen to mark through all proper names on the photocopy so the document will lose its identity. Write a brief paper giving the title and purpose of the document. Attach your photocopy.

3. Type one original copy of the Three-Day Notice to Pay Rent or Quit as shown on page 332. Substitute your city, state, and a logical ZIP code for those given in the notice. Use appropriate dates. Proofread carefully. If the notice is more than one page in length, staple the pages in correct legal style.

4. Type one original copy of the Power of Attorney as shown on page 338. Use client document typing style. (Omit the acknowledgment called for.)

6

Wills

Wills are one-party client documents. They are the most uniquely personal of all legal documents. Wills are prepared for individuals at their request and under their personal instructions. The purpose of a will is to dispose, as each maker wishes, of all of the real and personal property owned by the testator at the time of death.

Only he or she whose will it is need be given a copy of this legal paper. It is a private document, and no one other than the testator, the attorney who dictated it, and the legal secretary who typed it need know its contents until the death of the testator. It is a highly personal and confidential document.

DEFINITIONS

Before we can proceed into the subject of wills, we must discuss the vocabulary used.

Will. A will is the means whereby an individual predetermines the disposition of personal and real property upon death. If one dies leaving no will, all property owned by the individual at the time of death will be divided or disposed of in accordance with the laws of the state.

Codicil.   A codicil is an addendum to a will. By a codicil, a testator may add to, delete from, or otherwise change the provisions of the will.

Testator (masculine), testatrix (feminine).   The testator is the one who makes and signs a will disposing of all real and personal property owned at date of death. *Testator* is commonly used to include both the masculine and feminine. However, many law offices do use *testatrix* in the will of a woman client.

Witnesses.   The witnesses are those persons who, by their signatures, attest that they did attend and witness the signing of the will. There are some restrictions as to who may act as witnesses. One restriction is that one named as a beneficiary in a will may not also act as a witness to it.

Beneficiaries.   Parties named in the will to receive all or a portion of the testator's property upon death are beneficiaries. Beneficiaries may be individuals, companies, colleges, agencies, or institutions.

Executor (masculine), executrix (feminine).   The executor is the party named by the testator to act after the death of the testator and to carry out the terms of the will. *Executor* is commonly used to include both the masculine and the feminine. If a woman is named to serve in this capacity, many law offices do use the term *executrix*. If the testator names an individual to serve as executor, an alternate executor is usually also named; the one first named may not be able to act as such executor for any of several reasons:

- The executor may have predeceased the testator.
- The executor may have moved to a distant country or another state, and it would be inconvenient to serve.
- The executor may be ill and unable to act.
- The executor may decline to act for personal reasons.

Remember, many years may pass between the making of a will and the death of the testator. It is always wise to update a will as circumstances dictate.

Frequently, the executor named in a will is a trust department of a bank, a trust company, or other institution. Such an entity does not die or become ill or incapacitated. Neither does it move. For these reasons, such companies are often named executors or alternate executors.

The word *will* usually brings to mind the formal legal document, which is accurate and complete, precisely and carefully written. However, this is only one of the three general classifications of wills:

1. Holographic (hō-lō-GRAF-ik) wills
2. Nuncupative (NUN-kyu-pāt-iv) wills
3. Formal wills

Any of these wills, if they satisfy the legal requirements of the state, may be legal wills.

Holographic wills are those wills written entirely in the hand-writing of the testator or testatrix. This includes the date, signature, and body of the instrument.

One county clerk's office has on file an original holographic will that has been probated and that was and is a rather difficult filing problem. The will satisfies all the requirements of the law of the state in which it was filed for probate. It is dated and signed by the testator and is entirely in his handwriting. The problem is this: the will was written on a large plank of wood!

Wills such as this one may satisfy the state requirements, but they are often ambiguous and incomplete and require legal interpretation. Therefore, they may not truly reflect the wishes of the testator. Consider the following holographic will. Jurisdiction is unknown. Some say the document is fictitious. In either event, it is worth reading.

Last Will and Testament of Herman Obleweiss

I am writing of my will minselluf that dam lawyir want he should have too much money, he ask too many answers about the family. first thing i want i dont want my brother oscar get a god dam ting wot i got. he is a mumser he done me out of forty dollars fourteen years since.

I want it that hilda my sister she gets the north sixtie akers of at where i am homing it now i bet she dont get that loafer husban of hers to broke twenty akers next plowing time gonoph work. she cant have it if she lets oscar liver on it i want i should have it back if she does.

tell moma that six hundred dollars she been looking for for twenty years is berried from the backhouse behind about ten feet down she better let little frederick do the diggin and count it when he comes up.

Pastor lucknitz can have three hundred dollars if he kiss de book he wont preach no more dumhead talks about polotiks. he should a roof put on de medinghouse with and the elders should the bills look at.

moma the rest should get but i want that adolph shud tell her what not she should do so no more slick irishers sell her vokum cleeners day noise like hell and a broom dont cost so much.

I want it that mine brother adolph should be my exeter and i want it that the jedge should pleeze make adolph plenty bond put up and watch him like hell adolphus is a good bisness man but only a dumkopf would trust him with a busted pfennig.

I want dam sure that schliemical oscar dont nothing get tell adolph he can have a hundred dollars if he prove to jedje oscar dont get nothing. dat dam sure fix oscar.

Herman Obleweiss

Nuncupative wills are oral wills. Such wills should be reduced to writing as soon as possible, for they may be difficult to prove in a court of law. A possible valid nuncupative will might be one made by a dying victim of an automobile accident. Before those present at the scene the accident victim might state the names of the beneficiaries and the property they are to receive if the injured person dies. The statement, reduced to writing, could be presented to the probate court and witnessed by those having heard the will spoken.

Formal wills are those wills drawn or prepared in conformance with state law and prepared at the direction and request of the testator. State laws differ. One important example of such differences is in the matter of the witnesses to a will. Many states require that three persons witness the signing of a formal will; other states require only two witnesses.

THE FORMAL WILL

It is the formal will, dictated by the attorney and typed by the legal secretary, that will be discussed in some detail in this chapter. The completed will must be dated, signed by the testator, and signed by the number of witnesses required by state law.

Copies

As explained in Chapter 5, for all practical purposes the *minimum* number of copies of a will (a one-party client document) is three: an original executed copy and a conformed copy for the client, and an office file copy.

An original will is a valuable legal document and should be held in a safe place, accessible when needed. Many law offices, perhaps most, maintain an original will depository where executed wills may be held for safekeeping. The wills are then always readily available if the clients later wish to revise them, and they are always available for probate upon the death of the testators.

If a trust company or other institution is named executor of a will, it is not uncommon for the testator to have the original will delivered directly to the executor for safekeeping.

The testator may wish to retain the original will or have it held in the attorney's will file; he may wish to have a copy of the will delivered to the named executor; he may also wish a copy for his ready reference. This would, of course, require the preparation of still another copy of the will: the original for safekeeping, a white conformed copy for testator's reference, a white conformed copy for the executor, and a law office copy.

If, during dictation of the will, the legal secretary is in doubt as to the number of copies that should be prepared, the information should be sought from the attorney. Extra copies are delivered to no one other than the testator except by specific request of the testator. Decisions regarding such extra copies and their delivery are the responsibility of the attorney and are not within the scope of responsibility of the legal secretary.

NOTE: The law office file copy should contain a notation of the disposition of the original will. The testator may change the location of the original will many times or may leave it in its original location. In either event, the office files will contain one lead as to its whereabouts should the information be requested.

Paper and Style

A will is a client document. Therefore, it is typed on plain legal paper. Client document style is used.

Will Clauses

A formal will contains a title, signature lines, and the following clauses, each of which is a separate paragraph:

- Introductory clause
- Debt clause
- Residuary clause
- Clause naming executor or executrix (Bond is sometimes waived in this clause.)
- Signature clause
- Attestation clause

Other special clauses or paragraphs may be a part of a will, but the six listed above are the necessary clauses of a formal will. A simple will follows; it has been divided into sections for illustration and discussion.

Title and Introductory Clause

The title includes the name of the document and the name of the testator. The sample introductory paragraph includes the name of the testator, county and state of residence, and also includes information about the state of mind of the testator:

LAST WILL AND TESTAMENT

OF

FRANCIS PETER IRWYNE

I, FRANCIS PETER IRWYNE, now residing in the county of Fresno, state of California, and being of sound and disposing mind and memory and not acting under fraud, menace, duress or the undue influence of any person whomsoever, do hereby make, publish and declare this to be my last will and testament, and hereby expressly revoke any and all former wills and codicils to wills heretofore made by me.

DISCUSSION

1. The title, because of its length, is double spaced, and it is typed in all caps. This title style lends importance to the name of the document and to the testator's name: each has its own line of writing. Underscoring the title is extra, unnecessary typing, which not only requires extra time and offers added opportunity for type errors, but adds nothing to the legality of the document.

2. A triple space separates the title from the body of the will.

3. The proper name in the introductory clause is typed in all caps. It is surrounded by commas because it is in apposition with the pronoun *I*. The testator's name must be correctly spelled. If it is not, the document will have to be retyped. Imagine the embarrassment of the legal secretary if the testator has to call attention to such a type or spelling error!

4. When followed by the names of the county and the state, the words *county* and *state* are sometimes capitalized. Grammatically, it is unnecessary. Practically, it is faster not to capitalize the words.

5. Commas do not precede the *and* or *or* in either series. This is usual legal punctuation.

6. Compound words: *whomsoever, hereby, heretofore.*

7. Legal words: *duress, undue, testament, codicils.*

8. Legal phrases: *last will and testament; sound and disposing mind and memory; of any person whomsoever; make, publish and declare; codicils to wills.*

Numbered Clauses

All clauses in the will are numbered except the introductory, signature, and attestation clauses. Later, when the will is being probated, numbered clauses will facilitate finding and referring to specific provisions of the will. Numbered clauses may consist of more than one paragraph.

> FIRST: I declare that I am married and that my wife's name is
>
> MARY ADAMS IRWYNE. I further declare that I have two children, a son,
>
> JOHN HARRY IRWYNE, and a daughter, MARYANNE ELLEN IRWYNE.

DISCUSSION

1. Writing the paragraph numbers in words and in all caps is usual style. It lends an air of formality to the document. To underscore the number would only clutter the appearance and offer extra chance for type errors. Some offices use Roman numerals. Others use First, Article I, or Article One. Some offices prefer to center the paragraph number on a separate line.

2. The possessive case is used: *wife's name* means *the name of my wife.*

3. Proper names are typed in all caps. The legal secretary must check the spelling of all proper names for exactness and must check the typing for accuracy.

4. Commas surround JOHN HARRY IRWYNE because that name is in apposition with the word *son.* MARYANNE ELLEN IRWYNE is in apposition with the word *daughter.*

Debt Clause

The debt clause provides for the payment of debts of the testator upon his death. Special stipulations regarding payment of inheritance taxes from estate funds are sometimes included in this paragraph.

> SECOND: I hereby direct my executrix hereinafter named to pay all
>
> of my just, unsecured debts and the expenses of my last illness and funeral
>
> as soon as may be lawfully and conveniently done after my demise.

DISCUSSION

1. Some offices prefer that the words *executor* and *executrix* be capitalized. Grammatically, it is not necessary to capitalize the words. Practically, it is faster and offers fewer chances for type errors if the words are not capitalized. However, uniformity of style requires that if the words are capped any time in a document they must be capped every time in that document. *Uniformity of style marks the work of the professional legal secretary.*

2. Compound words: *hereby, hereinafter.*

3. Legal word: *demise* (used here it means death).

4. Legal phrases: *just, unsecured debts* (debts that are legally due and payable but that are not secured by a mortgage or a lien); *last illness and funeral.*

Clauses Granting Specific Bequests

Wills may include many clauses granting specific bequests to relatives, friends, colleges, charitable organizations. Technically, a *bequest* refers to a gift of personal property, a *devise* refers to a gift of real property, and a *legacy* refers to a gift of money. The joint use of the verbs *give, devise and bequeath* covers all of these nouns.

THIRD: I hereby give and bequeath to my son, JOHN HARRY IRWYNE, my coin collection.

FOURTH: I hereby give and bequeath to my daughter, MARYANNE ELLEN IRWYNE, the sum of Five Thousand Dollars ($5,000.00).

DISCUSSION

1. Specific sums of money should be typed in words followed by figures. Note the use of the complete figure including the two ciphers for the cents portion of the money amount.

Even in wills, some offices prefer that figures alone be used for money sums. It is extremely important that no corrections be made in any such numbers.

2. Compound word: *hereby.*

3. Legal phrase: *give and bequeath.*

4. If real property is given by will and the legal property description is included, the legal description should be single spaced and indented from each margin, i.e., a one-half-inch indention for long descriptions and a one-inch indention for short legal descriptions.

Proofreading is accomplished by a team of two, the typist reading from the original deed and the second party reading the description written into the will.

Residuary Clause

This clause disposes of all property of the decedent not specifically disposed of earlier in the will. The one named to receive the residuary (remaining) estate is called the *residuary beneficiary*.

> FIFTH: All of the rest, residue and remainder of my property,
> both real and personal, of whatsoever kind and character and wheresoever
> situated, I hereby give, devise and bequeath to my wife, MARY ADAMS IRWYNE,
> if she survives me, otherwise in equal shares to my surviving children
> and the descendants of any deceased child, per stirpes.

DISCUSSION

1. Observe the use of commas in this clause. No comma is used before the *and* in either series. All other commas add to the clarity of the statement.

2. Compound words: *whatsoever, wheresoever, hereby.*

3. Latin phrase: *per stirpes* (per STIR-pēs) (by right of representation; sharing an inheritance that a deceased ancestor had inherited).

4. Legal phrases: *rest, residue and remainder; kind and character; give, devise and bequeath.*

Clause Naming Executor or Executrix; Bond

In this clause is named the one who is to act as executor or executrix of the will upon the death of the testator. If a corporation is named as executor, an alternate executor is not usually named. If an individual is named to act as executor, however, an alternate is usually named. Co-executors are sometimes named to carry out the provisions of a will.

The bond required by law of all executors and administrators of estates may be waived by the testator in the will. Unless the bond is specifically waived in the will, the named executor will be required by law to be bonded before decedent's estate may be administered.

> SIXTH: I hereby nominate and appoint my said wife, MARY ADAMS

IRWYNE, as the executrix of this will and authorize her to act as such without bond. In the event of her failure to qualify or to complete her duties as such executrix, then I nominate and appoint my son, JOHN HARRY IRWYNE, to act as executor hereof without bond. In the event of his failure to qualify or to complete his duties as such executor, then I nominate and appoint THE TRUST COMPANY as such executor.

DISCUSSION

1. Observe the use of the word *executrix* in referring to the wife and *executor* in referring to the son. The correct form of the word, feminine or masculine, must be used in each instance unless the office uses *executor* to include both masculine and feminine.

2. Observe the use of the commas around the proper names. Those names are in apposition with the words immediately preceding them, i.e., wife, MARY ADAMS IRWYNE, and son, JOHN HARRY IRWYNE. Correct punctuation is as shown in this example.

3. Compound words: *hereby, hereof.*

4. Legal word: *bond* (a fidelity or good-faith bond).

5. Legal phrase: *nominate and appoint.*

Signature Clause and Signature Line

The signature clause includes the place and date the will was signed (executed).

IN WITNESS WHEREOF, I have hereunto set my hand and seal at City, State, this ____ day of _____, 19__.

_____
FRANCIS PETER IRWYNE

DISCUSSION

1. At least one line of the signature clause must be on a page with the numbered paragraphs of the will. At least one line of the signature clause must be with the testator's signature line. Obviously, placement of this clause is very important. Stretching or shortening of the final paragraphs of the will may be required to assure proper placement of this paragraph.

If it appears that the signature clause and signature line will fall well above the bottom of the page, there is no placement problem.

2. The introductory phrase, IN WITNESS WHEREOF, is typed in all caps and is followed by a comma.

3. Timing determines the manner of typing the data in this paragraph. If the will is to be signed the same day it is typed, the legal secretary will type the day, month, and year. If the exact date of signing is not known, the legal secretary will leave a blank line of about an inch for the date, but will type in both the month and the year. If the will is typed near the end of the month, the legal secretary will leave a blank line for the date, leave a longer blank line for the month, and type the year. If the will is typed near the end of the month of December, the legal secretary may leave a blank for the day, leave a longer blank for the month, and type 19——, leaving only enough space for the required numbers.

It is important to leave adequate space for the testator to fill in the required portions of the date. However, unnecessarily long lines are unattractive. Good judgment will dictate the proper line lengths that should be provided.

4. The signature line should be two double spaces below the last line of the signature clause and should begin about the middle of the page and extend to the right margin. The testator's name, as written in the title and the introductory paragraph, should be typed in all caps and centered directly below the signature line.

5. Many offices require the testator's initials or signature in the lower margin of each page of the will. A typed line may be provided for the convenience of the testator.

6. Compound words: *whereof, hereunto.*

7. Legal phrases: *in witness whereof, set my hand and seal.*

Attestation Clause and Signature Lines for Witnesses

The attestation clause is a declaration that the witnesses attended the signing of the will. It includes the date of the execution of the will or a reference to the date contained in the signature clause. It contains the name of the testator. It is not numbered. At least one line of the attestation clause must be on the page containing the signature of the testator.

Signature and address lines for the witnesses required by state law (two or three) should be typed below the attestation clause. Sufficient space must be allowed for the signatures and for the complete addresses: street, city, and state.

The foregoing instrument, consisting of two (2) pages, including this page signed by the witnesses, was on the date hereof signed by the said FRANCIS PETER IRWYNE and declared by him to be his last will and testament, and at his request, and in his presence, and in the presence of each other, we have subscribed our names as witnesses to the said will.

_____Address_____

_____

_____Address_____

_____

DISCUSSION

1. Careful study of the punctuation in this paragraph will reveal that it must be as shown to completely describe the conditions under which the document was executed; that is, that the testator and the witnesses were all present during the complete execution of the will.

2. At least the first line of the attestation clause must be typed on the same page as the testator's signature. If space permits, the attestation clause should begin three double spaces below the testator's signature line.

3. To conform to the double-spaced style used in wills, the attestation clause is double spaced. However, if space is limited, the attestation clause may be single spaced in order to avoid continuation of only a line or two plus signature lines to another page.

4. Since the total number of pages of the will is included as a part of the attestation clause, the legal secretary must exercise care to include the correct number of pages of the will as well as the correct phraseology. If only the first line of the attestation clause were included on the testator's signature page, the statement following the number of pages in the will would have to be changed to read: "including *the* page signed. . . ."

Study the preceding statement to make certain you have properly digested its contents. Such changes as this are the responsibility of the legal secretary. An attorney could not possibly dictate that change, for it would not be possible to predetermine just where in the typewritten page the attestation clause would fall.

5. Signature lines for two witnesses, together with lines for their addresses, are shown. In some states, three witness signature lines are required.

6. Compound words: *foregoing, hereof.*
7. Legal words: *said* (more specific than *the*), *subscribed.*

Proofreading the Will

When the will has been typed, the secretary should carefully proofread it for content, correct spelling of proper names, and type errors.

A will is a personal document, and the testator or testatrix will read it very carefully. It would be embarrassing if type or spelling errors were discovered by the testator. It would be more than embarrassing if a careless error gave property to the wrong individual or the right person were given the wrong property. An omission of a paragraph could deny a gift of great real or intrinsic value.

Wills are of exceptional importance to their owners and should look the part. They should be neat, accurate, and handsome.

Will Covers

Will covers and legal backs are identical in size. Will covers are, however, usually white. The paper is frequently better textured and of better quality than legal backs.

If a formal will cover is used, the data required on the outside of the cover should be completed and the original will placed in the will cover and stapled. A legal back, conformed to match exactly the formal will cover, should be made for the testator's reference will copy.

If formal will covers are not available, the title of the document, the name of the testator, the date of the instrument, and the firm's name and address should be added to the outside of two legal backs, one of which should also be marked "Copy." The original will should be placed in one legal back. The reference copy of the will should be placed in the cover marked "Copy."

The backs are folded once and typed *before* the copies of the will are stapled into place.

Notifying the Client of the
Completion of the Will

During the client's first visit to the law office, an appointment may have been made for the signing of the will. If so, it is the legal secretary's responsibility to have the will completed and ready when the client enters the office.

If an appointment has not been made, the attorney may telephone the client at the time the will is completed and set an appointment for the signing of the will. Or perhaps the legal secretary may be instructed by the attorney to make the phone call. If the client is not in, another call later in the day should be made. No one other than the client is ever given any information regarding business a client has with the law firm. If the client has given other instructions, however, they should be followed.

Executing the Will

When the client arrives at the office, he is given the original will to read. If it is satisfactory, the attorney, the secretary, and one other person, if state law requires, may act as the witnesses to the will. Sometimes two or more attorneys serve as witnesses.

The testator, seated comfortably for writing, will be asked by the attorney if this document is his will. He will also be asked by the attorney if he wishes those in attendance to witness the will. If both answers are affirmative, the attorney will suggest that the testator sign the will, using the same signature as that typed just below the signature line. The attorney will then ask the testator to fill in the date if any part of it has been left blank during the typing.

Using the same pen, the witnesses will sign their names and fill in their addresses. The testator and witnesses are all present during the complete execution of the will. The will has been executed when all signatures have been affixed, date completed, and addresses filled in.

Conforming Copies

Copies of the will must be conformed to match the original will exactly. If witnesses have used abbreviations in writing their addresses, the conformed copies will show the abbreviations. The copies should be immediately conformed on a typewriter while the original will is still in the law office.

Distribution of Copies

A signed will is an important document, and the testator should be instructed to keep it in a safe place. At the request of the testator, the original will may be held in the original will file or in the law office safe. In this event, a simple receipt should be prepared in duplicate:

At his request, the original will of FRANCIS PETER IRWYNE has been placed in this firm's will file.

Dated: month, day, year.

FIRM NAME

By_____

The receipt will be signed by the attorney or by the legal secretary acting as agent. As agent, the secretary will sign the attorney's name. Just below the name the initials of the legal secretary will be written. The original receipt will be given the client, and the conformed copy of the receipt will be placed in the office files or attached to the office copy of the will.

The conformed reference copy of the will should be given to the client. The office copy should be placed in the law office will file.

If a trust company or other institution has been named executor or alternate executor of the will, the client may wish a conformed copy of the will sent to the institution. A brief transmittal letter including the name of the testator and the date of the will should be sent with the conformed copy of the will.

The Trust Company
7123 Gentle Building
Fresno, California 00000

Re: Last Will and Testament of
Francis Peter Irwyne

Gentlemen:

Enclosed is a conformed copy of the Last Will and Testament of Francis Peter Irwyne, dated June 12, 19__. The Trust Company has been named alternate executor in this will.

Mr. Irwyne requested that a copy be sent to you.

Sincerely yours,

BROWN, BROWN and BROWN

By_____
John Henry Brown

ab
Enclosure

Codicils

If a testator wishes to make a change or changes in the will, a codicil may be drawn. A codicil is typed in the same formal style as a will. The title is

CODICIL TO LAST WILL AND TESTAMENT

OF

FRANCIS PETER IRWYNE

The introductory paragraph includes a reference to the last will and testament to which it is an addendum.

The original codicil is enclosed in a will cover and placed with the original will for safekeeping. A reference copy of the codicil is given to the testator. The office copy should be conformed and attached to the office copy of the original will.

Codicils are formal documents and must be witnessed in the same manner and by the same number of witnesses as the original will.

Major changes in a will may require a complete rewriting of the will. In this event, the office copy of the first will should show by a dated pencil notation that a later will exists. Usual practice is to staple the office copy of the new will on top of the office copy of the will it replaces.

SUMMARY

A will is a uniquely personal one-party client document. It consists of title, introductory clause, debt clause, residuary clause, clause naming executor (bond sometimes waived), signature clause and signature line, and attestation clause and witness signature lines.

For all practical purposes, the minimum copies prepared of a will are three: the original executed copy for safekeeping, a conformed copy for testator's reference, and an office file copy.

A codicil is a one-party client document by which a testator may supplement or modify the terms of a will.

Careful proofreading of both wills and codicils to wills is essential and cannot be overemphasized.

See Appendix B for complete wills.

SUGGESTED SPECIAL ASSIGNMENTS

1. Using client document style, make one original copy of the will shown on page 336 of the appendix. Change the city and state to your location. If it is necessary for three persons to witness a will in your state, make this change.

2. Type a reciprocal will for the husband of Natalie Deno Brown. This will be the *Last Will and Testament of William John Brown.* The executrix will be Natalie Deno Brown. All provisions of the will are the same as the will of Natalie Deno Brown. Caution: Make necessary changes from *executor* to *executrix* and from feminine to masculine pronouns. Proofread carefully.

7

Leases

A lease is a two-party client document. It may also be a multiparty client document if more than one person owns the lease property or more than one person or business is the lessee. One party, the lessor, for certain remuneration conveys (gives) to another party, the lessee, a portion of his interest in and to certain property.

A lease is written for a specified period of time, for specified remuneration, and to cover specific property. A lease is a contract. A lease agreement covering real property must be in writing as provided in the Statute of Frauds.

PARTIES TO A LEASE

The parties to a lease are the *lessor*, sometimes referred to as *landlord*, *owner*, or *party of the first part* (if named first in the lease agreement); and the *lessee*, sometimes referred to as *tenant*, *renter*, or *party of the second part*. It is important that the same reference terms, i.e., *lessor* and *lessee*, *owner* and *renter*, *landlord* and *tenant*, or *party of the first part* and *party of the second part*, be used throughout a document.

A mnemonic for distinguishing between *lessor* and *lessee* is this: the less*ee* is the one who r*ec*eives the use of the property. Notice the *e*'s in *lessee* and the *e*'s in *receives.* To carry the mnemonic a bit further: a *donee receives* the gift, the *donor* gives the gift; the *grantee receives*, the *grantor* gives.

FORM AND STYLE

A lease is a client document, and client document style is used. These instruments are double spaced and the margins are those used for all client documents.

Copies

The minimum copies required of a two-party client document are three: one executed copy for the client, one executed copy for the second party to the agreement, and one conformed copy for the law office files. However, *minimum* copies of a lease are usually *four:* one executed copy for the lessor, one executed copy for the lessee, one conformed copy for the client, and one conformed copy for the law office files. If real estate brokers or other attorneys are involved in the lease matter, still other conformed copies may be required for their files.

Duplicate Executed Copies

Both parties to a contract receive executed copies of the document. Therefore, both the lessor and the lessee will receive executed copies of the lease, and both will receive "originals."

To achieve this effect and yet type the document only one time, bond paper should be used for both the original and the first carbon copy of the lease. Lightweight paper should be used for all other carbon copies.

Upon completion of the lease, the two bond copies will be assembled and placed in legal backs. Each will be signed by all parties to the lease; each will be dated. All other copies of the lease will be conformed. Distribution of the copies will be: executed original for the client, executed bond carbon copy for the second party to the lease, *conformed* white onionskin copy for the client, and *conformed* yellow office file copy.

Executed copies of leases or other agreements or contracts are valuable legal documents. They should be placed in a safe deposit box or other place of safekeeping. Conformed copies delivered to clients have no real legal value, but they are extremely useful as reference copies.

The wise legal secretary will determine during dictation the maximum possible number of copies that may be required of a document, thus eliminating a possible retyping of a long, detailed paper. It is sometimes advisable to estimate the greatest possible number of copies that may be required and add one for good measure.

If an office copy machine is available, the legal secretary will type only the two copies that are to be executed and the office copy. All other copies may be quickly made on the copy machine from the unexecuted original or the conformed office copy.

Conforming Copies

As soon as the original agreements or leases have been executed and dated, all copies must be immediately conformed. When the originals have left the office, it is too late to conform copies. An unconformed office copy implies that the document was never executed.

It is a rarity for anyone to remind a legal secretary to conform copies of legal documents. Thus, this responsibility, which is both real and urgent, must be assumed by the secretary.

MAJOR SECTIONS OF A LEASE

A lease covering real property has been divided into sections for illustration and discussion:

- Title and introductory paragraph
- WHEREAS clauses
- NOW, THEREFORE, clause
- Term or condition paragraphs or clauses
- Signature clause and signature lines
- Acknowledgments

Title and Introductory Paragraph

The title identifies the document. The introductory paragraph includes the names and identifies the parties to the lease. It frequently also includes the date of the document.

LEASE

THIS LEASE, made and entered into this ＿＿＿ day of March, 19＿,

by and between FRANCIS PETER IRWYNE and MARY ADAMS IRWYNE, husband and wife,

as joint tenants, hereinafter referred to as "lessor," and JOHN HENRY JONES,

a single man, hereinafter referred to as "lessee,"

WITNESSETH:

DISCUSSION

1. The title is typed in all caps and is centered two inches from the top of the page.

2. *THIS LEASE*, the first words of the introductory paragraph, is typed in all caps. The first words might also have been *THIS AGREEMENT* or *THIS LEASE AGREEMENT*.

3. In our example, portions of the date have been left blank. These blanks would be filled in during execution of the lease. The date of an agreement is frequently dictated by the attorney, in which event lines would not be required. The date would be typed as part of the paragraph.

4. Proper names are always typed in all caps.

5. *Lessor* and *lessee* are placed in quotes in the first paragraph because of the grammatical construction. The quotation marks are omitted as the words appear later in the lease.

6. Commas surround the phrases, *husband and wife, as joint tenants, hereinafter referred to as "lessor,"* because these phrases describe FRANCIS PETER IRWYNE and MARY ADAMS IRWYNE. The phrases are in apposition with those proper names. Commas also surround *a single man* and *hereinafter referred to as "lessee"* for the same reason, i.e., they are in apposition with JOHN HENRY JONES.

The legal secretary must be able to recognize appositive words and phrases and correctly punctuate them. Incorrect punctuation could result in ambiguity and misinterpretation.

A discussion of appositional words or phrases is included in most desk dictionaries and in all reference manuals for stenographers. The inquisitive secretary might check the manual's index for "commas" and refer to the appropriate paragraphs in that section.

7. *WITNESSETH:* is written as a separate paragraph and is typed in all caps. Either punctuation is omitted or a colon is used. Spaces are sometimes left between the letters, i.e., *W I T N E S-S E T H.* WITNESS is frequently used in place of WITNESSETH.

WITNESSETH or *WITNESS* is sometimes added to the last line of the introductory paragraph. This is an acceptable style.

8. Compound word: *hereinafter.*

9. Legal words: *lease, lessor, lessee, witnesseth.*

10. Legal phrases: *made and entered into, by and between, husband and wife, joint tenants, a single man.*

WHEREAS Clauses

The WHEREAS paragraphs furnish facts and circumstances of the lease. Together, these paragraphs are the introduction or preamble to the document.

WHEREAS, the lessor owns and is willing to lease and let to lessee, upon the terms hereinafter provided, that certain unimproved parcel of real estate situate in the county of Los Angeles, state of California, and more particularly described as:

The Southwesterly 200 feet of the following described real property, to wit:

> That portion of the Garrett Tract, Rancho Santa Catalina, subdivided for the Santa Catalina Land Association, in the County of Los Angeles, State of California, as per map recorded in Book 1 Page 502 and in Book 32 Page 18 of Miscellaneous Records of said County, described as follows: Beginning at a point in the center line of the Santa Catalina Road, also called the Mills Road, and First Street, that is south 32° 14' 40" west, 529.9 feet from the most westerly corner of Tract No. 5793, as per map recorded in Book 79 Pages 60 and 61 of Maps, in the office of the County Recorder of said County, thence north 32° 04' 40" east, 399.77 feet; thence south 56° 43' 30" east, 124.34 feet; thence south 33° 57' 30" west, 399.69 feet to a point in the center line of said Santa Catalina Road; thence north 56° 43' 30" west along said center line, 127.79 feet, more or less, to the point of beginning, (more commonly known as 10501 Mills Road, Bell, California),

which property shall hereinafter be referred to as the "demised premises";

and

WHEREAS, the lessee is willing to take and hold possession of the demised premises upon said terms and conditions hereinafter provided for;

DISCUSSION

1. *WHEREAS* is typed in all caps and is followed by a comma.

2. There may be one WHEREAS clause, or there may be many such clauses. Each is a new paragraph.

3. WHEREAS paragraphs are frequently very long. They are often single sentences. Internal punctuation must be carefully used to assure clarity of the statements.

4. In this illustration, one WHEREAS paragraph describes the real property to be let (leased). The general location of the property, i.e., the county and state, is double spaced. Punctuation preceding the real property description is a colon.

5. Legal property descriptions furnish a complete and exact identification of the real property. They are single spaced and indented equally from *each* margin: one inch for short descriptions and one-half inch for long descriptions.

The real property descriptions should be copied *exactly* as they appear on the deeds or other documents from which they are taken. The legal secretary may *not* presume to change the spelling, punctuation, capitalization, or other particulars of a description without first verifying the change with the attorney. Any variance from the original description could result in confusion or in the transfer of another's property.

Legal property descriptions are sometimes very brief. Residential lot descriptions may simply read:

```
...real property situated in the city of Fresno, county of Fresno, state of

California, described as follows:

        Lot 72 of Tract No. 1888, Friendway Tract No. 10, according
        to the map thereof recorded in Book 20 Page 72 of Plats,
        records of said County.
```

Metes and bounds descriptions, on the other hand, are usually much longer. Metes (meaning measurements) and bounds (meaning boundaries) descriptions give exact measurements and boundaries of a parcel of real estate. The description included in this lease is a metes and bounds description.

The symbols used in a metes and bounds description to indicate exact direction are degrees (°), minutes ('), and seconds ("). Thus, *south 32° 04' 40"* would read "south thirty-two degrees, four minutes, forty seconds."

6. Proofreading legal property descriptions is as important as writing them. Even the slightest variance from the original description could result at least in embarrassment and possibly in a lawsuit.

Two persons should be involved in proofreading the descriptions. The secretary should follow the original deed or description. The assistant proofreader should read the secretary's newly typed description. Both will take turns reading aloud. All capital letters will be announced, as will punctuation marks, decimals, and the spelling of unusual or proper words. Long and involved real property descriptions should be proofread in this manner more than one time to assure complete accuracy.

If the secretary and attorney comprise the office force for the moment, the attorney will assist in proofreading real property descriptions. This professional is well aware of the need for accuracy.

7. The first letter of the phrase following the single-spaced legal description is not capitalized in the example. The phrase is properly a part of the very long one-sentence paragraph beginning "WHEREAS."

In another agreement, the real property description could very well be the end of the sentence. In that case, the first word of the following sentence would be capped. The careful, observant legal secretary studies and understands the wording and meaning of legal statements. This leads to correct punctuation.

8. In the example, the street address of the property has been included in the parentheses as part of the legal property description. Such a street address might be, instead, double spaced immediately following the single-spaced legal property description. Of course, it would be a duplication of effort as well as an error to show it in both places.

Including the street address is a public relations gesture. It permits easy identification of the real property. Few persons, if any, could locate real property from the legal description alone without reference to a land map.

9. Terminal punctuation for WHEREAS clauses is a semicolon followed by the word *and* (; *and*) for all but the final clause. Its terminal punctuation is a semicolon.

10. Compound words: *whereas, hereinafter.*

11. Legal words: *let, terms, situate.*

12. Legal phrases: *lease and let, hereinafter provided, unimproved parcel of real estate, more particularly described as, to wit, which property, demised premises, take and hold, said terms and conditions.*

NOW, THEREFORE Clause

This paragraph immediately follows the final WHEREAS paragraph. It introduces the terms and conditions of the lease.

NOW, THEREFORE, in consideration of the premises and the covenants of the parties each to the other herein made, the lessor hereby demises and leases to the lessee and the lessee takes and leases the property above referred to as the demised premises; and it is mutually agreed by and between the lessor and the lessee as follows:

DISCUSSION

1. *NOW, THEREFORE*, is typed in all caps, with commas surrounding *THEREFORE*.

2. The entire paragraph is one sentence, which is carefully punctuated to assure clarity. Terminal punctuation is a colon.

3. Compound words: *therefore, herein, hereby.*

4. Legal words: *premises, covenants, parties, demises.*

5. Legal phrases: *each to the other herein made, demises and leases, takes and leases, above referred to, mutually agreed, by and between.*

Condition Paragraphs

Condition paragraphs state the terms and conditions of the lease, i.e., length of the lease, rental fee, use of the property, and other terms. These paragraphs are frequently single spaced, particularly if they are long or great in number. However, *only* condition paragraphs and real property descriptions are single spaced. The remainder of the lease is double spaced.

```
        1. TERM. The term of this lease shall be five (5) years from
and after April 1, 19__; provided, however, that the lessee, being then in
good standing under the terms hereof, may at any time before January 1, 19__,
renew and extend this lease for an additional successive term of five (5)
years by serving lessor, in the manner hereinafter provided, with a written
notice that it elects to renew said lease and agrees to be bound by all of
its provisions for an additional successive term of five (5) years after
April 1, 19__.

        2. RENTAL. As rental hereunder, the lessee shall, without
deduction, offset or counterclaim, on the first day of each and every calendar
month of the term of this lease or any renewal or extension of the same, pay
to lessor, in cash or by check, at such time as the lessor may from time to time
in writing direct, the sum of Six Hundred Fifty Dollars ($650.00) for each month
in the five-year period commencing with the month of April, 19__, to and includ-
ing the month of March, 19__; and in the event that the lessee has exercised its
option to renew and extend this lease for an additional term of five (5) years
as provided for herein, then the rental shall be the sum of Seven Hundred Dollars
($700.00) for each month of the five-year term commencing with the month of
April, 19__, to and including the month of March, 19__.
```

DISCUSSION

1. Condition or term paragraphs are numbered and titled to facilitate reference to pertinent portions of the lease. Titles are in all caps and immediately follow the paragraph number.

2. Each paragraph in this sample lease is a single sentence. Paragraphs often contain several sentences; however, very long sentences are acceptable legal style.

3. Commas surround the year when it follows the month and day or just the month, i.e., April, 19——, and April 1, 19——.

4. Significant numbers are written in words followed by figures in parentheses.

5. Paragraph 1, the TERM paragraph, states that the length of the lease is five years, with an option for another five years. Dates must be carefully checked to assure that five-year periods have been designated.

6. The RENTAL paragraph contains an escalator clause, which provides for an increase or escalation in rent from $1250.00 a month during the first five-year period to $1500.00 a month during the next five-year period if the option is exercised. Money figures must be very carefully checked for accuracy.

7. Compound words: *hereof, hereinafter, hereunder, herein.*

8. Legal words: *term, elects, bound, same, option.*

9. Legal phrases: *from and after; in good standing; renew and extend; successive term; written notice; without deduction, offset or counterclaim; each and every; calendar month; renewal or extension; of the same; to and including; exercise its option.*

Signature Clause and Signature Lines

At least one line of the signature clause must appear on the page containing the signature lines. Preferred style is to include both the signature clause and signature lines on a page containing a line or more (preferably three lines or more) of the body of the lease.

IN WITNESS WHEREOF, the lessor and lessee have executed these

presents the day and year first above written.

```
_____        _____
     JOHN HENRY JONES              FRANCIS PETER IRWYNE
Lessee


                               _____
                                   MARY ADAMS IRWYNE
                               Lessor
EXECUTED IN DUPLICATE
```

DISCUSSION

1. *IN WITNESS WHEREOF* is typed in all caps and is followed by a comma.

2. Signature lines are 2½ or 3 inches long and two double spaces

apart if space permits that luxury. The names of the parties are typed in all caps just below the signature lines.

3. Lessor and lessee are readily identified if the signature lines for each are placed on opposite margins of the page as shown. The word "lessee" following the lessee's signature line correctly identifies that party. The word "lessor" following the lessor's signature lines correctly identifies that party.

4. If the lease is executed in duplicate or triplicate or quadruplicate, a statement to that effect is typed in all caps at the left margin one double space below the last signature line. This information tells everyone concerned how many signed copies of the document are in existence.

5. Legal words: *executed, presents.*

6. Legal phrases: *executed these presents, day and year first above written.*

Acknowledgments

An acknowledgment is a formal statement made before an authorized individual by which the signer acknowledges that he signed the document.

```
STATE OF CALIFORNIA   )
                      )  ss.
COUNTY OF LOS ANGELES )
```

On this _____ day of March, 19_, before me, the undersigned, a notary public in and for said county and state, personally appeared FRANCIS PETER IRWYNE and MARY ADAMS IRWYNE, known to me to be the persons whose names are subscribed to the within instrument, and acknowledged to me that they executed the same.

IN WITNESS WHEREOF, I have hereunto set my hand and affixed my official seal the day and year in this certificate first above written.

```
                                     _____
                                     Notary public in and for said county
                                              and state
```

DISCUSSION

1. An acknowledgment witnessed by an authorized person, most frequently a notary public, is a necessary part of any document transferring title to real property. This lease is such a document. *Ac-*

knowledgment receives its name from the word *acknowledged,* which appears near the end of the first paragraph of the acknowledgment.

2. A second acknowledgment, for JOHN HENRY JONES, changed to state "known to me to be the *person* whose *name is* subscribed to the within instrument, and acknowledged to me that *he* executed . . ." is required to complete the lease.

3. The acknowledgments may be on separate pages. However, if by single-spacing the acknowledgments they can be included on the signature page of the lease, this is a good style. Also, if many acknowledgments are required, they should be single spaced to avoid great bulkiness of the completed lease.

4. Each party will sign all "original" copies, as will the notaries public (or notary publics).

5. The state and county in which the document is executed and notarized appear in all caps in the place and style shown in the example.

6. The abbreviation *ss.* stands for *scilicet,* which is Latin for *namely.* This abbreviation follows to the right and center of the parentheses boxing the county and state. Lowercase *s*'s are used.

7. Compound words: *undersigned, within, hereunto.*

8. Legal words: *subscribed, instrument, acknowledged, executed, affixed, seal, certificate.*

9. Legal phrases: *notary public, in and for, first above written.*

PROOFREADING

After the lease has been typed, it must be carefully proofread. All dates must be checked to assure accuracy. Names must be correct and correctly spelled. All conditions of the lease that should be a part of it must be included. The real property description should be carefully proofed as described earlier.

CORRECTIONS

Corrections are tolerated if they are not visible and if they are not a part of a name, money figure, or date. They are *not* acceptable any place in the lease if they are visible. They are never acceptable if their presence jeopardizes the legality of the document.

LEGAL BACKS

Signed copies of the lease should be enclosed in legal backs. The outside of the legal backs should contain sufficient information to identify the contents. Many clients include among their papers various legal documents. The title of the instrument, names of the lessor and lessee, the date of the instrument, and the law firm's name and address would properly identify this lease.

RECORDATION

An original, executed copy of a document transferring title to real property is usually put on record in the recorder's or records office of the county in which the real property is located. A document designed to transfer title of ownership does not, in fact, change the ownership for public record until the document has been registered with the recorder's office. If the attorney determines that the lease, a document transferring only a portion of the title, should be recorded, an executed copy should be forwarded to the records office. (For various reasons, leases are not always recorded.)

The recording fee varies from county to county and state to state. It also varies with the length of the document to be recorded. The recordation fee is advanced by the law firm. The costs will be included in the client's statement.

Once recorded, the document is returned as requested by the sender. It is usually expedient to have the document returned to the law office. The legal secretary is then able to make note of the recording data (see Figure 7-1), which is stamped on the lease cover, and conform the office copy. This information includes the time, date, book and page of recordation, as well as the document number assigned to the lease.

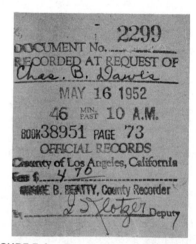

FIGURE 7-1   Completed recordation stamp

SUMMARY

A lease is a two-party client document by which a landlord conveys to a tenant an interest in and to certain named property. A lease contains the following: title; introductory paragraph; WITNESSETH or WITNESS; WHEREAS paragraphs; NOW, THEREFORE, paragraph; condition or term paragraphs; signature clause and signature lines; and acknowledgments.

A lease requires careful proofreading, with particular attention given to any real property descriptions that are a part of the lease.

If the document is placed on record with the records office of the county in which the property is located, the recordation information, when available, should be noted on the law office file copy of the document. The original document should be delivered to the client.

See Appendix B for a completed lease.

SUGGESTED SPECIAL ASSIGNMENTS

1. Make one original copy of the lease shown on pages 326–332. Proofread the metes and bounds description carefully, first by yourself, then with the assistance of a second person. Use care in completing the dates given to assure that you have a ten-year and not a nine- or eleven-year lease. The real property description must be indented and single spaced. The numbered paragraphs may be single or double spaced. The remainder of the lease must be double spaced. Assemble. Staple in correct legal style.

2. From a law office, a friend, a relative, or your own personal files, obtain a copy of a lease covering real property. Make one original copy using fictitious names. If the lease is unusually long, omit one or more of the term paragraphs. Proofread the real property description; proofread the completed lease. Assemble. Staple in correct legal style.

8

Letters, Memos, Wires, and Messages

To relegate law office correspondence to the unimportant would be similar to charging that the smartly decorated display windows of a major department store were valueless. Both are sources of information and advertising. Correspondence represents the attorney, as do the unwritten letters and the poorly written letters. But so, also, do the letters that reflect promptness, accuracy, and proficiency.

Written communications in a law office include letters, memos, wires, and telephone messages. Each, if important enough to write at all, is important enough for promptness, accuracy, and completeness.

PROMPTNESS

Since the various kinds of communication must all be handled eventually, why not handle them *now*? The same number of minutes or hours will be required whether they are prepared now or later — and the excellent public relations created by prompt action is inestimable.

Very large and successful business corporations have established definite periods of time within which incoming letters must be answered. Such a deadline is in use in some law offices. Clients who have taken their own time to write letters may reasonably expect replies within a week.

Sometimes the attorney has no news to report. Still, with the attorney's approval, a brief letter or phone call by the legal secretary could very well relieve a worried client who, without such communication, would feel neglected or forgotten. The letter would inform the client that nothing new had developed but that information would be forwarded as it was available. When such a communication has been approved, it should be typed for the attorney's signature.

You say, "Where will I find the time for this extra correspondence?" That is a problem. But a short note or phone call now may eliminate a much longer letter or phone call later. This PR technique will build goodwill for the office and for the profession.

ACCURACY

As in any paper work emanating from a law office, all written communications should be accurate in every respect, including dates, figures, names, titles, addresses, and quotations.

Dates.   If the dictator has said in a letter, ". . . meet with you at the Hotel Great on Friday, March 22," check your desk calendar to see if, in fact, March 22 does fall on Friday.

Figures.   If a money amount or other figure is used, check any notes the attorney may have on the matter to confirm the accuracy of the number.

Names.   Are you sensitive about the spelling of your name? So are others. Check spellings by referring to files, to incoming correspondence, to phone books, to city directories. If a prominent name is used and there is a question of the correct spelling, call the public library for assistance.

Titles.   A title should precede the name of the addressee. Perhaps the title is *The Honorable, Dr., Professor, Dean, The Reverend.* Or perhaps the title is simply *Mr., Ms., Miss,* or *Mrs.* Still, a title is a correct part of the first line of the inside address.

Addresses.   Street addresses must be checked and rechecked. A registered or a regular letter sent to a mistyped street address cannot be delivered. Think of the wasted time. The letter will be returned for a better address, and this time you will do the checking that should have been done the first time. Only this time you will be embarrassed about doing it.

Quotations.   If a quotation is included in a letter, double-proof it. You read the original quotation as another person checks your typed copy. Accuracy is all-important. Check and double-check. Once the habit is formed, you'll be surprised at your increased self-confidence.

COMPLETENESS

If an answer to an incoming letter is incomplete, a second letter will have to be dictated and transcribed. The secretary should share responsibility in avoiding unnecessary extra correspondence.

As the secretary opens and reads incoming mail, the particular items that require attention may be checkmarked in the margin or lightly underscored in pencil. When the answer to the letter has been dictated, the secretary can quickly check to make certain all information requested in the incoming letter was included in the dictated answer.

Occasionally incoming mail will include, as an afterthought, a request for information far removed from the original intent of the letter. It is these items that are sometimes overlooked by the dictator. It is these items the legal secretary should check. This extra quality in a secretary is an unusually valuable asset.

A telephone message that fails to include a name, a telephone number, date, or time of day is not complete, and an incomplete communication is sometimes valueless or even harmful.

Check the incoming letter, check instructions, check, check, and be certain the communication you are preparing is complete.

I suppose every attorney has, at one time or another, received a letter concerning a scheduled meeting but neglecting to include either the date, the time, or the location. Such an omission cannot happen if the attorney and secretary are both watchful in the preparation of correspondence.

LETTERS

Law office letters are as necessary to the law office as business letters are to the business office. Both serve the same purpose: to seek or to furnish information. Letters are emissaries of the office. They make either a favorable and lasting impression or an unfavorable and lasting impression. An unprofessional-appearing letter has been typed by an amateur; a professional-appearing letter has been typed by a pro.

A legal secretary can help make correspondence a valuable public relations tool by giving special attention not only to promptness, accuracy, and completeness, but also to letter style and form.

For discussion purposes, we will dissect a letter into twelve parts, as follows:

1. Paper, letterheads, carbon ribbons
2. Style
3. Date
4. Inside address and attention line
5. Subject line
6. Salutation
7. Body
8. Complimentary closing and signature line
9. Miscellaneous notations
10. Extra copies
11. Continuation sheets
12. Envelopes

Paper, Letterheads, Carbon Ribbons

Paper

Erasable white bond for originals and lightweight white and yellow paper for carbon copies are used in most offices. Some offices, possibly because of the slightly higher charge for erasable paper, use good quality bond. However, erasable paper of good quality is practical since it does permit invisible corrections if they are made before the printing has penetrated the finish. The secretary does not live who does not make an occasional typing error.

Letterheads

Letterheads used by law offices are conservative almost to the extreme. Printers offer a choice of several styles, but the popular choice is one that includes the firm's name, address, and telephone number in black print centered near the top of the paper. Names of partners are usually printed in the margins.

Lightweight letterhead paper is practical for overseas airmail use. Further, a multipage letter should be typed on onionskin paper to save weight. If page one of a letter is typed on letterhead bond, pages 2, 3, 4, and so on, will be typed on plain bond. If page one is typed on letterhead onionskin, all continuation pages will be typed on plain onionskin.

The first page of *carbon copies* of letters is typed on onionskin letterhead. All continuation pages, that is, pages 2, 3, 4, and so on, would be on plain onionskin paper.

Carbon copies of letters are always typed on onionskin paper. An exception to this statement is this: if two signed copies of a letter are required, then the original and first carbon of the letter would be typed on bond letterhead, with all continuation sheets on bond.

Carbon Ribbons

Correctable typewriters, whose carbon ribbons and lift-off tapes permit the *removal* of type errors, are an important part of law office equipment. However, you may find yourself assigned to a noncorrectable carbon ribbon typewriter. Correctable carbon ribbons and lift-off tabs are available for most carbon ribbon typewriters. Inquire about them at a stationery supply company. If they are available for your typewriter, you may be surprised at the convenience and efficiency of these ribbons and their separate lift-off tabs.

Style

The *semiblock style* with block paragraphs is usual for legal correspondence. The date is centered a double or triple space below the letterhead. A letter typed in semiblock style follows:

<pre>
                              May 12, 19__

     Clarenden Insurance Company
     316 West Olive Avenue
     City, State 00000

     Attention: Mr. M. R. Clarenden

                                Re: Robert Xix Account

     Gentlemen:

     Enclosed is trustee's check made payable to you in the sum of $202.02
     for Robert Xix's insurance with the Wendelworth Program.

     Please have the payment date changed from the first of the month to the
     tenth of the month. As you know, in the past whenever the payments
     were not made promptly on the first of the month, an overdue statement,
     plus additional charges, was sent.

     The funds that are made available for this payment are not received in
     this office until after the first of the month. Will you please change
     the date to the tenth so we may eliminate the additional charges.

                              Very truly yours,

                              BROWN, BROWN and BROWN

                              By_____
                                      John Henry Brown

     JHB:aa
     Enclosure
</pre>

Full-block style can be achieved by beginning every line of the letter at the left margin. This includes the date, subject line, and the complimentary closing. A triple space between the final line of the complimentary closing and the miscellaneous notations adds to the professional appearance of the letter.

Margins

During World War II, margins were standardized by the then War Department and other government agencies. A modification of that style developed and spread into business and industry because standardization is timesaving and, therefore, money-saving. Letters long and short may be written with standard margins of about one and one-quarter inches. The use of standardized margins will increase productivity.

Centering letters top to bottom is accomplished by varying the number of spaces between the letterhead and the first line of the inside address. If the letter is very long, few spaces are left. If the letter is very short, a great many spaces are left.

Watching the right margin to keep it equal to or slightly narrower than the left margin will center the letters left to right.

Centering a letter top to bottom is a skill that requires practice. However, even the most proficient sometimes misjudge. The complimentary closing and signature lines may be used as an elevator. If the letter is a little low on the page, less space should be left for the signature. Steno initials and miscellaneous notations should be placed at the left margin directly across from the signature line. If the letter is a little too high on the page, five or six spaces may be left for the signature, and steno initials may be dropped an extra space or two.

Date

Every letter must be dated the day it is to be mailed. On a full-block letter the date will begin at the left margin an inch or so above the inside address. For other letter styles, the date is usually centered about an inch below the letterhead. An acceptable alternate style is to place the date near the right margin.

Inside Address and Attention Line

Inside Address

Inside addresses may range from three lines to seven lines plus an attention line. Some business letterheads include general information not properly part of an inside address. Only the information necessary for the letter to reach its destination should be used. When both a street address and a post office box are included in the letterhead, only the post office box should be used. The street address is given for the use of those who wish to visit the establishment.

Attention Line

Law office correspondence is occasionally addressed to a firm, a corporation, or a government office with an attention line directing the letter to a particular individual or office. This attention line is part of the inside address and should be placed a double space below the inside address at the left margin. However, on the envelope the attention line is placed a single or double space *above* the address.

CAUTION: It is essential that the attention line be shown on the envelope.

Continuation Lines

If a line of the inside address is overlong, it should be continued to a second line and the continuation line indented sufficiently to show the continuation. On a standard typewriter, two spaces should be indented.

Letter	*Envelope*

Mr. Charles Henry Adams
General Manager and
    Vice-President
Blank Lumber Company
Post Office Box 000
City, State   00000
	Mr. Charles Henry Adams
	General Manager and
	    Vice-President
	Blank Lumber Company
	Post Office Box 000
	City, State 00000

Dear Mr. Adams:	

Blank Lumber Company
Post Office Box 000
City, State   00000
	Attention Mr. Charles Henry Adams
	            General Manager and
	                Vice-President

Attention Mr. Charles Henry Adams
        General Manager and
            Vice-President
	Blank Lumber Company
	Post Office Box 000
	City, State 00000

Gentlemen:	

Accuracy

Care must be used in checking inside addresses to assure complete accuracy. If a name is misspelled, the addressee could very well be offended. If the street address or city or state is incorrect, the letter will be delayed in reaching its destination.

It is good style to give every addressee a title: *Mr., Mrs., Miss, Ms., Dr.,* or other appropriate title. Correct forms of address for judges, members of the clergy, government officials, and many others are given in most desk dictionaries. Incorrectly addressing a client or associate implies carelessness. On the other hand, careful use of titles is a good public relations tool.

If a woman is married, her title is *Mrs.* If a woman is single her title is *Miss.* The correct title for a woman whose marital status is unknown is *Ms.*, a title that many women, married or single, adopt by personal preference.

A woman can assure that her preferred title will be used if the title is included as part of the *typed* signature of her letters; i.e., *Ms. Sara Jones, Miss Sara Jones, Mrs. Sara Jones.* The title *Mr.*, in parentheses, should precede the *typed* signature of a man whose given name is used for both masculine and feminine; i.e., *(Mr.) Connie Smith, (Mr.) Sandy Jones.* Otherwise, *Mr.* is omitted from the typed signature.

An earned title such as *M.D. (medical doctor)* and *Ph.D. (doctor of philosophy)* is included in the first line of the inside address; i.e., *Dr. Marilyn Smith* or *Dr. Henry Jones.* If one were to write *Dr. Marilyn Smith, M.D.,* or *Dr. Henry Jones, Ph.D.,* the title *doctor* would, in fact, have been written twice.

In England, a title used by solicitors and barristers is *Esquire,* abbreviated *Esq.* It is the equivalent of *Mr.* in the United States. *Esq.* follows the name, i.e., *John Barrister, Esq.* The title is sometimes used by United States attorneys. To use both *Mr.* and *Esq.* in addressing a letter would be the same as writing *Mr. John Smith, Mr.*

Subject Line

The subject line is used for immediate reference to the subject matter of the letter. Therefore, it should stand out. Where better than below the inside address and to the right, as in the letter on page 114? In this position, the subject line is surrounded by space on all sides.

Re, from *res*, Latin for *thing*, is followed by a colon. The subject (usually the title of a case) follows. If it is too long for one line, the continuation line begins under the first word of the subject, not under the *R* in *Re*.

        Re: Francis Peter Irwyne vs.
             WWW Railway

In legal correspondence, the subject line is usually placed a double space below the inside address and a double space above the salutation. In business correspondence, the subject line follows the salutation.

Salutation

Salutations used in law office letters are the same as those used in business letters. Common salutations are these:

Gentlemen:
Dear Mr. Jones:
Dear Mary:
Dear Judge Smith:

Special salutations are given in the *forms of address* sections of most desk dictionaries. These sections are indexed and are also shown on the contents page of the dictionaries.

The alert legal secretary will record in a handy notebook or an alphabet file the names and addresses of those persons frequently written to. A note should also be made of any special salutations such as

Dear Bob:	Dear Spoof:
Dear Mary:	Dear Rich:

To so address a person one time and not another would reflect a change in relationship between the addressor and the addressee. It is the secretary's responsibility to assure the same friendly salutation each time.

The middle words are not capitalized in such salutations as

My dear Joe: My good friend Ed:

Punctuation

A colon follows the salutation. However, if open punctuation is used (no punctuation following the salutation), a comma should not follow the complimentary closing. This open punctuation style is frequently used in law office correspondence.

Body

Either blocked or indented paragraphs are used in legal correspondence. However, blocked paragraphs are more efficient since they eliminate two steps: setting and striking the paragraph tab.

Letters are almost always single spaced with double spaces between paragraphs. An exception to this is the one-sentence letter, which should be double spaced unless the sentence is extremely long.

I know of an attorney, a very successful one, who insists that his correspondence all be double spaced. And why not? It is his office, his correspondence, and his signature at the bottom of the letters. But his is indeed an unusual style.

Minor Editing

At no time do I advocate changing dictation. This is the prerogative of the dictator only. I do suggest, however, that the legal secretary be alert to minor editing that would improve both the appearance and the sound of the correspondence.

Suppose the attorney has dictated, "Referring to the second paragraph of your letter, I refer you to. . . ." It is the secretary's editing duty to change one of the "refer" words. How about "Regarding the second paragraph of your letter, I refer you to. . . ."

Suppose the dictation reads, "Your gesture is sincerely appreciated. Sincerely yours." How about "Your gesture is very much appreciated. Sincerely yours." Or, "Your gesture is sincerely appreciated. Yours very truly."

Occasionally a dictator will overuse the words *I* or *we*. Sometimes a sentence can simply be turned around. "I hope you will plan to spend some time. . . ." may be changed to "When you are in the city next week, please plan to spend some time. . . ." Overuse of *I* and *we*, particularly if they happen to be the first words in each of several paragraphs, is somewhat stuffy. The thoughtful secretary can deftly alter the construction and eliminate the problem.

Plural subjects require plural verbs and singular subjects require singular verbs. If lengthy dictation separates the subject and the verb, the dictator may err in matching the verb to its subject. Editing such errors is the responsibility of the professional legal secretary.

Complimentary Closing and Signature Line

Sincerely yours is probably the most regularly used of all complimentary closings, but *very truly yours*, *yours truly*, *cordially yours*, and many others are also used. If the attorney enjoys using the friendly, old-fashioned phrase

I remain,

Yours very truly,

type it. However, you, the legal secretary, should not adopt this style in the letters you compose and write for the firm over your signature.

The complimentary closing is typed a double space below the body of the letter and begins at the center or a half-inch left of center to provide ample space for the dictator's signature.

Signature lines may include the firm name in all caps and the attorney's name and title. Or they may include only the attorney's name or title. Following are several styles used by law firms:

Sincerely yours,	Sincerely yours,
BROWN, BROWN and BROWN	BROWN, BROWN and BROWN
By_____ Charles W. Brown	By_____ Charles W. Brown Attorney at Law
Sincerely yours,	Sincerely yours,
BROWN, BROWN and BROWN	
By	John C. Attorney
Sincerely yours,	Sincerely yours,
John C. Attorney Attorney at Law	Attorney at Law

Variations in the spacing of complimentary closings and signature lines to improve the appearance of a poorly placed letter are suggested earlier in the chapter.

Miscellaneous Notations

Special notations regarding enclosures and mailing instructions for the letter are placed below the signature line and at the left margin. These notations are primarily for the use of the secretary, or, if the firm is very large, for the use of the mail-room employees.

If such notations are grouped together, a quick glance at that area will tell the secretary or mail clerk

- who dictated and who typed the letter
- whether enclosures are to be added

- whether the letter is regular, airmail, or special delivery
- whether the letter is registered or certified
- whether a return receipt is requested
- whether there are extra copies for delivery (Extra copies are discussed later in this chapter.)

Enclosure is used to indicate one or more enclosures. The word will remind the secretary to make the enclosure. If the body of the letter does not identify the enclosures, each should be described briefly or listed by title on the *office* copy of the letter. If the letter is going to the mailroom and enclosures (booklets, speeches, etc.) are held there, a notation identifying the enclosures to be added should be paperclipped to the letter.

Registered and certified mail must be taken to the post office for handling.

Some notations follow:

```
JWB:aa                              JWB:aa
Enclosure                           Enclosure
Airmail--Special Delivery           Certified--RRR

JWB:aa                              JWB:aa
Airmail                             Registered Mail
```

Personal, confidential, and *personal and confidential* notations are typed in all caps a double space above the inside address at the left margin. This notation is primarily for the use of the addressee and will, in this position, give immediate notice of the confidential nature of the letter. For the same reason, this notation appears a double space above the envelope address in all caps.

Extra Copies

Extra copies are an expedient used to furnish identical information to each of several persons by means of a single letter. Extra copies are required for open copies, blind copies, and letters with multiple inside addresses. Many offices make carbon copies; many offices use the copier for the extra copies. Onionskin paper is used for carbon copies *except* when more than one copy of a letter is to be signed.

Open Copies

If the addressee should be informed that a copy of the letter is being sent to another, the notation is shown just below the miscellaneous notations *on the original and all copies.* If the copy is a carbon copy, the notation is "cc Mr. John Jones." If the copy is made on a copier, the notation is "copy to Mr. John Jones."

Blind Copies (bc) and Blind Carbon Copies (bcc)

Blind copies are used when the information contained in a letter will be of interest to others, yet the addressee would not benefit by learning of the distribution. *The "blind" notation is not shown on the original letter.*

For example, the attorney sends Mrs. Prospective Client a letter confirming a morning telephone call. Another firm attorney and an insurance agent are to be informed of the letter's contents. If carbon copies are made, the carbon pack will consist of an original on bond letterhead, thin yellow for the office copy, and two white onionskin letterheads for the blind copies. (Copies to employees are often typed on plain white onionskin.)

The letter will be addressed to the client and typed in its entirety. The original will be removed from the typewriter. Below the necessary miscellaneous notations at the left margin will be typed "bcc Mr. Henry Insurance" followed by Mr. Insurance's complete address. The title "Mr." is used because Mr. Insurance is not a member of the law firm. The inside address is included for the information of the firm attorney and also for the later use of the dictator and the secretary.

One thin white copy of the letter will be removed from the typewriter. On the remaining white carbon copy and yellow office copy is shown "bcc Mary Attorney."

What do we have?

- For the client, the original with no copy notations.
- For the insurance agent, a white copy showing that a blind copy of the letter went to him.
- For the firm attorney, a white copy showing blind copies went to Mr. Henry Insurance and to Mary Attorney. The associate knows exactly who receives copies of the letter.
- The office copy tells the complete story.

If a copier is used for making the extra copies, they are made from the original letter. The necessary bc notations are added to the extra copies as indicated. The office copy contains all of the information.

Occasionally the writer will wish to add a message for one of the recipients of a blind copy. If such a notation were for the insurance agent, the notation would appear on all extra copies. If the message were for the associate attorney, the style would be the same, but the message would appear only on the attorney's copy and the office file copy.

Multiple Inside Addresses

There may be occasions when a letter will be addressed to two or more people with different addresses. The inside addresses will be typed, one under the other, and all copies will be signed by the dictator.

To eliminate any possible chance for offense, addressees should be listed alphabetically:

```
Mr. John Doe
576 Waters Street
City, State  00000

Mr. Richard Roe
245 Rivers Street
City, State  00000

                          Re:  Lake Street Contract

Gentlemen:
```

The carbon pack for a letter addressed to several people would be: original, thin yellow, and the required number of bond letterheads. If the copies required were too numerous to permit legible copies if made on bond, all copies of the letter, including the original, would be typed on onionskin letterhead.

The salutation, if all addressees were men, would be "Gentlemen." If both men and women were named, the simplest solution would be to eliminate the salutation entirely.

To assure that copies go to each addressee, a small but visible checkmark should be added immediately following the name of the one to whom that particular copy is to be delivered. Thus, each copy of the letter (except the office file copy) should have one checkmark saying, in effect, "Send me to. . . ."

Checkmarks

A checkmark following the insurance agent's name would reserve that copy for him. A checkmark following Mary Attorney's name would reserve that copy for her.

Suppose a letter were sent to an opposing counsel and blind carbon copies were to be typed for each of several persons, all of equal status. The names should be alphabetized and checkmarked, one checkmark to a copy. The checkmark simply means, "Send me to. . . ."

Complete addresses for those receiving blind carbon copies are included only when they would serve a definite purpose.

Appearance and Legibility

It is not possible to stress too much the importance of producing legible carbon copies. To help assure legibility, many offices use lightweight yellow paper for office copies. A carbon pack follows:

- Bond
- Lightweight yellow
- Lightweight white onionskin — as many as required within the limits of the typewriter

This assembling method assures a clear, legible office copy.

Continuation Sheets

Continuation sheets (pages 2, 3, and so on) should be the same quality paper as the first page. Each should contain a heading to identify it.

```
Mrs. Prospective Client
Page 2
Date
```

or

```
Mrs. Prospective Client          2                              Date
```

Envelopes

With the advent of the ZIP code, envelopes have taken on a new appearance. The ZIP code scanner reads from top to bottom of an envelope, then it returns to the bottom line of the envelope and reads across. If it does not find a ZIP code on that bottom line, it discards the envelope for manual sorting. This requires that the typist place *nothing* below the bottom line of the envelope address.

In view of the inflexibility of the scanner, those who address letters must, of necessity, be flexible. Miscellaneous information such as attention lines and air mail and certified RRR notations must be typed above the inside address.

Appearance. Envelopes should be neat and unsmudged, and should contain all information necessary to get the letter from the sender to the addressee quickly.

Mailing instructions such as special delivery are typed in the stamp area of the envelope. These notations are for the use of postal service employees and will be most readily seen in that area of the envelope.

Attention lines are properly a part of the inside address. They should be typed as the first or the second line of the envelope address, or a double space above the company name.

Personal and confidential notations must appear on the envelope as well as on the letter. What good are they if they are not immediately apparent to those handling the envelope at its destination? This notation should appear in all caps a double space above the envelope address.

IMPORTANT: The envelope address should be an exact duplicate of the inside address on the letter to facilitate proofreading of both. If notations are typed in all caps on the letter, they should be typed in all caps on the envelope.

MEMOS

Memos, short for memorandums or memoranda, are interoffice communications. They are informal, their style is carefully careless, and they are less time-consuming to dictate and to type than the formal, demanding business letters.

Memos must contain certain elements:

• Date
• Names of addressees
• Name of writer or originator
• Subject
• Message
• Dictator and steno initials

Style

The most efficient of the memo styles is that shown below. Only one tab need be set, and it can be quickly set by an experienced guess. Aligning the heading titles at the left margin and aligning the names and subject one directly beneath the other presents a neat, attractive appearance. Further, each of these items is quickly identifiable.

Double spaces separate each of the groups in the heading, and a triple space separates the subject from the single-spaced body of the memo. Paragraphs are not indented.

```
                                          Date

     To:          J. Doe
                  R. Roe

     From:        R. W. Smith

     Re:          Automatic typewriters


     Representatives of two typewriter companies will call at the office on
     Monday, April 17. The first will arrive at 2 p.m., and the second will
     arrive about 3 p.m.  Each will explain his company's automatic
     typewriters with special attention to use in a law office.

     If we can all meet with these gentlemen, we should be able to make our
     decision soon regarding the possible purchase of automatic typewriters
     for the office.

     RWS:aa
```

An original, thin white, and office copy of this memo would be typed. The original would be checkmarked for J. Doe, the white carbon copy would be checkmarked for R. Roe, and the yellow copy would be filed in the office files.

Names of Addressees Alphabetized

If a memo is addressed to more than one person, the names should be alphabetized. This is a simple but effective public relations tool. Let no one be offended because a name came last in a random listing of names. And let no one feel superior because a name came first. Further, names are quickly located in alphabetical lists.

Unsigned Communication

Memos are usually unsigned, although occasionally dictators do initial or sign them. A typed signature is extraneous on interoffice communications; the writer's name appears in the heading.

Identification Initials and Attachment Notation

Identification initials are typed at the left margin below the message. If appropriate, the word *attachment* is typed below the steno initials. Materials to be sent with a memo are stapled or paperclipped to the original. Therefore, the term *attachment* is appropriate.

Information Copies

A memo may be addressed to several people, each of whom must act on the information contained therein. A copy of the same memo might be sent to another in the office for information only. In this event, that person's name would be typed below the stenographer's initials as follows: *cc Robert Attorney.* This notation would appear on the original and on all copies of the memo.

Checkmarking the names to identify who gets which copy is as important on memos as it is on copies of letters.

WIRES

Wires (telegrams) are used if a message must be delivered quickly and a written record kept of it. Some kinds of messages sent by Western Union are straight telegrams, day letters, night letters, and cablegrams. Special information about service and delivery should be obtained directly from the local Western Union office.

Style

If Western Union blanks are available in the office, they should be used. Otherwise, a wire is typed in all caps on white bond. Since this copy remains in the office, it is the office copy. Western Union uses all caps for its messages, and any wires contained in the office files are more readily identified if they are typed in all caps. A telegram contains certain elements:

- Type of message: wire, night letter, or other
- Date
- Inside address
- Message
- Sender's name and company

Delivery

After the wire has been typed and approved by the dictator, it must be given to Western Union for transmittal to the addressee. The procedure follows:

- Dial Western Union.
- Ask for an operator and furnish such information as may be requested,

i.e., office telephone number, firm name, and so on.
- Read the operator the complete wire, including the inside address, message, and sender's name and company.
- Have the wire read back in its entirety to assure its accuracy.

At the conclusion of the phone call, a notation of the time, day, and initials of the one calling Western Union should be written on the face of the wire:

sent
10:10 a.m. 1/2/8——
aa

The notation may later be of very real importance. Further, it protects the secretary because it verifies that the wire was sent, when, and by whom. (Upon request, Western Union will mail the sender a copy of the wire. There is a nominal charge for this service.)

Western Union has available Telefax machines for the use of very large law offices requiring this service. If such a machine is available in an office, the wire will be typed over the Telefax machine, which will, in turn, transmit it to the local Western Union office for transmittal to its ultimate destination.

TELEPHONE MESSAGES

The receptionist, stenographer, or legal secretary who takes a telephone message is responsible for reporting it immediately and accurately. All messages should contain

- Date
- Time of day: hour and minute
- Whether the call is to be returned
- Name and telephone number of the caller
- Brief but clear summary of the message
- Name or initials of the one taking the message

Telephone messages are usually filed in the appropriate legal file folder. They have taken the time of office personnel. In addition, they may add to a pending legal matter an item of information that may not only have current value but be of importance later in the development of the case. Messages are made in duplicate in many law offices to avoid loss or misplacement.

SUMMARY

Legal secretaries are called upon to write letters, memos, wires, and telephone messages, all of which are included in office communications.

Letters are goodwill ambassadors of the law office. They are one of the means of advertising available to the office. It is incumbent upon the secretary to send out attractive, prompt, accurate, and complete letters. The time spent to achieve expertness and efficiency is time well spent.

The appearance of memos, wires, and telephone messages is secondary to the content, for office personnel alone will see these papers. However, always remembering the importance of neatness and exactness, the legal secretary will also prepare all of these forms of communication in careful fashion.

SUGGESTED SPECIAL ASSIGNMENTS

1. Type the letter to Clarendon Insurance Company given on page 114. Make an open copy for Mr. Robert Xix, 450 West Haven Avenue, City, State, ZIP, and an office file copy. This letter will require two envelopes: one for the insurance company and one for Mr. Xix. Use your city and state and an appropriate or fictitious ZIP code number. Caution: Checkmark the copy for Mr. Xix.

2. Type the multiple address letter to Hall, Keln, and Zolle, shown on page 347. Make appropriate extra copies and a file copy. Prepare the necessary envelopes. Use fictitious ZIP code numbers. Caution: Checkmark carefully and correctly.

3. Make the necessary copies of the memo on page 126 with an extra copy for Harriet Morton. (The notation *cc Harriet Morton* will show on the original and all copies just below the steno initials.)

PART TWO

Part Two will discuss the law and the courts;

The forms — printed and typed — so necessary to law office efficiency;

Court documents — prepared by the law office for the use of the courts;

Complaints and summonses — the first papers prepared in a lawsuit;

Answers — the defendant's response to the plaintiff's complaint;

Legal procedure — the steps necessary to commence, continue, and conclude a legal matter;

Probate court and probate procedure — the means established under law to permit one to administer another's estate.

9

The Law
and the Courts

Law is that set of rules or methods established to permit coexistence in a society. Without the law to guide and protect us, we could do as we pleased — right or wrong, helpful or destructive. But we do have the law. It protects both ourselves and our property, and it denies us the right to harm others or their property.

Courts, on the other hand, are that part of the government established to apply the law and to administer justice.

THE LAW

Law is a nebulous term. It may refer to the whole law, or it may refer to a broad or a fine classification of law, for the word *law* may be used in many ways. The legal secretary will wonder about and work with

- Sources of law and
- Classifications of law

and all that each includes.

Where did our laws originate? Are our laws static, remaining the same, decade in and decade out? Hardly. The dynamic character of the law is its most appealing quality. The sources of law in the United States of America vary. They are

- Constitution (constitutional law)
- Statutes (statutory law)
- Common law (in those states whose law is based on the English common law)
- Case law
- Napoleonic Code (used in Louisiana, which was a French colony and in its early history adopted the Napoleonic Code of France)
- Administrative agencies (administrative law)

Constitution

The Constitution of the United States of America is the supreme law of the land. All laws passed by the legislatures, both federal and state, and all decisions made by the courts must be within the meaning of the Constitution.

The fifty state constitutions are the supreme laws of each of those states. No state constitution may be in conflict with the provisions of the Constitution of the United States of America.

Constitutional law. This is the branch of public law dealing with the establishment and interpretation of the constitutions, federal or state. It determines the validity of acts and statutes as related to the meaning or interpretation of provisions of the constitutions.

Many law firms and many attorneys specialize in constitutional law.

Statutes

Statutes are the laws that come into existence via the lawmaking bodies of the nation, usually called the legislatures.

Federal statutes or laws. These laws are brought into existence by the Congress of the United States. Proposed laws are written, studied, and voted upon by the members of the Congress; if passed they become a part of the law of the nation. They may then be codified, that is, systematically added to the appropriate section of the United States Code. The United States Code, with annual supplements, is a compilation of the general and permanent laws of the United States.

State statutes or laws.   Enactments of the legislatures bring these laws into existence; they are applicable only in the state where enacted. As with federal laws, proposed state laws are written, studied, and voted upon by the state legislature, and if passed become a part of the general state law. They may then be codified or systematically added to the appropriate section of the state code. State code books, with supplements, are compilations of the general and permanent laws of the state.

State code books are kept current by pocket supplements issued annually. It is frequently a responsibility of the legal secretary to insert the pocket supplements into the pocket sections of the inside back covers of the appropriate code books. In this manner, code books may be brought up to date. Pocket supplements must be matched to the correct book and accurately and regularly filed.

Statutory law.   Law originating with the legislatures and found in the general laws of each state or in the appropriate United States Code or state code books is statutory law. This law is sometimes referred to as written law, since the laws are written for study, written at the time of passage, and written into the code books.

Local and municipal ordinances.   Laws passed by city or local councils are known as local and municipal ordinances. They are effective within the city limits. These laws, too, must be within the meaning of the state constitution and also within the meaning of the Constitution of the United States.

Common law

Common law is the body of law that originated and developed in England following the Norman Conquest in 1066. The Norman conquerors established courts and traveling judges. Decisions of a court were based upon the customs of the community, and these decisions served as precedents for similar problems that later came before the courts.

When the newly independent colonies of America formed their government, they chose to adopt the law with which they were most familiar — the English common law. Thus English common law was and is a source of law in this country. Where there is no written law, the common law continues.

Common law is sometimes called *unwritten law* because it originated from court decisions rather than from written statutes or decrees.

Present-day use of the common law principle.   A judge will make sufficient inquiry among the two parties to a legal dispute to discover the accepted practice in a particular trade or industry. Once satisfied that a certain practice is common among the people of that trade or industry, the judge accepts that practice as law and renders a decision accordingly.

Case Law

Case law refers to the reported cases that together form a body of law or precedence upon which decisions in later cases will be based. Most of the law books in an attorney's library are reports of cases decided by the courts. The judges in later cases will normally rely on the case law as reported in these law books.

The principle of *stare decisis* (STAR-ē dē-SĪ-sis), Latin for *to stand by a decision*, refers to the policy of the courts to stay with or stand by precedent. Thus, the rules of the law are applied in common to all persons.

Napoleonic Code

Napoleon founded in France the necessarily strong form of government required in order to establish a unified system of law. During the early part of the nineteenth century, France adopted what came to be known as the Napoleonic Code.

Louisiana, a French colony during the early history of this nation, adopted the Napoleonic Code. Many of Louisiana's laws have come from this Code rather than from the English common law adopted by other states of the Union.

Administrative Agencies

Administrative agencies are created by acts of Congress at the federal level and by acts of the legislature at the state level. The lawmaking bodies establish the area of control of the newly created agencies. Further, they often empower those agencies to make and enforce the rules necessary to accomplish their objectives.

The agencies are frequently empowered also to make investigations in the areas they cover and to prosecute violators of those rules or administrative laws.

Some administrative agencies are branches of executive departments and others are independent agencies of the federal or state government.

Independent agencies.   Among many others at the federal level of government are these independent administrative agencies:

- Federal Communications Commission
- National Aeronautics and Space Administration
- National Labor Relations Board
- Bureau of Indian Affairs
- Veterans Administration
- Environmental Protection Agency

Branches of executive departments. Here are only a very few of the federal administrative agencies that are branches of executive departments:

- Forest Service, a division of the United States Department of Agriculture
- Fish and Wildlife Service, a branch of the Department of the Interior
- Internal Revenue Service and
- United States Secret Service, both branches of the Department of the Treasury
- Social Security Administration, a division of the Department of Health and Human Services

State administrative agencies. Some administrative agencies created by action of the state legislatures are these:

- Departments of revenue
- Public utilities commissions
- Industrial relations departments
- Welfare departments
- Highway departments

Administrative law. To function properly and to achieve the objectives for which they were brought into existence, administrative agencies are frequently empowered to make laws, to establish procedure to gain their objectives, and to enforce their laws.

When differences arise between individuals or businesses and the administrative agencies, legal assistance may be required. Because of the individualistic nature of the procedure, laws, and forms of administrative agencies, many law firms have specialized in this branch of law, which continues to grow very rapidly.

The wise legal secretary will have immediately available the full names, telephone numbers, and addresses of the administrative agencies regularly contacted by the law office. If the firm specializes in administrative law, the legal secretary must become familiar with the forms and procedures of the agencies. Further, a reasonable supply of the agency forms regularly used in the office must be kept on hand.

Classifications of Law

A legal problem facing an attorney may involve law of one or several classifications. It may be a matter of federal, state, or municipal law; of public law or private law; of civil law or criminal law; and the solution will surely involve substantive and procedural law.

Federal, State, and Municipal Law

Federal laws. Certain laws are exclusively federal laws. Some such laws are bankruptcy laws, patent and trademark laws, laws passed by the Congress of the United States, and the law set forth in the Constitution. These laws have the same force and effect in all parts of the nation. They cross state lines and are enforced by federal officers.

State laws. These are laws passed by a state legislature. They are effective only in that state. It is true that the laws must be within the meaning of the United States Constitution, but they apply exclusively to the state and its people. They are enforced by state officers.

City ordinances. Laws enacted by city officials are city ordinances. They are effective within the boundaries of the city and are enforced by municipal officers.

Public Law and Private Law

Public law. That body of law directly involving the government is public law. Criminal law is a part of public law; i.e., when a suspect has been accused, the government brings suit. International law is a part of public law, as are administrative law and maritime law (law relating to navigation and business conducted at sea). Public law is also concerned with the authority of the federal and state governments to make laws and federal and state executives to issue orders.

Private law. The body of law having to do with relationships among or between people is private law. Included in private law are

- Real estate law
- Domestic relations
- Partnerships
- Law of contracts, which is concerned with the enforceability of agreements between people or institutions
- Tort law, which is concerned with the rights of individuals to be free from interference by others with regard to their persons, property, or reputations. Personal injury and property damage suits, slander, libel, and assault and battery lawsuits are tort actions.

Civil Law and Criminal Law

Civil law and criminal law are possibly most easily distinguishable by the consequences of the trial: The consequence of a civil trial is a money judgment, an order of the court for a party to the suit to do or not to do a thing, or a verdict for the defendant. The consequence of a criminal trial is a fine, imprisonment in a penal institution, or an acquittal.

Civil law. This field of law adjusts differences between people or institutions. It includes all the fields of law that involve business relationships, civil wrongs, and property ownership. The government may also be party to a civil suit; that is, an individual or institution could bring suit against the government.

Criminal law. This law includes as parties to the suit the government, on the one hand, as plaintiff, and an individual or institution, on the other hand, as defendant who has allegedly violated a law.

Substantive Law and Procedural Law

Substantive law. This is the great body of law. *Substance* is the word from which *substantive law* comes. Substantive law is that part of the law having to do with our rights and our obligations. It is the law as stated in the Constitution of the United States and in the state constitutions, in the federal and state statutes. It is the law established by administrative agencies, and it is the law included in the common law and in case law.

Until an attorney knows the facts of a matter, a determination cannot be made as to which part of the substantive law has been violated or if, in fact, there has been a violation. Knowledge of all the facts must be had before it can be determined whether there are grounds for a lawsuit. Facts are simply those circumstances, happenings, occurrences, statements, documents, articles, and other property that are real, that exist or did exist, and that are important to a particular legal matter.

Notice the word *matter*. It means *case* or *legal action*. It has a legal flavor that will be detected as these pages and chapters are read.

As the legal secretary works with various client and court documents, much substantive law will be learned by "osmosis." This knowledge may be instrumental in a later decision to earn a law degree, pass the bar, and practice law. This is a pattern followed by many legal secretaries. Further, the legal knowledge gained by the secretary may be of real value in anticipating and solving personal problems.

One thing the legal secretary will learn above all else: for legal advice, see an attorney.

Procedural law. Procedural law is also called *adjective* or *descriptive* law. This is the law that describes the procedure for preparing a case for court, continuing it through the court, and bringing it to a conclusion.

There are many statutes that limit the manner of filing cases. If these statutes are not complied with exactly, the attorney may lose the case at that stage regardless of the merits of the case. In appealing a case, for example, most states have statutes requiring that an appeal be filed within a given number of days. If the necessary documents are not filed with the clerk of the court within that period of time, there can be no appeal.

The Paris peace talks during the Vietnam War were greatly delayed because of procedural law. The shape of the conference table became a paramount issue: should it be round, oblong, square, U-shaped? This had nothing to do with substantive law; it was simply a procedural matter that had to be resolved before talks on substantive law could begin. All parties to the peace conference were involved in this matter of procedural law.

For the legal secretary, adjective law is the how-to of law: how to type a court document to meet the court's approval; how to commence, continue, and conclude a legal action; how to type a client document so that, if necessary, it will withstand litigation.

Adjective law (or procedural or descriptive law) is the first concern of the legal secretary. If there is uncertainty about how to do something in a law office, the legal secretary must know that there is a correct way to do it, as well as where to go to find that correct way.

Substantive law is the domain of the attorney. Procedural law is the concern of the legal secretary. But do not be misled. The attorney is responsible for both of these facets of law. The attorney cannot, does not, and will not relinquish responsibility for searching, sorting, and studying substantive law. The knowledge and the accompanying responsibility of procedural law are shared with the secretary.

Legal Actions

Legal actions are those court proceedings by which, in a *civil* action, one party seeks redress for a wrong or protection of a right (private law); and in a *criminal* action, the government prosecutes an individual or institution for the alleged commission of a crime (public law).

Civil Actions

Civil actions are lawsuits involving two parties; thus we will refer to them as two-party actions. A party may be an individual, partnership, corporation, or other individual or agency. Parties to the action are the *plaintiff*, who brings the action, and the *defendant*, against whom the action is brought.

A divorce or dissolution action is a civil matter. It may dissolve a marriage. One partner sues the other. Separation is legalized, property is divided, and the welfare of the children is the serious and usually first concern of the court.

A personal injury lawsuit is a civil action. One party, the plaintiff, sues the other party, the defendant, to recover for damages sustained.

A breach of contract suit is a civil action. One party sues the other for alleged violation of a contract.

Criminal Actions

When a court document reads, "The People of the United States of America, Plaintiff, versus John Doe, Defendant," or "The People of the State of Michigan, Plaintiff, versus John Doe, Defendant," that document is a part of a criminal matter. Two parties are involved: the government and the accused. We will also, therefore, refer to these actions as two-party suits.

When an individual is accused of committing a crime, the opponent is all of the people of the country in a federal matter or all of the people of a state in a state case. Representing the people of the nation (plaintiff) is the Attorney General of the United States. Representing the accused (defendant) is the individual's attorney. Representing the people of any state (plaintiff) is that state's district attorney, also sometimes called state's attorney or county attorney. Representing the accused (defendant) is the individual's attorney.

Crimes are classified as felonies or misdemeanors, depending upon the seriousness of the crime.

Felonies. These are serious crimes, and punishment may be death or imprisonment in a state penitentiary. One who has been accused of murder has been charged with committing a felony. One who has, by illegal means, taken large sums of money could be charged with the commission of a felony.

Misdemeanors. These crimes are less serious, but they are crimes nevertheless. Punishment therefor (for them) may be fine or imprisonment in a city or county jail, or both fine and imprisonment. One who has been found guilty of loitering in an unauthorized area is involved in a misdemeanor count and may be fined or imprisoned in a city or county jail.

141

Now is the time to note that a criminal matter receives precedence over a civil matter in the court systems. The Constitution of the United States guarantees an accused person the right to a speedy trial. This, then, accounts for the long delays sometimes experienced by those involved in civil lawsuits. Civil suits are frequently delayed to permit early hearings of criminal cases.

THE COURTS

The court system is that part of the government structure that has been established to apply the law and administer justice. Our courts alone of all the courts in the world are empowered to declare legislation to be unconstitutional and void. In the United States of America, there are fifty-one separate court systems: the federal court system and fifty state court systems. The fifty state court systems are similar in design to the federal court system. All include a highest court — usually called the supreme court — courts of appeal, and trial courts.

Federal Court System

The court system of the United States of America includes the following:

- The Supreme Court of the United States, which is the highest court in the nation and therefore sometimes referred to as the court of last resort
- United States Courts of Appeal
- Unites States District Courts (trial courts)
- Many special courts including Court of Claims, Court of Customs and Patent Appeals, and Bankruptcy Court

Some of the legal actions that would be heard in a federal court are: lawsuits between states, lawsuits with the federal government as party to the action, or matters having to do with such federal laws as patent and copyright laws, bankruptcy law, or maritime law.

A legal matter heard in a federal court could be appealed to the United States Courts of Appeal; and then, if warranted, litigant (party to a lawsuit) could petition the United States Supreme Court for permission to appeal to that body.

State Court Systems

The state court systems have, under various names, all of the following courts:

- Supreme courts

- Courts of appeal
- Trial courts
- Lower or inferior courts
- Probate courts

New York and other states have surrogate courts or orphans' courts, where probate matters are heard. In many states, probate matters are heard in a branch of the state superior court.

NOTE: It is incumbent upon the legal secretary to be able to distinguish between the two court systems — federal and state. A legal document to be filed in a federal court carries that court's title and is filed (deposited) in the clerk's office for that court, which will be located nearby. A legal paper to be filed in a state court carries that court's title and is filed in the clerk's office for that court, located nearby.

Courts of Original Jurisdiction and Courts of Appeal

Courts of original jurisdiction are trial courts. They hear a lawsuit the first time it is in court. Appellate courts are those that review both the testimony given in the court of original jurisdiction and that court's verdict.

Courts of original jurisdiction.   If Mr. West Neighbor and Mr. East Neighbor, both residing in Fresno, California, became involved in a lawsuit because Mr. East Neighbor had inadvertently caused the destruction of Mr. West Neighbor's elaborate new brick barbecue, the lawsuit would be heard in a state trial court in Fresno. The two neighbors, witnesses, and the officers of the court (the judge, the attorneys, clerk of the court, sheriff, marshal, and sometimes a bailiff or constable) would be in attendance. Testimony would be heard and a decision reached. A jury might or might not be present, depending upon the wishes of the parties to the action.

Appellate court.   Suppose Mr. West Neighbor lost the case and was unhappy with the verdict. If Mr. West Neighbor appealed the case, it would be reviewed by a court of appeal, which is a higher court. The appellate court would review the trial held in the court of original jurisdiction by reviewing the record of the case, reading the briefs prepared by the attorneys for the parties, and hearing the arguments of the attorneys for the parties.

The court would then decide the issues raised on the appeal. If the appellate court found that no material error had been committed during the trial, the decision of the trial court would be affirmed. If a material error had been committed in the trial court, the appellate court could either grant a judgment for the appellant (the one appealing) or set aside the judgment of the lower court and send the case back for retrial.

NOTE: Either party could appeal the verdict of an appellate court to the state supreme court. If warranted, litigant could petition the Supreme Court of the United States to appeal to that body.

It is highly unlikely that the fictitious barbecue case would find its way to that august body!

Courts of Record and Courts Not of Record

A written record is kept of the proceedings held in a court of record. No written record is kept of the proceedings held in a court not of record.

Courts of record. Procedure in a court of record requires the use of written court documents; further, the proceedings of the court are recorded for possible later use. Trial courts are courts of record, as are all appellate courts and supreme courts.

Matters serious in nature or involving rather large sums of money are held in courts of record. A court of record includes in its personnel a court reporter who takes verbatim testimony. The certified court reporter is a highly skilled technician who is able to take shorthand, usually machine shorthand, in excess of two hundred words a minute. If a case is appealed, it is the reporter's immediate duty to transcribe all the records taken during the proceeding in proper form for transmittal to the judges and attorneys who are interested.

Courts not of record—inferior courts. These courts include, among others, municipal court, traffic court, and small claims court. Matters involving relatively small sums of money or lesser infractions of the law are heard in these courts. Written court documents are not required as a part of the procedure in the inferior courts, and no written record is made of the proceedings.

SUMMARY

Law is that set of rules or methods established to permit coexistence in a society. Some kinds of law that are of interest to the legal secretary are: sources of law; federal law and state law; public law and private law; civil law and criminal law; substantive law and procedural law.

The legal secretary is particularly concerned with procedural law, which is the how-to of law: how to commence, continue, and conclude a matter in the courts.

Legal actions are court proceedings by which one party seeks redress for a wrong or protection of a right, or by which the government prosecutes an accused individual or institution for the commission of a crime.

The courts are that part of the government established to apply the law and administer justice. There are fifty-one court systems: one federal system and fifty state systems. All court systems include courts of original jurisdiction and appellate courts.

The federal courts are courts of record. State courts include both courts of record and courts not of record. The inferior courts, which are courts not of record, hear relatively minor matters such as traffic violations and cases involving small sums of money, which may be heard in a municipal court.

SUGGESTED SPECIAL ASSIGNMENTS

1. Library study. List ten independent federal agencies and ten independent state agencies.

2. Library study. List ten federal branches of executive departments and ten state branches of executive departments.

3. Write a one-page, double-spaced essay explaining how the state constitutions and the Constitution of the United States differ in their application to *all* of the people of the United States of America.

10

Forms–
Printed and Typed

Printed forms are used in business, government, education, and law to facilitate communication. From the one-by-two-inch wallet identification cards to the multipage tax forms, corporation forms, work application forms, and college entrance forms, printed forms have become an integral part of our communications system.

The elimination of forms for communication would be tantamount to the elimination of the automobile for transportation.

REDUCING INFORMATION TO A FORM

The initial process of reducing basic information to a form is tedious, time-consuming, and all-important. Those who design forms must determine, first, what the form should accomplish, and second, how to accomplish it. They must consider

- Using words economically
- Standardizing style
- Including all necessary information

146

- Wording statements and questions clearly
- Producing a document that, when used by the consumer, will accomplish the purpose for which it was intended

IMPORTANCE OF FORMS

Forms save time. This is the key to their popularity. Forms are accurate and reliable. This, too, accounts for their popular use.

Members of the Internal Revenue Service receive and check vast numbers of tax returns annually. All returns are printed forms, some of them many pages long. The IRS agents need not read the printed portion of the tax returns; they know what it says. Only the data supplied by the taxpayer need be checked by IRS personnel. Think of the time saved that federal agency by the use of forms!

In a law office, the use of legal forms, sometimes called law blanks, results in a similar saving of time. The attorney need furnish only the information required in the spaces of the law blank. Lengthy dictation is eliminated. The secretary need fill in only the blank lines of the form and proofread the typing. Long transcription and proofreading sessions are eliminated.

IDENTIFICATION OF FORMS

Forms, whether in a business or law office, are usually identified in two ways: by title and by identification number.

Title

The attorney will indicate the form to be used by referring to its exact name or title. The legal secretary will carefully select from among the many legal forms the document that carries that exact title.

A *subpoena* is a *subpoena; a subpoena duces tecum* is a *subpoena duces tecum.* These are entirely different forms. An individual *grant deed* is an individual *grant deed; a corporation grant deed* is a *corporation grant deed.* Each serves a particular purpose.

Identification Number

In fine print in one corner of most forms is the identification number. This identification usually includes the issuing agency's form number and the date of the latest printing or revision of the form.

The identification number is important to the legal secretary. Titles may be identical, but a difference in any part of two identification numbers indicates both that the forms were printed at different times and that the contents of the documents may be dissimilar.

If duplicates of a form are to be typed, the legal secretary must make certain forms with identical identification numbers are used.

While the legal secretary is replenishing the supplies of forms, the identification numbers should be checked. If the new forms show a change in the identification number, they should be used and the entire supply of the old form should be destroyed.

SOURCES OF LEGAL FORMS OR LAW BLANKS

Legal forms may be obtained from many sources and may be classified into five groups.

- Commercial forms
- Special business office forms (See Appendix E.)
- Government forms (See Appendix E.)
- Court forms (See Appendix E.)
- Law office forms and form procedures

Commercial Forms

Commercial forms are those sold by stationery stores. These include

- Rental forms
- Lease forms
- Various contract forms
- Deeds
- Mortgages
- Bankruptcy forms
- Wills
- Agreements
- and a host of others

Clients sometimes purchase commercial forms and bring them to the law office for completion. If practical, the form will be used by the attorney. Frequently, however, the form is so general in nature or lacking in specific clauses that it is not used; instead, a document tailored to the problem is dictated for transcription by the legal secretary.

Special Business Office Forms

Title and abstract companies are in the business of recording and determining historical and current title to real property; that is, it is their business to know who did own and who does now own any parcel of real estate. Each time real property changes ownership, the change in title is noted by these companies by means of a direct or indirect search of the official records maintained in the local records office.

Both title and abstract companies supply, free of charge, legal forms that relate to real estate transactions. Among others, these forms include deeds of many kinds, including quitclaim deeds and grant deeds; mortgage forms of various kinds; and notes secured by deeds of trust or mortgages.

Banks and insurance companies are other businesses that may have forms useful to and usable by the law office. Forms from these sources are also furnished free of charge.

Business office legal forms are carefully identified as to the source; i.e., if XYZ Abstract Company supplied the form, XYZ Abstract Company's name would appear in bold type in a prominent place on the document. The forms are a means of advertising for the business.

Use of these business forms is widespread in law offices because of the easy accessibility of the forms, their accuracy and completeness, and the fact that they are free.

Government Forms

Forms are usually provided free of charge by the various federal, state, and local governmental agencies. A few of the many agencies and departments that supply forms are

- Internal Revenue Service
- Social Security Administration
- Veterans Administration

Since government and other forms are frequently revised, it is unwise to accumulate an unrealistically large supply of forms. The latest revisions and newest forms are always available for the asking.

Court Forms

Court forms are furnished by the clerk's office, usually free of charge. These forms include

- Probate forms
- Divorce and marriage dissolution forms
- Subpoenas
- Summonses
- Jury instructions
- and countless others

Use of the court forms is encouraged — nay, almost demanded — by the clerk's office and the court (judge). Any of these forms, if typed in its entirety, would require endless proofreading and checking to determine if all statements required under the law were included.

The forms, as printed and provided by the clerk's office, are accurate and complete. When correctly filled in by the law office, the forms accomplish the job for which they were intended — and they eliminate time-consuming proofreading. Only the filled-in portions need be checked — by the attorney, the legal secretary, personnel at the court clerk's office, and the judge.

Law Office Forms and Form Procedures

Some law offices use forms of their own making — for example, vacation schedule forms, procedural check lists, or telephone message forms.

However, the forms that are of more value than any other are, in fact, not printed forms at all. They are the court and client documents contained in the law office files, any of which may be used as reference material.

Most court and client documents are a combination of form paragraphs and specially dictated paragraphs. Together they make the new document the unique instrument it must be if it is to accomplish its special purpose.

Formal wills, discussed in a previous chapter, contain many paragraphs that, except for a change in name, relationship, address, or kind of property, may be used as form paragraphs for other wills produced in a law office.

Leases prepared by an attorney are a combination of form paragraphs, which may be taken from already existing leases, and newly dictated paragraphs or clauses, which will cover the specific requirements of the new lease contract.

Court documents, including complaints, answers, motions, and notices, among others, include in their contents many form paragraphs. A combination of the form paragraphs and the new, specially dictated paragraphs results in a court document tailored to the matter at hand.

Care and judgment in selecting the appropriate form paragraphs for inclusion in the newest document are the forte of the attorney. By training, research, and knowledge of the facts, the attorney is able to select the correct form paragraphs, add the special dictation required, and produce the proper legal document.

It is the legal secretary's responsibility to note well and carefully which paragraphs from which documents are to be copied into the new document and to make careful notes of changes in wording indicated during dictation.

Further, it is the legal secretary's responsibility to make minor changes in any form paragraphs; that is, change *he* to *she*, or *he* to *they*, or *her* to *his*, or *defendant* to *defendants*, or *plaintiff* to *plaintiffs*, or *is* to *are*, if the new document requires such changes. These minor changes could become major problems if not correctly made during the typing of the document.

Automatic Typewriters and
Word Processing Equipment

Automatic typewriters and word processing equipment with their "memory" capabilities serve an extremely useful purpose in the area of form paragraphs.

The equipment permits paragraphs that are common to particular documents to be placed in memory, by tape or other means, for indefinite retention. Tapes are filed between uses. When a document containing any of the recorded form paragraphs is to be used, the memory element is activated; the appropriate buttons are pushed; and the typing or printout is made accurately and at a speed upwards from 180 words a minute.

The memory may be programmed to stop at critical points to permit the addition of names, dates, addresses, or other information required to complete the new document. Following their use, tapes are refiled for later use.

The permanently filed tapes contain only standardized portions of court and client documents. A tape containing standardized will clauses would be correctly filed under "wills" in the tape file. The tape containing standardized portions of other documents regularly written in the law office would be filed by subject matter.

Some law offices have reduced portions of many documents to forms for use on the automatic typewriters. Others have not yet begun using this device for increasing production. The aggressive, progressive legal secretary will investigate the possibilities inherent in the use of automatic typewriters and other word processing equipment.

Of course, a great deal of the work produced in law offices is from straight dictation. Letters emanating from a law office could scarcely be reduced to forms. But documents produced again and again, which repeat standardized paragraphs, may be adapted to taped or automatic typing.

USING FORMS

Every legal secretary discovers, with time, the best method for using forms. Following are some suggestions for most easily and efficiently producing accurate and attractive completed forms.

Dictation

During dictation, both the attorney and the legal secretary should have in their hands identical copies of the form to be used. As the attorney dictates the data to be added to the form, the secretary will record the information in a shorthand notebook or on machine shorthand tape, carefully identifying each blank and the information to be added.

Should the attorney fail to refer to any part of the form, the legal secretary will mention the omission. A statement such as, "Should item 4 be completed?" will alert the attorney.

Sometimes a blank space is left open with good reason. Such a line should show just enough typing to indicate to the reader that the line was purposely left unanswered (incomplete). The symbol *N/A* (not applicable) or two or three hyphens is all that is necessary. The symbol should be placed at the approximate center of the line so that it is easily visible.

Identification of Dictated Information

It is important to clearly identify each item of information and the blank it is to fill. This may be accomplished by the use of various symbols. For example, a penciled (a) on the blank line of the form and an identical (a) preceding the notes for that space tie the two together. A penciled (b) on the next blank line and a (b) preceding the appropriate notes will identify these notes as properly belonging in that space. The legal secretary must exercise great care in properly identifying the notes and the blanks they are to fill.

A manual shorthand operator would be wise to skip a line in the notebook between the various items in the form. The machine shorthand operator would be wise to show adequate blank space between items of information in order to distinguish the items clearly. The information dictated to complete the forms is rarely in the form of complete sentences. Without clear means of demarcation, the novice secretary could make serious errors in typing even the simplest forms.

ASSEMBLING A FORM CARBON PACK

At least one copy of every paper leaving a law office is prepared for the law office files. If the firm regularly uses a photocopy machine for such copies, only the original form need be typed. Any necessary copies would be made on the copy machine.

If, however, carbon copies of the forms are to be prepared, all copies must be carefully aligned to assure that the information typed on a line on the original document will fall on exactly the same line on all copies. Such alignment may be assured by

1. Inserting the carbon pack into the machine minus the carbon paper.
2. Inserting the carbon paper. It need not reach the uppermost edge of the paper and should not, in fact, be within a half-inch of that top edge. This placement facilitates removal of the carbon paper. The secretary need only hold the pack at the upper left corner, and quickly remove all pieces of carbon paper at one stroke with the other hand.
3. Aligning the pack so the lines on the form are straight with the line of typing. Some forms are printed slightly askew.
4. Typing a period at the end of one of the lines on the form.
5. Checking all carbon copies to assure that the period is identically placed on all copies.
6. Adjusting the sheets of the carbon pack to correct the placement if the period is high or low in relation to the placement on the original. This adjustment is accomplished by releasing the paper, raising or lowering the carbon copy that is out of line, striking another period, and checking the results.
7. Repeating all the steps, 1 through 6, if necessary.

Such care may seem extreme to the uninitiated. However, the printing on otherwise identical forms may be higher or lower on one page than on its counterparts, Thus, typed information on the original could very well fall on incorrect lines on the carbon copies. The carbon copies would certainly not be true copies of the original and would, in fact, misinform the reader. Such misinformation could have serious consequences in a law office.

SPACING ON FORMS

Some forms are prepared with typewriters in mind. For these forms the secretary need only set the typewriter for single or double spacing and proceed with the typing. Other forms are less thoughtfully prepared. For these, the secretary must use the line finder of the typewriter for each line of typing if an accurate and attractive form is to be produced.

Typing on a Line

The typed line is correctly placed slightly above the printed line. A faint glimmer of white should show between the line and the bottom of the typed material. If the line of type is placed too low, the printed line itself will partially obscure the typed letters. If too high, the form will appear to be carelessly prepared.

Signature Lines

The typed signature should be placed a *single* space below the signature line and typed in all caps. This is a good public relations technique. The signer knows exactly how the document is to be signed: full name, initials and last name, or whatever. Further, anyone referring to the document knows who signed it. It is not always possible to decipher signatures!

I recall delivering a court document to an attorney. I extended to him his copy of the paper as well as the original copy that he was to sign in order to show he had received the paper. He grabbed the copies from me, turned the original sideways on his desk, and scribbled a series of rapid back and forth strokes. Then he straightened the paper, placed two dots above what were, I guessed, *i*'s, and handed the paper back to me. Not even he could have read that signature!

Z-Mark

Some forms provide more blank space than is generally required to complete a particular document. To eliminate a later addition of unwanted or unauthorized information, the legal secretary will use a ruler and add a Z-mark to fill the space. The top line of the Z will begin at the end of the last line of typing and extend to the right margin. The bottom line of the Z will begin at the left margin about a single space above the first line of printing following the form's blank space. The line will continue to the right margin. A diagonal line will join the two opposite ends of the horizontal lines to form a Z.

The Z-mark must be in ink and must show on *all* copies of the form.

PROOFREADING

Forms must be carefully proofread by the secretary — both the printed and the typed portions — to assure that

- Every printed line of the form contains typing, whether it is the information requested or an N/A or a series of hyphens to indicate that the line was purposely left unanswered
- The information has been placed on the correct lines
- The carbon copies are true copies of the original
- Names are spelled correctly, dates are accurate, typing is perfect

TYPING DOCUMENTS CONTAINING FORM PARAGRAPHS

A legal document consisting of form paragraphs taken from each of several legal papers and also containing original paragraphs dictated for the new document requires

- Care in reading and observing dictation notes that indicate *which* paragraph from *which* document goes *where* in the new legal paper.
- Attention to paragraph numbering. A form paragraph may carry one number in one document and another number in the new document.
- Attention to minor revisions such as *plaintiff* for *plaintiffs*, with the appropriate change in the verb form.
- Careful proofreading for content, for typing and spelling errors, and for completeness of the document. Proofreading will include continual reference to notes and to the various documents containing the form paragraphs that are to become a part of the new document.

FORM FILES

A legal secretary's form file consists of extra copies of typical documents that make up the daily production work. The form file is a master guide and a ready reference for the law office in which it is prepared.

Preparing a Form File

Suppose the legal secretary has been dictated a very long will that disposes of the testator's property and sets up a trust with long and complicated trust provisions. Suppose, too, that this is the first such will the secretary has been asked to type.

As each carbon pack is assembled, the legal secretary will add an extra sheet of lightweight white paper. When the will is completed, the secretary will assemble the extra copy, staple it, and add it to the form file. (If a copier is available, the extra copy will be made from the original will.)

Later, when a similar will is to be prepared, immediately at hand is a will that may be helpful to the attorney as the new document is being dictated. It will certainly be helpful to the legal secretary. Neither the legal secretary nor the attorney need search a bulky will file to find a document with such trust provisions. A copy is available in the legal secretary's own form file.

Of course, not all the provisions of the will in the form file will be included in the new document, nor will all provisions be identical, but the will in the form file may be used as a valuable guide in the preparation of the new document.

Student Form File

The legal trainee or student would be wise to assemble a personal form file by making extra thin white copies of the various documents typed in class. The extra copies could be bound together at center top with Acco fasteners. Such a form file would verify an applicant's production ability and familiarity with legal language and style. The form file should accompany the applicant during employment interviews.

Weeding Out Old Forms

Form files may become bulky and inefficient if they contain too many documents. They should properly include only typical legal papers that are valuable for reference purposes. The wise legal secretary will review the form file occasionally and remove old, torn copies. Through constant use, the forms may become dog-eared and neither handsome to look at nor pleasant to handle.

Accessibility of Forms in the Form File

A new form file may be assembled in rather haphazard order and still serve a good purpose. However, as it grows in size, documents similar in nature should be grouped together and bound at the center top by Acco fasteners. Complaints in personal injury and property damage suits could be assembled in one pack. Other documents should be similarly assembled.

The real value of the form file lies in its easy accessibility to certain legal documents. The more efficient and simple the form file, the better.

Form files are most frequently kept in the legal secretary's own desk drawers for ready reference.

Form File — Value and Appropriateness

A complete and well-assembled form file is an irreplaceable and valuable asset to a legal secretary. I once asked a successful legal secretary whether she owned a form file. "Form file?" she replied. "It's the very last thing I'd want to lose!"

A neophyte in the business of legal secretaryship questioned, "What is a form file, and how do I go about gathering one?" Some time later she telephoned to tell me how large her form file was (I believe she said "two inches thick"!) and how very valuable it was to her.

Among other uses, the form file reminds the legal secretary of exact style for any of the documents it contains.

Both the new and the experienced legal secretary may find it helpful to note in the margins of some documents such information as the number of copies to be prepared or other data that might be helpful.

CAUTION: A form file assembled in one law office is not necessarily valuable in another. Style and wording vary from office to office and attorney to attorney. A new form file should be started with each new position.

Lawyers agree, almost unanimously, that they prefer to train their own secretaries. This simply means that an attorney wishes papers emanating from the office to bear the distinctive tone and appearance of that office. Sometimes an experienced legal secretary is faulted for forcing a personal style (one learned in another office) on a new employer. This is a severe and serious criticism.

Skill and knowledge gained in a law office are especially valuable in another law office if the legal secretary is flexible and able to adapt both skill and knowledge to the requirements of the new employer.

Form files, therefore, are of real value only in the office where they were assembled. The professional legal secretary will not be found guilty of attempting to force a familiar style onto an attorney who already has a perfectly good style.

SUMMARY

In our society, forms are as important to communication as automobiles are to transportation. They serve a two-fold purpose — speed and accuracy.

Forms are identified by both title and identification number. Both should be identical if exact copies of a law blank are desired.

Legal forms may be classified as commercial, business, government, court, and law office. Law office forms are both printed and typed forms. Typed forms encompass the use of standard or form paragraphs and original dictation.

The professional legal secretary transcribes and proofreads forms with the same care given any legal document. A special effort is exerted to ensure that all dictated information is included in its proper place on the form.

A form file is a personal and valuable collection for use in a particular law office. If the legal secretary changes positions, the training and knowledge accumulated in this field of legal secretaryship are carried to the new office. But a new form file is begun at the new office.

The professional legal secretary is flexible and able to adapt to the form, style, and requirements peculiar to a new law office.

SUGGESTED SPECIAL ASSIGNMENTS

1. Visit an abstract or title company office. Obtain copies of brochures or pamphlets that describe the services offered. Ask for a copy of their most-used form for transferring title to real estate from one individual to another. Write a one-page, single-spaced paper describing your experience. Attach a form and any brochures you may have received.

2. Obtain a copy of one of the forms used by the Internal Revenue Service or other government agency. Write a short essay describing the purpose of the form and attach the form.

11

Court
Documents

Court documents are those legal papers prepared for the use of the courts. Client documents, as discussed in an earlier chapter, are prepared primarily for the use of the clients. Court documents are filed with the court; client documents are delivered to clients.

PLEADINGS AND OTHER COURT DOCUMENTS

Pleadings are court documents that either present or answer contentions in a legal matter. They "plead" that a wrong be remedied, or they "plead" that there was no wrong committed. Some pleadings are

- Complaints
- Answers
- Demurrers
- Cross-complaints

Among the *other court documents* are

- Notices
- Motions
- Affidavits
- Summonses
- Subpoenas

Court Designation

All court documents are a part of the machinery necessary to pursue a legal matter from its inception to its conclusion. These papers are prepared for use in a particular court; that is, if a case is heard (held) in a superior court, that court's title will appear on all documents filed in the matter. If the case is to be heard in a municipal court, that court's title will appear on all documents filed in the matter.

Client Copies

Court documents are prepared for the use of the courts. A complaint, for example, is filed with the court. But it is filed on behalf of the client.

Whether the client receives copies of legal papers is a matter of law office policy. Some offices, assuming that the clients are not interested in the legal jargon of the contents, send no copies to their clients. Other offices, possibly more sharply aware of the communications gap between the lawyer and the layman, send copies of all documents in any given matter to the client. This policy accomplishes a great deal: it bridges the gap between the lawyer and the layman; it informs the client of the volume of work and paperwork entailed during the course of a lawsuit or a probate matter; it keeps the client informed of the progress of the legal problem; it leads to a general understanding and appreciation of legal language by lay persons; and it serves to justify and clarify the statement at billing time.

Paper

Good quality, erasable bond paper is used for original copies. Erasable onionskin paper is used for carbon copies. Most jurisdictions use 8½-by-13-inch legal paper; however, some jurisdictions either accept or require court documents prepared on lettersize (8½-by-11-inch) paper.

A perusal of the legal periodicals regularly arriving at the law office will keep the legal secretary abreast of possible changes in paper styles, procedural changes, and new form requirements. It is sometimes difficult for the legal secretary to justify using office time to read the legal journals, but it is time well spent. The professional legal secretary must be well informed.

Legal Paper

Three styles of legal paper are available: plain, ruled, and ruled and numbered. (See Figure 11-1.) The particular style of paper specified by the court is the paper that must be used for documents filed with that court.

To identify the source of the document, the law firm's name and address are frequently printed in the left margin or lower left corner of the paper. This printed paper may be used either for page one only, or for all pages of the court document.

Ruled-and-numbered paper.   A double ruled line, 1¼ inches from the left edge of the paper, determines the left margin. A single ruled line ⅜ inches from the right edge of the paper determines the right margin. All typewriting is contained between these ruled margins.

Double-spaced numbers from 1 through 32 (legal size) or 1 through 28 (letter size), just to the left of the double ruled margin, number the lines of typing for later possible reference. Whether the communicating persons are together in an office or a continent apart speaking over the telephone, immediate reference to a particular word or clause may be made: "Page 5, line 13, fourth word should be changed from 'concedes' to 'accepts.'" Such preciseness could not be misunderstood. This could be a very real advantage in the discussion of wording and content.

Only with single-spaced material, such as legal property descrip-

Ruled and numbered   Ruled   Plain

FIGURE 11-1   Legal paper

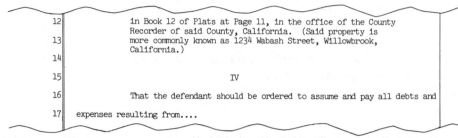

12	in Book 12 of Plats at Page 11, in the office of the County Recorder of said County, California. (Said property is
13	more commonly known as 1234 Wabash Street, Willowbrook, California.)
14	
15	IV
16	That the defendant should be ordered to assume and pay all debts and
17	expenses resulting from....

FIGURE 11-2   Correct use of numbered paper

tions, are the unnumbered spaces used. If single-spaced material terminates on an unnumbered space, the following numbered space will be skipped and the double-spaced material will continue on the next numbered space. (See Figure 11-2.)

The first line of a paragraph may begin on line 32, or 28 of the short paper. However, if a numbered paragraph ended on line 31, or 27 of the short paper, it would obviously be poor style to place a paragraph number alone on line 32 or 28, the last line of the paper. To eliminate the problem, three or four hyphens centered on the last numbered line would inform the reader that the line was noted and purposely left unused.

The only typing below the final numbered line is the page number, which is centered a triple space below the final numbered line on the page.

Ruled paper.   This paper has the ruled margins but no numbers. Typing must be contained within the ruled margins. If typing extends beyond the lines, the entire page will appear to have been carelessly typed. Carelessness in any sense is unacceptable in a law office.

Plain paper.   In areas where unruled, unnumbered paper is used for court documents, the same good-quality, erasable plain paper is used for both client and court documents.

Style

Pica (not elite) type, double spacing, and one-inch paragraph indentions are used in typing court documents. These permit quick and easy perusal of the contents. *Margins are predetermined on ruled and ruled-and-numbered paper.* If plain paper is used, the margins are the same as those used for client documents.

left margin: one inch
right margin: one inch, more or less (Overall appearance of right margin should be slightly narrower than the left margin.)

top margin: first page — two inches; following pages — one and one-half inches

bottom margin: one inch

Copies

The minimum number of copies required of most court documents is three.

- The original to be filed with the court
- Conformed white carbon copy to be delivered to opposing counsel
- Office file copy

If law office policy dictates that copies of all documents should be furnished the client, the necessary extra copy would be prepared. For any of many reasons, several copies of court documents may be required. Before beginning to type, the legal secretary should determine the maximum number of copies that may be required. This determination may eliminate the unpleasant task of retyping a very long document needlessly.

Copy machines are a basic part of the equipment of almost every law office. If it is agreeable to the attorney, the secretary may type an original and file copy, or type only an original and make all other copies on the photocopying machine.

Conforming Copies

All copies of court documents must be conformed to include dates, signatures, and other data shown on the original document.

Pagination

The first page may or may not be numbered; the choice is the secretary's. However, the title page is obviously page one, and the addition of the page number adds nothing to the appearance.

All continuation pages are numbered at the bottom center of the page, a triple space above the bottom of the page. Page numbers should fall directly one under the other, an effect achieved by setting a tab for the center of the page.

Title Page and Caption

The title page of every court document contains certain specific information that, taken together, is the caption of the document. In most states, the caption is typed in the upper portion of the first

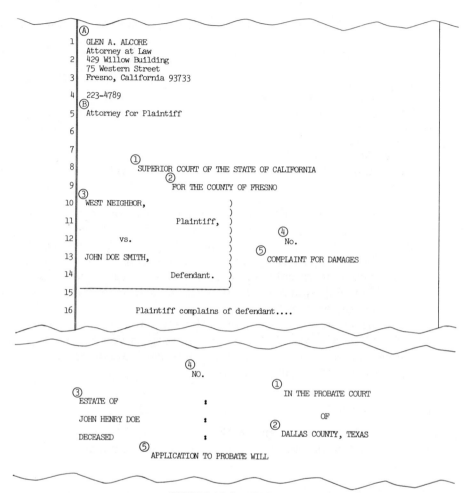

FIGURE 11-3 Captions

page, with the body of the document immediately following on the same page. In some jurisdictions, however, a separate title page, unnumbered, carries the caption; the body of the court document begins on a new page, which is page one.

Placement of the caption data varies with the states, but all the following information, excluding only *A* and *B*, must always be included on the title page:

1. Jurisdiction
2. Venue
3. Case title
4. Court or docket number

5. Title of court document
A. Attorney's name, address, and telephone number
B. Client identification (Attorney for_____)

Figure 11-3 illustrates two title page styles. The circled numbers and letters are used for reference purposes only.

DISCUSSION

1. *Jurisdiction.* This line names the court where the legal matter will be heard.
2. *Venue.* This line gives the county (geographical) location.
3. *Case title.* The title of the case includes

- The name of the plaintiff or petitioner who initiated the suit
- The word *plaintiff* or *petitioner* (usually but not always shown in all jurisdictions)
- *Versus* or *vs.* or *v.* or *against*
- The name of the defendant or respondent
- The word *defendant (if plaintiff was used)* or *respondent* (if *petitioner* was used)

The plaintiffs or petitioners and defendants or respondents may be plural in number, in which event the words themselves would be plural. Proper names are typed in all caps.

If the names of the plaintiffs or defendants are too long to be typed on one line, they should be single spaced. The remainder of the caption, however, is double spaced.

```
WEST NEIGHBOR,

                    Plaintiff,

        vs.

JOHN DOE SMITH, RICHARD ROE,
and MAUDE ELLEN ROE,

                    Defendants.
```

A proper name may be divided, i.e., first name on one line and other names on a continuation line. It is never correct style to hyphenate proper names, although space limitations may lead a secretary to consider this possibility.

For reasons of law, it is sometimes necessary to include in the case title fictitious names such as JOHN DOE or DOE I, DOE II, or

DOE ONE, DOE TWO, DOE THREE, or DOES ONE through TEN. These fictitious names (in all caps because they substitute for proper names) permit later insertion of true names as parties to the action.

```
JOHN BROWN,

                    Plaintiff,

     vs.

MARY SMITH, DOE ONE, DOE TWO,
DOE THREE,

                    Defendants.
```

Other court documents, including some petitions and decrees, may show only one party in the case title.

```
Guardianship of

RICHARD ROE, JR,

A minor.
```

Whether the case title is boxed as shown in Figure 11-3, or unboxed, it is usually clearly separated from the court number and document title.

4. *Court or docket number.* The first paper filed in any court matter will not have a court or docket number. The number must be assigned by the court clerk's office. However, space for the case number should be provided by the secretary by typing *No.* and allowing ample space for the later addition of the number. The court number, when assigned, should be shown on all subsequent court documents in the matter.

5. *Title of pleadings or other court documents.* The document title is typed in all caps, sometimes to the right of the case title and sometimes a double space below it. Placement is determined by local practice. If the title is long, it may be single or double spaced on two or more lines. Avoid hyphenating at the end of the line.

```
CROSS-COMPLAINT IN             DEMURRER TO COMPLAINT
                                        AND
    INTERPLEADER                POINTS AND AUTHORITIES
                                 IN SUPPORT THEREOF
```

6. Item A gives the name, address, and telephone number of the attorney or the attorney and law firm represented. This information must be included as a part of all court documents. In California,

placement is as shown in Figure 11-3. Some jurisdictions prefer that the information be shown near the signature line at the end of the document.

Without this identifying information, the court would be at a loss to know the originator of the document.

For identification purposes in transferring data to a computer system, some jurisdictions may require the attorney's American Bar Association number (or other number) immediately following the attorney's name in this portion of the document.

7. Item B of Figure 11-3 designates the party represented by the named attorney. This information is sometimes shown in the signature area of the document.

If several plaintiffs or defendants are named, this line should read *Attorney for Plaintiff, MORTON NELSON* or *Attorney for Defendant, MAUDE ELLEN ROE.* This will indicate the particular plaintiff or defendant represented by the law firm.

8. Preparation of the first pleading in any legal matter requires extreme care on the part of the legal secretary to ensure the use of correct names and correct spelling of names. The caption used in the first pleading will be copied on all later documents in the case.

9. Legal words: *defendant, plaintiff, complaint.*

Introductory Statement or Paragraph

The introductory statement or paragraph begins a triple space below the last line of the caption. It is an unnumbered paragraph. If ruled-and-numbered paper is used, each line of type must begin on a numbered line.

Some court documents in all jurisdictions, and all court documents in some jurisdictions, introduce the body of the document with what might be compared to the "To" line of a memo or the inside address of a letter. Four examples follow:

TO: DEFENDANT AND HIS ATTORNEY OF RECORD:

TO THE SUPERIOR COURT OF THE STATE OF WASHINGTON, IN AND FOR THE COUNTY OF BLANK:

TO THE SURROGATE COURT OF THE COUNTY OF BLANK:

TO THE HONORABLE JUDGE OF SAID COURT:

In many jurisdictions, the addressee is omitted from pleadings and the introductory paragraph begins a double or a triple space below the caption. Three introductory paragraphs follow:

> Comes now plaintiff above named, by and through its [a company]
> attorney, JOHN SMITH, and, complaining against defendants, alleges as follows:

> Come now defendants, JOHN JOHNSON and MARY JOHNSON, and, in answer
> to the complaint heretofore filed, allege as follows:

> The petition of MARY ADAMS IRWYNE, as executrix of the will of
> FRANCIS PETER IRWYNE, deceased, respectfully shows:

Body Style of Pleadings and Other Court Documents

The statements and allegations that comprise the body of pleadings are usually numbered paragraphs. During dictation, the attorney will indicate the paragraphs and their numbers. If the numbers are not given, the legal secretary may assume that the paragraphs will be indented but not numbered.

Most *pleadings* — i.e., complaints, answers, petitions — have numbered paragraphs. Most other court documents — i.e., motions, notices, affidavits — do not.

If paragraphs are numbered, Roman numerals, centered above the paragraphs, are most commonly used. They are aligned from the left, as follows:

I
II
III
XXII

An introductory paragraph and numbered paragraphs follow:

> Comes now plaintiff above named, by and through its attorney,
> ROBERT R. ROOBEY, and, complaining against defendants, alleges as follows:
>
> I
>
> Plaintiff is a corporation organized and existing under the laws
> of the state of Hawaii, whose principal place of business is in Honolulu,
> city and county of Honolulu, state of Hawaii. Defendants, RICHARD RICHARDS
> and JOHN JOHNSON, are residents of Honolulu, aforesaid.

II

That on or about December 1, 19__, plaintiff and defendants,

RICHARD RICHARDS and JOHN JOHNSON, executed a lease, plaintiff as lessor and

defendants as lessee, of certain property described in said lease, a copy of

which is attached hereto, marked Exhibit A, and made a part hereof by reference.

DISCUSSION

1. The introductory paragraph is unnumbered. The proper name is typed in all caps.

2. Roman numerals are used to number the paragraphs in this pleading. They are aligned at the left and centered.

3. The phrase *RICHARD RICHARDS and JOHN JOHNSON* is surrounded by commas to clarify that these names are in apposition with the word *defendants*.

4. Compound words: *aforesaid, hereto, hereof.*

5. Legal words: *plaintiff, defendants, executed, lease, lessor, lessee.*

6. Legal phrases: *comes now, alleges as follows, organized and existing, principal place of business, on or about, made a part hereof by reference.*

Prayer

The prayer is a request for relief for a wrong done or committed. It is the final paragraph of a *pleading*. It will include, in paragraph style or in outline form, the specific relief requested. A prayer follows:

WHEREFORE, premises considered, the plaintiff prays that the

defendant be cited to appear and answer herein; and that upon final hearing

hereof, the plaintiff have and recover judgment against the defendant in the

sum of $9,370.00, together with interest, attorneys' fees as alleged

hereinabove, and all costs herein incurred; and for such other and further

relief, at law or in equity, to which the plaintiff may show himself justly

entitled.

DISCUSSION

1. The prayer begins with *WHEREFORE* in all caps followed by a comma.

2. The prayer almost always contains the word *pray* or *prays*.

3. Semicolons separate *that* clauses and specific items of relief requested.

4. Compound words: *herein, hereof, hereinabove.*

5. Legal words: *premises, prays, cited, answer, hearing, alleged, incurred.*

6. Legal phrases: *premises considered, have and recover, costs herein incurred, and for such other and further relief, at law or in equity, may show himself justly entitled.*

The same prayer, in outline form, follows:

WHEREFORE, premises considered, the plaintiff prays that the defendant be cited to appear and answer herein; and that upon final hearing hereof, the plaintiff have and recover judgment against the defendant as follows:

1. The sum of $9,370.00, together with interest;

2. Attorneys' fees as alleged hereinabove;

3. Costs herein incurred;

4. For such other and further relief, at law or in equity, to which the plaintiff may show himself justly entitled.

DISCUSSION

When the outline style is used in setting up the prayer, Arabic numbers are used.

Signature Lines

The signature of the client is required on some court documents in addition to the signature of a member of the law firm. Some court documents require only the signature of the attorney.

With no preplanning, the body of the court document could end on the last line or near the last line of the page, with no space for required signatures. However, as with client documents, at least one line of type and preferably three, in addition to the date line if there is one, must be included on the signature page. Preplanning, which might include the use of either stretching or shortening the typed material, will help to eliminate the problem of completing the document but having no space for signatures.

Signature lines begin at the center of the page and extend to the right margin, thus allowing ample space for even a very large signature. Four examples of signature lines follow:

DATED: December 21, 19__.

```
_____
          Robert H. Roobey
        Attorney for Defendant
```

as the court may deem proper.

JOHNSON, JOHNSON and JOHNSON

```
By_____
          John H. Johnson
        Attorneys for Plaintiff
```

to the court seems meet and proper in the premises.

CALLAHAN, HARRINGTON, WISE, BROWN,
GLENN, WINSTON and CLINTON

```
By_____
       Attorneys for Cross-Complainant
```

to which the plaintiff may show herself entitled.

```
_____
        ROSEMARY SMITH, Plaintiff
```

```
_____
        Robert R. Roobey
      Attorney for Plaintiff
```

DISCUSSION

Even with ruled-and-numbered paper, the lower one-inch margin may be used for the signature line, if spacing requires such placement.

Verifications

A verification is a sworn confirmation of the truth of the statements contained in a document. By signing the verification attached to the document, the client confirms the authenticity of the allegations contained in that document.

Certain pleadings must include verifications; and if an initial pleading contains a verification, the answering pleading usually must include a verification.

The verification immediately follows the signature line. If space permits, the verification may be typed on the signature page of the document, or it may be started on the signature page and continued to another page. It may also be typed on a separate numbered page, and if a printed verification is used, it is numbered and attached as the last page of the court document.

Two verifications, one sworn to before a notary public and the other containing a *penalty of perjury statement,* follow:

```
STATE OF CALIFORNIA  )
                     ) ss.
COUNTY OF BLANK      )
```

MARY ADAMS IRWYNE, first being duly sworn, deposes and says:

That she is the plaintiff in the above entitled action; that she has read the foregoing Complaint for Damages and knows the contents thereof; that she certifies that the same is true of her own knowledge, except as to the matters which are therein stated upon her information or belief, and as to those matters, she believes it to be true.

```
                                _____
                                     MARY ADAMS IRWYNE
Subscribed and sworn to before me
this _____ day of November, 19__.

_____
        Notary Public
My commission expires_____.
```

I, the undersigned, certify and declare as follows:

That I am one of the plaintiffs in the within and above entitled action; that I have read the within and foregoing Complaint for Damages and know the contents thereof; that the same is true of my own knowledge, except as to those matters which are therein stated on my information and belief, and as to those matters, I believe it to be true.

I declare under penalty of perjury that the foregoing is true and correct.

Dated this _____ day of November, 19__.

```
                                _____
                                     JOHN HENRY JONES
```

DISCUSSION

1. The verification signed before a notary public begins with the geographical information, *STATE OF CALIFORNIA, COUNTY OF BLANK*, and includes the notary's statement and signature line. The date is included in the notary's statement.

2. The verification containing the penalty of perjury clause, acceptable in some states, includes that clause as a final paragraph of the verification. It is followed by a date line and signature line. *Introductory state and county designation is not required on this verification.*

3. The legal secretary must use care in typing verifications. If the plaintiff in a matter were JACK ADAMS, either of the sample verifications could be used *as a form*. However, the wording of the first verification would have to be changed to the masculine. In the second verification, the words "one of the plaintiffs" would have to be changed to "the plaintiff."

These seemingly minor changes are of major importance to the accuracy of the court document.

PUBLIC RELATIONS AND COURT DOCUMENTS

The court documents represent the law firm, the attorney, and the legal secretary. The reputation of each is affected by the appearance, neatness, completeness, and accuracy of the court papers.

To paraphrase a superior court judge as he addressed students of a class in legal secretaryship:

> When I see certain firm names on documents, I read those papers in order as they appear before me. Historically, those offices have submitted accurate, well-written documents to the court. Documents submitted by other offices, however, require more careful scrutiny, because past experience tells me the documents are poorly and even carelessly prepared. Those documents I place at the bottom of the papers before me. I read them when I have the time to scrutinize them carefully.

What reputation are you, the secretary, going to help make for your law firm? The opinion of this public, the court, is of primary concern to the firm, the attorney, and the secretary.

Appearance of Court Documents

The appearance of court documents must tell the reader that time and effort were involved in the preparation. Every court document has a purpose. If the document is important enough to write at all, it is important enough to write well.

The same rules for corrections govern in the preparation of court documents as in the preparation of client documents: Noticeable corrections are not acceptable, and there should never be corrections in names, numbers, or money amounts.

Legal Covers (Backs)

Some jurisdictions require that the original court documents be placed in legal backs. Other jurisdictions have abandoned this requirement because it is believed that the covers serve no real purpose, but only consume valuable file space.

If used, the covers are attached in the same manner as they are to client documents.

SUMMARY

Court documents are those legal papers prepared for the use of the court. Pleadings are those court documents that present or answer contentions in a legal matter. Complaints, answers, demurrers, and cross-complaints are examples of pleadings. Notices, motions, and affidavits are examples of other court documents, but they are not pleadings.

A pleading may be separated into the following parts for discussion: caption (consisting of jurisdiction, venue, case title, court or docket number, and title of court document); attorney's name, address, and telephone number; client identification; introductory statement or paragraph; body of the document; prayer; signature line(s); and verification (if required).

Other court documents, such as notices and motions, will contain neither a prayer nor a verification. They might contain no special introductory statement other than the use of all caps for the first several words of the first paragraph of the document.

Accuracy, completeness, and neatness are important in the preparation of all court documents.

See Appendix D for sample court documents.

SUGGESTED SPECIAL ASSIGNMENTS

1. Visit a stationery store, the clerk's office, a law office, or otherwise determine the kind of legal stationery used in your jurisdiction. Learn the price per ream of the best quality erasable paper. Write a brief essay describing your experience. Attach a sample of the correct legal stationery.

2. Visit the clerk's office, a law office, or otherwise determine the style and data used on the title page and included in the caption of a court document in your jurisdiction. Type a title page and/or caption that will satisfy the requirements of the courts in your area.

3. Make one copy of the verification on page 172. Use the typing style accepted in your jurisdiction. Change the name to Robert Steven Thomas. Make all necessary changes in the personal pronouns.

12

Complaint and Summons-Civil Suit

How many times have you heard the expression, "I feel like suing him." The speaker could be the pedestrian waiting at the crosswalk on a rainy day, soaking wet because a speeding automobile has just passed and thoroughly splashed him. It could be a discouraged, angry customer talking about a sales clerk. Or it could be a homeowner looking at his flower beds, torn and flattened by his neighbor's dog.

It's a long, long way from the casual, "I feel like suing him," to a court of law.

Suppose Harold Homeowner's flower beds contained exotic trees and shrubs, many imported. Suppose he supplemented his income by occasionally selling plants from his garden. If the damage was great and Donald Dogbreeder was adamant in denying responsibility for it, Mr. Homeowner could very well decide to call an attorney.

Once the decision is made, the legal secretary becomes involved by

* Handling the initial telephone call with the prospective client

- Making an appointment for him to see the attorney
- Introducing the client and the attorney at appointment time
- Taking the dictation and writing the complaint if the matter is to be litigated
- Preparing the summons

COMPLAINT

Appointment

When Harold Homeowner, a new client, arrives for his appointment, the attorney will discuss the legal problem with him. During their conversation, the attorney will take rather extensive notes on a legal-size pad of yellow, lined notepaper. (The legal secretary must make certain that an adequate supply of the notepads is always available in the attorney's desk.)

As the client leaves the office at the termination of his talk with the attorney, good manners and therefore good public relations will cause the legal secretary to look up from the desk long enough to nod or say "Goodbye." After all, in the future the secretary will be both seeing him and talking with him by telephone. The friendlier the atmosphere of the office (quiet, not boisterous), the warmer the relationship between the office and the client.

Fiduciary Relationship

Between the attorney and the client there exists a fiduciary or trust relationship. Any information given the attorney by the client is confidential. The client may rely upon the good faith and confidentiality of the relationship.

Calculated Delay in Commencing Legal Action

Attorneys, in their natural role as counselors, sometimes wait a day or more before commencing work on a new case. Why? A client may arrive at a law office in a fine, white heat of anger or may be otherwise emotionally disturbed. A request will be made that the lawsuit be commenced NOW. However, once that original burst of temper or emotional crisis has passed, the client may wish to drop all action.

In retrospect, the client may realize some personal dereliction of duty or may simply have a change of heart. Later, the client may telephone the attorney and ask if there is any way the whole matter can be forgotten. In all probability, the answer will be "yes." There need not be a lawsuit. The attorney has not yet incurred any court expenses, and the client will be billed only for the office consultation.

A delay in the preparation of the initial court papers can be a very real accommodation to the client.

Urgency in Commencing Action

If the damage is great and the client, after serious deliberation, has come to the attorney, the attorney will begin work on the matter as soon as possible. The facts will be studied and a determination made as to whether there are sufficient grounds for a lawsuit. If so, the attorney will call in the legal secretary for dictation. Dictating equipment is sometimes used, but often the dictation is given directly to the secretary.

Statutes of Limitations

The statute of limitations in each of the states sets forth the periods of time within which a plaintiff (or petitioner or complainant) must begin the lawsuit. Suppose, in our fictitious case, the statute of limitations specified that the suit must be commenced within three years for that kind of civil action. If Mr. Homeowner has waited until the three years have almost passed before visiting the attorney, dictation, preparation, filing, and service of the complaint and summons would be most urgent.

As soon as a court document is dictated, it becomes urgent, and the legal secretary must type it as quickly as possible.

Definitions

Before we can intelligently discuss complaints and summonses, we must discuss the vocabulary special to these documents.

Complaint.   The complaint is a court document and is the first pleading in a civil suit. It is prepared on behalf of the plaintiff. It contains the facts or allegations upon which the plaintiff bases the lawsuit. The complaint, when served upon the defendant, will inform the defendant of the facts.

The initial pleading may also be called a declaration, a petition, or a bill. The exact title is determined by local jurisdiction and the legal matter itself.

Summons. A summons is a legal form that, when served upon the person named therein, is notification that an action has been commenced in the court named on the form. Further, it is notification that the defendant is to appear within a certain period of time and answer the complaint. The defendant's failure to answer the complaint on time harms no one but the defendant: The suit may be lost by default.

Plaintiff. The plaintiff is the person who begins or brings the action. The plaintiff's name appears first in the case title. There may be one or many plaintiffs in a single legal matter. In some jurisdictions, the term *petitioner*, not *plaintiff*, is used in referring to the party who initiates the lawsuit.

Defendant. The defendant is the one being sued. The defendant's name follows the plaintiff's in the case title. There may be one or many defendants in a lawsuit. In those jurisdictions using *petitioner* in referring to the party bringing the suit, the responding party may be called the *respondent* instead of the defendant.

Cause of action. Defined broadly, the cause of action is the event or act, or series of events or acts, upon which the lawsuit is based. A single cause of action or several causes of action may be included in one complaint.

Filing. *Filing* has two distinct meanings in law: first, depositing a court document with the court clerk's office for inclusion in a permanent file in that office; second, placing a copy of a document or other paper in a law office file.

Filing fee. A fee paid to the court clerk's office each time a new matter is filed with that office.

Dictation of the Complaint or Petition

A dictation session may be very long or very brief. In either event, the wise legal secretary should be prepared. If a shorthand notebook is nearing completion, an extra one should be on hand. The machine shorthand operator will check the supply of tape to make certain it is adequate. Both make sure that pens or pencils are readily available.

Since the complaint or petition is the first pleading in a new case, all names, dates, and places must be checked and double-checked for accuracy. Correspondence and later court documents will be based upon the information contained in this initial pleading. There is no place for laxity in its preparation.

Caption

The caption will be dictated and will include

- Jurisdiction
- Venue
- Case title
- Document title

The case or docket number cannot be dictated since the court has not yet assigned a number. The number will be assigned when the initial pleading is filed at the court clerk's office.

Introductory Information

The introduction will be dictated. In some jurisdictions, the initial pleading includes addressee data, which is followed by the introductory paragraph. Other jurisdictions omit the addressee data, and the introductory paragraph immediately follows the caption.

Body of the Complaint

The body of the complaint will be dictated and will include the facts and circumstances upon which the suit is based. The attorney will use reference materials to be certain that all of the allegations required by the laws of the state have been included.

Portions of the body of the complaint will be dictated by the attorney's saying, "Copy paragraph four of this complaint," indicating both the complaint and the paragraph to be copied. The legal secretary's notes must adequately identify both the paragraph to be copied and the complaint from which it is to be copied. For example, a notation, "Copy paragraph four of Bell versus White complaint," would adequately identify both the paragraph and the document. The paragraph, whatever its number in the Bell versus White complaint, will assume its own number in the new complaint.

If an excerpt from a book or a contract is included in the dictation, the book or contract must be identified in the secretary's notes. Exact excerpts may be indicated by noting the page number and indicating the first few and last several words of the material to be copied.

The attorney is even more concerned than the secretary about the accuracy of the new document. The attorney, therefore, will keep all reference materials in proper order and hand them to the secretary during dictation or at the completion of the dictation session.

As the attorney dictates, the legal secretary must make certain that all the dictation has been understandable. If it is unclear to the secretary, it may be unclear to the defendant's (or respondent's) attorney.

The new legal secretary may ask a great many questions. The important thing to remember is this: It is all right to ask questions, but it is unprofessional to have to ask the same question more than once.

If the dictation is not quite clear, the legal secretary simply asks, "May I read a paragraph back to you?" Upon hearing it, the attorney may make a change. On the other hand, because of knowledge and understanding of legal rhetoric, the attorney may know that the statement is entirely satisfactory, and so indicate. Back at the desk the legal secretary should read and reread the questioned portion until it is completely understood.

Legal language is sometimes difficult to comprehend. It requires concentration and understanding. However, the experienced legal secretary uses legal terms in office conversation.

The allegations contained in a complaint are written in numbered paragraphs for quick and certain identification by both attorneys and court personnel. During dictation, the attorney will indicate the paragraphs and their numbers. If a number is inadvertently skipped or repeated, the secretary carefully records the correct number. The numbering change is called to the attorney's attention only if it will be helpful during dictation.

Prayer

The prayer is the final paragraph of the complaint. It is unnumbered. It sets forth the relief requested by the plaintiff. The concluding statement of the prayer, sometimes called the "omnibus clause," is all-inclusive. By its wording, it permits the court to grant relief other than that specifically requested in the prayer.

Verification

A verification is a sworn statement as to the correctness or truth of an accompanying document. Verifications are required on many pleadings. If the attorney does not indicate whether a verification is to be attached, the legal secretary should ask about it. If a verification is required, the secretary will type it, using as a guide a verification contained in the form file. All changes necessary to make the verification fit the new complaint will be made by the secretary.

Form Paragraphs and Legal Documents

Given the facts, and using the form file, the experienced legal secretary is able to prepare many court documents with little dictation from the attorney. These are the truly competent, experienced legal secretaries. It is they who have escalated legal secretaryship into a profession.

Typing the Complaint

Once dictated, the complaint should be transcribed as soon as possible. It takes precedence over much of the other work in the office.

Copies

An original and two are the minimum copies required. The original will be filed with the clerk's office, a white carbon copy will be served on the defendant, and the third copy (yellow) is for the law office files. Of course, if there are several defendants, additional copies of the complaint must be made. If it is the policy of the office to send copies of all legal papers to clients, still one more copy of the complaint will be made for this purpose.

If a copy machine is available, perhaps only the original complaint will be typed. All other copies will be made on the copy machine.

If carbon copies are to be typed, the carbon pack will be white bond, yellow onionskin, and white onionskin copies, in that order, to assure a legible office copy. This order is particularly important if many carbon copies are required of the document. The carbon pack will be inserted into the typewriter, the carbon inserted, and left and top edges of the paper evened — and the secretary is ready for transcription.

The new legal secretary will refer to the form file for guidance in the matter of style. The form file may also be of help in the deciphering of unclear shorthand notes. If a form file is not yet available, the new legal secretary should refer to an office file containing a similar document.

Appointment Calendar or Diary

When the complaint has been typed, proofread, assembled, and stapled, the original is taken to the attorney for perusal and signature. The attorney — or the legal secretary, if the attorney so directs — will then telephone the client to come to the office if a signature is required on the complaint or the verification or both.

The legal secretary, in making the call to the client, simply tells him, "Mr. Homeowner, could you call at the office? The papers are ready for your signature."

If the client is not at home or is unable to come to the telephone, the legal secretary will thank the answering party, but will place the call later in the day when the client is likely to be available. It is always wise to assume that the client's business with the law firm is personal and that not even a spouse or secretary knows of it.

When the client has been reached, the legal secretary arranges an appointment time and immediately writes the time on the diaries or desk calendars to avoid possible conflicts in appointments. Some law offices use diaries to record appointments, others use desk calendars, and still others use both. (See Figure 12-1.)

Occasionally, a legal secretary will make an appointment notation on the calendar and fail to mark it immediately on the attorney's calendar. In the meantime, the attorney may have talked to a client or associate and made an appointment for the same time. It may be necessary for one or the other appointment to be changed. Guess who will probably have to make that phone call?

It is important that the desk or appointment calendars of the

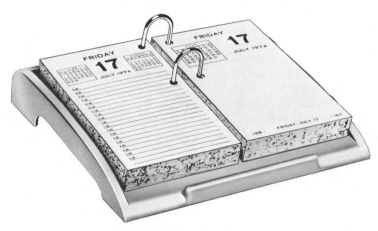

FIGURE 12-1   Desk Calendar

attorney and the legal secretary be identical in almost every respect. (The attorney's personal engagements, golfing dates, and similar appointments need not show on the secretary's calendar. And the attorney's calendar need not show the secretary's dates and other personal engagements.)

Client's Signature on the Complaint

When the client arrives at the office to sign the complaint or verification, he will be asked to read the complaint. If he is to sign the verification truthfully, he must know what is contained in the complaint to which it is attached.

If the verification contains a penalty of perjury clause, the client's signature is all that is required to complete the verification. If the verification requires a notary public's signature, the client must sign the verification in the presence of a notary public, and the notary must also sign and date the verification.

If it is required, the client will sign the complaint. All copies of the complaint must be conformed.

When the complaint has been completely signed, it is ready for filing. But the complaint is of little value without the summons.

SUMMONS

The summons is a court form that the attorney need not dictate. Only the caption need be typed, and it should be an exact duplicate of the caption on the complaint.

Copies

A minimum of three copies of the summons will be prepared in the law office: an original (to be later filed with the court clerk), a copy for service on the defendant, and a copy for the office files. Extra copies are prepared if several defendants are named or if a copy is to be delivered to the client for information. Each defendant named in a lawsuit must be served with a copy of the summons.

FILING THE COMPLAINT AND SUMMONS

To this point, a lawsuit has not yet officially begun. The case becomes a matter of record when the complaint has been filed and a number assigned to it by the court.

Now the court costs will begin. These costs, beginning with the filing fee, are paid out of law office funds and charged to the client's account. The client will be billed for them later.

A law firm check for the exact amount of the filing fee will be prepared for delivery to the court clerk. The check stub should show the case title for billing purposes. Filing fees are set by law, and fee schedules are available at the court clerk's office.

The attorney, legal secretary, law clerk, or a messenger service may take the complaint, summons, and check to the clerk's office. The check covers the plaintiff's appearance in the lawsuit. Filing of the first papers and payment of the fee are together referred to as *making an appearance.*

At the courthouse, the court clerk will accept the original complaint, the original summons, and the check. The clerk will make and return a receipt for the filing fee.

A file stamp and case number will be placed on the original complaint. The court clerk will retain the original complaint for the court files. The case number will be stamped on the original summons and returned to the one acting as messenger. The case number should be stamped on all copies of the summons and complaint in the possession of the messenger. If all copies have been left at the office, they must be conformed to show the case number as soon as the number is available to the secretary.

SERVICE OF SUMMONS AND COMPLAINT

To this point, Mr. Dogbreeder, our defendant, is not involved in a lawsuit. If Mr. Homeowner decided to call the whole thing off, Mr. Dogbreeder might never know that an action had been filed against him.

To involve him, he must be served; that is, he must be given a copy of the summons. When he reads it, he knows he is party to a lawsuit, and he knows who has brought the action against him.

Jurisdictional Differences for Service

In some jurisdictions, a copy of the complaint and a copy of the summons must be served on the defendant at the same time. In some jurisdictions, only the summons need be served; the defendant's copy of the complaint may be obtained by defendant or counsel at the clerk's office. In some jurisdictions, the complaint is not filed with the court until after service of the summons upon the defendant.

Time Runs

In every case, however, the defendant must be served with a summons. When service has been made, time begins to run. Note that phrase. It simply means that beginning with that date, the defendant has a certain number of days (specified in the summons) within which to answer the complaint. If it is left unanswered, the defendant will probably lose the case by default.

In most jurisdictions, the day of service of the summons is not included in the counting of time. Assume a ten-day period is specified on the summons as the time within which the defendant must make an answer in the matter. If service was made on Monday, December 1, then Tuesday, December 2, would begin the count. December 11, a Thursday, would be the last day of the ten-day period. On December 12, the defendant would be in default if an answer or other appearance had not been made in the matter.

If the period ends on a holiday or on a Sunday, the count extends to the following day. Intervening holidays or Sundays are counted as any other days.

Serving the Summons and/or
Summons and Complaint

When the summons has been typed and copies of the complaint have been conformed, service may be made on the defendant, who is, in our fictitious case, Mr. Dogbreeder.

Process Servers

The Yellow Pages of the telephone directory list names of individuals and companies whose business it is to serve legal papers. From among the several process servers listed, the attorney will choose one or more and use the services consistently.

Sometimes the attorney calls the process server. Frequently, however, the attorney asks the legal secretary to make the telephone call requesting the process server to call at the office.

Usually, *copies* of the summons and/or complaint and summons (the jurisdictional requirement) are given to the process server at the law office. The proof of service or affidavit of service, which is a part of the original summons, will be completed by the process server and returned to the law office after a copy of the summons has been served upon the defendant.

Locating the Defendant

The process server must locate the defendant and hand him a copy of the summons or copies of the summons and complaint (jurisdictional requirement). The more information the process server has regarding the defendant and his possible whereabouts, the quicker and easier the service and the lower the service charge will be. Included in the information that should be furnished the process server are:

- Name of the defendant
- Residence address
- Business address
- Hours during which defendant might be located at either of the above addresses
- Any other helpful information

Frequently the plaintiff or complainant bringing the suit is able to provide the law office with all the information necessary for service.

When service has been made (copies of the appropriate documents have been handed to the defendant), the process server will complete the information on the back of the original summons. This includes the name of the defendant served, the address where the paper was served, and the date and hour of service. The process server will then sign the original summons and return it to the law office. The charge for service will be paid by the law firm. The client's account will be charged, and he will later be billed for the amount of the service fee.

NOTE: Summonses may also be served by other qualified persons. Service is not limited solely to process servers. In some jurisdictions, summons may be served by mail. Special mailing requirements must be adhered to.

When all copies of the summons have been conformed, the original summons is ready for filing with the court clerk's office. One conformed copy is placed in the law office file.

See Appendix E for *summons* and *proof of service*.

Marking Calendar with Date of Service and Return Day

The legal secretary must record in the office diary or on the desk calendars the date of service of the summons and the return day, which is the final date before default action may be taken. If the latter date is not noted, time could pass, the case could be forgotten in the rush of other matters, and the plaintiff's legal needs would not have been adequately handled.

To avoid a possible oversight in recording the dates, the legal secretary should not file the office copy of the summons until the dates have been noted on the calendar. The wise legal secretary records the dates *as soon as* the original summons has been returned to the office by the process server.

SUMMARY

The complaint and the summons are the two papers prepared first in a civil suit. The complaint states the facts upon which the action is founded. It is a pleading and contains the following: caption; introductory paragraph; body of complaint, including a statement of facts that constitute a cause of action or causes of action; prayer; signature line(s); and verification (if required).

The summons is a printed form that contains the same caption as the complaint. It notifies the defendant of the time within which the complaint must be answered.

Service is complete when a copy of the summons (or copies of the complaint and summons) has been handed to the defendant and the original summons properly completed by the process server.

The date of service and the date default action may be taken must be recorded on the office calendars or in the office diary to assure prompt follow-up of the matter.

SUGGESTED SPECIAL ASSIGNMENTS

1.   From a law office, a form book in the law library, the clerk's office, or your own personal files, obtain a copy of an initial pleading. Prepare one original copy. (Substitute the fictitious names of Allen B. Colder, plaintiff, and Frank Gary Hall, defendant, for those shown in your original pleading.) Proofread carefully. Assemble and staple.

2.   Obtain a copy of a summons from the court clerk's office. Complete the summons. The plaintiff is Allen B. Colder and the defendant is Frank Gary Hall.

3.   Prepare one original copy of the complaint shown on page 350. Use the typing style acceptable in your jurisdiction. Proofread carefully. Assemble and staple.

4.   Read Canon 4 of the Code of Professional Responsibility of the American Bar Association (pages 298–300). Write a brief summary of this canon.

13

Answers

Mr. Dogbreeder, just served with a summons, is no doubt alarmed, angry, or bewildered. It is one thing to subconsciously expect to be named defendant in a lawsuit. It is quite another for it to become a reality.

Whom should he see? This may be the first time in his life that he has felt the need for the services of an attorney. From names recommended to him by neighbors, friends, fellow employees, church members, or the local legal reference association, Mr. Dogbreeder will choose a law firm to represent him.

THE CLIENT

That first call to a law office can be satisfying, or it can be a frustrating, unhappy experience. A great deal depends upon the receptionist or secretary who answers the telephone. Careful use of good public relations techniques, in this case simply good manners and a quiet, businesslike attitude and voice over the telephone, will reassure the prospective client that he is in good hands. If the secretary will use the client's name once or twice during the short telephone conversation, he will be reassured that he has called the right office for help with his legal problem.

No matter how small or how large the problem, the legal secretary is still in the business of helping people. That help begins with the first phone call or unannounced office call of a new client.

Handling Client's First Telephone Call

If the attorney is in the office, the phone call should be transferred immediately. If the attorney is not in the office at that moment, the prospective client should be assured that his call will be returned immediately upon the attorney's return to the office.

One bit of information the secretary might elicit from Mr. Dogbreeder, if he has indicated his problem, is the exact date service of the summons was made on him. After checking the appointment calendar, the secretary might make a tentative appointment for Mr. Dogbreeder to see the attorney.

The telephone message the secretary makes of this phone call should be accurate and legible. It should contain the date, the time, and the correct name and phone number of the caller. And it should indicate the date the summons was served on the client, if this information is available.

When the attorney returns to the office, it is the legal secretary's responsibility to follow up on Mr. Dogbreeder's call. Perhaps the attorney would like a telephone call placed to Mr. Dogbreeder. After all, the secretary promised the client that the attorney would return the call. It is the secretary's responsibility to keep the promise.

Appointment

The same fiduciary or trust relationship exists between the defendant and the attorney as exists between the plaintiff and the attorney. EC (Ethical Consideration) 5-15 of the Code of Professional Responsibility of the American Bar Association states in part:

A lawyer should never represent in litigation multiple clients with differing interests; and there are few situations in which he would be justified in representing in litigation multiple clients with potentially differing interests.[1]

[1] Excerpted from the *Model Code of Professional Responsibility*, as amended February, 1979, ©, American Bar Association.

Therefore, an attorney may, in any lawsuit, represent either a plaintiff or a defendant, but not both the plaintiff and the defendant.

During the defendant's visit with the attorney, the attorney will take notes as the defendant explains the problem to be litigated. The notes will be written on the ever-present yellow lined legal notepad.

The complaint and summons will be left with the defendant's attorney for reference and use. If, for some reason, the client wishes copies of the summons and complaint, a good public relations gesture would be to run copies on the office copying machine. The wise secretary would make a pencil notation on the complaint or summons retained in the office to indicate that copies were delivered to the client and the date of their delivery.

As the client leaves the office, the legal secretary will smile and nod or pleasantly say "Goodbye."

APPEARANCE

The *plaintiff* made an appearance in this matter when the complaint and summons were filed in the court clerk's office by the attorneys.

The *defendant* will make an appearance when a court document has been filed by defendant's attorney, and the filing fee, if required, has been paid. The court document may be one of many, each serving a different purpose, but each qualifying to make an appearance for the defendant. These include, among others:

- Answer (a pleading answering plaintiff's complaint)
- Demurrer (a pleading questioning that the facts stated in the complaint are of sufficient legal consequence to require an answer)
- Notice of appearance (used in those jurisdictions where the summons alone is served on the defendant)
- Answer and cross-complaint (a pleading answering plaintiff's complaint and including defendant's own complaint, which is called a cross-complaint)

We will assume that the *answer* is the court document used to make Mr. Dogbreeder's appearance in this matter.

Urgency

It is important that the legal secretary make note in the office diary or on the desk calendars of the final date (return date) by which defendant must answer the complaint. If an appearance has not been made by that date, the defendant could lose the suit by default. The error resulting from the failure to make a proper notation of the date would rest squarely on the shoulders of the legal secretary. Of course, the attorney would be finally at fault, and the office would suffer the consequences.

It is the legal secretary's responsibility, as well as the attorney's, to check the calendar or diary and call attention to the passage of time and the approaching last day to answer.

Extending Time to Answer

If an extension of time beyond the answer or return date is required, the defense attorney could very well telephone plaintiff's attorney and request an extension of time.

It is not uncommon for a trial attorney to be involved in a lawsuit that requires full time in court for a period of several days. The attorney's hours away from the courtroom are frequently filled with details incidental to the trial. Thus there is very little time to devote to other law office problems during that period of time. Each attorney recognizes that such a situation may occur at any time. Such extensions of time are necessary if attorneys are to prepare their cases properly.

A *stipulation* confirming the extension of time and setting a new date would be prepared by the defendant's attorney. (See Appendix D.) The new date would be noted in the office diary or on the desk calendars.

After the defense attorney had signed the stipulation, it would be delivered to the plaintiff's counsel for signature, and a copy would be delivered to plaintiff's counsel for the files. The fully executed original document would then be filed with the court, but only after the office copy had been conformed.

COMMUNICATION BETWEEN THE ATTORNEYS

When defendant has selected an attorney, all future communication between the parties is through the attorneys. The plaintiff's attorney will communicate with the plaintiff. The defendant's attorney will communicate with the defendant. However, all communication between the parties should be through the attorneys.

Subsequent legal papers in the matter will be delivered to the attorneys, not to the individuals whom the attorneys represent. Copies of all court documents may be given the client for his information if this is the policy of the office.

The defendant's attorney will dictate the answer to the legal secretary, using the client's (defendant's) copy of the complaint as a reference. In addition, the attorney may refer to other files and materials as a court document is dictated that will adequately answer the allegations contained in the complaint.

At the conclusion of the dictation, the attorney will hand the secretary the complaint and summons to use in preparing an office file for the new case. As the answer to the complaint is typed, the secretary will refer to the complaint and summons in order to confirm the accuracy of names, dates, locations, and other facts contained in these documents and included in the answer.

Caption

Dictation will include reference to the case title. The secretary's notes need show only "Homeowner vs Dogbreeder" or a similar identifying notation. The document title will be dictated. The remainder of the caption will be taken directly from the complaint.

Introduction

The introductory paragraph will be dictated. It is an unnumbered paragraph announcing that the defendant is making an answer.

Body

In this pleading, as in the initial pleading (complaint), all paragraphs are numbered. The attorney will painstakingly review each paragraph of the complaint. During dictation, reference will be made to specific paragraphs of the complaint, admitting or denying the contents. It is of utmost importance that the legal secretary record accurately all paragraph numbers dictated. Serious confusion could result if a careless type or transcription error admitted allegations in a paragraph that, in fact, had been denied in the attorney's dictation.

If a question should arise in the secretary's mind as to the clarity or completeness of a portion of the dictation, the questioned statement should be called to the attorney's attention. "May I read a sentence (or paragraph) back to you?" is sufficient.

Dictation should be punctuated as it is taken in shorthand or as it is heard on the transcriber. The drop and rise of the dictator's voice usually indicate commas and other punctuation as clearly as though they had been verbally included.

Prayer

The attorney will dictate the prayer, which is an unnumbered paragraph and usually begins with the word WHEREFORE.

Date Line

If a verification is not a part of the answer, a date line usually follows the prayer. The attorney will dictate the date line if one is to be included. As is usual in writing date lines, portions of the date may be left blank if it is not known just when the document will be signed.

Verification

If the complaint was verified, the answer must also usually be verified. The verification may or may not be dictated. However, the competent legal secretary will check the complaint, and if a verification is included, the attorney should be consulted. With the attorney's approval, the secretary will add a verification to the answer.

TYPING THE ANSWER

As in the preparation of a complaint, the answer, once dictated, should be typed as soon as possible. It, too, takes precedence over most of the work in the office. If the final date for answering the complaint is today, the answer must be typed, signed, served, and filed TODAY.

Copies

If a copy machine is available, perhaps only an original of the answer will be typed. All other copies will be run off on the copy machine. If a copy machine is not available, the minimum copies in the carbon pack will be: an original for the court clerk's office, a copy for service on the plaintiff's attorney, and an office file copy. If more than one person is to be served, other copies of the answer will be required. If the client is to receive a copy, still another copy must be prepared.

Typing Style

The new legal secretary may refer to an answer contained in the form file. The style of the complaint will not necessarily be followed since it might vary slightly or widely from that used in this attorney's office.

Legal secretaries sometimes question the differences in style used in law offices within the same jurisdiction. These differences may result from the varied educational backgrounds of the attorneys. An attorney who obtained a law degree from an Eastern college may prefer certain wording and certain format. An attorney who graduated from a law school in another part of the country may use somewhat different legal language and prefer a slightly different format.

It is true that all attorneys who pass the bar of a state and practice therein must conform to the rules of practice for that state. However, the rules are not so stringent that they fail to allow for differences in training and background of the myriad attorneys who practice in the state.

It is not the legal secretary's prerogative to impose the legal language and style learned in one office on another attorney or office. Each office is unique and need not follow precisely the wording and style of other offices. All attorneys, however, must follow such wording and style as is required by the court and state in which they practice.

Firm Name and Address

The firm name and address will appear on the first or signature page of the answer, or on the printed back if one is used. This identifies the defendant's attorney for both the court and the plaintiff's attorney.

Caption

Data for the caption will be taken from the complaint. The *case title* and *number* shown on the complaint will be typed on the answer and on all succeeding court papers in the case.

If the case title included several plaintiffs or several defendants, it is sufficient in most states to shorten the title on all succeeding documents.

```
JOHN JONES, WEST NEIGHBOR,
and HAROLD HOMEOWNER,

            Plaintiffs,


    vs.

MARY SMITH, EAST NEIGHBOR,
and DONALD DOGBREEDER,

            Defendants.
```

may be shortened to:

JOHN JONES, et al.,

Plaintiffs,

vs.

MARY SMITH, et al.,

Defendants.

The *document title* will be written exactly as it is dictated by the attorney.

Introduction

The introductory paragraph begins a double space below the last line of the caption, or on the first numbered space below the caption if ruled-and-numbered paper is used. Some examples of the introductory statements in an answer follow:

Comes now the defendant, DONALD DOGBREEDER, and, in answer to the complaint heretofore filed, alleges as follows:

Comes now the defendant, DONALD DOGBREEDER, and, answering the complaint on file herein, admits, denies and alleges as follows, to wit:

Defendant, DONALD DOGBREEDER, answers the allegations of the alleged first cause of action of the complaint herein as follows:

[The preceding statement may be used if the complaint contains more than one cause of action.]

The defendant, DONALD DOGBREEDER, answering the complaint herein by his attorneys, JONES and JONES, alleges:

DISCUSSION

1. Observe that all proper names are in all caps. (Some law offices prefer that the firm name be typed in lower case.) Unless you have instructions to the contrary, a practical, consistent rule to follow is: type all proper names in all caps in all legal documents.

2. Observe the commas surrounding the defendant's name. His name is in apposition with the word *defendant*. Rules of grammar dictate the use of commas.

3. Observe the commas surrounding "in answer to the complaint heretofore filed" in the first example and "answering the complaint on file herein" in the second example. Both are parenthetical phrases inserted into the sentences, which would be complete without the statements. The first example, without the inserted phrase, would read: "Comes now the defendant, DONALD DOG-BREEDER, and alleges as follows." The complete parenthetical phrase should be enclosed in commas, not just a portion of it. It is a rather common error to omit the first comma—but it is still an error.

4. In the series, "admits, denies and alleges," the comma is omitted before the *and*.

Body of the Answer

The body of the answer is transcribed as dictated by the attorney. The legal secretary may refer to the form file for the style used by the office. The body of the answer begins a double space below the last line of the introduction. Two examples follow:

I

Defendant admits paragraphs I and II of the complaint.

II

In answer to the allegations of paragraphs III and IV, this

answering defendant denies that any obligation was....

---

1. Defendant admits paragraphs I and II of the complaint.

2. Defendant admits so much of paragraph III as alleges that

the plaintiff....

DISCUSSION

1. The first example uses Roman numerals to number the paragraphs of the answer. They are also used to refer to the paragraphs of the complaint. *This indicates that the paragraphs of the complaint were numbered with Roman numerals.*

2. Observe that the Roman numerals are centered and are aligned at the left. It is a simple matter to set a tab at the approxi-

mate center of the page and type the number. No backspacing is required.

3. In the second example, *Arabic* numbers are used to identify the paragraphs in the answer. However, *this example indicates that Roman numerals were used to number paragraphs in the complaint.*

4. Periods follow Arabic numbers when they are used to number paragraphs. Periods do not follow Roman numerals.

Prayer

The prayer will be transcribed as dictated. Two styles of prayers follow:

WHEREFORE, defendant prays that the complaint be dismissed; and that he have and recover his costs; and for such other and further relief as the court deems proper.

WHEREFORE, defendant prays judgment as follows:

1. That plaintiff take nothing by his action;

2. For costs of suit;

3. For such other and further relief as the court deems just and proper in the premises.

DISCUSSION

1. *WHEREFORE* is in all caps and is followed by a comma.

2. The prayer may be typed in paragraph form or in outline form, as shown in the two examples. It need not follow the style used in the complaint. Rather, it follows the form used in the law office where it is prepared.

If the legal secretary has a choice in the matter, the second or outline form shown above should be used, for the very obvious reason that each request is itemized and the style is easy to proofread for both accuracy and completeness.

3. The final statement in the prayer is the omnibus clause. It is usually included as a part of the prayer to permit such relief as may be granted by the court but that is not specifically set forth in the prayer.

Date Line

A date line follows the prayer if a verification is not to be included. Three date line styles follow:

Dated: Honolulu, Hawaii, December ___, 19__.

Dated this _____day of December, 19__.

Dated at Cincinnati, Ohio, December 12, 19__.

DISCUSSION

1. Observe the punctuation. Commas surround *Hawaii* and *Ohio*.

2. If the answer is to be signed the day it is typed, the complete date may be typed. If there is even a slight chance that it will not be signed that day, blanks should be provided for later addition of the date. The date will be filled in by the signer when the document is executed.

The date lines should be realistic in length. If the date to be filled in later is the day of the month, a one-inch line is adequate. However, if the document is prepared near the end of the month, and the month is also to be filled in later, a line should be left that is long enough to accommodate the name of the month.

Aren't you momentarily disturbed when you are confronted with a form with insufficient space for the data requested? So are your clients.

Signature Line

The firm name is typed with the signature line regularly used by the office and the attorney.

Verifications

Verifications should be transcribed as dictated. If the complaint contains a verification, but one was not dictated or even alluded to during the dictation, the legal secretary will type a proper verification as part of the answer. As the answer is handed to the attorney for signature, mention should be made that a verification was added. If, for some reason, one should not have been included, the attorney is forewarned.

The verification should be carefully proofread for content as well as for type or punctuation errors. If a "he" is to sign it, all references to the signer should be "he" or "his." If a "she" is to sign it, all references to the signer should be "she" or "her." It is embarrassing for all concerned if the client has to call such proofreading errors to the attention of either the attorney or the secretary.

Signatures

When complete, the answer is taken to the attorney for perusal and signature.

If a verification is a part of the answer, the client will be asked to come to the office. The telephone call, if made by the secretary at the attorney's request, should be brief but pleasant. If there is an urgency about the signing, this information must be tactfully conveyed to the client.

Conforming Copies

When the answer has been signed and dated, all copies must be conformed to match the original exactly.

Serving the Answer

In most jurisdictions, the answer may be served upon the plaintiff in either of two ways:

1. By serving a copy of the answer personally on plaintiff's attorney or someone acting as agent (the secretary). Acknowledgment of such service should be made on the original answer by having plaintiff's attorney or agent sign a simple receipt: "Copy of this Answer was received on _____ (date) _____."

When the original answer has been returned to the office, the legal secretary will immediately conform the office copy to match exactly the receipt on the original copy of the answer.

2. By mailing a copy of the answer to plaintiff's attorney. An affidavit of service by mail will then be made by the person who places the copy in the mail. Copies of the affidavit will be attached to all copies of the answer. When the copy of the answer has been mailed, the affidavit attached to the original answer will be completed and signed by the one who mailed the copy, usually the legal secretary. Other copies will be conformed.

DEFENDANT'S APPEARANCE

When the answer has been served on plaintiff's attorney and all copies have been conformed, the original answer is ready for filing with the court clerk's office. In most states, a fee is charged for the first appearance of the defendant in the matter.

The original answer and a law firm check to cover the filing fee will be taken to the court clerk's office. The clerk will accept the check and original answer and return a receipt for the fee. (The receipt will be placed in the office file.) Defendant has made an appearance.

The client will be billed later for costs advanced by the firm.

SUCCEEDING STEPS

Before placing the office copy of the answer in the file, the legal secretary will check with the attorney to learn the date of the next action in the matter. That date must be noted in the office diary or on the desk calendars. If a follow-up date was not noted and the answer was filed in the office files, the matter could lie unattended until the plaintiff's attorney or the client raised the question of further action on the matter.

Recording the dates for action, follow-ups, court appearances, and so on, is a primary part of the legal secretary's work.

SUMMARY

Defendant's appearance in a civil matter may be made in various ways, including answer, demurrer, notice of appearance, and answer and cross-complaint.

An answer consists of the following, which will be typed in the style used by the defense attorney's office (it may or may not be the same style as that of the complaint): caption, introductory paragraph, body, prayer, signature lines, and verification (if required).

When the answer has been completed, proofread, and signed, it is served on plaintiff's attorney, either in person or by mail.

The original answer showing service upon plaintiff's attorney and a check covering the fee for defendant's appearance in the matter are taken to the courthouse for filing. This constitutes the defendant's appearance in the lawsuit.

SUGGESTED SPECIAL ASSIGNMENTS

1. Obtain a copy of the second pleading in a lawsuit (answer, response, or possibly a demurrer) from a law firm, a form book at the law library, a friend or family member, or your own personal files. Type one original copy of the pleading. Substitute fictitious names for those in the original pleading. Proofread. Assemble and staple.

2.   Type one original copy of the answer on page 357. Make the necessary changes in style to conform to the requirements in your jurisdiction. Proofread. Assemble and staple.

3.   Type one original copy of the stipulation in Appendix D. Make the necessary changes to conform to your jurisdiction. Proofread carefully.

14

Legal Procedure

There are procedures for many, perhaps most, of our daily activities. Something as commonplace as beginning the day is, in a sense, procedural: we awaken, leave the bed, shower or bathe, dress, breakfast, and enter the student or the working world. Each of us has a particular ritual or procedure that we follow.

In a business matter as routine as depositing money in a checking account at Bank XYZ, certain procedure must be followed. With money to deposit, we take the following steps:

1. Complete Bank XYZ's deposit slip in a manner suitable to the bank.
2. Deliver the deposit slip and the money to the bank *simultaneously*.
3. Accept a deposit receipt.

All steps must be completed before the money is placed in the account of the depositor.

DEFINITION OF LEGAL PROCEDURE

Although it is complicated and varied, legal procedure is basically those steps necessary under the law to commence, continue, and a certain procedure; patents are granted only after the proper procedural steps have been followed.

SOURCE AND IMPORTANCE
OF LEGAL PROCEDURE

Legal procedure is established by law. Each step follows another because some place, some time, those steps and the order of those steps were set by law. If time limits are part of the procedure, they must be recognized and adhered to. For example, if state law provides that six months must elapse between the service of a complaint on a defendant and the issuance of the decree of divorce, no shorter time is legally acceptable in that state.

The legal procedure that is established must be followed. Further, if established procedure is changed by law, the new legal procedure must be followed the day it becomes law.

LEGAL PROCEDURE AND THE NEW SECRETARY

The novice legal secretary, either interested in a particular branch of law or employed by specialists, will benefit by carefully preparing a list of all steps of the procedure in that special area of law. Time periods that must be observed and titles of all documents that might be used during the course of the action should be included in the list. The legal secretary will not only become familiar with procedure, but, when dictated a document, may recognize the step of procedure in the matter simply by the title of the court document to be prepared.

Procedural information may be obtained in various ways, three of which are

1. Source books in the law office library or the local law library
2. The attorney, who may take the time to explain legal procedure to the secretary who expresses special interest in the work
3. On-the-job experience — learning legal procedure by working daily with various legal problems

DIFFERENCES IN LEGAL PROCEDURE

The steps necessary to process a *civil* matter through the courts are different from the steps necessary to process a *criminal* matter through the courts. These are, in turn, different from the steps necessary to bring a corporation into existence or to commence, continue, and conclude a bankruptcy matter. An adoption follows conclude a particular legal problem. It is a method for processing the client's problems through the courts.

Cursory outlines of civil procedure, divorce and dissolution procedure, criminal procedure, bankruptcy procedure, and corporation procedure are given in this chapter. The five vary greatly in procedural requirements and in the statutory time periods that must be recognized under the law. Probate procedure is included in some detail in Chapter 16.

Statutory Time Periods

No attempt will be made in this volume to list specific time periods required by law between various procedural steps. They vary. One state may require a period of ten days and another twenty days between similar steps; one, six months, another a year between other steps.

Statutory time periods are established for the protection of all interested parties to the action. All such persons are given ample time to take such action as is necessary to protect their interests—to make an appearance, to request that they be notified of activity in certain matters, or to protect their investment or property.

When served with a summons, the defendant has from ten days in some states to thirty days in other states in which to answer (make an appearance). An individual served with a notice to vacate the premises has a statutory period of time before forced eviction. In a forced sale of real property, both the seller and the buyer benefit by the statutory period of time that must run between the publication of notice of sale and the actual sale. Statutory periods of time that are a part of probate procedure protect the rights of both creditors and beneficiaries of the decedent.

Document Titles

Specific titles of court documents will not be used here. They differ. For example, in a civil action the plaintiff's initial court document stating the cause of action is called, in some states, a *complaint;* in others, a *petition;* in others, a *declaration;* in others, a *bill;* and in still others it is referred to as a *narration.* The titles differ, but the function is the same: to initiate a lawsuit.

Procedural Steps

Specific steps of procedure will not be given. Only the broad steps necessary to illustrate procedural differences in civil, divorce and dissolution, criminal, bankruptcy, and corporation procedures will be listed. The steps vary. Size or geographical spread may result in slight procedural differences between jurisdictions within a state.

CIVIL PROCEDURE

A civil suit is a legal action with individuals, corporations, partnerships, or agencies suing or being sued to protect a right or prevent a wrong.

Such suits may result from

- An automobile accident (personal injury and property damage suit)
- Failure of one party or the other to live up to the terms of a contract (breach of contract suit)
- Husband or wife suing the other to end the marriage (divorce or marriage dissolution matter)
- A landlord suing a tenant to regain possession of property (unlawful detainer suit)
- or other cause of action

Civil procedure, very briefly, consists of

1. Preparation and filing of complaint or original petition
2. Issuance of summons
3. Service of summons (or summons and complaint) on defendant
4. Answer by defendant within statutory period of time (If defendant fails to make an appearance [answer] within the statutory period of time, plaintiff may take judgment by default.)
5. Plaintiff's answer to the cross-complaint, made within the statutory period of time, if a cross-complaint is filed and served by defendant
6. Pretrial
7. Trial
8. Judgment
9. Appeal, if one is made by either party to the suit

Calendaring Civil Suits

In some states the court system includes separate courts for criminal and civil cases. In many states, however, one court — for example, the superior court or the circuit court — will hear both civil and criminal matters. Under the Constitution of the United States, civil suits are secondary to criminal suits in gaining a place on the court calendar. If the court calendar has a sudden influx of criminal cases to be heard, civil suits already scheduled will be recalendared for hearing at a later date.

The Constitution of the United States of America declares in Article VI of the Bill of Rights:

> In all criminal prosecutions, the accused shall enjoy the right to a speedy and public trial, by an impartial jury of the State and district wherein the crime shall have been committed, which district shall have been previously ascertained by law, and to be informed of the nature and cause of the accusation; to be confronted with the witnesses against him; to have compulsory process for obtaining witnesses in his favor, and to have the Assistance of Counsel for his defense.

For the reasons given in this section of the Bill of Rights, together with the heavy overloading of most court calendars, civil matters may wait months or even years before they are heard in a court of law, when one court is charged with hearing both civil and criminal matters.

DIVORCE AND DISSOLUTION PROCEDURE

Divorce procedure separates a man and wife in most states. This is an *adversary proceeding* and assumes that one party is right and one party is wrong. One or more of several grounds for divorce (adultery, extreme cruelty, etc.) recognized by the state may be given in the initial court document, which is sometimes called a bill of divorcement, a complaint for divorce, or other similar title.

Among the data that must be included in the original pleading are the following:

- Residence of one or both of the parties
- Place and date of the marriage
- Date of the separation
- Minor children
- Property of the parties
- Grounds for divorce

As in other civil suits, the initial pleading and/or summons is served on the defendant. If default is to be avoided, the initial pleading must be answered. This is accomplished by the defendant's attorney, who prepares and files an answer within the time period shown on the summons.

A final decree of divorce is granted when all statutory requirements have been met, including the calendar time that must pass between the filing of the initial pleading and the granting of the final decree.

In most states, pleadings and other legal documents used in

divorce proceedings are typed out in full and follow the same style used in other civil matters. However, printed forms such as the *summons*, the *interlocutory decree* (if there is one) and the *final decree of divorce* are sometimes used.

Dissolution of marriage is a *nonadversary proceeding* and is sometimes referred to as "no-fault" divorce. The purpose of the dissolution proceeding is to permit separation of husband and wife without placing blame. Dissolutions were introduced first in California and became effective there in January 1971.

Among the many changes effected to lessen the emotional trauma of divorce was the use of less abrasive legal terms.

- *Petitioner* for *plaintiff*
- *Respondent* for *defendant*
- *Petition* for *complaint*
- *Response* for *answer*

In California, the only grounds for dissolution are

- irreconcilable differences that have caused the irremediable breakdown of the marriage; and
- incurable insanity

As in divorce procedure, the initial pleading and summons are served on the respondent, who must answer within the time shown on the summons.

From the initial petition and summons to the final judgment of dissolution, printed forms are used. Only rarely is a court document typed in its entirety.

See Appendix E for several California dissolution forms.

CRIMINAL PROCEDURE

When the *people of the nation* or the *people of a state*, as plaintiffs, bring suit against an individual, an agency, or a company for the commission or omission of an act *in violation of the law*, a criminal action is instituted. The case title might read:

```
THE PEOPLE OF THE STATE OF
CALIFORNIA,

                    Plaintiff,


        vs.


JOHN DOE,

                    Defendant.
```

When a crime has been committed, and the accused has been located, the steps of criminal procedure are, briefly

1. Warrant of arrest issued
2. Arrest — individual taken into custody
3. Arraignment — prisoner taken before the court to answer the criminal charge
4. Preliminary examination or preliminary trial
5. Trial
6. Judgment or verdict — individual found guilty or not guilty by the court or by the jury
7. Appeal, if filed

During the course of a criminal action, the legal papers prepared by the secretary are relatively few when compared with those required for most civil actions. Of those prepared, most are printed legal forms.

BANKRUPTCY PROCEDURE

Bankruptcy is a *federal* matter and is heard in a United States Bankruptcy Court. Bankruptcy proceedings may be initiated by the bankrupt's creditors; involuntary bankruptcy proceedings will ensue. If bankruptcy proceedings are initiated by the bankrupt, voluntary bankruptcy proceedings will follow.

Voluntary Bankruptcy

When a person accumulates debts and finds that he is unable to pay them, he may voluntarily file a petition asking that he be declared a bankrupt. Bankruptcy forms are sold in stationery stores.

Procedural steps in a voluntary bankruptcy matter follow:

1. Bankrupt files a debtor's petition in bankruptcy with the clerk of the United States Bankruptcy Court. (Chapter 7 bankruptcy requires that an original and one copy be filed with the Bankruptcy Court. Chapter 11 bankruptcy requires that an original and five copies be filed with the Bankruptcy Court.) A copy is retained in the attorney's files. Attached to the petition are

   - Summary of debts and assets of the petitioner (bankrupt)
   - Schedule listing in detail all debts of the petitioner

- Schedule listing in detail all property of the petitioner
- Mailing list of all creditors

2. A filing fee is required at the time the petition is filed in Bankruptcy Court.

3. A meeting of all creditors is scheduled and all creditors are sent notices.

4. Creditors' meeting is held and a trustee is elected.

5. Each creditor submits a proof of claim of the amount owed by the debtor.

6. The trustee administers the estate.

7. If sufficient funds are available, debts of a priority status and secured and unsecured debts are paid, in that order.

8. When a discharge has been entered, bankrupt is relieved of the burden of his debts as presented by his creditors, unless objections have been filed.

NOTE: Bankruptcy procedure is the same in every state, since it is a federal matter and is heard in the United States Bankruptcy Court.

CORPORATION PROCEDURE

Corporations are established under state law, which differs from state to state. Following are some of the steps usually common to the procedure for organizing and establishing a new corporation:

1. Reserve a name for the new corporation. The new corporation's name must be unique; it may not duplicate any other name on file in the state office of corporations.
2. Prepare, execute, and file articles of incorporation.
3. Prepare by-laws.
4. Conduct first meeting of the directors of the corporation and prepare minutes of the meeting.
5. Apply for permission to issue stock.

Corporations have an indefinite life, but may be dissolved upon proper application to the state department for corporations.

PUBLICATION OF NOTICES AND
OBSERVANCE OF TIME PERIODS

Publication of notices and care in observing statutory time periods are extremely important if included as procedural steps in any legal matter. The able legal secretary will assume a share of the responsibility. The secretary is also responsible for following correct form and style in the preparation of the legal documents required as a part of the procedure.

Publication

Publication of legal notices is required to give public notice of impending legal action to all interested persons.

When the procedure requires the printing of a notice or other legal paper in a publication of general circulation, the attorney will make the printing assignment. It is the legal secretary's responsibility to make certain the publication takes place, by checking the daily office copies of the newspaper.

If the notice is to be published for a period of three weeks, the legal secretary makes certain it is so published, again by checking the office copies of the newspaper. Furthermore, if affidavits of publication are to be filed by the newspaper, the filing of the affidavits should be verified. If the newspaper had published the notice, but through an error of a new employee or other inadvertence an affidavit had not been filed with the court, there could be a delay in the next procedural step.

The secretary will find the legal newspaper personnel so efficient in their performance that there could be an inclination to forego checking on them. However, there is always the possibility of oversight or error, which the legal secretary must try to eliminate.

Time

When a lapse of time is required between procedural steps, the legal secretary will note on the calendar or diary the exact expiration date of the time period. As the date approaches, the legal secretary will call the attorney's attention to the matter, so that if legal forms or documents must be prepared, there will be ample time to prepare them.

Care must be exercised at all times to follow each step of legal procedure and to follow it within the time periods established by law.

FORM AND STYLE

Legal procedure includes the use of correct legal forms and court documents prepared in an acceptable style. If the incorrect form is submitted, or a form is not properly completed or executed, a correction will have to be made, thus delaying the next procedural step.

If a complaint or a petition requires a verification signed by the complainant or the petitioner, failure to include the verification would, of course, delay the matter until the oversight could be corrected.

SUMMARY

Exact conformance to procedure in any legal matter is a paramount responsibility of the attorney and is, therefore, a paramount responsibility of the legal secretary.

Careful attention to recording and observing dates of hearings, dates for beginning each succeeding step in the procedure — all dates pertaining to the matter — is a major concern of the legal secretary.

Procedure in any legal problem is similar in all states, but the details differ, particularly the statutory time periods between steps and the exact titles of the many court documents and legal forms. The number of steps and the number of documents required from the inception of the legal matter to its conclusion varies with the states.

It is important to the legal secretary to know that there is such a thing as legal procedure, that it must be followed exactly, and that it will probably vary from state to state and sometimes between jurisdictions within a state.

The legal secretary with experience in one state must become acquainted with the procedure of any other state where employment is desired. However, a basic understanding of legal procedure, of forms, of the importance of time and of dates, and of legal secretaryship generally will permit an experienced legal secretary to move from one state to another, confident that legal secretaryship experience is a transferable commodity.

SUGGESTED SPECIAL ASSIGNMENTS

1. List the procedural steps in a divorce or dissolution matter (as followed in your state).

2. On separate papers, type a caption for a criminal matter and a caption for a civil matter. Use the style accepted in your jursidiction. Proofread carefully for style and accuracy.

15

Probate Court

When Mr. Francis Peter Irwyne dies and is no longer here to take care of his property, someone will have to act for him. When Mr. West Neighbor's elderly father, because of the infirmities caused by old age, is incapable of handling his property, someone will have to do it for him. If a minor is suddenly bereft of parents, he is neither legally able to manage the assets he may have inherited nor legally able to care for himself. Someone will have to be appointed to take care of both the youngster and his property.

In most states, all these matters would be handled in probate court. This court is primarily concerned with estates or property of individuals who, for reasons of age, illness, incompetence, or death, are unable to administer their own property.

In some states, special courts called *probate, surrogate,* or *orphans'* courts hear the matters. In other states, they are heard in a special probate department of the superior or other court.

Included among the matters handled in probate court may be:

- Conservatorships
- Guardianships

- Intestate matters
- Testate matters

DEFINITIONS

Definitions for some of the special legal terms used in probate are furnished here, in order to relate the correct terms to the appropriate legal category, to identify the parties in various probate matters, to identify the letters of authority granted each appointee who is to administer property in probate, and to present the special legal significance of each of the terms.

Conservatorships

Conservatorships are established to conserve or protect the property of those who, for reasons of health or old age infirmity, are unable to manage their property.

The *conservatee* is the one who owns the property but is incapable of managing it.

The *conservator* is the one appointed by the court to manage the property. The conservator may also be named to care for the conservatee personally as the guardian or protector.

Letters of conservatorship, a legal form, are issued by the court to the conservator. The letters authorize the conservator to care for and manage the conservatee's property.

Guardianships

Guardianships are established to protect the property of minors and others who, for various legal reasons, are unable to administer their affairs.

A *guardian* is the one legally responsible for the care of the person *and* property or the person *or* property of another who, because of age, incompetence, or other condition, is unable to administer his/her own affairs.

A guardian may be appointed to care for both the estate and the person of an individual. Or a guardian, perhaps an institution, may be appointed to manage the estate, while another guardian, an individual, may be appointed to care for the individual's personal needs.

A *minor* or *infant* is the one who is under the age of legal competence — that is, one who has not yet reached the age of majority as established by state law. If the need arose, a guardianship, not a conservatorship, would be established for a minor.

An *incompetent* is one who is incapable of managing his/her own affairs because of insanity, feeblemindedness, or similar condition. Some states establish guardianships, others establish conservatorships in order legally to administer the property of the incompetent.

Letters of guardianship, a court form, are issued by the court to the guardian. The letters authorize the guardian to care for and administer the property of the minor (or incompetent).

Intestate Matters

A person who dies without leaving a will dies intestate. (*Testate* is derived from a Latin word *testari* which means "to make a will." *In-* is a prefix meaning "not," as in *inactive*.)

A *decedent* is one who is deceased. In law, it has the special meaning of one who has recently died. (The mnemonic for remembering how to spell *decedent* is "all *e*'s.")

An *administrator*, in probate law, is the one appointed *by the court* to administer the estate of a decedent. The feminine of the word is *administratrix*. Included in the administrator's duties are these:

- Locating all assets of the estate
- Paying debts of the decedent and the estate
- Distributing the remainder of the estate to the *heirs at law*; that is, the heirs as determined by state law

Letters of administration are issued by the court to the administrator. (See Appendix E.) The letters authorize the administrator to administer the decedent's estate.

Testate Matters

One who dies and leaves a valid will is said to have died testate.

An *executor* is the one named in the testator's will to carry out the provisions of the will. The feminine of the word is *executrix*.

Letters testamentary are issued by the court to the executor. (See Appendix E.) The letters authorize the executor to administer decedent's estate in accordance with the provisions of the will. Included in the executor's duties are these:

- Locating all assets of the estate
- Paying debts of the decedent and the estate
- Distributing the remainder of the estate to the beneficiaries named in the will

If the executor named in the will is unable to act as such executor for any of several reasons such as death, illness, or distance, an *administrator with will annexed* is appointed *by the court* to carry out the provisions of the testator's will. The three terms, *administrator with will annexed, administrator cum testamento annexo,* and *administrator cta,* are synonymous. *Cum testamento annexo,* shortened to *cta,* is Latin for "with will annexed."

Not infrequently, a will prepared elsewhere than in a law office fails to carry a provision naming an executor. The court would then appoint an administrator with will annexed.

Holographic wills sometimes fail to name an executor. The court would appoint an administrator with will annexed.

Letters of administration with will annexed would be issued by the court. (See Appendix E.) The letters authorize the administrator with will annexed to administer the decedent's estate. The duties are identical to those of an executor.

PROBATE COURT DOCUMENTS

The legal papers in probate matters are one-party court documents. The name appearing in the caption is that of the person whose property or well-being is the concern of the court.

Estate of

FRANCIS PETER IRWYNE,

Deceased.

Guardianship of the person and estate of

JOHN E. YOUNGSTER,

Minor.

Original Petition or Application

In the first or original petition filed in a probate matter, the petitioner requests authority to administer or manage the estate and further requests that *letters* be issued for this purpose.

Letters

At the court hearing on the petition or application, the appropriate letters of conservatorship, letters of guardianship, letters of administration, letters testamentary, or letters of administration with will annexed will be issued by the court. They will be issued only if the petitioner is deemed qualified to act in such capacity.

The letters, which are printed court forms, will be completed by the legal secretary. At the court hearing on the petition, the letters will be delivered to the court for issuance (approval and signature of the judge). Letters must be issued (dated and signed by the judge) before the petitioner or applicant may act in an official capacity. Certified copies of letters may be ordered by the attorney for the use of the petitioner. These are evidence of the petitioner's authority to act in the probate matter.

Locating Assets

A major responsibility of the one to whom letters have been issued is the locating and listing of all assets of the estate. A complete inventory must be made of all real and personal property owned by the one whose name appears in the caption of the court document. The inventory will list all property, including real estate, interest in real estate, patent rights, businesses, money, jewelry, and all other personal property.

The party to whom letters are issued is responsible for handling estate property carefully and judiciously. The property may not be disposed of, manipulated, or additional property purchased without the court's approval. Estate property must be kept separate and apart from the individual's own property. The two may not be commingled (combined).

Paying Debts

All debts or expenses, including property and income taxes, will be paid out of estate funds by the one to whom letters were issued.

Distributing the Property

Conservatorship. In a conservatorship, if the conservatee regains good health and is again able to manage the property, it will be returned by court action.

Guardianship. In a guardianship for a minor, the assets of the estate will be transferred when the individual reaches the age of majority (comes of age).

In a guardianship for an incompetent person, the assets of the estate will be returned when, in the opinion of the court, the person is able to manage the property.

Intestate Matter. In an intestate matter, decedent's property will be distributed to the heirs at law in accordance with the laws of the state.

Testate Matter.   In a testate matter, decedent's property will be distributed in accordance with the wishes expressed by the testator in the will.

Forms

Both court forms and tax forms are widely used in probate work. These forms provide efficiency in the preparation of probate papers and permit uniformity of style and information in petitions, orders, tax forms, letters, and other papers required during the course of an estate matter. They also enable the new legal secretary to understand general probate procedure and requirements.

SUMMARY

Probate courts are sometimes called surrogate courts or orphans' courts, or they may be branches of superior or other courts.

Some of the matters heard in probate court are

- Conservatorships — established to protect the property of adults who are incapable of managing their property
- Guardianships — established to protect the property of minors and others who are unable to manage their property
- Intestate matters — established to administer the estates of those who have died leaving no wills
- Testate matters — established to administer the estates of those who have died and left valid wills

Letters are the court forms that, when issued, authorize a party to administer or manage an estate. Such a party is responsible for collecting assets of the estate, paying estate debts, managing the property, and distributing the property.

Estate property is distributed according to law. In a conservatorship or guardianship, the property may, by court order, be returned to the control of the owner. In a testate or intestate matter, the property will be distributed to the legal beneficiaries.

Rigidity of statutory requirements in probate permits and requires the use of many legal forms in this branch of the law.

SUGGESTED SPECIAL ASSIGNMENTS

1.   Obtain a copy of letters of guardianship, letters of conservatorship, or letters of administration. Complete the caption using one of the following names: Leland Mark Norris, Ellen Fay Goodwin, or Celia Dawn Ellis.

2. From a law office, a form book in a law library, the clerk's office, or other source, obtain a copy of an initial petition in a guardianship, conservatorship, or intestate matter. Type one original copy, using one of the names in Suggested Special Assignment 1 as the minor, the incompetent or conservatee, or the decedent. (If the initial petition is a law blank or form, obtain a copy and complete it according to the style on file in the clerk's office.)

16

Probate Procedure– A Testate Matter

Obviously, the procedure in each of the matters in the preceding chapter is much more complicated than is indicated in the discussion. To illustrate the complexity of probate procedure and the importance of the passage of statutory time periods in some probate matters, this chapter follows a testate matter through its major steps.

LANGUAGE AND STYLE

The legal rhetoric, special words, and style used in the various forms and petitions in a testate matter are similar to those used in guardianships, conservatorships, and intestate matters.

Caption styles follow jurisdictional requirements and vary in each of the fifty states. It is not feasible to include here fifty captions or fifty of each of the many papers required in any matters. Therefore, representative legal documents will be used to illustrate major steps in the procedure followed in a testate matter.

In almost every state, there is an attempt being made to modernize the legal rhetoric, to omit redundant phraseology, to streamline style, and generally to move into the computer age. Yet it is necessary to retain much of the original if we are to maintain the law.

THE CLIENT

The client who visits the law office carrying a will of a recently deceased relative or friend may be a lonely, lost individual. The understanding and friendliness of the legal secretary are undeniably important.

Often, only in the law office are people able to speak somewhat unemotionally of a recent bereavement. Possibly it is the rather formal surroundings. Possibly it is because there they feel they are still near and serving the decedent.

At any rate, the legal secretary who, by attitude and attention, gives recently bereaved persons some comfort is serving the client and, indirectly, the attorney at a most sensitive time. Too much attention and conversation would be ill-mannered. A nod, pleasant replies to questions, and undivided attention, if warranted, are the most useful public relations techniques.

Appointment

During the first interview with Ned David Bent, named by his father, Norton David Bent, to act as the executor of his estate, the attorney will obtain from him both the original will and a great deal of miscellaneous and statistical information.

Forms

If the secretary has placed on the attorney's desk the forms that must be completed early in the probate of the estate, a special request for them will have been eliminated. The forms might include the original petition (if a court form is used) and the information forms required by the state inheritance tax department.

Information Required

With the forms as a guide, the attorney, using a yellow lined legal notepad, will obtain from the client the information necessary to begin probate proceedings. This includes

- Full name of the decedent and any and all other names by which he may have been known or under which he may have owned property. Norton David Bent might also have been known as Norton D. Bent, N. David Bent, N. D. Bent, or even Dave Bent.
- Date and place of death.
- Heirs at law, even though they may not have been mentioned in the will. This would include other children of the decedent, were there any.
- Complete names, addresses, ages, and relationships of all persons named in the will as beneficiaries.
- Kinds and approximate value of property owned by decedent at date of death.
- Special information necessary to complete inheritance tax forms.

The will named Ned David Bent as executor of the estate. His current address and telephone number should be a matter of record in the office files.

Dictation

Less verbatim dictation is required in probate matters than in many other legal matters, because of the rigidity of the statutory requirements and the fact that in most jurisdictions many of the court documents have been reduced to legal forms.

Dictation is frequently a matter of the attorney's furnishing the legal secretary with facts to be added to forms, copies of which each has available during the dictation period.

COURT DOCUMENTS – PROBATE

Probate papers are one-party court documents. They are typed on legal paper regularly used by the local courts. It may be ruled-and-numbered paper, ruled paper, or plain paper. It may be legal size or letter size. The kind of paper depends upon the court requirements and office preference.

Copies Required of Court Documents

Minimum copies required are two: an original copy for the court clerk's office and an office file copy. If law firm policy dictates that copies of legal papers be sent to clients, extra copies of all documents must be made and delivered to the named executor.

Special Notice

During the course of settling the estate, one or more of the heirs may hire counsel to represent their interests. The attorney for the heir will file with the court a request for special notice of all activities of the estate. The attorney representing the executor will send copies of all court documents filed in the estate to the heir's attorney. That attorney will, in turn, keep the heir informed of all action in the estate.

COURT FORMS

The increasing number of estates being probated has encouraged the courts to turn to the use of forms wherever feasible. The forms are usually prepared and provided by the clerk's office, often at no charge to the law office, and are, in turn, completed by the law office for court use. In some states the probate forms are available at book or stationery stores for a nominal fee.

Some court forms used in testate matters are

- Petition for probate of will and for letters testamentary, also sometimes called an application for letters (see pages 226-227.)
- Order admitting will to probate and for letters testamentary and order approving appraiser (Some jurisdictions use separate orders: an order for letters and an order appointing appraiser.) (see page 230.)
- Letters testamentary
- Creditor's claim
- Inventory and appraisement

(See Appendix E.)

COPIES OF THE WILL

As soon as the original will is available, the legal secretary will prepare several copies. If a copy machine is available, the copies may be made on it. If not, the copies must be typed to conform exactly to the original will. They will, therefore, require careful proofreading.

If a holographic will is to be probated, the secretary will make a typewritten copy for filing with the original holographic will. This provides a typed interpretation of sometimes difficult or almost illegible handwriting.

OPENING A FILE

Each new case requires a new case file. If the numerical filing system is used in the office, the file folder will be appropriately identified with both the office file number and the names of the decedent and the executor.

Filed materials will be securely attached to the folder by Acco fasteners. The first papers placed in the new office file will be the attorney's notes, a copy of the original will, and a conformed copy of the petition for probate of will with a copy of the will attached thereto. All later papers will be added in chronological order. Each will be placed on the top of the last and attached to the file with the Acco fastener.

SEQUENCE OF EVENTS IN A TESTATE MATTER

As is true of other probate court matters, a natural sequence of events and documents is required to prove a will and probate an estate. This procedure has been established by law and runs

- Petition for probate of will
- Order admitting will to probate and order appointing appraiser
- Letters testamentary
- Notice to creditors
- Creditors' claims
- Inventory and appraisement
- State inheritance tax papers
- Federal estate tax forms
- Petitions requesting authority of the court:
  - for the sale of real property
  - for the sale of securities or other personal property
  - for disposition of problems arising during probate
- Orders of the court regarding the petitions
- Estate accounting
- Petition for distribution
- Decree of distribution
- Distribution receipts
- Discharge of executor

In some states the majority of these court documents are typed in their entirety. However, in many states court forms (law blanks) are used.

Petition for Probate of Will

In a lawsuit where one party is suing another, the complaint is the first court document filed. In a probate matter where the will of a decedent is being proved, the petition for probate of will is the first court document filed. The title of this initial document varies with the states, but the function is the same.

If a situation is unusually complicated, the original petition or application may be dictated and typed in its entirety. If a court form is available from the court clerk's office, however, it should be used. Figure 16-1 shows a completed petition for probate of will and for letters testamentary used in California.

DISCUSSION

1. The information required for probating a will in all states is similar. Please compare the California form (Figure 16-1) with a like form for your jurisdiction.

2. If boxes are provided, the *x* should be placed carefully *within* the box so there can be no question which box is intended. If lines are to be filled in, the necessary information should. be placed carefully on the line so there can be no question about the line intended.

3. If a blank is to be unanswered, an *N/A* (not applicable) or two or three hyphens should be placed in the space to indicate that the item has received proper attention.

4. In Figure 16-1, the figures shown in 3b must be aligned as shown to facilitate addition of the items. This is true any time figures are placed in columns.

5. Figure 16-1 requires the names and the addresses of those benefiting under the will.

Names. Names must be correctly spelled to identify properly those named to inherit under the will.

Ages.   If a minor inherits substantial property, a guardian must be appointed before the inheritance will be distributed. The court must therefore be informed of the ages of the beneficiaries as required by the form.

Relationship.   This information is required for the court's use and for the computation of state inheritance taxes. The relationship required is the blood relationship, i.e., brother, father, daughter, or other relationship; or the marriage relationship, husband or wife. All others are termed "strangers," indicating neither a blood nor a marriage relationship. The word *stranger* as we use it in our everyday lives is quite different in meaning from the word *stranger* as used to indicate legal relationship.

6. Figure 16-1 (California) includes a penalty of perjury declaration which is to be signed by the petitioner. This statement is not signed before a notary public. In most states, the petitioner must sign a verification before a notary public.

NAME AND ADDRESS OF ATTORNEY	TELEPHONE NO	FOR COURT USE ONLY

BENJAMIN C. DOLL
450 Winton Building   209-224-1111
Fresno, California 00000

ATTORNEY FOR   Petitioner

SUPERIOR COURT OF CALIFORNIA, COUNTY OF FRESNO
1100 Van Ness Avenue, P.O. Box 1628
Fresno, California 93717

CLK 4000.00 E08 70 R07 75

ESTATE OF

NORTON DAVID BENT, also known as NORTON D. BENT, N. DAVID BENT, N. D. BENT
and DAVE BENT,

DECEDENT

	[X] PROBATE OF WILL AND FOR LETTERS TESTAMENTARY	CASE NUMBER
	[ ] PROBATE OF WILL AND FOR LETTERS OF ADMINISTRATION WITH WILL ANNEXED	
PETITION FOR	[ ] LETTERS OF ADMINISTRATION	HEARING DATE
	[ ] SPECIAL LETTERS OF ADMINISTRATION	
	[ ] AUTHORIZATION TO ADMINISTER UNDER THE INDEPENDENT ADMINISTRATION	DEPT TIME
	OF ESTATES ACT (Prob C 591 et seq.) (Complete Item 6 below)	

1. Attorney requests publication in (Name of newspaper):   Fresno Daily Legal Report

   BENJAMIN C. DOLL   *Benjamin C. Doll*
   (Type or print name)   (Signature of attorney)

2. Petitioner (Name of each. See footnote* before completing):   NED DAVID BENT
   requests
   a. [X] The decedent's will and codicils if any be admitted to probate.
   b. [ ] (Name):   NED DAVID BENT
      be appointed (1) [X] executor   (3) [ ] administrator
                   (2) [ ] administrator with will annexed   (4) [ ] special administrator;
      and letters issue upon qualification.
   c. [ ] Authority to administer under The Independent Administration of Estates Act.
   d. [X] Bond not be required. [ ] Bond be fixed at $ _____ to be furnished by an authorized
                    surety company or as otherwise provided by law.

FACTS CONCERNING PETITION

3. a. Jurisdictional facts concerning the decedent   c. Bond
   (1) Decedent died on (Date): March 24, 19__   (1) [X] Will waives bond.
      i. [X] a resident of the above named County   (2) [ ] Receipts for deposits to reduce bond will
         of the State of California.   be filed.
      ii. [ ] a nonresident of California and left an   (3) [X] Petitioner is sole [X] heir.
         estate in the above named County.   [ ] beneficiary.
   b. Character and estimated value of the property of   d. Testacy or intestacy
      the estate   (1) [X] Presented herewith are decedent's will
      (1) Real property $ 500,000.00   dated: 6/11/78 and [ ] codicils dated
      (2) Personal property $ 200,000.00
      (3) Annual income from real   copies of which are attached.
         and personal property $ 90,000.00   (2) [ ] Decedent died intestate
      (4) Total of (2) and (3) $ 290,000.00

(Continued on Reverse Side)

* The declaration must be signed in California (CCP 2015.5). Affidavit required when signed outside of California. No attachment permitted less than on a full page (California Rule of Court 201(b)). All petitioners must sign the petition. Only one need sign the declaration.

Form Approved by the
Judicial Council of California
Effective July 1, 1975

PETITION FOR PROBATE

Prob C 228, 229, 326, 327, 362
400-410, 420, 423, 440
460, 591-591.7

FIGURE 16-1A Petition for probate of a decedent's estate — California form (front)

e. Appointment of personal representative
  (1) Appointment of executor, or administrator with will annexed
    i. [X] Petitioner is named as executor in the will.
    ii. [ ] No executor is named in the will.
    iii. [ ] Petitioner is a nominee (See attachment 3e)
    iv. [ ] Other named executors will not act because of [ ] death [ ] declination [ ] other reasons as set forth in attachment 3e(iv).

(2) Appointment of administrator
    [ ] Petitioner is a nominee (See attachment 3e(2)).
    [ ] Petitioner is related to the decedent as:

(3) [ ] Appointment of special administrator requested (See attachment 3e(3) for grounds and requested powers).
f. Petitioner is a [X] resident of California.
    [ ] nonresident of California.

FACTS CONCERNING HEIRS

(Complete in all cases.)

4. a. The decedent is survived by
    (1) [ ] spouse. [X] no spouse.
    (2) [X] child. [ ] no child.
    (3) [ ] issue of predeceased child. [X] no issue of predeceased child.
    (4) [ ] parent. [X] no parent.
  b. No surviving child or issue of a predeceased child has been omitted from the list of heirs.

(Complete only if no spouse or issue survived the decedent.) (Prob C 228, 229)
  c. The decedent
    (1) [ ] had no predeceased spouse.
    (2) [ ] had a predeceased spouse whose heirs are named in the list of heirs.

(Complete only if no parent or issue survived the decedent.)
  d. The decedent is survived by
    (1) [ ] a brother or sister or issue of a predeceased brother or sister and none has been omitted from the list of heirs.
    (2) [ ] no brother or sister or issue of a predeceased brother or sister.

5. The names, addresses, relationships and ages of heirs, devisees and legatees so far as known to petitioner are. (List additional names, addresses, relationships, and ages of heirs, devisees, and legatees in attachment 5.)

Name and Address	Relationship	Age
NED DAVID BENT 255 Whitley Street Fresno, California 00000	son	adult
HELEN BENTWORTH HAWSON 9388 Candlewood Road Cincinnati, Ohio 00000	stranger	adult
ROREY JACKSON 9005 Calendar Highway Fresno, California 00000	stranger	adult

ADDITIONAL FACTS CONCERNING THE INDEPENDENT ADMINISTRATION OF ESTATE

6. a. [ ] Decedent's will does not preclude independent administration of this estate under Prob C 591 et seq.
   b. [ ] Decedent died intestate.

Dated: April 2, 19__

NED DAVID BENT
(Type or print name)   (Signature of Petitioner)

I certify (or declare) under penalty of perjury that the foregoing is true and correct and that this declaration is executed on (Date): April 2, 19__ at (Place): Fresno, California.

NED DAVID BENT
(Type or print name)   (Signature of petitioner)

FIGURE 16–1B   Petition for probate of a decedent's estate — California form (reverse)

7. The completed petition shown in Figure 16-1 includes a penciled "X" on each line requiring a signature. The *X*'s may be removed or may remain after the appropriate signatures have been made.

Copies

The minimum copies required are an original and one office copy, unless the law office follows a policy of providing copies to clients. In this event, an extra copy of the petition would be prepared for the client.

Petitioner's Appearance

When the petition has been typed and signed, it will be filed with the clerk of the court. In some states only the petitioner signs the petition, in some states only the attorney signs the petition, in some states both the petitioner and the attorney sign the petition. At the clerk's office, the case will be given a *court number*, also sometimes called a *docket number*, which will be noted by the legal secretary and included on all succeeding documents in the matter.

The *hearing date* set by the court clerk will also be noted by the legal secretary, who will record it on the office diary or desk calendar, whichever is regularly used by the office for the noting or recording of hearing dates, dates of expiration of statutory time periods, and other dates important to the proper functioning of the law office. On the hearing date the attorney usually must appear in court for the hearing on the petition.

Notice of Hearing

To assure that all interested persons are notified of the time and date of the impending hearing, notices are sent as follows: The court clerk will notify all persons listed in the petition as heirs, devisees, and legatees. A notice will be published in the local legal newspaper, which will give public notice of the hearing. The law office will authorize this publication. The legal secretary will scan the office copies of the newspaper to assure that publication is being made. Publication costs are paid from estate funds.

Hearing

At the court hearing on the petition or application for probate of the will, the petitioner and the witnesses to the will may be required to appear with the attorney. If their appearance is necessary, the legal secretary, with the approval of the attorney, will assume the responsibility for notifying these individuals of the time and date of the hearing. Appropriate letters may be dictated by the attorney, or the legal secretary may be expected to write letters for the attorney's signature without benefit of dictation.

The legal secretary will refer the file to the attorney a few days prior to the hearing. All persons who are to appear at the hearing will be notified, usually by telephone, to remind them of the hearing date.

At the hearing, the will must be proved by witnesses to the will testifying in person as to its authenticity, or by affidavits testifying to the authenticity of the will and signed by the witnesses in lieu of their personal appearance. (See Appendix E.)

If the court finds the will is authentic, an order will be issued to that effect (see page 230), letters testamentary will be issued (see Appendix E), and the executor will assume the responsibility of carrying on for the decedent.

Bond

To protect the interests of all heirs, the law provides that, *unless specifically waived in a will*, a fidelity bond must be posted by the one named to administer an estate. Bond premiums are paid from estate funds.

The bond was waived in the will of Norton David Bent. The residuary beneficiary is also the executor. If he misused estate funds, only he would suffer.

However, another decedent's will might name one executor and several residuary beneficiaries. Suppose the estate consisted of several hundred thousand dollars in cash deposited in various savings and checking accounts. Suppose several nephews had been named to inherit equally under the will. Suppose, further, that one nephew had been named executor without bond.

If the nephew, upon receiving letters testamentary, transferred all funds to his account as executor and then absconded with the money, the remaining nephews would not receive their inheritances. A fidelity bond would protect the interest of the nephews.

Order for Probate

The order for probate grants authority for the petitioner to act as executor of the estate and authorizes the issuance of letters testamentary. Figure 16-2 shows a completed order for probate. It is the

NAME AND ADDRESS OF ATTORNEY:	TELEPHONE NO.:	FOR COURT USE ONLY:
BENJAMIN C. DOLL 450 Winton Building Fresno, California 00000 ATTORNEY FOR: Executor	209-224-1111 CALIF. BAR ASSOC. NO. 000000	

SUPERIOR COURT OF CALIFORNIA, COUNTY OF FRESNO
1100 Van Ness, P.O. Box 1628, Fresno, California 93717

CLK 4001.00 E09-61 R07-77

ESTATE OF:

NORTON DAVID BENT, aka NORTON D. BENT, N. DAVID BENT, N. D. BENT and
DAVE BENT,

DECEDENT

ORDER FOR PROBATE:	CASE NUMBER:

[X] ORDER APPOINTING   [X] EXECUTOR
                    [ ] ADMINISTRATOR WITH WILL ANNEXED
                    [ ] ADMINISTRATOR
                    [ ] SPECIAL ADMINISTRATOR
[ ] ORDER AUTHORIZING INDEPENDENT ADMINISTRATION OF ESTATE
	0000000

1. Date of hearing: 4/27/__   [ ] Dept. [ ] Div. [ ] Room No.:   Judge:

THE COURT FINDS:

2. a. All notices required by law have been given.
   b. Decedent died on (date): March 24, 19__
      (1) [x] a resident of the above-named county of the State of California.
      (2) [ ] a nonresident of California and left an estate in the above-named county.
3. [x] The decedent's will dated: June 11, 1978
      and each codicil dated: N/A
      was admitted to probate by Minute Order on (date):

IT IS ORDERED:

4. (name): NED DAVID BENT
   is appointed
   a. [X] Executor of the decedent's will   d. [ ] Special Administrator
   b. [ ] Administrator with will annexed   (1) [ ] with general powers
   c. [ ] Administrator   (2) [ ] with special powers as specified in Attachment 4d
   and letters shall issue on qualification.   (3) [ ] without notice of hearing
5. [ ] Authority is granted to administer estate under The Independent Administration of Estates Act.
6. Bond is
   a. [x] not required.
   b. [ ] fixed at: $ to be furnished by an authorized surety company or as otherwise provided by law.
7. [x] The inheritance tax referee appointed is (name): JOHN JOHNSON

Dated: . . . .

_____
Judge of the Superior Court
[ ] Signature follows last attachment.

8. Total number of pages attached: 0

No attachment permitted on less than a full page (California Rule of Court 201(b)).

Prob C 329, 351, 362
407, 409, 410
461, 462, 465, 541
591, 605, 1220-1224
1240

Form Approved by the
Judicial Council of California
Effective July 1, 1977

ORDER FOR PROBATE

FIGURE 16-2   Order for probate

court's answer to the petition for probate shown in Figure 16-1. The order is prepared in the law office.

Letters authorizing the executor to act for the decedent cannot be issued until the order for probate has been signed by the judge. An inheritance tax referee or appraiser is appointed by the order of the court. The appraiser named in the order is a state officer and will be the official appraiser of all of the assets of the estate. Some states, if certain conditions exist, permit the executor to name the appraiser.

DISCUSSION

1. In those states where probate forms are not used, the order is typed out in its entirety in the law office for the court's signature. The form or the wholly typed document is taken to the court by the attorney usually on the day of the hearing. It is left there for the judge's approval and signature.

2. In some jurisdictions the bar association number of the attorney is required.

3. Note that the attorney is now the attorney for the *executor*.

4. The caption has been changed by the substitution of *aka* for *also known as*. The abbreviation may be used on all court documents following the original petition.

5. Introductory statements such as *THE COURT FINDS* and *IT IS ORDERED* are printed in all caps as they would be typed in all caps if the order were typewritten.

6. Prior to the hearing, when the order is being prepared in the law office, it is not known which judge will hear the petition and sign the order. A typed signature is not placed below the signature line.

7. Legal words: referee, surety.

8. Legal phrases: date of hearing, admitted to probate.

Letters Testamentary

Letters testamentary (see Appendix E), when signed by the judge, authorize the executor to act for the decedent. When decedent's checking and savings accounts have been released by state tax authorities, the executor will transfer the funds to a new account titled, "Ned David Bent, as executor of the estate of Norton David Bent, deceased."

To simplify the preparation of the estate accounting, which must be completed before an estate may be closed, the executor should be instructed

- To write estate checks for even small amounts of money leaving the estate
- To keep an accurate and complete record of the source of all funds coming into the estate account (These could be dividends, interest, rental income, or other income.)
- To maintain complete records of every estate transaction
- To handle estate funds and property cautiously

NOTE: Ned David Bent, as executor of the estate and residuary beneficiary, may waive an accounting of the estate of his father, Norton David Bent. He may do this only if the estate has ample funds to pay all expenses, taxes, fees, and cover specific bequests.

Following is a discussion of the letters testamentary shown in Appendix E.

1. Letters testamentary are filled in at the law office by the legal secretary. They are delivered to the court by the attorney at the time of the hearing.

2. When letters have been properly executed (by the judge in some jurisdictions and by the executor and the county clerk in other jurisdictions), certified copies may be ordered. The letters serve as identification and authority for the executor. They must be shown before the executor can

- Transfer funds on deposit in decedent's name to his name as executor of the estate
- Sell or transfer stocks or bonds belonging to the estate
- Cash certain insurance policies
- Conduct various kinds of estate business

If the assets and composition of the estate property warrant, the attorney may order one or more certified copies of letters following the hearing. Charges for the certified copies are paid from estate funds.

Notice to Creditors

Immediately following appointment, the executor is required to notify the decedent's creditors that all just debts will be received and paid by the estate. Notice is accomplished by publishing a notice to creditors in a newspaper of general circulation. Arrangements for publication are made by the attorney. Publication costs are paid from estate funds.

Creditors must file claims within a statutory period of time following the date of publication of notice to creditors. Both the date of the first publication and the expiration date of the statutory time period must be recorded in the diary or on the desk calendars. Both dates must be noted prominently in the file, either on the inside of the file cover or on an office probate procedure form contained in the file.

Despite the reliability of legal newspaper personnel, the legal secretary should check the daily office copy of the paper to determine that publication has, in fact, been made. If, through error, notice to creditors was not published early in the estate proceedings, it would still have to be published and the statutory period of time allowed to run before the assets of the estate could be distributed and the estate closed.

Not only would such an error be embarrassing to the law firm, it would be a real annoyance to the client and all beneficiaries awaiting distribution of the assets of the estate.

On the expiration date of the statutory period of time allowed for notice to creditors, the file will be reviewed by the attorney to determine whether steps may be taken toward closing the estate.

Creditors' Claims

A creditor's claim is prepared and signed by each creditor. (See Appendix E.) It is then given to the executor for approval. As the claims are approved by the executor and the court, they are paid from estate funds.

Among the claims presented to the executor for payment are the bills of decedent due at the date of death, such as utility, rental, and other regular monthly bills; hospital and doctor bills for the last illness; and sums due for funeral and interment.

Inventory

Very soon after the hearing on the petition for probate of will, the executor will begin a listing of all assets of decedent's estate. From this list, the legal secretary will type the inventory. (See inventory forms in Appendix E.)

Copies of the inventory will be required for the court, the inheritance tax appraiser, and the law office files. In addition, the executor and heirs may request copies.

Inventoried items must be carefully itemized. Each inventoried item is consecutively numbered, adequately identified, and followed by a space for the appraised value as made by the court-appointed appraiser. Known sums of money, such as bank account balances at the date of death, are filled in by the legal secretary. Real property is identified by both the street address and the legal property description.

Appraisal and Determination of Tax

The original and a copy of the inventory are sent to the appraiser's office. The original inventory will be returned to the law office when all items have been appraised as of the date of death and the total assets of the estate determined by the appraiser. The copy will be retained by the appraiser.

NOTE: The legal secretary must conform the office copy of the inventory as soon as the original has been completed by the appraiser and returned to the law office. Following a careful proofreading, a tape should be run on the adding machine to check out the total of the estate's assets.

In addition to the inventory, the appraiser must have a copy of the will in order to determine who the beneficiaries are and what each will inherit. The appraiser must also be provided, usually in duplicate, the completed tax information forms. These forms contain personal and statistical information on the decedent and beneficiaries under the will.

Necessary inheritance tax forms are furnished in all states. Two of the forms provided by the Division of Inheritance and Gift Tax of California (a community property state) for the use of law offices are

1. Inheritance Tax Declaration, Form IT-22. This is a four-page questionnaire requesting detailed information necessary to determine the inheritance tax due from each beneficiary. (See Appendix E.)
2. Marital Property Declaration, Form IT-3. This is a questionnaire to determine whether all or part of the estate is community property. (See Appendix E.) Such a declaration or affidavit is not used in non-community property states.

Determination of State Inheritance Taxes

When the state inheritance taxes are charged to each beneficiary, the tax is computed based on the relationship of the beneficiary to the decedent and the value of the individual inheritance. It is necessary, therefore, for those computing the inheritance tax to have

- A copy of the will
- Information as to the relationship of the heirs of the decedent
- Value of the property to be received by each beneficiary

The appraiser's office will prepare and return to the law office a statement showing the taxes due the state from each beneficiary. If no taxes are due, the law office will also be informed.

The appraiser's fee is paid from estate funds.

Payment of State Inheritance Tax

Unless the will contains a provision that all taxes will be paid from estate funds, each beneficiary usually must pay the taxes due the state before the bequest is made. To avoid penalties for late payment, the taxes due from each beneficiary might be advanced by the estate. Each beneficiary could reimburse the estate during probate. Or, if it is agreeable to the beneficiaries, the taxes due from each may be deducted from the individual's share prior to distribution. The heir would not then have to advance funds for payment of the tax.

Time

To assure prompt payment of taxes, a state may grant a small discount for early payment or charge a fee for late payment. If for some reason the law office is dilatory in preparing papers, having the property appraised and the taxes computed, the attorney may be liable for the charge.

It is the legal secretary's responsibility to note the time period from the date of death when the taxes are due and to make certain that any available discount is obtained and possible late charges avoided.

Federal Estate Tax

The federal estate tax, applicable in every state of the nation, is computed on the total value of the decedent's estate and is a debt of the estate.

United States Estate Tax Return, Form 706, must be filed for the estate of every citizen or resident of the United States whose gross estate at date of death is in excess of the maximum tax-free amount currently allowed by the Congress. (During the 1970s this amount rose from $60 thousand to $175 thousand after December 31, 1980.)

Form 706 must be completed and sent to the United States Internal Revenue Service within nine months of the decedent's death, and any taxes due must be paid within the same period of time. The form is available from the Internal Revenue Service offices. (See Appendix E for pages 1, 2, and 3 of Form 706.)

This tax return is a bulky, multipage booklet, which must be disassembled in order that each page may be inserted into the typewriter for completion. If a decedent died testate, a certified copy of the will must be filed with this tax return. A copy of the completed form should be retained in the office files.

It is frequently the legal secretary's duty to work with the attorney in computing the tax and preparing the tax form. In complicated estate matters, the tax return may be prepared by a tax accountant.

The federal estate tax is paid out of estate funds. *It is not a tax levied against individual beneficiaries.* Unless an extension of time has been granted, the tax must be paid within nine months of the date of death or a penalty will be levied. Here again, it is the attorney's and thus the legal secretary's duty to see that the return is filed or an extension obtained and the tax paid within the required period.

Changing (Reducing) Assets to Cash

Frequently, cash funds in the estate are not sufficient to pay all creditors' claims, court costs, attorney and executor fees, taxes, and money bequests. In this event, the executor will decide which of the assets of the estate must be sold to acquire the necessary cash funds.

Securities

To sell securities that were issued in the decedent's name, the transfer agents (banks or firms named on stock certificates and authorized to transfer stock from one person to another) may each require

- A copy of the death certificate
- A certified copy of the decree granting court approval of the sale of the securities
- Certified copy of letters testamentary
- Other miscellaneous information

It is the legal secretary's responsibility to assure that all necessary papers are available. Further, a check must be made to make certain that the executor has signed the stock certificates if such signature is required.

When the money from the sale of the securities has been received, it will be accepted by the executor and placed in the estate checking account.

Real Estate

If it becomes necessary to sell real estate, either because cash is needed in the estate or because it is the wish of the beneficiaries under the will, court approval must be obtained and notice given in a newspaper of general circulation.

First, a petition requesting permission to sell the real estate is prepared in the law office and filed with the court. At the hearing on the petition, the order approving (or denying) the sale will be signed by the court. The order is also prepared in the law office. The petition will be signed by the petitioner or the petitioner and the attorney. The order will be signed by the judge. It will authorize or *order* the sale of the real property.

Closing the Estate

Steps may be taken to distribute the assets of the estate in accordance with the will and to close the estate when

- Statutory time for notice to creditors has passed
- Statutory time for contesting the will has passed
- All taxes have been paid
- All debts of the estate have been paid

Accounting for the Estate Property

Before distribution of the assets may be made to the heirs, a complete accounting must be made to the court for all transactions and for all real and personal property of the estate. (The accounting may be waived under special circumstances.)

The accounting is a detailed listing of the assets of the estate, all incoming money or property, all outgoing money or property, and the money or property remaining for distribution.

The accounting must be complete, must balance, and must receive the court's approval. In some jurisdictions, receipts for all disbursements of estate funds must accompany the copy of the accounting that is filed with the court clerk's office. Some jurisdictions, however, because of the bulk, prefer that the receipts remain in an accessible, permanent file in the attorney's office.

If a bank or trust company is serving as executor, that entity will usually prepare the accounting. Otherwise, the accounting is prepared by the legal secretary under the instruction and supervision of the attorney.

Petition for Distribution or Discharge

In some jurisdictions, a petition for distribution of the estate will be dictated by the attorney and typed by the legal secretary. A copy of the accounting will be attached, unless it has been waived.

In other jurisdictions, a court form variously called *application* or *petition for discharge* is available.

These petitions set forth the names and inheritances of all beneficiaries and ask for approval for the payment of attorney and executor fees, as set by state statute, from estate funds.

Extraordinary fees may be requested for either the executor or the attorney, or both, if unusual or special legal work has been required of them.

Decree of Distribution or Discharge

When the petition has been completed and executed, it is filed with the court clerk and set for hearing. The *order* or decree granted at the hearing is similar in wording to the petition, except that it *grants* all requests in the petition. The order is dictated and typed in the law office for the signature of the judge.

If, for reasons of law, the court were to deny all or part of the petition, the order would be rewritten to include the changes.

Since probate matters proceed under the continuous scrutiny of the court, the final petition and order are, to the specialists in this field, rather routine (though complicated and time-consuming) legal documents.

Distribution of the Estate

Court receipts are required of all beneficiaries at the time of delivery of their property to them. The original receipts are filed with the court clerk. Law office file copies are conformed and filed in the case file.

Discharge of the Executor

When the estate property has been distributed, receipts filed, and estate checking account closed, the estate may be closed and the executor discharged of duties. However, if a federal estate tax was paid, funds are retained in the estate's checking account and the estate is held open until there is assurance that the federal tax return was correct.

With the assurance that the federal estate tax return was accepted by the Internal Revenue Service, the final discharge of the executor may be filed with the clerk of the court. The office case file will be closed and transferred to the inactive office files.

TRANSFERRING A FILE TO CLOSED STATUS

Prior to transferring a file from active to closed status, the legal secretary should take the time required to search the file for unnecessary papers that could be eliminated in an effort to reduce the size of the file. Some papers that might be removed and destroyed are

- Extra copies of various legal documents that may have been prepared
- Copies of miscellaneous transmittal letters
- Unimportant telephone messages and memos

Most law offices retain closed case files for indefinite periods of time. There is always the possibility that a later legal matter could be facilitated by reference to a prior case handled in the office. Such reference could be to the style or wording of various documents contained in the file, or it could be to the parties or property that are a part of the file — information that could be valuable in a new legal matter involving the same individuals or property.

SUMMARY

Probate procedure in testate matters varies from state to state. Statutory time periods vary. Appointment of appraisers varies. Style and document titles vary. However, all testate matters in all states have in common the following:

- Appointment of a person or institution as executor to administer decedent's estate
- Publication of notice to creditors of the decedent
- Assembling of estate assets and preparation of the inventory
- Appraisal of estate assets as of the date of death
- Payment of debts of the decedent and the estate
- Payment of taxes
- Payment of court costs
- Accounting of all property and money transactions
- Distribution of estate property

- Filing of the receipts of beneficiaries
- Final discharge of the executor

With the closing of the estate, the office file should be searched for extraneous papers, which should be removed and destroyed. The file should then be transferred to the file section containing closed office files.

SUGGESTED SPECIAL ASSIGNMENTS

1. From the clerk's office (or stationery store, if forms are located there), obtain a copy of the first petition in probate (a form) used in your jurisdiction. Complete the form, using the data included in Figure 16-1.

2. If in your jurisdiction most of the court documents used in a probate proceeding are typed in their entirety, obtain a copy of the first petition and type one original copy. Use fictitious names in your petition. Proofread. Assemble and staple.

PART THREE

Part Three discusses matters of special significance to the legal secretary:

Law books — their value, their classification, and their contents;

Finding, keeping, and leaving a position — suggestions for accomplishing each of these in an efficient, successful manner;

Tips to try — miscellaneous minor and major suggestions for easing the task of the legal secretary.

17

Law Books

A lawyer could practice law without an office. A lawyer could practice law without a secretary. But a lawyer could not practice law without law books.

The law books upon which the attorney depends may be found in the office library, in the local law library, in the law library of an established law school. But law books must be available.

In any discipline, in any profession, books and periodicals are a source of information and authority. However, nowhere but in law is the promptness of publication of such primary consideration. A principle of law that has been followed and relied upon may be changed by a decision of a higher court, perhaps the United States Supreme Court. A law enacted by a state or the national legislature may be rescinded or superseded by another statute of the legislative body. The earlier court decision or statute can no longer be used as law; rather, the later legislation on its effective date, or the latest court decision, must be followed.

Court decisions (judicial opinions) reversing earlier legal decisions and new legislation (statutes) must be published and made

available to the profession. Only by prompt publication may lawyers and judges alike have access to the latest statutes and judicial
opinions.

The attorney's special forte is the knowledge and ability to ex-
tract from among the mountains of law books and periodicals the
cases, the statutes, the opinions that must be cited as authority to
support a cause in a court of law.

POCKET SUPPLEMENTS OR POCKET PARTS

An ingenious device for keeping law books current is the pocket part
or pocket supplement. These paper-bound supplements contain the
most recent court decisions or recently enacted legislation assembled
in a logical manner, printed, and bound with an insert tab at the
back. Each pocket supplement is assembled for attachment to a
particular volume of a law book series. The pocket part is identified
with a code as to the volume to which it should be affixed.

By placing the insert tab of the pocket part into the pocket that
is bound into the inside back cover of law books, the supplement
may be securely affixed to the volume. If the pocket supplements
are promptly filed, the law books to which they are attached will be
current. When a supplement reaches an unreasonable size, the volume
of which it is a part will be revised to delete the outdated portions
and include the latest data.

Pocket supplements are useless and the law books out of date if
the two are not immediately united. This is the task of the legal
secretary — placing the pocket supplement in the appropriate volume
and destroying the pocket part it supersedes.

LOOSE-LEAF SERVICES

Business, labor, legal, and tax information is made available in loose-
leaf form by Prentice-Hall, Inc., Loose-Leaf Services. The contents
of the loose-leaf binders are kept up to date by weekly report bulle-
tins. As changes in the law, in the tax law, or other subject areas
occur, the old pages are pulled from the binders and the new pages
are inserted.

CAUTION: Prior to destroying the old pages, the secretary should
double check to make certain that no errors have occurred either in
inserting or in removing the pages.

The secretary must have some knowledge of law books to fulfill the role of legal secretary. Some pleadings will include "citations." What are they and why are they important to a legal matter?

Citation as used here refers specifically to the *abbreviation* of the information necessary to identify a source of legal data. For example, the citation *Apex v. Gordon, 119 Mo. 114, 89 S.W. 1025, 109 Am. St. Rep. 700*, translated, reads: Apex versus Gordon, Volume 119 of Missouri (reports) at page 114, Volume 89 of the South Western Reporter at page 1025, Volume 109 of American State Reports at page 700.

This case has been reported in each of the three volumes. The attorney may have one, none, or all of the law books in the office. However, the volumes will be available through the services of the county law library.

Definition

A citation is a reference to a statute or to a reported case and its location in a legal volume.

An error in any portion of the citation, whether it is an error of the dictator or an error of the typist, would refer the reader to the incorrect and inappropriate case or statute. *Citations must be accurate.* If the law books are available, the legal secretary should check all citations for accuracy before typing them. If the law books are not available (the attorney may have researched the material in the county law library), the secretary should check all dictation against the attorney's handwritten notes to avoid possible errors in either the dictation or transcription.

LAW BOOK CLASSIFICATIONS

Most of the law books and legal writings found in any law library, large or small, will fit into one of the following classifications:

- Encyclopedias
- Digests
- Reported cases (Reporters)
- Code books and statutory compilations
- Citators
- Legal newspapers and periodicals

- Form books
- Dictionaries

Encyclopedias

If a client enters the law office with what appears to be a litigable problem, the attorney listens attentively, takes rather copious notes, and at the termination of the meeting arranges for a later appointment. In the interim, legal research will be conducted to determine if the facts as presented by the client are, in fact, sufficient grounds for a lawsuit. Further, the legal principle or principles (also referred to as legal doctrines) must be found that might be used to get the matter before the courts.

If the legal problem involves a contract that has not been honored for any of several reasons, the attorney will begin research by going to the appropriate volume of a legal encyclopedia, in this case to the volume containing the title *contracts*. There, alphabetically by title, will be found a legal principle or doctrine or several of them that seem to fit the client's problem. One such might be the legal doctrine of *breach of contract*. The facts of the new matter might fall into this legal principle and others as well.

Perhaps a legal problem had to do with an act of arson. The attorney would refer to the volume of an encyclopedia containing the word *arson*. A search would then be made through the detailed subtitles following the main topic itself. The encyclopedia, in summary, furnishes the searcher a general review of an area of law that previously might have been unfamiliar.

After reading the cases cited in the encyclopedia and the brief paragraphs following each citation, the searcher will go to the digests. The digests will provide a detailed report of the case or cases which the searcher believes most nearly match the case and are favorable to it.

The principal legal encyclopedias are *American Jurisprudence (Am. Jur.)*, 58 volumes, and *American Jurisprudence 2d (Am. Jur. 2d)*, over 80 volumes, with multivolume general indexes, and *Corpus Juris Secundum (C.J.S.)*, which consists of well over 100 text volumes plus a multivolume general index.

The encyclopedias are kept up to date by annual cumulative pocket supplements.

American Jurisprudence and *American Jurisprudence 2d* cover both procedural and substantive law and include legal maxims and legal definitions of words and phrases.

Digests

The case digest is an index to the reported cases that comprise case law. Reported cases are those cases that have been heard in an appellate court and reported in the case books or reporter series. The cases are reported and published chronologically. Because of their vast number, an index of the cases and their judicial opinions is required if they are to be available for reference and authority. *The digests are the indexes to the reported cases.*

The *American Digest System* is considered the major index to case law in the United States. Other digests cover the various units of the *National Reporter System.*

Digests are peculiarly the tool of the lawyer, who is schooled in the specific skills and techniques necessary to use these volumes properly.

The encyclopedias lead the researcher to the digests. The digests lead the researcher to the volumes of the *National Reporter System* that contain the cases in point with the researcher's legal problem.

Reported Cases (Reporters)

Reported cases, or *Reporters*, are primary legal authority. The cases reported in them are those that have been heard in an appellate court. The decision of the trial court may have been affirmed, reversed, or otherwise modified by the appellate court.

The reported cases form the body of case law on which our judicial system relies as precedent. The great bulk of the books in an office of a lawyer in general practice is usually composed of this type of book.

The reported cases that an attorney, through research, finds to support the legal position of the client are the cases that will be cited and relied upon.

Published Report

The published report of the case in the *Reporter Series* includes the case title, the court and date of the appeal, and a brief statement of the facts of the case. This is followed by a brief, concise summary of each of the significant legal points that were decided. The summaries are usually in brackets or italics. They are the publisher's interpretation of the points that are significant in the case.

By scanning the summary, an attorney is able to discover the principal legal doctrines thought to be involved in the reported case, the decision of the court, and possible reasons for the court's decision.

The written opinion following the summary was prepared by a judge holding with the majority who was appointed by the chief appellate justice to write the majority opinion.

In a case of some magnitude, a judge representing the minority opinion may also be asked to write that opinion for the report.

National Reporter System

Case reports of federal courts and all state appellate courts are privately published in the *National Reporter System*. The *System* is divided into both regional divisions and states. Reported cases within a state or region are included in that region's *Reporter Series.*

A particular service of the *National Reporter System* is the relative speed with which reported cases are published and made available for the use of the courts and the attorneys.

Only a few of the many multivolume editions of the *National Reporter System* are

- *Atlantic Reporter* (includes all important court decisions in the Atlantic Seaboard states of Connecticut, Delaware, Maine, Maryland, New Hampshire, New Jersey, Pennsylvania, Rhode Island, and Vermont)
- *California Reporter* (includes all important court decisions in the state of California)
- *North Eastern Reporter* (includes important court decisions in Illinois, Indiana, Massachusetts, New York, and Ohio)
- *Texas Reporter* (includes important court decisions in the state of Texas)
- *Supreme Court Reporter* (contains United States Supreme Court cases)
- *Federal Reporter* (contains federal appellate court cases)

The law office library of an attorney in general practice would probably include the *Reporter Series* for the state and region and any others frequently referred to.

Abbreviations

The acceptable abbreviation for each series of law books may be found in a law dictionary or in the law book itself.

Points and Authorities

The cases the attorney believes support the current case are those cited in Points and Authorities following the body and signature lines of the pleading.

Code Books and Statutory Compilations

The statutes passed by the state and national legislatures are added to the already existing laws of the state or nation. So that they may be accessible, the laws are codified by subject matter. In some states, separate code books are published — i.e., the laws having to do with probate are bound together in a state probate code book; legislation relating to criminal law may be bound in a criminal or penal code book; revenue and taxation statutes may be included in a code book by that name. In other states, a multivolume code book may include all code sections.

The state codes or statutes may be obtained either in annotated or unannotated editions. The annotated editions are more valuable to the attorney, as they furnish explanatory historical notes, cross-references to related laws, and other supplemental information.

Federal statutes are included in the *United States Code*, a series of law books also available at a law library.

Citators

Citators or citation books are those books that, if properly used, will tell the lawyer if the statutes and cases cited as authority are still valid or if they have been superseded by later statutes or, in case law, reversed or modified by later judicial decisions.

Legal Newspapers and Periodicals

Legal newspapers serve the legal profession by keeping the practitioners (attorneys) informed of the latest in the business of law. Local procedural changes, court dockets, and items of interest to local attorneys are included in the contents, as are the legal notices that must be, by law, published in a newspaper of general circulation.

Legal periodicals offer varied and scholarly writings on selected legislation and judicial opinions. The legal periodicals originate with the various bar associations, commercial publishers, and law schools.

The *law school review* is, typically, a scholarly magazine sponsored by a law school and edited and published by honor students selected to be on the staff of the law review. The law reviews of major law schools are highly respected scholarly publications.

The law school review usually includes penetrating discussions of several carefully chosen cases. It may also include book reviews and special articles written by law school teachers, justices, and attorneys.

The value of the periodicals in presenting scholarly reports on minute aspects of the law, in offering discussions of newly enacted legislation, in discussing principles and basic issues of various decided cases, and in affording an outlet for discussion and opinion of honor law students is recognized within the profession.

The law reviews are widely published. Their articles and discussions are listed in various indexes and digests that permit both the student and the attorney access to the contents of all the reviews.

Form Books

The attorney who has researched a case has yet to get it before the courts. This must be accomplished in wording and style acceptable in the jurisdiction where the matter is to be heard.

General form books consist of printed forms with wording and style that may be adapted to fit a particular situation. A local form book contains forms acceptable in that jurisdiction.

Form books are available from various sources, including bar associations, state judicial councils, and private publishing companies. These books are part of many law office libraries and of all law school and county law libraries.

Dictionaries

Legal terminology or rhetoric is precise language. The exact legal meanings of that language are available in law dictionaries.

A good law dictionary provides an exact legal definition of each word or phrase it contains and gives citations to support the definition. Unlike a general dictionary of the American-English language, which furnishes meanings acceptable in various disciplines, connotations, and geographical areas, the legal dictionary furnishes only the precise legal definition or definitions and use.

Black's Law Dictionary is one of the leaders in this field. In addition to the legal words and phrases it defines, it includes legal abbreviations and pronunciations of unusual legal words.

SUMMARY

Law books are the tools of the lawyer's trade. Without them an attorney could not practice law.

Most of the thousands upon thousands of law books and periodicals that have been and will be published may be classified as one of the following: encyclopedias, digests, reported cases (Reporters), code books and statutory compilations, citators, legal newspapers and periodicals, form books, and dictionaries.

The forte of the attorney is the ability to locate from among the mountains of law books the statute or case in point that may be relied upon to win the lawsuit.

SUGGESTED SPECIAL ASSIGNMENT

1. Visit a law library. Write a one-page, single-spaced paper describing your experience. Include as much specific information about the law library as you were able to obtain. Example: a) number of employees; b) financial support; c) access to lay persons as well as attorneys; d) number of volumes; e) other information.

18

Finding, Keeping, Leaving Your Position

Of finding, keeping, and leaving a position, one who has not yet found the first job as a legal secretary is certain to believe that finding the position is the most difficult.

The neophyte on the job, who has not yet discovered the sense of security that will eventually develop, who knows well neither the language of the law nor legal procedure, will believe that keeping the position is by far the most difficult of the three.

But the pro who has worked happily as a legal secretary, who knows the joy of helping others, who has experienced the camaraderie of law office associates and the feeling of indispensability occasioned by having been a part of the law firm, will know that leaving such a position is the most difficult of the three.

Perhaps this discussion will dispel some worries, or present new ones, or merely arouse an awareness of the importance of each of these steps in the working life of a legal secretary.

LENGTH OF TENURE

An individual who has accepted a position with a firm owes the employer at least three years of loyal service. The first year is devoted to learning as well as working, the second year is a production year, the third year the employee is truly valuable to the firm. Now the legal secretary is able to accept responsibility, to handle many matters with little guidance, and to handle routine office duties in a professional manner.

If at the end of three years the secretary is dissatisfied with the position, with the salary, with the particular kind of work, some thought should be given to moving on to another position. Moving for moving's sake is not wise. A change in positions should be considered only if the new position offers improved working conditions, a better salary, an increase in responsibility, or greater convenience.

The adage, "A rolling stone gathers no moss," is worth thinking about.

Low pay is a valid reason for leaving an office at any time. But the employee must be certain that a new position is available and that the pay increase is substantial.

FINDING A POSITION AS A LEGAL SECRETARY

Finding a position as a legal secretary is perhaps the most difficult step. It can be a rather traumatic experience if it is the first position ever sought by the applicant and if the search is approached with fear instead of expectation. It can be a real adventure if approached positively.

Sources of Employment

For one with no experience to offer but with an education beyond high school, good or above-average skills, and a pleasing personality; for one with previous business office experience only; for a legal secretary new to a geographical area; or for the experienced legal secretary in search of a new position in the same city or town — any or all of these sources of employment might be tried:

- Friends and relatives
- College placement office
- State employment office
- Commercial employment offices
- Want ad sections of local newspapers
- Yellow Pages of the telephone directory (for law office addresses and telephone numbers)
- Legal Secretaries Association employment officer (a service available only to members of the Association)

Friends and Relatives

A student once said to me, quite self-righteously, "My uncle said he might be able to help me find a job after I graduate. I won't let him. I want to find a job on my own."

What this student failed to realize is that the uncle would be helping not only her, but the prospective employer as well. And the uncle could enjoy the pleasant feeling that comes with helping others.

Let your friends and relatives know that you are trained and ready for work and that you will appreciate a good word wherever they may have connections. They may be your introduction to the very position that suits you best. Your friend or relative will have done both you and your employer a very real favor.

College Placement Office

For the student with a major or training in legal secretaryship, the college placement office should be the first stop in the search for a position as legal secretary.

Some college placement offices have conscientiously cultivated the office and law office segments of the community to develop employment opportunities for students. These college employment offices will be eager for applicants and will be helpful in placing those students who take advantage of their services.

Whatever the situation at your college, try this source of employment. It is possible that the ideal position for you will be waiting at your college placement office.

Tests are usually not required of applicants, and no fee is charged for the placement service.

State Employment Office

The state employment office, also sometimes called the office of human resources, is, in most cities, an excellent source of employment opportunities. Attorneys searching for either legal secretarial trainees or experienced legal secretaries frequently make their first calls to the state office of employment, and they are usually assured of receiving several applicants from this source. A person searching for a position in a law office would be wise to take advantage of this service.

Suitability of the applicant for an office position is determined by written tests and typewriting tests. Shorthand tests are usually included. As with the college placement office, no fee is charged.

Commercial Employment Offices

Attorneys who have exhausted other sources in their search for legal secretaries frequently turn to commercial employment agencies. Once having learned that these agencies screen the applicants before referring them for interviews, and having had successful experience with the services of a commercial agency, some attorneys rely solely on these offices to help them in their search for office personnel. Prospective legal secretaries are shortsighted if they fail to consider this source of employment.

Commercial agencies test and interview all who apply to them for secretarial positions. They screen the applicant and the employer, hoping to match the personality and skills of the applicant to the employer and the existing vacancy.

Charge. The single drawback to this otherwise excellent source of employment is the fee charged. It must be pointed out, however, that testing costs money, that interviews take time and cost money, that the overhead of a business office costs money, and that someone has to pay for it. That someone is the person who benefits by the service.

The fee varies with the geographical location. To one who would much prefer to receive a full pay check from the beginning of employment, the fee is a sizable sum of money. On the other hand, the applicant has, in effect, hired an agent. Both time and temper are saved and countless fruitless interviews are eliminated. Perhaps this source of employment is best for some job hunters. If the applicant finds an acceptable position, the money has been well spent.

It should be pointed out that on occasion the employer, happy to have found *the* secretary who will exactly fill the position, will pay the employment fee. This is by no means standard procedure, but it is a distinct possibility. Occasionally the agency charges the employer for the service, and thus it is free to the employee.

Fees charged by commercial employment agencies are based upon the monthly salary the new employee will receive. It follows, therefore, that the agencies will obtain the highest possible salaries for their applicants.

Before signing with a commercial agency, the applicant should take the usual precaution of reading the contract carefully. It is also advisable to make a comparison among several agencies regarding the fees charged, kinds of positions offered, length of the term of the contract, and other conditions of importance to the applicant.

Want Ad Sections of Local Newspapers

In some cities the want ad sections of the newspapers are excellent sources of employment. Ads inserted by attorneys and by commercial agencies serve as guides to the salaries that prospective legal secretaries or trainees may expect in a particular geographical area.

Want ads of private employers should be answered immediately. Promptness indicates interest; delay could mean a lost opportunity.

Yellow Pages of the Telephone Directory

Under "Attorneys" in the Yellow Pages of the telephone directory are listed the names, addresses, and telephone numbers of most of the attorneys and law firms in the area.

Having decided whether to seek employment in a small law office or a large law firm, the job seeker might use the Yellow Pages to great advantage.

First, several firms could be selected and a note made of the complete names and telephone numbers. With this ammunition in hand, the prospective legal secretary might telephone each law office, offer a proper introduction, state the purpose of the call, and ask to speak to the office manager (if it is a large firm) or the attorney (if it is a small office).

When the office manager or the attorney answers the telephone, the applicant should

- Make an introduction (name)
- State the purpose of the call (employment as a legal secretary)
- Ask about job possibilities (present or future openings)

When a negative response has been given — and it is important that the applicant be ready for a "no," for that is almost certainly what will be heard — this question should be asked: "Do you know of a law firm that might have an opening?" The question may or may not lead to a position, but it is a positive approach to job hunting. The *next* call may be the call that produces results.

This method costs nothing but time and patience. Many phone calls may have to be made before an appointment for an interview is granted. Once that appointment is made, however, the first step toward obtaining a position has been taken — and you have done it all yourself!

A second method is to select several firms and write down the names and addresses, then make a personal visit to each firm. This is a time-consuming process but may very well be worth while. Who knows, the first call may find you with an interview. With persistance, this approach to job hunting may produce the results you desire: an interview and the promise of employment.

Find an approach that best suits you, but don't give up.

The *Martindale-Hubbell Law Directory*, available at law libraries and most law offices, lists law firms and attorneys, rates them, and lists the branches of law that are their specialties. The cautious applicant might wish to visit a law library and refer to the listings of each of the firms or attorneys before accepting a position.

An applicant who wishes to work in a law office specializing in criminal law, environmental law, corporate law, or other special area of the law should refer to the *Martindale-Hubbell Law Directory*.

Legal Secretaries Association Employment Officer

Many local branches of the National Association of Legal Secretaries (International) annually appoint employment officers. The members of the Association know better than most which law offices are looking for new employees. With this information, the employment officer is able to be of service to both applicants and employers.

Any member of NALS may take advantage of this service at no charge, whether employment is sought locally or in a new geographical area.

Resumes

A resume is also sometimes called a vita sheet or a data sheet. Its purpose is to provide a prospective employer with a brief history of an applicant's qualifications for a particular position.

A resume must accompany a letter of application. Further, a resume should accompany an applicant who appears for a job interview.

The content and style of a resume are left to the discretion of the applicant. Nothing negative should be included. Nothing extraneous should be included. Nothing untrue should be included. However, all of the information that will "sell" a prospective employer on the applicant as an employee must be included.

Figure 18-1 is a sample resume. It includes information that would be helpful to a prospective employer.

Figure 18-2 is a sample letter of application (or cover letter for the resume). If appropriate, this letter may state

R E S U M E

of

Miss Caroline Lee Carswell
7790 North Gentle Avenue
Fresno, California 00000
Telephone: 209-222-3333

position   Legal secretary

personal   Born June 20, 19__, Denver, Colorado. 5" 5".
data   120 pounds. Caucasian. Protestant. Single.
                (Race, religion, and marital status may be
                omitted. It is the choice of the applicant.)

education   A. S., Blank Junior College, Denver, Colorado,
                19__, with a major in legal secretaryship.

                Presently taking refresher courses at California
                State University, Fresno.

business experience

present   Part-time secretary to John A. Adams, owner, Adams
                Parts Stores, 811 Charles Place, Fresno, California.
                Telephone: 000-333-4444

19__-__   Secretary to Miss Margaret A. Peterson, instructor,
                Blank Junior College, 4500 Mellon Avenue, Denver,
                Colorado 0000. Telephone: 000-666-7777.

personal references   Mr. Charles A. Widdoms (pastor)
                11337 Cary Avenue
                Fresno, California 00000
                Telephone: 000-222-3333

                Dr. Barry A. Williams
                California State University, Fresno
                North Maple and East Shaw Avenues
                Fresno, California 00000
                Telephone: 000-777-9999

                Mrs. Janell Johnson
                7789 Eastland Avenue
                Fresno, California 00000
                Telephone: 000-111-2222

other data   In August of last year I began attending
                California State University, Fresno, as a part-
                time student in the School of Business. I have
                also been working as a part-time secretary. I am
                now eager for full-time employment as a legal
                secretary.

                My typing speed is about 70 words a minute, and
                my shorthand speed is over 120 words a minute.
                I have worked with transcribing equipment and
                am familiar with word processing equipment.

                In addition to legal secretaryship and advanced
                secretarial, shorthand, and typing courses, I
                have taken courses in accounting, business
                communications, data processing, English, filing
                and finding, and word processing.

FIGURE 18-1   Sample resume

May 22, 19__

Mr. Gerald J. Georges
Office Manager
Carlton, Brown and Gaynes
Attorneys at Law
75 Fulton Avenue
San Francisco, California   00000

Dear Mr. Georges:

I am applying for a position as legal secretary with your
firm. The enclosed resume lists my qualifications and
gives personal information, personal references, and
business experience.

Not included on the resume is my special interest in the
legal profession. The work and the special language of law
appeal to me, and I should very much like to be employed
full time as a legal secretary.

I will be in San Francisco the week of June 7. May I have
an appointment for an interview? I will telephone you on
Tuesday, June 8. I am very much interested in a position
with your firm and will appreciate the opportunity to talk
with you about it.

Sincerely yours,

Caroline Carswell

Miss Caroline Lee Carswell
7790 North Gentle Avenue
Fresno, California   00000
Telephone: 209-222-3333

Enclosure

FIGURE 18-2   Sample letter of application

- Why you are interested in working for this firm
- How you learned about the position
- That you are enclosing a resume
- When you are available for an interview
- Your particular interest in law and the legal profession

Application Forms, Tests, and Interviews

The adventure of finding the first position — or, for the experienced legal secretary, the perfect position — is challenging and exciting. The temperament, ingenuity, training, ability, and skill of the applicant are tested by the application forms, tests, and interviews that are all a part of the adventure.

Application Forms

Only when applying for work in a legal department of a business, agency, or institution or in a very large law firm will an applicant for a position as legal secretary be required to complete an application form. Most law offices select personnel by means of interviews and a review of letters or short legal papers that the applicant transcribes from the dictation of the interviewing attorney.

If an applicant is given a form to complete, it should receive full attention. This will be the first paper in the hands of the interviewer and will help form the first judgment of the applicant. It is important, then, that a neat, complete, and accurate application be submitted.

Prior to writing on the application form, the applicant should take the precaution of reading the entire form carefully. This will eliminate the common error of putting too much or too little information on a line. It is wise to first jot on a notepad the answers to certain items to assure completeness and accuracy of the answers.

Some application forms require last name, first name, and middle name in that order. Others require first name, middle name, and last name in that order. These are simple matters, but once begun, the order cannot be neatly changed.

It is helpful to have readily available a complete list of schools with dates attended and employers with dates of employment. Complete names, addresses, and telephone numbers should be included, as necessary. The list would permit accuracy, consistency, and speed in completing application forms.

Testing

Testing may come in a variety of ways. Large firms or legal departments may require written tests that include punctuation, spelling, and questions to determine applicant's attitude and ability to handle various office situations.

Testing may include a five- or ten-minute typewriting test. If given the opportunity, the applicant should become acquainted with the typewriter to be used so that its peculiarities are not a complete surprise. An accomplished typist controls the machine; the poor or average typist lets the machine take control. Test results will more closely resemble the true capabilities of the applicant who has studied the typewriter prior to taking the test.

Testing sometimes includes a dictation test. This may be a formal three- or five-minute dictation test followed by complete transcription in manuscript style. Or it may consist of a dictated letter or short legal document to be transcribed in an acceptable style.

Use of the correct style for either the letter or the document, accuracy in spelling, good use of punctuation principles, and the absence of unsightly corrections will assure success on the dictation-transcription test.

CAUTION: Pen, pencil, notebook, and correcting materials should accompany an applicant at both interviews and testing situations.

The wise applicant with shorthand ability will have given this skill special attention prior to appearing for a test. If tapes or records containing timed dictation are not available, the next best thing is a shorthand session with the evening news. Or perhaps the job seeker can find someone who will read a newspaper article aloud to permit shorthand practice and the recall of shorthand symbols that may not have been used recently.

A half hour at a typewriter immediately prior to leaving for a job interview will limber fingers and prepare the applicant for the expected typing and transcription tests.

Whatever the testing situation, tell yourself this: "If I am nervous and do poorly, I am hurting only myself." If you let your nerves jeopardize your obtaining a desirable position, you and you alone are responsible. Do your best on the test—then go home and collapse if you must!

Interviews

It is the interview that finally determines which of the several applicants will be named to fill a position. The interview is that brief period during which the employer and the applicant judge each other.

The applicant will be looking for

- An employer who is considerate, interesting, successful or capable of succeeding
- A position that is interesting, challenging, and offers a chance for growth
- A salary commensurate with ability, with regular pay increases assured

The employer wishes to know if the applicant will

* Be an asset to the office
* Be helpful in difficult situations
* Fit in with other office personnel
* Be able to communicate with both office personnel and clients
* Be alert to ask necessary questions and benefit by the information given
* Be a good employee

The special qualities looked for are

* Positive attitude
* Poise
* Pleasant appearance
* Proper use of the American-English language
* Appropriateness of questions
* Aptness of answers to questions

Positive attitude. Attitude is first, for the applicant who fails here has failed the interview. An attorney once told me that attitude was the *single* quality by which secretaries were selected in that office.

This attorney said that the person who expressed interest in the position, that is, *genuine* interest in the position, was the one chosen. Some applicants express an interest in the money, the hours, the appearance of the office, possibilities of advancement, and fringe benefits. But they never once, by statement or question, show that they are interested in learning the work, in doing the work, or in extending themselves beyond the minimum work required.

Further, this attorney does not choose to work with these people. What this office needs is someone who really wishes to become a legal secretary, who wishes to become involved in the position, and who is at least as much interested in the work as in the pay check.

Applicants, then, must convey to interviewers by their questions and their answers to interviewers' questions that they are interested in the position for what they can bring to it—not solely for what they can get out of it.

Interviewers' questions should be answered briefly and to the point. These persons do not have time for long, involved answers and opinions. Too much conversation has cost many applicants the very positions they were trying to "talk themselves into."

The shy, too-quiet applicant must cultivate a voice expressing confidence. One means of accomplishing this is to increase voice volume slightly. If the interviewer is unable to hear the applicant, snap judgment will be, "This person will never be able to communicate with others."

Attitude—let your attitude show. Let your attitude be positive. Let your attitude win you the position.

Poise. Poise is second in importance. A prospective employer is searching for a secretary with sufficient self-confidence to inspire confidence in others.

An applicant must make a favorable impression on the one whose opinion will be sought and freely given: the receptionist or legal secretary who is already a part of the firm. The applicant can make a favorable impression by

- Entering the office quietly
- Making a businesslike introduction
- Referring to the appointment (if an appointment was made)
- Stating the purpose of the call
- Being seated in the waiting room, unless the interviewer is immediately available

The tension felt by any applicant can be relieved somewhat by absorption in any interesting article in one of the office magazines. When called in for the interview, the applicant will be relaxed.

During the interview, sit with your hands in your lap and a pleasant expression on your face. Be as relaxed as possible. You will already have made a positive impression on the interviewer.

Finger tapping, fidgeting, snapping and unsnapping a briefcase or a handbag, chewing gum—all are *verboten!* These are immediate indicators of a nervous, unreliable, insecure individual. Before the interview, make certain these are not part of your interviewing personality.

Pleasant appearance. Appearance is important. It tells all who see you that you are or are not aware of the appropriate dress for an occasion. Women cannot wear jeans or shorts; neither can men. The applicant must dress as if going to visit any business office. Dress must follow current style trends but remain on the conservative side. Office costume is as individual, varied, yet standard as is evening costume, skiing costume, or swimming costume. These various kinds of costumes are not interchangeable.

The employer is looking for a secretary, not a clotheshorse. If the applicant's costume draws more attention than attitude, skills, and other qualifications, the sympathy of present office employees will already have been lost. The interviewing attorney will probably look but not hire.

It is important to dress well. The applicant who is either ultra-conservative or extremely modern in dress will not have as great appeal to the interviewer as will the applicant who uses moderation and good taste.

Proper use of the American-English language.   Proper use of the American-English language is very important for the legal secretary. The applicant should speak carefully, avoiding the use of slang and extreme terms. It is important to speak naturally, to appear at ease, to use the language correctly. This can be most easily accomplished by speaking quietly and sparingly.

Those who are not sure of their ability to use the language correctly would do well to take one or more of the speech, linguistics, or English courses offered at adult schools or at any of the local colleges.

The interviewer who detects serious grammatical errors in an applicant's speech patterns will question, and rightly, the individual's ability to understand and use the difficult legal rhetoric legal secretaries face.

Appropriateness of the applicant's questions.   The applicant's questions will help the interviewer evaluate tact, awareness, attitude, self-importance, self-esteem, and desire for the position.

Suitable questions to the employer could be:

- Is the practice general, criminal, probate? (This will open the door for the attorney to discuss the work of the office and may lead the applicant to other appropriate questions regarding the office.)
- Does the attorney dictate to the secretary or use dictating equipment? (This is a particularly good question if the applicant is skillful both with shorthand and in the use of dictating equipment.)
- Other appropriate questions referring to the position —*not* to the welfare of the applicant.

If, during the interview, such questions as hours and days of employment, salary, and vacation have not been discussed by the attorney, the applicant must introduce these subjects before the conclusion of the interview. Failure to discuss them early in the interview could be an oversight on the part of the attorney. But the applicant must have all the facts regarding the position. The questions should wait until late in the interview. They should not be among the applicant's first questions.

REMEMBER: The attorney is looking for someone who will be an asset to the office and who will be concerned with the office and its problems.

Aptness of the applicant's answers to the interviewer's questions. The importance of this point is self-evident. If the attorney asks where the applicant went to college, the appropriate reply would be the name of the college. It is not necessary to begin with grammar school and work up to junior high school, high school, and finally to college. If the attorney seeks information about work experience, the proper reply would be a brief description of the work experience, not a potpourri of anecdotes along the way.

KEEPING YOUR POSITION AS A LEGAL SECRETARY

An experienced legal secretary once said to me, "Don't baby your students. Give them the most difficult work you can find. They will certainly be ready for legal work then." And she proceeded to tell me of her first day in the office. It included

- Dictation and transcription of a complicated agreement (Both the wording and style were new to her.)
- Completion of a deed of trust form (She had never before seen a real property description.)
- Filing, telephone calls, incoming and outgoing mail, and miscellaneous details that are a necessary part of office work

The variety of work, the complexity of the dictation, and the activity of the office combined to make this secretary wonder just how long she would last as a legal secretary. Many years have passed and she is still working as a legal secretary. The variety, complexity, and activity made the position exciting, challenging, and interesting to her.

The secretary who will not have to wonder how to keep a position is the one who

- Does the best work possible
- Asks necessary questions and makes notes of the answers
- Learns to anticipate the needs of the attorney, the client, and the office itself
- Uses good public relations techniques in dealing with all of the publics
- Enjoys the work
- Takes pride in the work

Does the best work possible. The secretary who really tries, who does the best work possible, who benefits by daily work experience and by the mistakes that may have been made, who is loyal, who is thoughtful, who is generous with time and effort — that secretary will be an asset and will not easily be replaced.

Asks necessary questions and makes notes of the answers.   No one, in whatever capacity, knows all there is to know about anything. The legal secretary, whether a neophyte or a pro, will have questions that must be asked if the task at hand is to be completed accurately, efficiently, and on time.

The secretary whose future holds success is the one who keeps a notebook or memo system for recording items of interest and of importance to office efficiency. Answers to such questions as who gets how many copies of letters and documents should be recorded in a notebook.

Later on, making and referring to these handy notes may not be quite as necessary as they are early in a career, but until that period of expertise arrives, the notes in the "memory" notebook will be a valuable aid.

Everyone expects the new employee to ask questions. No one expects the same question to be asked again and again.

Learns to anticipate the needs of the attorney, the client, and the office itself.   Some fortunate few have an innate sense of anticipating the needs of others. The less fortunate must acquire the habit.

Each morning the secretary should anticipate that the attorney will be taking notes during conversations with clients. Therefore, pens, pencils, and yellow lined legal notepads must be made easily available. If the attorney indicates that a document in a certain legal matter should be dictated, the thoughtful secretary will immediately locate the appropriate file and place it on the attorney's desk. To anticipate means simply to help before such help has been requested.

I suppose we are all aware of those who "overanticipate" — the kind of people who so want to help that they complete the sentences we are desperately trying to complete ourselves. One who overanticipates may seem officious.

The secretary who anticipates the needs of the office is the one who anticipates that

- Supplies need replenishing
- Stationery needs reordering
- Reception office chairs need straightening when they have been shuffled about by one or another of the clients
- Pencils need sharpening
- Calendars need ordering in ample time for the new year
- Countless other tasks require regular attention

Uses good public relations techniques in dealing with all of the law office publics.　This quality is vitally important if the secretary is to become essential to the smooth functioning of the law office.

The public relations techniques used may be those used by many others, or they may be those peculiarly personal. Wise use of good public relations techniques will make the legal secretary indispensable to the many publics, including the attorney.

Enjoys the work.　One need never ask if a legal secretary enjoys the work. It shows. And unhappiness also shows.

The secretary who enjoys the work is almost always doing it well. One does not enjoy participating in sports when success is not experienced. This reaction is equally true of occupational enjoyment.

Takes pride in the work.　The secretary who takes pride in the work will improve daily, will learn for personal satisfaction, will enjoy making friends and putting people at ease, and will take pride in the reputation for efficiency, accuracy, and consideration that the firm enjoys.

A position is only as important as its owner believes it to be. If by action and deed an employee implies that a position is the best in the world, who can disagree? Some will be envious. Some will aspire to finding a similar position.

An employee can make a position large or small, important or unimportant. By attitude and actions, the employee can make the position seem to be the most nearly perfect position of all — or the worst. To quote Elbert Hubbard in his essay titled "Loyalty":

> If — you work for a man, in heaven's name work for him; speak well of him and stand by the institution he represents.
> Remember — An ounce of loyalty is worth a pound of cleverness.
> If — you must growl, condemn, and eternally find fault, why — resign your position and when you are on the outside, damn to your heart's content — but as long as you are a part of the institution do not condemn it; if you do, the first high wind that comes along will blow you away, and probably you will never know why.

LEAVING YOUR POSITION

How can one maintain goodwill, good fellowship, and good reputation when leaving a position that has been

- Interesting, exciting, challenging, enjoyable, and entirely satisfactory?
- Tolerable, dull, only occasionally interesting?
- Boring, unpleasant on occasion, entirely unsatisfactory?

Each situation presents a different problem. Yet the departing secretary must keep a good reputation intact. Later employers, whether ten days, ten months, or ten years later, may contact any or all previous employers for recommendations. A poor report along the way could jeopardize the secretary's later employment.

Interesting Position

The secretary who has thoroughly enjoyed a position, enjoyed the friendship of fellow employees, enjoyed associating with clients and the many others who are a part of the law office publics will find it difficult to say goodbye to it all.

The departing secretary must

- Explain the reasons for leaving so there will be no misunderstanding
- Give ample notice and offer to train a replacement
- Do everything possible to assure continuation of goodwill
- Convey appreciation for everything learned and gained from the association with the office
- Use the same public relations skill in leaving the position that was used in obtaining it

Occasionally Interesting Position

The secretary who is leaving a position that has been only mildly interesting, even bordering on the dull side, must hide the relief that must surely be felt at terminating the employment. This secretary, too, must give ample notice, offer to train a replacement, and in every way be helpful and cooperative during the final days with the firm.

At no time can this secretary afford the luxury of telling the employer that the job was unsatisfactory or dull. This employer may be listed as a reference on future application forms for later employment. The door must be left open for a good recommendation if one is ever required.

Totally Unsatisfactory Position

The unfortunate secretary who, during the initial interview, failed to evaluate the employer or the position correctly need not stay on the job "for the experience" or "out of loyalty." The position that is totally unacceptable for one person may be totally acceptable for another.

Most people who work do so from necessity. It would be a hardship for most of us to be without employment for any length of time. A secretary who has accepted an entirely unsatisfactory position should begin to search for another position quietly and unannounced while remaining at the job.

One of the hazards of this kind of job hunting is that the prospective new employer will wish to call the present employer for a recommendation. The prospective employer will also wish to have the new employee begin work as soon as possible. Both situations must be handled fairly. The prospective employer must be told that the current employer does not yet know of the applicant's plans for a change in positions and that two weeks' notice must be given. The prospective employer will appreciate this display of loyalty.

Applicants who in any way fault previous employers or positions are, in effect, suggesting that they might also find fault with new situations. At no time may applicants place blame — not on themselves, not on their employers, not on their positions.

Some reasons for changing positions might be

- There is no chance for advancement in their present positions.
- They want more responsibility.
- They prefer employment nearer home.
- They wish to change the kind of employment.

These are only a few of the many reasons that could be used. Resourceful applicants will have logical, honest reasons ready for the prospective employers.

I knew a secretary who arrived at work one morning to discover that the office furniture had been rearranged, her working area moved, and her proximity to her employer drastically changed. The furniture arrangement suggested that she had been replaced by another as secretary to the supervisor.

As she realized the import of the change, she grew angry, then very angry. Thinking no farther ahead than the tip of her nose, she strode into the supervisor's office and loudly demanded the reason for the change. Her attitude aroused a like attitude in the supervisor, and they were soon shouting each other down. Loudly she announced, "I'll quit before I let you move me around that way!" Her employer shouted back, "I accept your resignation!"

The secretary resigned and her resignation was accepted. But this loss of temper had its aftereffects. She had been employed by the firm for over ten years. In her search for employment she had to list the firm, if not the former employer, as part of her previous employment. Ten years is much too long a period to pass over in an application. The employer, slow to forgive, would not recommend his former secretary. A long period of time passed before she was again able to find employment.

The story would have been much different had she not lost her temper. She could have quietly begun searching for a new position. Later, when the incident lay safely in the past, she could have resigned, secure in her knowledge that she would have at least a reasonable recommendation for her ten years of employment.

No one, but no one, can afford the luxury of shouting, of destroying another's image, of losing self-control. An employee may resign, but the resignation must be made so the door is always open for a possible return. Who knows? The position left now may sometime in the future be just the one that would best fit new circumstances.

SUMMARY

Finding, keeping, and leaving a position are all difficult. Each requires the use of tact, good judgment, and good public relations techniques.

To find a position, the legal secretary must use every source of employment available. Care must be exercised in taking tests, in completing application forms, and in participating in interviews.

Keeping the position is easy for the one who honestly does the very best, asks necessary questions and makes notes of the answers, anticipates the wishes of others, uses good public relations techniques, and enjoys and takes pride in the work.

Leaving a position requires skill, good manners, and the use of good public relations techniques. The legal secretary must leave a position in such a way that the door will always be open for a possible return. Recommendations of past employers are the keys to future employment.

SUGGESTED SPECIAL ASSIGNMENTS

1. Visit your college placement office. Inquire about the possibility of part-time employment while you are a student and full-time employment when you graduate. Write a one-page essay describing your experience and including the information you have gained.

2. Visit a commercial placement office. Obtain an application form. Ask for information regarding fees, length of contract, and

other items of importance to you. Write a one-page essay describing your experience. Attach a copy of the application form to your essay.

3. Visit the local state, county, or city employment office. Inquire about the availability of full-time positions for legal secretaries. Inquire about testing and interviews. Obtain an application form and any printed information that may be available. Write a one-page essay describing your experience. Attach to the essay a copy of the application form and any printed information you may have received.

19

Tips to Try

All pros have special tricks that helped them move into the professional category. Their shortcuts sped them on their way; their creativity eased the tedious steps that are part of every endeavor. By their attention to detail the professional secretaries produce accurate, attractive, professional-appearing papers.

Try these tips where practical and develop your own tricks of the trade as well. Good luck!

ABBREVIATIONS

"Occupant" mail is replete with abbreviations. The emphasis is speed, not quality. The legal secretary must emphasize both speed and quality, but quality comes first.

Such abbreviations as *Mr.*, *Mrs.*, *Dr.*, *Inc.*, and *Ltd.* are acceptable ones. Others, such as *N.* for *North*, *Enc.* for *Enclosure*, are shortcuts seldom used by professional secretaries.

In letters that originate in offices of the presidents of large corporations, chairmen of boards of directors, reputable and well-known law firms, the word *Enclosure* is spelled out, as are *North, South, Street, Avenue,* and other words commonly a part of street addresses.

This attention to detail marks the secretary who aspires to perfection.

COLOR CODING

Color coding is used to achieve immediate recognition of coded items. It is an excellent time-saving device. Consistency in the use of certain colors for certain matters is all-important.

Try color-coding file folders by using various colored labels. White could be used for the general office files, pink for probate, blue for corporation matters, and so on. If your office specializes in one kind of law, the first sections of files could be one color, second section of the same file another color, third still another. As the cases grew to three, four, five sections, the color of the file label would indicate immediately which section of the file was being used.

Yellow three-by-five cards could list names and addresses of all persons on the office Christmas card list. Pink three-by-five cards could list the names and addresses and phone numbers of those individuals and firms regularly written to or telephoned.

DRY CLEANING DIRTY FINGERS

Smudgy fingers may result from working with typewriter ribbons or handling carbon ribbons or paper. No matter the proximity of the wash basin, it is still farther from the secretary than the desk paper supply. Any soil that will come off on a typed page will also come off on a plain piece of paper.

Use a clean sheet of paper and briskly rub your fingers. Presto! Clean fingers! This technique will save many trips to the wash basin. Of course, paper does not do the complete job of soap and water, but it does remove the excess smudge that could spoil an otherwise perfect piece of work.

ENCLOSURE

The word *Enclosure* on a letter covers one or several enclosures. This notation is primarily for the use of the secretary as a reminder to enclose the necessary material.

The dictator might state in a letter that "material is enclosed" and indicate the enclosures to the secretary. As the letter is signed, the dictator could very well have a change of mind and decide to include only one of the papers. The letter is still correct, and so is the *Enclosure* notation if it has been written without an *s* to make it plural.

If enclosures must be identified or the number of enclosures noted, the information should be shown on the yellow office copy only. Deletions or additions to a list naming the enclosures can be made on the office copy. Such changes are not possible on the signed copy of the letter, which would have to be retyped and signed again.

ERASING

Erasing is a skill that proficient secretaries have already perfected. Following are some tips even they may be able to use:

1. Use three erasers: art gum eraser to remove smudges, soft eraser to remove heavy ink and carbon, ink eraser to remove the remainder of the type error.
2. Clean erasers by rubbing them briskly over a clean piece of paper or very fine sandpaper.
3. Use an erasing shield to protect adjoining letters from smears and smudges.
4. Practice the following procedure, which will, in time, produce invisible erasures:
   a. Press the soft eraser against the type error with an up-and-down motion, or roll it across the word to be removed. Look at the eraser. It will contain an imprint of the letters. Clean the eraser. Blot again.
   b. Use the ink eraser to remove the remainder of the letter or word. Rub briskly but lightly. The goal is to remove the letters, not the paper.
   c. Use the art gum eraser to remove smudges that might appear near the erasure or elsewhere on the paper.
5. Erase the original first. Both ink and carbon erase more easily if they are removed immediately.
6. Carbon copies should be erased as neatly and with the same care as the original. This advice especially includes the office copy, which is the one the attorney and other office personnel will handle.

NOTE: Correctable typewriters almost eliminate erasing.

EXTRA CARBONS

If a letter is two or more pages long and there is any possibility that an extra copy might later be required for reference or for transmittal to another party, make an extra copy for the office file. The extra copy should be on white paper and should be placed in the file folder next to but *under* the yellow office copy.

NOTE: This precaution is unnecessary if a copy machine is available.

FORM FILES AS
EMPLOYMENT REFERENCES

The student who has not yet worked in a law office should assemble a form file consisting of accurate, attractive legal documents prepared as class assignments.

Such a form file will indicate far better than words that the student is familiar with legal documents and legal terminology. The quality of the work will introduce the interviewing attorney to the kind of work the applicant is able to produce.

The form file will be only a skeleton form file containing one copy of each of the various documents typed in class.

OPENING MAIL

The envelope that, in one motion, is opened *across* the top then *down* one side is fully opened. Checks, calling cards, clippings, photographs, and other small enclosures will be readily seen and removed.

Just one experience of discarding an envelope that did contain or could possibly have contained such an enclosure is ample proof of the value of this tip. Not every incoming letter is written by an experienced letter writer. Occasionally enclosures not referred to in the letter will be included in an envelope. It is essential that each envelope be completely empty when it is discarded.

PROOFREADING

Proofreading is critical in legal work. What might seem a minor discrepancy to the secretary could very well be the basis of litigation for the law firm. The following tips may be of some help.

Hold line-for-line typed copy against the original copy to ascertain that the newly typed copy has as many lines as the original. This will insure that no line of the original copy has been omitted in the retyping.

Proofread for sense. Such type errors as *the* for *then* or *an* for *and* are difficult to discover because both the type error and the correct word are true words. This kind of error can be caught only if the proofreader "listens" to the content as it is silently proofread.

Real property descriptions and quoted material should be proofread twice. The first proofreading should be by the secretary who typed the material, the second by two people. The original material should be read by the secretary, the newly typed copy by the assistant proofreader (attorney, another legal secretary, or other available office employee). The secretary should read aloud. If the copy is long, the two proofreaders should take turns reading.

Capital letters, marks of punctuation, and abbreviations must be read aloud in proofreading real property descriptions or other technical material. Nontechnical material may be read aloud with no reference made to punctuation, which is indicated by voice tone.

ROUND-TABLE DISCUSSIONS

A public relations tool used by many offices, large and small, is the round-table discussion. If properly structured, this meeting gives all employees an opportunity to let off steam, to share ideas for improving or altering office procedures, to discuss vacation and salary scheduling and problems, and to discover new methods of sharing the work load.

Such discussions could be suggested by the office manager or a legal secretary with long employment with the firm. If the discussion is to be valuable, all employees must participate, with the attorney or attorneys acting as mediator.

If properly structured and regularly held, round-table discussions develop and maintain mutual understanding and respect, esprit de corps, and pride in the firm.

Such meetings could be regularly scheduled the last hour of the day the first or last working day of each month. A box of candy, soft drinks, or similar refreshments would lessen the tensions of the day.

SCRAPBOOKS

Begin an office scrapbook. Kept up to date, it will become an interesting and important source of information. Contents must be added in chronological order and should include all news items that contain the firm name or the names of the attorneys.

Suppose your attorney is appointed chairman of an important civic committee or speaks before a service organization. Suppose the firm name is used in a newspaper report of a trial. These items should be clipped and added to the scrapbook.

Before suggesting a scrapbook for the firm, clip and collect news items for a period of several weeks or months. Each must be carefully identified as to date and source. With clippings in hand, approach the attorney with your suggestion. Both your idea and your interest in the firm will be noted.

The size of the firm and the nature of the practice will determine the size of the scrapbook.

In mounting new clippings

- Cut items carefully along column lines.
- Clip the entire article, including pictures and continuation columns.
- Arrange the article in a manner that provides continuous reading top to bottom and left to right.
- Center date and source above the item:

The Fresno Bee

January 3, 19——

- Obtain two copies of the newspaper or periodical if a news item begins on one page and is continued on the reverse of the article.
- Use a good quality glue to mount clippings or photographs.

The newsy items of the civic activities of the attorneys will always be interesting to members of the firm. News items of court cases in which the firm is interested may be of more than passing value to the office.

Occasionally an article must be sent to a client or another attorney. The article should be clipped, then neatly centered and mounted on a letter-size sheet of plain paper for transmittal. Photocopies may be made of the mounted article.

SHORTHAND

Both manual and machine shorthand operators should create their own shorthand symbols for the words and phrases that recur frequently in legal dictation. Each shorthand system has its own brief forms and phrasing principles. In devising new shortcuts, the legal secretary must abide by the principles of the shorthand system.

In Gregg shorthand, the intersecting principle may be used with confidence in devising new legal shorthand symbols. *P* intersected *p* ($\mathcal{E}$) for *personal property*, *r* intersected *p* ($\mathcal{L}$) for *real property*, *l* intersected *t* ($\swarrow$) for *last will and testament* are excellent shortcuts.[1]

The machine shorthand operator can greatly increase the flexibility of that shorthand by spending some time sharpening "pencil shorthand" skills. "Pencil shorthand" is simply machine shorthand symbols written manually in a shorthand notebook or on other paper. Time spent developing this extra skill will be time well spent by the machine shorthand operator.

STAPLING LETTERS

Rarely are letters misstapled, but the following suggestions are for those few who are unsure of correct practice.

The first and continuation sheets of the original letter are NEVER stapled together. First and continuation sheets of all carbon copies of letters are ALWAYS stapled together. There is no particular reason for this practice; it is simply standard style.

Enclosures are not stapled to the letterhead. The enclosures that are the same size or longer than the letterhead are placed beneath the letter and folded with it. Small enclosures are placed within the folded letter.

If a stamp is enclosed, a tiny corner of the stamp should be moistened and adhered to the top of the letterhead.

STREET ADDRESSES

Use the local telephone directory to determine complete and correct addresses. The address must identify whether the street is an *avenue*, *boulevard*, *way*, *square*, *circle*, *lane*, or some other designation.

Telephone directories include as part of the street address every designation except *Street*. Example: *1234 Main* in the telephone directory would be written *1234 Main Street* in an inside address. Other street designations would be printed in the telephone directory as follows: *1234 Harper Wy* (Way), *1234 Charleston Dr* (Drive), *1234 Herndon Av* (Avenue). Street names and designations are often abbreviated in phone directories but not in inside addresses.

[1] Gregg Shorthand outlines reproduced with the permission of Gregg Division, McGraw-Hill, Inc., publishers and proprietors of Gregg Shorthand.

The street name *Broadway* requires no additional designation. This street name has been compounded to form a single word.

Street designations should be included in inside addresses because it is common practice in most cities to use the name with various designations; i.e., *1234 Harper Street, 234 Harper Way, 12345 Harper Lane* may all be good addresses in a single city. An envelope addressed to 12345 Harper would be delayed in delivery until the correct street designation could be determined by postal employees.

STRIKEOVERS

On most typewriters, an *o* can be typed over a *c* and an *e* can be typed over a *c;* a comma, colon, semicolon, or exclamation point can be typed over a period.

On your own typewriter, you may discover other symbols that can be typed over with no strikeover effect.

Obvious strikeovers are blemishes on the typewritten work of the secretary. Strikeovers that are not discernible are timesavers.

CAUTION: Test this strikeover method prior to adopting it for your use.

TOOLS OF THE TRADE

Ever thought of yourself as a carpenter or mechanic? If not, you haven't truly evaluated your position. In these capacities, your tools will be pliers, sandpaper, screwdriver, and waxed paper. There will be many uses for these tools other than those given here.

Pliers will loosen file drawer rods. They are crucial in fitting file drawers with the support systems for hanging files. (The manila folders are placed into the hanging file folders.)

Sandpaper will remove from both wood and metal desks and chairs the rough edges that cut and scratch flesh and damage clothing.

Screwdrivers will loosen set screws on adjustable chairs, ease or release tight-fitting drawers, and tighten loose screws on typewriters and on dictating and other equipment.

Waxed paper lubricates metal support rods for hanging files as well as metal channels for sliding glass doors, windows, and file drawers. A brisk rub of the waxed paper across the metal parts provides ample lubrication.

Additional lubricants are liquid and powdered graphite and light-weight oil. Screeching chairs, doors, and drawers may be eliminated if the lubricant is lightly applied.

TYPEWRITER REPAIRS

When your typewriter will not space or spaces too much; when a letter prints too dark, too light, or not at all; when the underscore key cuts the paper; or when the margins are uneven — keep samples showing the problem. Call the service representative and provide your samples. With these in hand, this expert can intelligently go about the business of repairing your typewriter.

As with a small child who will not show off before guests, a typewriter frequently will not demonstrate its idiosyncrasies before a qualified service representative.

WASTE OR USED PAPER

Destroy any used or waste papers by tearing them in two and then tearing those pieces once again. You'll find that wastebaskets will not fill as quickly as they do when such papers are wadded and then discarded. This practice also insures that papers are truly destroyed, and the chance of unscrupulous perusal of office waste paper is lessened.

SUMMARY

Shortcuts that improve efficiency and increase production are discovered regularly by the secretary who is consciously searching for ways to make the work load lighter.

Knowledge and use of special tricks are the mark of the professional in any trade or activity.

SUGGESTED SPECIAL ASSIGNMENTS

1. Experiment with any of the several tips given in this chapter. By oral presentation share your experiences with other students.

2. By oral presentation share with students any tips you have devised or have learned in other classes or on the job. How valuable have they been to you?

PART FOUR

Part Four comprises Appendixes containing the necessary information to serve the legal secretary adequately:

Model Code of Professional Responsibility of the American Bar Association. *The Code is included to acquaint the legal secretary with the standards that attorneys have set for themselves and by which they abide, and to introduce the reader to terms and phrases that typify legal correspondence and conversation. The special attitudes and routines peculiar to a law office are explained in the numbered Ethical Considerations that follow each Canon. Disciplinary Rules are not included here.*

Client documents, correspondence, court documents, and forms or law blanks. *A cross-section of examples of these will supplement the briefer samplings in the text.*

Glossary. *The Glossary was assembled from the pages of this volume to include those words and phrases requiring special definition.*

Bibliography. *The Bibliography was carefully selected to include reference books that would be interesting and valuable to the student and the legal secretary.*

Appendix A

Model Code
of Professional
Responsibility, American
Bar Association

PREAMBLE AND PRELIMINARY STATEMENT

PREAMBLE

The continued existence of a free and democratic society depends upon recognition of the concept that justice is based upon the rule of law grounded in respect for the dignity of the individual and his capacity through reason for enlightened self-government. Law so grounded makes justice possible, for only through such law does the dignity of the individual attain respect and protection. Without it, individual rights become subject to unrestrained power, respect for law is destroyed, and rational self-government is impossible.

Lawyers, as guardians of the law, play a vital role in the preservation of society. The fulfillment of this role requires an understanding by lawyers of their relationship with and function in our legal system. A consequent obligation of lawyers is to maintain the highest standards of ethical conduct.

In fulfilling his professional responsibilities, a lawyer necessarily assumes various roles that require the performance of many difficult tasks. Not every situation which he may encounter can be foreseen, but fundamental ethical principles are always present to guide him. Within the framework of these principles, a lawyer must with courage and foresight be able and ready to shape the body of the law to the ever-changing relationships of society.

The Code of Professional Responsibility points the way to the aspiring and provides standards by which to judge the transgressor. Each lawyer must find within his own conscience the touchstone against which to test the extent to which his actions should rise above minimum standards. But in the last analysis it is the desire for the respect and confidence of the members of his profession and of the society which he serves that should provide to a lawyer the incentive for the highest possible degree of ethical conduct. The possible loss of that respect and confidence is the ultimate sanction. So long as its practitioners are guided by these principles, the law will continue to be a noble profession. This is its greatness and its strength, which permit of no compromise.

PRELIMINARY STATEMENT

In furtherance of the principles stated in the Preamble, the American Bar Association has promulgated this Code of Professional Responsibility, consisting of three separate but interrelated parts: Canons, Ethical Considerations, and Disciplinary Rules. The Code is designed to be adopted by appropriate agencies both as an inspirational guide to the members of the profession and as a basis for disciplinary action when the conduct of a lawyer falls below the required minimum standards stated in the Disciplinary Rules.

Obviously the Canons, Ethical Considerations, and Disciplinary Rules cannot apply to non-lawyers; however, they do define the type of ethical conduct that the public has a right to expect not only of lawyers but also of their non-professional employees and associates in all matters pertaining to professional employment. A lawyer should ultimately be responsible for the conduct of his employees and associates in the course of the professional representation of the client.

The Canons are statements of axiomatic norms, expressing in general terms the standards of professional conduct expected of lawyers in their relationships with the public, with the legal system, and with the legal profession. They embody the general concepts from which the Ethical Considerations and the Disciplinary Rules are derived.

The Ethical Considerations are aspirational in character and represent the objectives toward which every member of the profession should strive. They constitute a body of principles upon which the lawyer can rely for guidance in many specific situations.

The Disciplinary Rules, unlike the Ethical Considerations, are mandatory in character. The Disciplinary Rules state the minimum level of conduct below which no lawyer can fall without being subject to disciplinary action. Within the framework of fair trial, the Disciplinary Rules should be uniformly applied to all lawyers, regardless of the nature of their professional activities. The Code makes no attempt to prescribe either disciplinary procedures or penalties for violation of a Disciplinary Rule, nor does it undertake to define standards for civil liability of lawyers for professional conduct. The severity of judgment against one found guilty of violating a Disciplinary Rule should be determined by the character of the offense and the attendant circumstances. An enforcing agency, in applying the Disciplinary Rules, may find interpretive guidance in the basic principles embodied in the Canons and in the objectives reflected in the Ethical Considerations.

CANON 1

A Lawyer Should Assist in Maintaining
the Integrity and Competence
of the Legal Profession

Ethical Considerations

EC 1-1   A basic tenet of the professional responsibility of lawyers is that every person in our society should have ready access to the independent professional services of a lawyer of integrity and competence. Maintaining the integrity and improving the competence of the bar to meet the highest standards is the ethical responsibility of every lawyer.

EC 1-2   The public should be protected from those who are not qualified to be lawyers by reason of a deficiency in education or moral standards or of other relevant factors but who nevertheless seek to practice law. To assure the maintenance of high moral and educational standards of the legal profession, lawyers should affirmatively assist courts and other appropriate bodies in promulgating, enforcing, and improving requirements for admission to the bar. In like manner, the bar has a positive obligation to aid in the continued improvement of all phases of preadmission and post-admission legal education.

EC 1-3   Before recommending an applicant for admission, a lawyer should satisfy himself that the applicant is of good moral character. Although a lawyer should not become a self-appointed investigator or judge of applicants for admission, he should report to proper officials all unfavorable information he possesses relating to the character or other qualifications of an applicant.

EC 1-4   The integrity of the profession can be maintained only if conduct of lawyers in violation of the Disciplinary Rules is brought to the attention of the proper officials. A lawyer should reveal voluntarily to those officials all unprivileged knowledge of conduct of lawyers which he believes clearly to be in violation of the Disciplinary Rules. A lawyer should, upon request, serve on and assist committees and boards having responsibility for the administration of the Disciplinary Rules.

EC 1-5   A lawyer should maintain high standards of professional conduct and should encourage fellow lawyers to do likewise. He should be temperate and dignified, and he should refrain from all illegal and morally reprehensible conduct. Because of his position in society, even minor violations of law by a lawyer may tend to lessen public confidence in the legal profession. Obedience to law exemplifies respect for law. To lawyers especially, respect for the law should be more than a platitude.

EC 1-6   An applicant for admission to the bar or a lawyer may be unqualified, temporarily or permanently, for other than moral and educational reasons, such as mental or emotional instability. Lawyers should be diligent in taking steps to see that during a period of disqualification such person is not granted a license or, if licensed, is not permitted to practice. In like manner, when the disqualification has terminated, members of the bar should assist such person in being licensed, or, if licensed, in being restored to his full right to practice.

CANON 2

A Lawyer Should Assist the Legal Profession in Fulfilling Its Duty to Make Legal Counsel Available

Ethical Considerations

EC 2-1   The need of members of the public for legal services is met only if they recognize their legal problems, appreciate the importance of seeking assistance, and are able to obtain the services of acceptable legal counsel. Hence, important functions of the legal profession are to educate laymen to recognize their problems, to facilitate the process of intelligent selection of lawyers, and to assist in making legal services fully available.

Recognition of Legal Problems

EC 2-2   The legal profession should assist laypersons to recognize legal problems because such problems may not be self-revealing and often are not timely noticed. Therefore, lawyers should encourage and participate in educational and public relations programs concerning our legal system with particular reference to legal problems that frequently arise. Preparation of advertisements and professional articles for lay publications and participation in seminars, lectures, and civic programs should be motivated by a desire to educate the public to an awareness of legal needs and to provide information relevant to the selection of the most appr priate counsel rather than to obtain publicity for particular lawyers. The problems of advertising on television require special consideration, due to the style, cost, and transitory nature of such media. If the interests of laypersons in receiving relevant lawyer advertising are not adequately served by print media and radio advertising, and if adequate safeguards to protect the public can reasonably be formulated, television advertising may serve a public interest.

EC 2-3   Whether a lawyer acts properly in volunteering in-person advice to a layperson to seek legal services depends upon the circumstances. The giving of advice that one should take legal action could well be in fulfillment of the duty of the legal profession to assist laypersons in recognizing legal problems. The advice is proper only if motivated by a desire to protect one who does not recognize that he may have legal problems or who is ignorant of his legal rights or obligations. It is improper if motivated by a desire to obtain personal benefit, secure personal publicity, or cause legal action to be taken merely to harass or injure another. A lawyer should not initiate an in-person contact with a non-client, personally or through a representative, for the purpose of being retained to represent him for compensation.

EC 2-4   Since motivation is subjective and often difficult to judge, the motives of a lawyer who volunteers in-person advice likely to produce legal controversy may well be suspect if he receives professional employment or other benefits as a result. A lawyer who volunteers in-person advice that one should obtain the services of a lawyer generally should not himself accept employment, compensation, or other benefit in connection with that matter. However, it is not improper for a lawyer to volunteer such advice and render resulting legal services to close friends, relatives, former clients (in regard to matters germane to former employment), and regular clients.

EC 2-5   A lawyer who writes or speaks for the purpose of educating members of the public to recognize their legal problems should carefully refrain from giving or appearing to give a general solution applicable to all apparently similar individual problems, since slight changes in fact situations may require a material variance in the applicable advice; otherwise, the public may be misled and misadvised. Talks and writings by lawyers for laypersons should caution them not to attempt to solve individual problems upon the basis of the information contained therein.

Selection of a Lawyer

EC 2-6   Formerly a potential client usually knew the reputations of local lawyers for competency and integrity and therefore could select a practitioner in whom he had confidence. This traditional selection process worked well because it was initiated by the client and the choice was an informed one.

EC 2-7   Changed conditions, however, have seriously restricted the effectiveness of the traditional selection process. Often the reputations of lawyers are not sufficiently known to enable laypersons to make intelligent choices. The law has become increasingly complex and specialized. Few lawyers are willing and competent to deal with every kind of legal matter, and many laypersons have difficulty in determining the competence of lawyers to render different types of legal services. The selection of legal counsel is particularly difficult for transients, persons moving into new areas, persons of limited education or means, and others who have little or no contact with lawyers. Lack of information about the availability of lawyers, the qualifications of particular lawyers, and the expense of legal representation leads laypersons to avoid seeking legal advice.

EC 2-8   Selection of a lawyer by a layperson should be made on an informed basis. Advice and recommendation of third parties — relatives, friends, acquaintances, business associates, or other lawyers — and disclosure of relevant information about the lawyer and his practice may be helpful. A layperson is best served if the recommendation is disinterested and informed. In order that the recommendation be disinterested, a lawyer should not seek to influence another to recommend his employment. A lawyer should not compensate another person for recommending him, for influencing a prospective client to employ him, or to encourage future recommendations. Advertisements and public communications, whether in law lists, telephone directories, newspapers, other forms of print media, television or radio, should be formulated to convey only information that is necessary to make an appropriate selection. Such information includes: (1) office information, such as name, including name of law firm and names of professional associates; addresses; telephone numbers; credit card acceptability; fluency in foreign languages; and office hours; (2) relevant biographical information; (3) description of the practice, but only by using designations and definitions authorized by [the agency having jurisdiction of the subject under state law], for example, one or more fields of law in which the lawyer or law firm practices; a statement that practice is limited to one or more fields of law; and/or a statement that the lawyer or law firm specializes in a particular field of law practice, but only by using designations, definitions and standards authorized by [the agency having jurisdiction of the subject under state law]; and (4) permitted fee information. Self-laudation should be avoided.

Selection of a Lawyer: Lawyer Advertising

EC 2-9   The lack of sophistication on the part of many members of the public concerning legal services, the importance of the interests affected by the choice of a lawyer and prior experience with unrestricted lawyer advertising, require that special care be taken by lawyers to avoid misleading the public and to assure that the information set forth in any advertising is relevant to the selection of a lawyer. The lawyer must be mindful that the benefits of lawyer advertising depend upon its reliability and accuracy. Examples of information in lawyer advertising that would be deceptive include misstatements of fact, suggestions that the ingenuity or prior record of a lawyer rather than the justice of the claim are the principal factors likely to determine the result, inclusion of information irrelevant to selecting a lawyer, and representations concerning the quality of service, which cannot be measured or verified. Since lawyer advertising is calculated and not spontaneous, reasonable regulation of lawyer advertising designed to foster compliance with appropriate standards serves the public interest without impeding the flow of useful, meaningful, and relevant information to the public.

EC 2-10   A lawyer should ensure that the information contained in any advertising which the lawyer publishes, broadcasts or causes to be published or broadcast is relevant, is disseminated in an objective and understandable fashion, and would facilitate the prospective client's ability to compare the qualifications of the lawyers available to represent him. A lawyer should strive to communicate such information without undue emphasis upon style and advertising strategems which serve to hinder rather than to facilitate intelligent selection of counsel. Because technological change is a recurrent feature of communications forms, and because perceptions of what is relevant in lawyer selection may change, lawyer advertising regulations should not be cast in rigid, unchangeable terms. Machinery is therefore available to advertisers and consumers for prompt consideration of proposals to change the rules governing lawyer advertising. The determination of any request for such change should depend upon whether the proposal is necessary in light of existing Code provisions, whether the proposal accords with standards of accuracy, reliability and truthfulness, and whether the proposal would facilitate informed selection of lawyers by potential consumers of legal services. Representatives of lawyers and consumers should be heard in addition to the applicant concerning any proposed change. Any change which is approved should be promulgated in the form of an amendment to the Code so that all lawyers practicing in the jurisdiction may avail themselves of its provisions.

EC 2-11   The name under which a lawyer conducts his practice may be a factor in the selection process. The use of a trade name or an assumed name could mislead laypersons concerning the identity, responsibility, and status of those practicing thereunder. Accordingly, a lawyer in private practice should practice only under a designation containing his own name, the name of a lawyer employing him, the name of one or more of the lawyers practicing in a partnership, or, if permitted by law, the name of a professional legal corporation, which should be clearly designated as such. For many years some law firms have used a firm name retaining one or more names of deceased or retired partners and such practice is not improper if the firm is a bona fide successor of a firm in which the deceased or retired person was a member, if the use of the name is authorized by law or by contract, and if the public is not misled thereby. However, the name of a partner who withdraws from a firm but continues to practice law should be omitted from the firm name in order to avoid misleading the public.

EC 2-12   A lawyer occupying a judicial, legislative, or public executive or administrative position who has the right to practice law concurrently may allow his name to remain in the name of the firm if he actively continues to practice law as a member thereof. Otherwise, his name should be removed from the firm name, and he should not be identified as a past or present member of the firm; and he should not hold himself out as being a practicing lawyer.

EC 2-13   In order to avoid the possibility of misleading persons with whom he deals, a lawyer should be scrupulous in the representation of his professional status. He should not hold himself out as being a partner or associate of a law firm if he is not one in fact, and thus should not hold himself out as a partner or associate if he only shares offices with another lawyer.

EC 2-14   In some instances a lawyer confines his practice to a particular field of law. In the absence of state controls to insure the existence of special competence, a lawyer should not be permitted to hold himself out as a specialist or as having official recognition as a specialist, other than in the fields of admiralty, trademark, and patent law where a holding out as a specialist historically has been permitted. A lawyer may, however, indicate in permitted advertising, if it is factual, a limitation of his practice or one or more particular areas or fields of law in which he practices using designations and definitions authorized for that purpose by [the state agency having jurisdiction]. A lawyer practicing in a jurisdiction which certifies specialists must also be careful not to confuse laypersons as to his status. If a lawyer discloses areas of law in which he practices or to which he limits his practice, but is not certified in [the jurisdiction], he, and the designation authorized in [the jurisdiction], should avoid any implication that he is in fact certified.

EC 2-15   The legal profession has developed lawyer referral systems designed to aid individuals who are able to pay fees but need assistance in locating lawyers competent to handle their particular problems. Use of a lawyer referral system enables a layman to avoid an uninformed selection of a lawyer because such a system makes possible the employment of competent lawyers who have indicated an interest in the subject matter involved. Lawyers should support the principle of lawyer referral systems and should encourage the evolution of other ethical plans which aid in the selection of qualified counsel.

Financial Ability to Employ Counsel: Generally

EC 2-16   The legal profession cannot remain a viable force in fulfilling its role in our society unless its members receive adequate compensation for services rendered, and reasonable fees should be charged in appropriate cases to clients able to pay them. Nevertheless, persons unable to pay all or a portion of a reasonable fee should be able to obtain necessary legal services, and lawyers should support and participate in ethical activities designed to achieve that objective.

Financial Ability to Employ Counsel:
Persons Able to Pay Reasonable Fees

EC 2-17   The determination of a proper fee requires consideration of the interests of both client and lawyer. A lawyer should not charge more than a reasonable fee, for excessive cost of legal service would deter laymen from utilizing the legal system in protection of their rights. Furthermore, an excessive charge abuses the professional relationship between lawyer and client. On the other hand, adequate compensation is necessary in order to enable the lawyer to serve his client effectively and to preserve the integrity and independence of the profession.

Ec 2-18   The determination of the reasonableness of a fee requires consideration of all relevant circumstances, including those stated in the Disciplinary Rules. The fees of a lawyer will vary according to many factors, including the time required, his experience, ability, and reputation, the nature of the employment, the responsibility involved, and the results obtained. It is a commendable and long-standing tradition of the bar that special consideration is given in the fixing of any fee for services rendered a brother lawyer or a member of his immediate family.

EC 2-19   As soon as feasible after a lawyer has been employed, it is desirable that he reach a clear agreement with his client as to the basis of the fee charges to be made. Such a course will not only prevent later misunderstanding but will also work for good relations between the lawyer and the client. It is usually beneficial to reduce to writing the understanding of the parties regarding the fee, particularly when it is contingent. A lawyer should be mindful that many persons who desire to employ him may have had little or no experience with fee charges of lawyers, and for this reason he should explain fully to such persons the reasons for the particular fee arrangement he proposes.

EC 2-20   Contingent fee arrangements in civil cases have long been commonly accepted in the United States in proceedings to enforce claims. The historical bases of their acceptance are that (1) they often, and in a variety of circumstances, provide the only practical means by which one having a claim against another can economically afford, finance, and obtain the services of a competent lawyer to prosecute his claim, and (2) a successful prosecution of the claim produces a *res* out of which the fee can be paid. Although a lawyer generally should decline to accept employment on a contingent fee basis by one who is able to pay a reasonable fixed fee, it is not necessarily improper for a lawyer, where justified by the particular circumstances of a case, to enter into a contingent fee contract in a civil case with any client who, after being fully informed of all relevant factors, desires that arrangement. Because of the human relationships involved and the unique character of the proceedings, contingent fee arrangements in domestic relation cases are rarely justified. In administrative agency proceedings contingent fee contracts should be governed by the same consideration as in other civil cases. Public policy properly condemns contingent fee arrangements in criminal cases, largely on the ground that legal services in criminal cases do not produce a *res* with which to pay the fee.

EC 2-21   A lawyer should not accept compensation or any thing of value incident to his employment or services from one other than his client without the knowledge and consent of his client after full disclosure.

EC 2-22   Without the consent of his client, a lawyer should not associate in a particular matter another lawyer outside his firm. A fee may properly be divided between lawyers properly associated if the division is in proportion to the services performed and the responsibility assumed by each lawyer and if the total fee is reasonable.

EC 2-23   A lawyer should be zealous in his efforts to avoid controversies over fees with clients and should attempt to resolve amicably any differences on the subject. He should not sue a client for a fee unless necessary to prevent fraud or gross imposition by the client.

Financial Ability to Employ Counsel:
Persons Unable to Pay Reasonable Fees

EC 2-24   A layman whose financial ability is not sufficient to permit payment of any fee cannot obtain legal services, other than in cases where a contingent fee is appropriate, unless the services are provided for him. Even a person of moderate means may be unable to pay a reasonable fee which is large because of the complexity, novelty, or difficulty of the problem or similar factors.

EC 2-25   Historically, the need for legal services of those unable to pay reasonable fees has been met in part by lawyers who donated their services or accepted court appointments on behalf of such individuals. The basic responsibility for providing legal services for those unable to pay ultimately rests upon the individual lawyer, and personal involvement in the problems of the disadvantaged can be one of the most rewarding experiences in the life of a lawyer. Every lawyer, regardless of professional prominence or professional workload, should find time to participate in serving the disadvantaged. The rendition of free legal services to those unable to pay reasonable fees continues to be an obligation of each lawyer, but the efforts of individual lawyers are often not enough to meet the need. Thus it has been necessary for the profession to institute additional programs to provide legal services. Accordingly, legal aid offices, lawyer referral services, and other related programs have been developed, and others will be developed, by the profession. Every lawyer should support all proper efforts to meet this need for legal services.

Acceptance and Retention of Employment

EC 2-26   A lawyer is under no obligation to act as adviser or advocate for every person who may wish to become his client; but in furtherance of the objective of the bar to make legal services fully available, a lawyer should not lightly decline proffered employment. The fulfillment of this objective requires acceptance by a lawyer of his share of tendered employment which may be unattractive both to him and the bar generally.

EC 2-27   History is replete with instances of distinguished and sacrificial services by lawyers who have represented unpopular clients and causes. Regardless of his personal feelings, a lawyer should not decline representation because a client or a cause is unpopular or community reaction is adverse.

EC 2-28   The personal preference of a lawyer to avoid adversary alignment against judges, other lawyers, public officials, or influential members of the community does not justify his rejection of tendered employment.

EC 2-29   When a lawyer is appointed by a court or requested by a bar association to undertake representation of a person unable to obtain counsel, whether for financial or other reasons, he should not seek to be excused from undertaking the representation except for compelling reasons. Compelling reasons do not include such factors as the repugnance of the subject matter of the proceeding, the identity or position of a person involved in the case, the belief of the lawyer that the defendant in a criminal proceeding is guilty, or the belief of the lawyer regarding the merits of the civil case.

EC 2-30   Employment should not be accepted by a lawyer when he is unable to render competent service or when he knows or it is obvious that the person seeking to employ him desires to institute or maintain an action merely for the purpose of harassing or maliciously injuring another. Likewise, a lawyer should decline employment if the intensity of his personal feeling, as distinguished from a community attitude, may impair his effective representation of a prospective client. If a lawyer knows a client has previously obtained counsel, he should not accept employment in the matter unless the other counsel approves or withdraws, or the client terminates the prior employment.

EC 2-31   Full availability of legal counsel requires both that persons be able to obtain counsel and that lawyers who undertake representation complete the work involved. Trial counsel for a convicted defendant should continue to represent his client by advising whether to take an appeal and, if the appeal is prosecuted, by representing him through the appeal unless new counsel is substituted or withdrawal is permitted by the appropriate court.

EC 2-32   A decision by a lawyer to withdraw should be made only on the basis of compelling circumstances, and in a matter pending before a tribunal he must comply with the rules of the tribunal regarding withdrawal. A lawyer should not withdraw without considering carefully and endeavoring to minimize the possible adverse effect on the rights of his client and the possibility of prejudice to his client as a result of his withdrawal. Even when he justifiably withdraws, a lawyer should protect the welfare of his client by giving due notice of his withdrawal, suggesting employment of other counsel, delivering to the client all papers and property to which the client is entitled, cooperating with counsel subsequently employed, and otherwise endeavoring to minimize the possibility of harm. Further, he should refund to the client any compensation not earned during the employment.

EC 2-33   As a part of the legal profession's commitment to the principle that high quality legal services should be available to all, attorneys are encouraged to cooperate with qualified legal assistance organizations providing prepaid legal services. Such participation should at all times be in accordance with the basic tenets of the profession: independence, integrity, competence and devotion to the interests of individual clients. An attorney so participating should make certain that his relationship with a qualified legal assistance organization in no way interferes with his independent professional representation of the interests of the individual client. An attorney should avoid situations in which officials of the organization who are not lawyers attempt to direct attorneys concerning the manner in which legal services are performed for individual members, and should also avoid situations in which considerations of economy are given undue weight in determining the attorneys employed by an organization or the legal services to be performed for the member or beneficiary rather than competence and quality of service. An attorney interested in maintaining the historic traditions of the profession and preserving the function of a lawyer as a trusted and independent advisor to individual members of society should carefully assess such factors when accepting employment by, or otherwise participating in, a particular qualified legal assistance organization, and while so participating should adhere to the highest professional standards of effort and competence.

CANON 3

A Lawyer Should Assist in Preventing the Unauthorized Practice of Law

Ethical Considerations

EC 3-1   The prohibition against the practice of law by a layman is grounded in the need of the public for integrity and competence of those who undertake to render legal services. Because of the fiduciary and personal character of the lawyer-client relationship and the inherently complex nature of our legal system, the public can better be assured of the requisite responsibility and competence if the practice of law is confined to those who are subject to the requirements and regulations imposed upon members of the legal profession.

EC 3-2   The sensitive variations in the considerations that bear on legal determinations often make it difficult even for a lawyer to exercise appropriate professional judgment, and it is therefore essential that the personal nature of the relationship of client and lawyer be preserved. Competent professional judgment is the product of a trained familiarity with law and legal processes, a disciplined, analytical approach to legal problems, and a firm ethical commitment.

EC 3-3   A non-lawyer who undertakes to handle legal matters is not governed as to integrity or legal competence by the same rules that govern the conduct of a lawyer. A lawyer is not only subject to that regulation but also is committed to high standards of ethical conduct. The public interest is best served in legal matters by a regulated profession committed to such standards. The Disciplinary Rules protect the public in that they prohibit a lawyer from seeking employment by improper overtures, from acting in cases of divided loyalties, and from submitting to the control of others in the exercise of his judgment. Moreover, a person who entrusts legal matters to a lawyer is protected by the attorney-client privilege and by the duty of the lawyer to hold inviolate the confidences and secrets of his client.

EC 3-4   A layman who seeks legal services often is not in a position to judge whether he will receive proper professional attention. The entrustment of a legal matter may well involve the confidences, the reputation, the property, the freedom, or even the life of the client. Proper protection of members of the public demands that no person be permitted to act in the confidential and demanding capacity of a lawyer unless he is subject to the regulations of the legal profession.

EC 3-5   It is neither necessary nor desirable to attempt the formulation of a single, specific definition of what constitutes the practice of law. Functionally, the practice of law relates to the rendition of services for others that call for the professional judgment of a lawyer. The essence of the professional judgment of the lawyer is his educated ability to relate the general body and philosophy of law to a specific legal problem of a client; and thus, the public interest will be better served if only lawyers are permitted to act in matters involving professional judgment. Where this professional judgment is not involved, non-lawyers, such as court clerks, police officers, abstracters, and many governmental employees, may engage in occupations that require a special knowledge of law in certain areas. But the services of a lawyer are essential in the public interest whenever the exercise of professional legal judgment is required.

EC 3-6   A lawyer often delegates tasks to clerks, secretaries, and other lay persons. Such delegation is proper if the lawyer maintains a direct relationship with his client, supervises the delegated work, and has complete professional responsibility for the work product. This delegation enables a lawyer to render legal service more economically and efficiently.

EC 3-7   The prohibition against a non-lawyer practicing law does not prevent a layman from representing himself, for then he is ordinarily exposing only himself to possible injury. The purpose of the legal profession is to make educated legal representation available to the public; but anyone who does not wish to avail himself of such representation is not required to do so. Even so, the legal profession should help members of the public to recognize legal problems and to understand why it may be unwise for them to act for themselves in matters having legal consequences.

EC 3-8   Since a lawyer should not aid or encourage a layman to practice law, he should not practice law in association with a layman or otherwise share legal fees with a layman. This does not mean, however, that the pecuniary value of the interest of a deceased lawyer in his firm or practice may not be paid to his estate or specified persons such as his widow or heirs. In like manner, profit-sharing retirement plans of a lawyer or law firm which include non-lawyer office employees are not improper. These limited exceptions to the rule against sharing legal fees with laymen are permissible since they do not aid or encourage laymen to practice law.

EC 3-9   Regulation of the practice of law is accomplished principally by the respective states. Authority to engage in the practice of law conferred in any jurisdiction is not per se a grant of the right to practice elsewhere, and it is improper for a lawyer to engage in practice where he is not permitted by law or by court order to do so. However, the demands of business and the mobility of our society pose distinct problems in the regulation of the practice of law by the states. In furtherance of the public interest, the legal profession should discourage regulation that unreasonably imposes territorial limitations upon the right of a lawyer to handle the legal affairs of his client or upon the opportunity of a client to obtain the services of a lawyer of his choice in all matters including the presentation of a contested matter in a tribunal before which the lawyer is not permanently admitted to practice.

CANON 4

A Lawyer Should Preserve the Confidences and Secrets of a Client

Ethical Considerations

EC 4-1   Both the fiduciary relationship existing between lawyer and client and the proper functioning of the legal system require the preservation by the lawyer of confidences and secrets of one who has employed or sought to employ him. A client must feel free to discuss whatever he wishes with his lawyer and a lawyer must be equally free to obtain information beyond that volunteered by his client. A lawyer should be fully informed of all the facts of the matter he is handling in order for his client to obtain the full advantage of our legal system. It is for the lawyer in the exercise of his independent professional judgment to separate the relevant and important from the irrelevant and unimportant. The observance of the ethical obligation of a lawyer to hold inviolate the confidences and secrets of his client not only facilitates the full development of facts essential to proper representation of the client but also encourages laymen to seek early legal assistance.

EC 4-2   The obligation to protect confidences and secrets obviously does not preclude a lawyer from revealing information when his client consents after full disclosure, when necessary to perform his professional employment, when permitted by a Disciplinary Rule, or when required by law. Unless the client otherwise directs, a lawyer may disclose the affairs of his client to partners or associates of his firm. It is a matter of common knowledge that the normal operation of a law office exposes confidential professional information to non-lawyer employees of the office, particularly secretaries and those having access to the files; and this obligates a lawyer to exercise care in selecting and training his employees so that the sanctity of all confidences and secrets of his clients may be preserved. If the obligation extends to two or more clients as to the same information, a lawyer should obtain the permission of all before revealing the information. A lawyer must always be sensitive to the rights and wishes of his client and act scrupulously in the making of decisions which may involve the disclosure of information obtained in his professional relationship. Thus, in the absence of consent of his client after full disclosure, a lawyer should not associate another lawyer in the handling of a matter; nor should he, in the absence of consent, seek counsel from another lawyer if there is a reasonable possibility that the identity of the client or his confidences or secrets would be revealed to such lawyer. Both social amenities and professional duty should cause a lawyer to shun indiscreet conversations concerning his clients.

EC 4-3   Unless the client otherwise directs, it is not improper for a lawyer to give limited information from his files to an outside agency necessary for statistical, bookkeeping, accounting, data processing, banking, printing, or other legitimate purposes, provided he exercises due care in the selection of the agency and warns the agency that the information must be kept confidential.

EC 4-4   The attorney-client privilege is more limited than the ethical obligation of a lawyer to guard the confidences and secrets of his client. This ethical precept, unlike the evidentiary privilege, exists without regard to the nature or source of information or the fact that others share the knowledge. A lawyer should endeavor to act in a manner which preserves the evidentiary privilege; for example, he should avoid professional discussions in the presence of persons to whom the privilege does not extend. A lawyer owes an obligation to advise the client of the attorney-client privilege and timely to assert the privilege unless it is waived by the client.

EC 4-5   A lawyer should not use information acquired in the course of the representation of a client to the disadvantage of the client and a lawyer should not use, except with the consent of his client after full disclosure, such information for his own purposes. Likewise, a lawyer should be diligent in his efforts to prevent the misuse of such information by his employees and associates. Care should be exercised by a lawyer to prevent the disclosure of the confidences and secrets of one client to another, and no employment should be accepted that might require such disclosure.

EC 4-6   The obligation of a lawyer to preserve the confidences and secrets of his client continues after the termination of his employment. Thus a lawyer should not attempt to sell a law practice as a going business because, among other reasons, to do so would involve the disclosure of confidences and secrets. A lawyer should also provide for the protection of the confidences and secrets of his client following the termination of the practice of the lawyer, whether termination is due to death, disability, or retirement. For example, a lawyer might provide for the personal papers of the client to be returned to him and for the papers of the lawyer to be delivered to another lawyer or to be destroyed. In determining the method of disposition, the instructions and wishes of the client should be a dominant consideration.

CANON 5

A Lawyer Should Exercise
Independent Professional Judgment
on Behalf of a Client

Ethical Considerations

EC 5-1   The professional judgment of a lawyer should be exercised, within the bounds of the law, solely for the benefit of his client and free of compromising influences and loyalties. Neither his personal interests, the interests of other clients, nor the desires of third persons should be permitted to dilute his loyalty to his client.

*Interests of a Lawyer That May
Affect His Judgment*

EC 5-2   A lawyer should not accept proffered employment if his personal interests or desires will, or there is a reasonable probability that they will, affect adversely the advice to be given or services to be rendered the prospective client. After accepting employment, a lawyer carefully should refrain from acquiring a property right or assuming a position that would tend to make his judgment less protective of the interests of his client.

EC 5-3   The self-interest of a lawyer resulting from his ownership of property in which his client also has an interest or which may affect property of his client may interfere with the exercise of free judgment on behalf of his client. If such interference would occur with respect to a prospective client, a lawyer should decline employment proffered by him. After accepting employment, a lawyer should not acquire property rights that would adversely affect his professional judgment in the representation of his client. Even if the property interests of a lawyer do not presently interfere with the exercise of his independent judgment, but the likehood of interference can reasonably be foreseen by him, a lawyer should explain the situation to his client and should decline employment or withdraw unless the client consents to the continuance of the relationship after full disclosure. A lawyer should not seek to persuade his client to permit him to invest in an undertaking of his client nor make improper use of his professional relationship to influence his client to invest in an enterprise in which the lawyer is interested.

EC 5-4   If, in the course of his representation of a client, a lawyer is permitted to receive from his client a beneficial ownership in publication rights relating to the subject matter of the employment, he may be tempted to subordinate the interests of his client to his own anticipated pecuniary gain. For example, a lawyer in a criminal case who obtains from his client television, radio, motion picture, newspaper, magazine, book, or other publication rights with respect to the case may be influenced, consciously or unconsciously, to a course of conduct that will enhance the value of his publication rights to the prejudice of his client. To prevent these potentially differing interests, such arrangements should be scrupulously avoided prior to the termination of all aspects of the matter giving rise to the employment, even though his employment has previously ended.

EC 5-5   A lawyer should not suggest to his client that a gift be made to himself or for his benefit. If a lawyer accepts a gift from his client, he is peculiarly susceptible to the charge that he unduly influenced or over-reached the client. If a client voluntarily offers to make a gift to his lawyer, the lawyer may accept the gift, but before doing so, he should urge that his client secure disinterested advice from an independent, competent person who is cognizant of all the circumstances. Other than in exceptional circumstances, a lawyer should insist that an instrument in which his client desires to name him beneficially be prepared by another lawyer selected by the client.

EC 5-6   A lawyer should not consciously influence a client to name him as executor, trustee, or lawyer in an instrument. In those cases where a client wishes to name his lawyer as such, care should be taken by the lawyer to avoid even the appearance of impropriety.

EC 5-7   The possibility of an adverse effect upon the exercise of free judgment by a lawyer on behalf of his client during litigation generally makes it undesirable for the lawyer to acquire a proprietary interest in the cause of his client or otherwise to become financially interested in the outcome of the litigation. However, it is not improper for a lawyer to protect his right to collect a fee for his services by the assertion of legally permissible liens, even though by doing so he may acquire an interest in the outcome of litigation. Although a contingent fee arrangement gives a lawyer a financial interest in the outcome of litigation, a reasonable contingent fee is permissible in civil cases because it may be the only means by which a layman can obtain the services of a lawyer of his choice. But a lawyer, because he is in a better position to evaluate a cause of action, should enter into a contingent fee arrangement only in those instances where the arrangement will be beneficial to the client.

EC 5-8   A financial interest in the outcome of litigation also results if monetary advances are made by the lawyer to his client. Although this assistance generally is not encouraged, there are instances when it is not improper to make loans to a client. For example, the advancing or guaranteeing of payment of the costs and expenses of litigation by a lawyer may be the only way a client can enforce his cause of action, but the ultimate liability for such costs and expenses must be that of the client.

EC 5-9   Occasionally a lawyer is called upon to decide in a particular case whether he will be a witness or an advocate. If a lawyer is both counsel and witness, he becomes more easily impeachable for interest and thus may be a less effective witness. Conversely, the opposing counsel may be handicapped in challenging the credibility of the lawyer when the lawyer also appears as an advocate in the case. An advocate who becomes a witness is in the unseemly and ineffective position of arguing his own credibility. The roles of an advocate and of a witness are inconsistent; the function of an advocate is to advance or argue the cause of another, while that of a witness is to state facts objectively.

EC 5-10   Problems incident to the lawyer-witness relationship arise at different stages; they relate either to whether a lawyer should accept employment or should withdraw from employment. Regardless of when the problem arises, his decision is to be governed by the same basic considerations. It is not objectionable for a lawyer who is a potential witness to be an advocate if it is unlikely that he will be called as a witness because his testimony would be merely cumulative or if his testimony will relate only to an uncontested issue. In the exceptional situation where it will be manifestly unfair to the client for the lawyer to refuse employment or to withdraw when he will likely be a witness on a contested issue, he may serve as advocate even though he may be a witness. In making such decision, he should determine the personal or financial sacrifice of the client that may result from his refusal of employment or withdrawal therefrom, the materiality of his testimony, and the effectiveness of his representation in view of his personal involvement. In weighing these factors, it should be clear that refusal or withdrawal will impose an unreasonable hardship upon the client before the lawyer accepts or continues the employment. Where the question arises, doubts should be resolved in favor of the lawyer testifying and against his becoming or continuing as an advocate.

EC 5-11   A lawyer should not permit his personal interests to influence his advice relative to a suggestion by his client that additional counsel be employed. In like manner, his personal interests should not deter him from suggesting that additional counsel be employed; on the contrary, he should be alert to the desirability of recommending additional counsel when, in his judgment, the proper representation of his client requires it. However, a lawyer should advise his client not to employ additional counsel suggested by the client if the lawyer believes that such employment would be a disservice to the client, and he should disclose the reasons for his belief.

EC 5-12   Inability of co-counsel to agree on a matter vital to the representation of their client requires that their disagreement be submitted by them jointly to their client for his resolution, and the decision of the client shall control the action to be taken.

EC 5-13   A lawyer should not maintain membership in or be influenced by any organization of employees that undertakes to prescribe, direct, or suggest when or how he should fulfill his professional obligations to a person or organization that employs him as a lawyer. Although it is not necessarily improper for a lawyer employed by a corporation or similar entity to be a member of an organization of employees, he should be vigilant to safeguard his fidelity as a lawyer to his employer, free from outside influences.

Interests of Multiple Clients

EC 5-14   Maintaining the independence of professional judgment required of a lawyer precludes his acceptance or continuation of employment that will adversely affect his judgment on behalf of or dilute his loyalty to a client. This problem arises whenever a lawyer is asked to represent two or more clients who may have differing interests, whether such interests be conflicting, inconsistent, diverse, or otherwise discordant.

EC 5-15   If a lawyer is requested to undertake or to continue representation of multiple clients having potentially differing interests, he must weigh carefully the possibility that his judgment may be impaired or his loyalty divided if he accepts or continues the employment. He should resolve all doubts against the propriety of the representation. A lawyer should never represent in litigation multiple clients with differing interests; and there are few situations in which he would be justified in representing in litigation multiple clients with potentially differing interests. If a lawyer accepted such employment and the interests did become actually differing, he would have to withdraw from employment with likelihood of resulting hardship on the clients; and for this reason it is preferable that he refuse the employment initially. On the other hand, there are many instances in which a lawyer may properly serve multiple clients having potentially differing interests in matters not involving litigation. If the interests vary only slightly, it is generally likely that the lawyer will not be subjected to an adverse influence and that he can retain his independent judgment on behalf of each client; and if the interests become differing, withdrawal is less likely to have a disruptive effect upon the causes of his clients.

EC 5-16   In those instances in which a lawyer is justified in representing two or more clients having differing interests, it is nevertheless essential that each client be given the opportunity to evaluate his need for representation free of any potential conflict and to obtain other counsel if he so desires. Thus before a lawyer may represent multiple clients, he should explain fully to each client the implications of the common representation and should accept or continue employment only if the clients consent. If there are present other circumstances that might cause any of the multiple clients to question the undivided loyalty of the lawyer, he should also advise all of the clients of those circumstances.

EC 5-17 Typically recurring situations involving potentially differing interests are those in which a lawyer is asked to represent codefendants in a criminal case, co-plaintiffs in a personal injury case, an insured and his insurer, and beneficiaries of the estate of a decedent. Whether a lawyer can fairly and adequately protect the interests of multiple clients in these and similar situations depends upon an analysis of each case. In certain circumstances, there may exist little chance of the judgment of the lawyer being adversely affected by the slight possibility that the interests will become actually differing; in other circumstances, the chance of adverse effect upon his judgment is not unlikely.

EC 5-18 A lawyer employed or retained by a corporation or similar entity owes his allegiance to the entity and not to a stockholder, director, officer, employee, representative, or other person connected with the entity. In advising the entity, a lawyer should keep paramount its interests and his professional judgment should not be influenced by the personal desires of any person or organization. Occasionally a lawyer for an entity is requested by a stockholder, director, officer, employee, representative, or other person connected with the entity to represent him in an individual capacity; in such case the lawyer may serve the individual only if the lawyer is convinced that differing interests are not present.

EC 5-19 A lawyer may represent several clients whose interests are not actually or potentially differing. Nevertheless, he should explain any circumstances that might cause a client to question his undivided loyalty. Regardless of the belief of a lawyer that he may properly represent multiple clients, he must defer to a client who holds the contrary belief and withdraw from representation of that client.

EC 5-20 A lawyer is often asked to serve as an impartial arbitrator or mediator in matters which involve present or former clients. He may serve in either capacity if he first discloses such present or former relationships. After a lawyer has undertaken to act as an impartial arbitrator or mediator, he should not thereafter represent in the dispute any of the parties involved.

Desires of Third Persons

EC 5-21 The obligation of a lawyer to exercise professional judgment solely on behalf of his client requires that he disregard the desires of others that might impair his free judgment. The desires of a third person will seldom adversely affect a lawyer unless that person is in a position to exert strong economic, political, or social pressures upon the lawyer. These influences are often subtle, and a lawyer must be alert to their existence. A lawyer subjected to outside pressures should make full disclosure of them to his client; and if he or his client believes that the effectiveness of his representation has been or will be impaired thereby, the lawyer should take proper steps to withdraw from representation of his client.

EC 5-22 Economic, political, or social pressures by third persons are less likely to impinge upon the independent judgment of a lawyer in a matter in which he is compensated directly by his client and his professional work is exclusively with his client. On the other hand, if a lawyer is compensated from a source other than his client, he may feel a sense of responsibility to someone other than his client.

EC 5-23 A person or organization that pays or furnishes lawyers to represent others possesses a potential power to exert strong pressures against the independent judgment of those lawyers. Some employers may be interested in furthering their own economic, political, or social goals without regard to the professional responsibility of the lawyer to his individual client. Others may be far more concerned with establishment or extension of legal principles than in the immediate protection of the rights of the lawyer's individual client. On some occasions, decisions on priority of work may be made by the employer rather than the lawyer with the result that prosecution of work already undertaken for clients is postponed to their detriment. Similarly, an employer may seek, consciously or unconsciously, to further its own economic interests through the action of the lawyers employed by it. Since a lawyer must always be free to exercise his professional judgment without regard to the interests or motives of a third person, the lawyer who is employed by one to represent another must constantly guard against erosion of his professional freedom.

EC 5-24 To assist a lawyer in preserving his professional independence, a number of courses are available to him. For example, a lawyer should not practice with or in the form of a professional legal corporation, even though the corporate form is permitted by law, if any director, officer, or stockholder of it is a non-lawyer. Although a lawyer may be employed by a business corporation with non-lawyers serving as directors or officers, and they necessarily have the right to make decisions of business policy, a lawyer must decline to accept direction of his professional judgment from any layman. Various types of legal aid offices are administered by boards of directors composed of lawyers and laymen. A lawyer should not accept employment from such an organization unless the board sets only broad policies and there is no interference in the relationship of the lawyer and the individual client he serves. Where a lawyer is employed by an organization, a written agreement that defines the relationship between him and the organization and provides for his independence is desirable since it may serve to prevent misunderstanding as to their respective roles. Although other innovations in the means of supplying legal counsel may develop, the responsibility of the lawyer to maintain his professional independence remains constant, and the legal profession must insure that changing circumstances do not result in loss of the professional independence of the lawyer.

CANON 6

A Lawyer Should Represent a Client Competently

Ethical Considerations

EC 6-1   Because of his vital role in the legal process, a lawyer should act with competence and proper care in representing clients. He should strive to become and remain proficient in his practice and should accept employment only in matters which he is or intends to become competent to handle.

EC 6-2   A lawyer is aided in attaining and maintaining his competence by keeping abreast of current legal literature and developments, participating in continuing legal education programs, concentrating in particular areas of the law, and by utilizing other available means. He has the additional ethical obligation to assist in improving the legal profession, and he may do so by participating in bar activities intended to advance the quality and standards of members of the profession. Of particular importance is the careful training of his younger associates and the giving of sound guidance to all lawyers who consult him. In short, a lawyer should strive at all levels to aid the legal profession in advancing the highest possible standards of integrity and competence and to meet those standards himself.

EC 6-3   While the licensing of a lawyer is evidence that he has met the standards then prevailing for admission to the bar, a lawyer generally should not accept employment in any area of the law in which he is not qualified. However, he may accept such employment if in good faith he expects to become qualified through study and investigation, as long as such preparation would not result in unreasonable delay or expense to his client. Proper preparation and representation may require the association by the lawyer of professionals in other disciplines. A lawyer offered employment in a matter in which he is not and does not expect to become so qualified should either decline the employment or, with the consent of his client, accept the employment and associate a lawyer who is competent in the matter.

EC 6-4 Having undertaken representation, a lawyer should use proper care to safeguard the interests of his client. If a lawyer has accepted employment in a matter beyond his competence but in which he expected to become competent, he should diligently undertake the work and study necessary to qualify himself. In addition to being qualified to handle a particular matter, his obligation to his client requires him to prepare adequately for and give appropriate attention to his legal work.

EC 6-5 A lawyer should have pride in his professional endeavors. His obligation to act competently calls for higher motivation than that arising from fear of civil liability or disciplinary penalty.

EC 6-6 A lawyer should not seek, by contract or other means, to limit his individual liability to his client for his malpractice. A lawyer who handles the affairs of his client properly has no need to attempt to limit his liability for his professional activities and one who does not handle the affairs of his client properly should not be permitted to do so. A lawyer who is a stockholder in or is associated with a professional legal corporation may, however, limit his liability for malpractice of his associates in the corporation, but only to the extent permitted by law.

CANON 7

A Lawyer Should Represent a Client Zealously Within the Bounds of the Law

Ethical Considerations

EC 7-1 The duty of a lawyer, both to his client and to the legal system, is to represent his client zealously within the bounds of the law, which includes Disciplinary Rules and enforceable professional regulations. The professional responsibility of a lawyer derives from his membership in a profession which has the duty of assisting members of the public to secure and protect available legal rights and benefits. In our government of laws and not of men, each member of our society is entitled to have his conduct judged and regulated in accordance with the law; to seek any lawful objective through legally permissible means; and to present for adjudication any lawful claim, issue, or defense.

EC 7-2   The bounds of the law in a given case are often difficult to ascertain. The language of legislative enactments and judicial opinions may be uncertain as applied to varying factual situations. The limits and specific meaning of apparently relevant law may be made doubtful by changing or developing constitutional interpretations, inadequately expressed statutes or judicial opinions, and changing public and judicial attitudes. Certainty of law ranges from well-settled rules through areas of conflicting authority to areas without precedent.

EC 7-3   Where the bounds of law are uncertain, the action of a lawyer may depend on whether he is serving as advocate or adviser. A lawyer may serve simultaneously as both advocate and adviser, but the two roles are essentially different. In asserting a position on behalf of his client, an advocate for the most part deals with past conduct and must take the facts as he finds them. By contrast, a lawyer serving as adviser primarily assists his client in determining the course of future conduct and relationships. While serving as advocate, a lawyer should resolve in favor of his client doubts as to the bounds of the law. In serving a client as adviser, a lawyer in appropriate circumstances should give his professional opinion as to what the ultimate decisions of the courts would likely be as to the applicable law.

Duty of the Lawyer to a Client

EC 7-4   The advocate may urge any permissible construction of the law favorable to his client, without regard to his professional opinion as to the likelihood that the construction will ultimately prevail. His conduct is within the bounds of the law, and therefore permissible, if the position taken is supported by the law or is supportable by a good faith argument for an extension, modification, or reversal of the law. However, a lawyer is not justified in asserting a position in litigation that is frivolous.

EC 7-5   A lawyer as adviser furthers the interest of his client by giving his professional opinion as to what he believes would likely be the ultimate decision of the courts on the matter at hand and by informing his client of the practical effect of such decision. He may continue in the representation of his client even though his client has elected to pursue a course of conduct contrary to the advice of the lawyer so long as he does not thereby knowingly assist the client to engage in illegal conduct or to take a frivolous legal position. A lawyer should never encourage or aid his client to commit criminal acts or counsel his client on how to violate the law and avoid punishment therefor.

EC 7-6   Whether the proposed action of a lawyer is within the bounds of the law may be a perplexing question when his client is contemplating a course of conduct having legal consequences that vary according to the client's intent, motive, or desires at the time of the action. Often a lawyer is asked to assist his client in developing evidence relevant to the state of mind of the client at a particular time. He may properly assist his client in the development and preservation of evidence of existing motive, intent, or desire; obviously, he may not do anything furthering the creation or preservation of false evidence. In many cases a lawyer may not be certain as to the state of mind of his client, and in those situations he should resolve reasonable doubts in favor of his client.

EC 7-7   In certain areas of legal representation not affecting the merits of the cause or substantially prejudicing the rights of a client, a lawyer is entitled to make decisions on his own. But otherwise the authority to make decisions is exclusively that of the client and, if made within the framework of the law, such decisions are binding on his lawyer. As typical examples in civil cases, it is for the client to decide whether he will accept a settlement offer or whether he will waive his right to plead an affirmative defense. A defense lawyer in a criminal case has the duty to advise his client fully on whether a particular plea to a charge appears to be desirable and as to the prospects of success on appeal, but it is for the client to decide what plea should be entered and whether an appeal should be taken.

EC 7-8   A lawyer should exert his best efforts to insure that decisions of his client are made only after the client has been informed of relevant considerations. A lawyer ought to initiate this decision-making process if the client does not do so. Advice of a lawyer to his client need not be confined to purely legal considerations. A lawyer should advise his client of the possible effect of each legal alternative. A lawyer should bring to bear upon this decision-making process the fullness of his experience as well as his objective viewpoint. In assisting his client to reach a proper decision, it is often desirable for a lawyer to point out those factors which may lead to a decision that is morally just as well as legally permissible. He may emphasize the possibility of harsh consequences that might result from assertion of legally permissible positions. In the final analysis, however, the lawyer should always remember that the decision whether to forego legally available objectives or methods because of non-legal factors is ultimately for the client and not for himself. In the event that the client in a non-adjudicatory matter insists upon a course of conduct that is contrary to the judgment and advice of the lawyer but not prohibited by Disciplinary Rules, the lawyer may withdraw from the employment.

EC 7-9   In the exercise of his professional judgment on those decisions which are for his determination in the handling of a legal matter, a lawyer should always act in a manner consistent with the best interests of his client. However, when an action in the best interest of his client seems to him to be unjust, he may ask his client for permission to forego such action.

EC 7-10   The duty of a lawyer to represent his client with zeal does not militate against his concurrent obligation to treat with consideration all persons involved in the legal process and to avoid the infliction of needless harm.

EC 7-11   The responsibilities of a lawyer may vary according to the intelligence, experience, mental condition or age of a client, the obligation of a public officer, or the nature of a particular proceeding. Examples include the representation of an illiterate or an incompetent, service as a public prosecutor or other government lawyer, and appearances before administrative and legislative bodies.

EC 7-12   Any mental or physical condition of a client that renders him incapable of making a considered judgment on his own behalf casts additional responsibilities upon his lawyer. Where an incompetent is acting through a guardian or other legal representative, a lawyer must look to such representative for those decisions which are normally the prerogative of the client to make. If a client under disability has no legal representative, his lawyer may be compelled in court proceedings to make decisions on behalf of the client. If the client is capable of understanding the matter in question or of contributing to the advancement of his interests, regardless of whether he is legally disqualified from performing certain acts, the lawyer should obtain from him all possible aid. If the disability of a client and the lack of a legal representative compel the lawyer to make decisions for his client, the lawyer should consider all circumstances then prevailing and act with care to safeguard and advance the interests of his client. But obviously a lawyer cannot perform any act or make any decision which the law requires his client to perform or make, either acting for himself if competent, or by a duly constituted representative if legally incompetent.

EC 7-13   The responsibility of a public prosecutor differs from that of the usual advocate; his duty is to seek justice, not merely to convict. This special duty exists because: (1) the prosecutor represents the sovereign and therefore should use restraint in the discretionary exercise of governmental powers, such as in the selection of cases to prosecute; (2) during trial the prosecutor is not only an advocate but he also may make decisions normally made by an individual client, and those affecting the public interest should be fair to all; and (3) in our system of criminal justice the accused is to be given the benefit of all reasonable doubts. With respect to evidence and witnesses, the prosecutor has responsibilities different from those of a lawyer in private practice: the prosecutor should make timely disclosure to the defense of available evidence, known to him, that tends to negate the guilt of the accused, mitigate the degree of the offense, or reduce the punishment. Further, a prosecutor should not intentionally avoid pursuit of evidence merely because he believes it will damage the prosecutor's case or aid the accused.

EC 7-14   A government lawyer who has discretionary power relative to litigation should refrain from instituting or continuing litigation that is obviously unfair. A government lawyer not having such discretionary power who believes there is lack of merit in a controversy submitted to him should so advise his superiors and recommend the avoidance of unfair litigation. A government lawyer in a civil action or administrative proceeding has the responsibility to seek justice and to develop a full and fair record, and he should not use his position or the economic power of the government to harass parties or to bring about unjust settlements or results.

EC 7-15   The nature and purpose of proceedings before administrative agencies vary widely. The proceedings may be legislative or quasijudicial, or a combination of both. They may be *ex parte* in character, in which event they may originate either at the instance of the agency or upon motion of an interested party. The scope of an inquiry may be purely investigative or it may be truly adversary looking toward the adjudication of specific rights of a party or of classes of parties. The foregoing are but examples of some of the types of proceedings conducted by administrative agencies. A lawyer appearing before an administrative agency, regardless of the nature of the proceeding it is conducting, has the continuing duty to advance the cause of his client within the bounds of the law. Where the applicable rules of the agency impose specific obligations upon a lawyer, it is his duty to comply therewith, unless the lawyer has a legitimate basis for challenging the validity thereof. In all appearances before administrative agencies, a lawyer should identify himself, his client if identity of his client is not privileged, and the representative nature of his appearance. It is not improper, however, for a lawyer to seek from an agency information available to the public without identifying his client.

EC 7-16   The primary business of a legislative body is to enact laws rather than to adjudicate controversies, although on occasion the activities of a legislative body may take on the characteristics of an adversary proceeding, particularly in investigative and impeachment matters. The role of a lawyer supporting or opposing proposed legislation normally is quite different from his role in representing a person under investigation or on trial by a legislative body. When a lawyer appears in connection with proposed legislation, he seeks to affect the lawmaking process, but when he appears on behalf of a client in investigatory or impeachment proceedings, he is concerned with the protection of the rights of his client. In either event, he should identify himself and his client, if identity of his client is not privileged, and should comply with applicable laws and legislative rules.

EC 7-17   The obligation of loyalty to his client applies only to a lawyer in the discharge of his professional duties and implies no obligation to adopt a personal viewpoint favorable to the interests or desires of his client. While a lawyer must act always with circumspection in order that his conduct will not adversely affect the rights of a client in a matter he is then handling, he may take positions on public issues and espouse legal reforms he favors without regard to the individual views of any client.

EC 7-18   The legal system in its broadest sense functions best when persons in need of legal advice or assistance are represented by their own counsel. For this reason a lawyer should not communicate on the subject matter of the representation of his client with a person he knows to be represented in the matter by a lawyer, unless pursuant to law or rule of court or unless he has the consent of the lawyer for that person. If one is not represented by counsel, a lawyer representing another may have to deal directly with the unrepresented person; in such an instance, a lawyer should not undertake to give advice to the person who is attempting to represent himself, except that he may advise him to obtain a lawyer.

Duty of the Lawyer to the
Adversary System of Justice

EC 7-19   Our legal system provides for the adjudication of disputes governed by the rules of substantive, evidentiary, and procedural law. An adversary presentation counters the natural human tendency to judge too swiftly in terms of the familiar that which is not yet fully known; the advocate, by his zealous preparation and presentation of facts and law, enables the tribunal to come to the hearing with an open and neutral mind and to render impartial judgments. The duty of a lawyer to his client and his duty to the legal system are the same: to represent his client zealously within the bounds of the law.

EC 7-20   In order to function properly, our adjudicative process requires an informed, impartial tribunal capable of administering justice promptly and efficiently according to procedures that command public confidence and respect. Not only must there be competent, adverse presentation of evidence and issues, but a tribunal must be aided by rules appropriate to an effective and dignified process. The procedures under which tribunals operate in our adversary system have been prescribed largely by legislative enactments, court rules and decisions, and administrative rules. Through the years certain concepts of proper professional conduct have become rules of law applicable to the adversary adjudicative process. Many of these concepts are the bases for standards of professional conduct set forth in the Disciplinary Rules.

EC 7-21   The civil adjudicative process is primarily designed for the settlement of disputes between parties, while the criminal process is designed for the protection of society as a whole. Threatening to use, or using, the criminal process to coerce adjustment of private civil claims or controversies is a subversion of that process; further, the person against whom the criminal process is so misused may be deterred from asserting his legal rights and thus the usefulness of the civil process in settling private disputes is impaired. As in all cases of abuse of judicial process, the improper use of criminal process tends to diminish public confidence in our legal system.

EC 7-22   Respect for judicial rulings is essential to the proper administration of justice; however, a litigant or his lawyer may, in good faith and within the framework of the law, take steps to test the correctness of a ruling of a tribunal.

EC 7-23   The complexity of law often makes it difficult for a tribunal to be fully informed unless the pertinent law is presented by the lawyers in the cause. A tribunal that is fully informed on the applicable law is better able to make a fair and accurate determination of the matter before it. The adversary system contemplates that each lawyer will present and argue the existing law in the light most favorable to his client. Where a lawyer knows of legal authority in the controlling jurisdiction directly adverse to the position of his client, he should inform the tribunal of its existence unless his adversary has done so; but, having made such disclosure, he may challenge its soundness in whole or in part.

EC 7-24   In order to bring about just and informed decisions, evidentiary and procedural rules have been established by tribunals to permit the inclusion of relevant evidence and argument and the exclusion of all other considerations. The expression by a lawyer of his personal opinion as to the justness of a cause, as to the credibility of a witness, as to the culpability of a civil litigant, or as to the guilt or innocence of an accused is not a proper subject for argument to the trier of fact. It is improper as to factual matters because admissible evidence possessed by a lawyer should be presented only as sworn testimony. It is improper as to all other matters because, were the rule otherwise, the silence of a lawyer on a given occasion could be construed unfavorably to his client. However, a lawyer may argue, on his analysis of the evidence, for any position or conclusion with respect to any of the foregoing matters.

EC 7-25   Rules of evidence and procedure are designed to lead to just decisions and are part of the framework of the law. Thus while a lawyer may take steps in good faith and within the framework of the law to test the validity of rules, he is not justified in consciously violating such rules and he should be diligent in his efforts to guard against his unintentional violation of them. As examples, a lawyer should subscribe to or verify only those pleadings that he believes are in compliance with applicable law and rules; a lawyer should not make any prefatory statement before a tribunal in regard to the purported facts of the case on trial unless he believes that his statement will be supported by admissible evidence; a lawyer should not ask a witness a question solely for the purpose of harassing or embarrassing him; and a lawyer should not by subterfuge put before a jury matters which it cannot properly consider.

EC 7-26   The law and Disciplinary Rules prohibit the use of fraudulent, false, or perjured testimony or evidence. A lawyer who knowingly participates in introduction of such testimony or evidence is subject to discipline. A lawyer should, however, present any admissible evidence his client desires to have presented unless he knows, or from facts within his knowledge should know, that such testimony or evidence is false, fraudulent, or perjured.

EC 7-27   Because it interferes with the proper administration of justice, a lawyer should not suppress evidence that he or his client has a legal obligation to reveal or produce. In like manner, a lawyer should not advise or cause a person to secrete himself or to leave the jurisdiction of a tribunal for the purpose of making him unavailable as a witness therein.

EC 7-28   Witnesses should always testify truthfully and should be free from any financial inducements that might tempt them to do otherwise. A lawyer should not pay or agree to pay a non-expert witness an amount in excess of reimbursement for expenses and financial loss incident to his being a witness; however, a lawyer may pay or agree to pay an expert witness a reasonable fee for his services as an expert. But in no event should a lawyer pay or agree to pay a contingent fee to any witness. A lawyer should exercise reasonable diligence to see that his client and lay associates conform to these standards.

EC 7-29   To safeguard the impartiality that is essential to the judicial process, veniremen and jurors should be protected against extraneous influences. When impartiality is present, public confidence in the judicial system is enhanced. There should be no extrajudicial communication with veniremen prior to trial or with jurors during trial by or on behalf of a lawyer connected with the case. Furthermore, a lawyer who is not connected with the case should not communicate with or cause another to communicate with a venireman or a juror about the case. After the trial, communication by a lawyer with jurors is permitted so long as he refrains from asking questions or making comments that tend to harass or embarrass the juror or to influence actions of the juror in future cases. Were a lawyer to be prohibited from communicating after trial with a juror, he could not ascertain if the verdict might be subject to legal challenge, in which event the invalidity of a verdict might go undetected. When an extrajudicial communication by a lawyer with a juror is permitted by law, it should be made considerately and with deference to the personal feelings of the juror.

EC 7-30   Vexations or harassing investigations of veniremen or jurors seriously impair the effectiveness of our jury system. For this reason, a lawyer or anyone on his behalf who conducts an investigation of venirement or jurors should act with circumspection and restraint.

EC 7-31   Communications with or investigations of members of families of veniremen or jurors by a lawyer or by anyone on his behalf are subject to the restrictions imposed upon the lawyer with respect to his communications with or investigations of veniremen and jurors.

EC 7-32   Because of his duty to aid in preserving the integrity of the jury system, a lawyer who learns of improper conduct by or towards a veniremen, a juror, or a member of the family of either should make a prompt report to the court regarding such conduct.

EC 7-33   A goal of our legal system is that each party shall have his case, criminal or civil, adjudicated by an impartial tribunal. The attainment of this goal may be defeated by dissemination of news or comments which tend to influence judge or jury. Such news or comments may prevent prospective jurors from being impartial at the outset of the trial and may also interfere with the obligation of jurors to base their verdict solely upon the evidence admitted in the trial. The release by a lawyer of out-of-court statements regarding an anticipated or pending trial may improperly affect the impartiality of the tribunal. For these reasons, standards for permissible and prohibited conduct of a lawyer with respect to trial publicity have been established.

EC 7-34 The impartiality of a public servant in our legal system may be impaired by the receipt of gifts or loans. A lawyer, therefore, is never justified in making a gift or a loan to a judge, a hearing officer, or an official or employee of a tribunal except as permitted by Section C(4) of Canon 5 of the Code of Judicial Conduct, but a lawyer may make a contribution to the campaign fund of a candidate for judicial office in conformity with Section B(2) under Canon 7 of the Code of Judicial Conduct.

EC 7-35 All litigants and lawyers should have access to tribunals on an equal basis. Generally, in adversary proceedings a lawyer should not communicate with a judge relative to a matter pending before, or which is to be brought before, a tribunal over which he presides in circumstances which might have the effect or give the appearance of granting undue advantage to one party. For example, a lawyer should not communicate with a tribunal by a writing unless a copy thereof is promptly delivered to opposing counsel or to the adverse party if he is not represented by a lawyer. Ordinarily an oral communication by a lawyer with a judge or hearing officer should be made only upon adequate notice to opposing counsel, or, if there is none, to the opposing party. A lawyer should not condone or lend himself to private importunities by another with a judge or hearing officer on behalf of himself or his client.

EC 7-36 Judicial hearings ought to be conducted through dignified and orderly procedures designed to protect the rights of all parties. Although a lawyer has the duty to represent his client zealously, he should not engage in any conduct that offends the dignity and decorum of proceedings. While maintaining his independence, a lawyer should be respectful, courteous, and above-board in his relations with a judge or hearing officer before whom he appears. He should avoid undue solicitude for the comfort or convenience of judge or jury and should avoid any other conduct calculated to gain special consideration.

EC 7-37 In adversary proceedings, clients are litigants and though ill feelings may exist between clients, such ill feelings should not influence a lawyer in his conduct, attitude, and demeanor towards opposing lawyers. A lawyer should not make unfair or derogatory personal reference to opposing counsel. Haranguing and offensive tactics by lawyers interfere with the orderly administration of justice and have no proper place in our legal system.

EC 7-38 A lawyer should be courteous to opposing counsel and should accede to reasonable requests regarding court proceedings, settings, continuances, waiver of procedural formalities, and similar matters which do not prejudice the rights of his client. He should follow local customs of courtesy or practice, unless he gives timely notice to opposing counsel of his intention not to do so. A lawyer should be punctual in fulfilling all professional commitments.

EC 7-39   In the final analysis, proper functioning of the adversary system depends upon cooperation between lawyers and tribunals in utilizing procedures which will preserve the impartiality of tribunals and make their decisional process prompt and just, without imping-ing upon the obligation of lawyers to represent their clients zealously within the framework of the law.

CANON 8

A Lawyer Should Assist in Improving the Legal System

Ethical Considerations

EC 8-1   Changes in human affairs and imperfections in human institutions make necessary constant efforts to maintain and improve our legal system. This system should function in a manner that com-mands public respect and fosters the use of legal remedies to achieve redress of grievances. By reason of education and experience, lawyers are especially qualified to recognize deficiencies in the legal system and to initiate corrective measures therein. Thus they should partici-pate in proposing and supporting legislation and programs to improve the system, without regard to the general interests or desires of clients or former clients.

EC 8-2   Rules of law are deficient if they are not just, understand-able, and responsive to the needs of society. If a lawyer believes that the existence or absence of a rule of law, substantive or procedural, causes or contributes to an unjust result, he should endeavor by law-ful means to obtain appropriate changes in the law. He should en-courage the simplification of laws and the repeal or amendment of laws that are outmoded. Likewise, legal procedures should be im-proved whenever experience indicates a change is needed.

EC 8-3   The fair administration of justice requires the availability of competent lawyers. Members of the public should be educated to recognize the existence of legal problems and the resultant need for legal services, and should be provided methods for intelligent selec-tion of counsel. Those persons unable to pay for legal services should be provided needed services. Clients and lawyers should not be penalized by undue geographical restraints upon representation in legal matters, and the bar should address itself to improvements in licensing, reciprocity, and admission procedures consistent with the needs of modern commerce.

EC 8-4   Whenever a lawyer seeks legislative or administrative changes, he should identify the capacity in which he appears, whether on behalf of himself, a client, or the public. A lawyer may advocate such changes on behalf of a client even though he does not agree with them. But when a lawyer purports to act on behalf of the public, he should espouse only those changes which he conscientiously believes to be in the public interest.

EC 8-5   Fraudulent, deceptive, or otherwise illegal conduct by a participant in a proceeding before a tribunal or legislative body is inconsistent with fair administration of justice, and it should never be participated in or condoned by lawyers. Unless constrained by his obligation to preserve the confidences and secrets of his client, a lawyer should reveal to appropriate authorities any knowledge he may have of such improper conduct.

EC 8-6   Judges and administrative officials having adjudicatory powers ought to be persons of integrity, competence, and suitable temperament. Generally, lawyers are qualified, by personal observation or investigation, to evaluate the qualifications of persons seeking or being considered for such public offices, and for this reason they have a special responsibility to aid in the selection of only those who are qualified. It is the duty of lawyers to endeavor to prevent political considerations from outweighing judicial fitness in the selection of judges. Lawyers should protest earnestly against the appointment or election of those who are unsuited for the bench and should strive to have elected or appointed thereto only those who are willing to forego pursuits, whether of a business, political, or other nature, that may interfere with the free and fair consideration of questions presented for adjudication. Adjudicatory officials, not being wholly free to defend themselves, are entitled to receive the support of the bar against unjust criticism. While a lawyer as a citizen has a right to criticize such officials publicly, he should be certain of the merit of his complaint, use appropriate language, and avoid petty criticisms, for unrestrained and intemperate statements tend to lessen public confidence in our legal system. Criticisms motivated by reasons other than a desire to improve the legal system are not justified.

EC 8-7   Since lawyers are a vital part of the legal system, they should be persons of integrity, of professional skill, and of dedication to the improvement of the system. Thus a lawyer should aid in establishing, as well as enforcing, standards of conduct adequate to protect the public by insuring that those who practice law are qualified to do so.

EC 8-8   Lawyers often serve as legislators or as holders of other public offices. This is highly desirable, as lawyers are uniquely qualified to make significant contributions to the improvement of the legal system. A lawyer who is a public officer, whether full or part-time, should not engage in activities in which his personal or professional interests are or foreseeably may be in conflict with his official duties.

EC 8-9   The advancement of our legal system is of vital importance in maintaining the rule of law and in facilitating orderly changes; therefore, lawyers should encourage, and should aid in making, needed changes and improvements.

CANON 9

A Lawyer Should Avoid Even the Appearance of Professional Impropriety

Ethical Considerations

EC 9-1   Continuation of the American concept that we are to be governed by rules of law requires that the people have faith that justice can be obtained through our legal system. A lawyer should promote public confidence in our system and in the legal profession.

EC 9-2   Public confidence in law and lawyers may be eroded by irresponsible or improper conduct of a lawyer. On occasion, ethical conduct of a lawyer may appear to laymen to be unethical. In order to avoid misunderstandings and hence to maintain confidence, a lawyer should fully and promptly inform his client of material developments in the matters being handled for the client. While a lawyer should guard against otherwise proper conduct that has a tendency to diminish public confidence in the legal system or in the legal profession, his duty to clients or to the public should never be subordinate merely because the full discharge of his obligation may be misunderstood or may tend to subject him or the legal profession to criticism. When explicit ethical guidance does not exist, a lawyer should determine his conduct by acting in a manner that promotes public confidence in the integrity and efficiency of the legal system and the legal profession.

EC 9-3   After a lawyer leaves judicial office or other public employment, he should not accept employment in connection with any matter in which he had substantial responsibility prior to his leaving, since to accept employment would give the appearance of impropriety even if none exists.

EC 9-4   Because the very essence of the legal system is to provide procedures by which matters can be presented in an impartial manner so that they may be decided solely upon the merits, any statement or suggestion by a lawyer that he can or would attempt to circumvent those procedures is detrimental to the legal system and tends to undermine public confidence in it.

EC 9-5   Separation of the funds of a client from those of his lawyer not only serves to protect the client but also avoids even the appearance of impropriety, and therefore commingling of such funds should be avoided.

EC 9-6   Every lawyer owes a solemn duty to uphold the integrity and honor of his profession; to encourage respect for the law and for the courts and the judges thereof; to observe the Code of Professional Responsibility; to act as a member of a learned profession, one dedicated to public service; to cooperate with his brother lawyers in supporting the organized bar through the devoting of his time, efforts, and financial support as his professional standing and ability reasonably permit; to conduct himself so as to reflect credit on the legal profession and to inspire the confidence, respect, and trust of his clients and of the public; and to strive to avoid not only professional impropriety but also the appearance of impropriety.

Appendix B

Client Documents

Refer to Chapter 5 for the preferred typing style for these client documents.

Variations in style and wording will be found throughout the nation as a result of jurisdictional preferences. However, the legal secretary or prospective legal secretary who has begun to assimilate and comprehend legal rhetoric, of whatever jurisdiction, will be prepared for the variations.

The following client documents are included:

- Bill of Sale and acknowledgment
- Deed and acknowledgment
- Lease and two acknowledgments
- Notice to Pay Rent or Quit
- Stock Pledge Agreement
- Promissory Note
- Will
- Power of Attorney (Special)

NOTE: These documents are included in this volume to acquaint readers with legal style and vocabulary. They are not to be construed as being complete and exact legal papers.

BILL OF SALE

KNOW ALL MEN BY THESE PRESENTS:

That we, JOHN DOE and JANE SMITH DOE, husband and wife, of the city of Modesto, county of Stanislaus, state of California, for good and valuable consideration, receipt of which is hereby acknowledged, do hereby grant, sell, transfer and deliver unto JAMES ROE, an individual, and RICHARD SMITH, an individual, as tenants in common, in equal shares, the following described personal property:

1 — Ford tractor, Model 0000

1 — Ferguson tractor, Model 0000

1 — 1960 Chevrolet pickup truck, Motor No. 000000

We hereby covenant with the grantees that we are the lawful owners of said personal property; that said personal property is free from all encumbrances; that we have good right to sell the same as aforesaid; and that we will warrant and defend the same against the lawful claims and demands of all persons.

IN WITNESS WHEREOF, we have hereunto set our hands this _____ day of _____, 19____.

_____
JOHN DOE

_____
JANE SMITH DOE

STATE OF CALIFORNIA   )
) ss.
COUNTY OF STANISLAUS)

On this _____ day of _____, 19____,
before me, a notary public in and for the state of California, with principal offices in Stanislaus County, personally appeared JOHN DOE and JANE SMITH DOE, known to me
to be the persons described in the within instrument, and
acknowledged that they executed the same.

IN WITNESS WHEREOF, I have hereunto set my hand
and affixed my official seal the day and year in this certificate first above written.

_____
Notary public in and for the
county of Stanislaus

D E E D

THIS DEED, made and entered into this 16th day of
October, 19____, by and between JOHN DOE and JANE SMITH
DOE, his wife, parties of the first part, and WILLIAMSON
AND COMPANY, a limited Virginia partnership, party of the
second part,

WITNESSETH:

That for and in consideration of the sum of Ten
Dollars ($10.00) cash in hand paid, and other good and
valuable consideration, receipt of all of which is hereby
acknowledged, the parties of the first part hereto do

hereby grant, bargain, sell and convey with general warranty of title unto the said party of the second part, all of that certain lot or parcel of land situate and being in the county of Fairfax, state of Virginia, more particularly described as follows:

Lot 1, Section 3, Mary Morrow Estates, as the same is duly platted, dedicated and recorded in Deed Book 136 at Page 29 among the land records of Fairfax County, Virginia.

And being the same property conveyed to the parties of the first part hereto by deed dated February 6, 1935, and recorded among the land records of Fairfax County, Virginia in Deed Book 1333 at Page 497.

LESS AND EXCEPT THEREFROM that portion thereof conveyed to the Commonwealth of Virginia in Deed Book 1900 at Page 400 for proposed Route 66.

This conveyance is made subject to the restrictions and conditions contained in the deeds forming the chain of title to this property.

SAID PARTIES OF THE FIRST PART COVENANT that they have the right to convey the said land unto the party of the second part; that they have done no act to encumber the same; that the said party of the second part shall have quiet possession of the land, free from all encumbrances; and that the said parties of the first part will execute such further assurances of the land as may be requisite.

WITNESS the following signatures and seals:

_____(SEAL)
JOHN DOE

_____(SEAL)
JANE SMITH DOE

COMMONWEALTH OF VIRGINIA)
) ss.
COUNTY OF FAIRFAX   )

I, _____, a notary public in and for the county aforesaid, whose commission as notary expires _____, do hereby certify that JOHN DOE and JANE SMITH DOE, his wife, whose names are signed to the foregoing deed bearing date on the 16th day of October, 19____, have acknowledged the same before me in my county aforesaid.

GIVEN under my hand and seal this _____ day of _____, 19 ____.

_____
Notary Public

LEASE

THIS LEASE, made and entered into this _____ day of _____, 19____, by and between JOHN DOE and JANE SMITH DOE, husband and wife, as joint tenants, hereinafter referred to as "lessor," and STATE COMPANY, doing business as GREAT STATE COMPANY, hereinafter called "lessee,"

WITNESS:

WHEREAS, the lessor owns and is willing to lease and let to lessee upon the terms hereinafter provided that certain real property (land and building) located in Bell, Los Angeles County, California, more particularly described as:

The Southwesterly 200 feet of the following described real property, to wit:

That portion of the Garrett Tract, Rancho Santa Catalina, subdivided for the Santa Catalina Land Association, in the County of Los Angeles, State of California, as per map recorded in Book 1 Page 502 and in Book 32 Page 18 of Miscellaneous Records of said County, described as follows:

Beginning at a point in the center line of the Santa Catalina Road, also called the Mills Road, and First Street, that is south 32° 14' 40" west, 529.9 feet from the most westerly corner of Tract No. 5793, as per map recorded in Book 79 Pages 60 and 61 of Maps, in the office of the County Recorder of said County, thence north 32° 04' 40" east, 399.77 feet; thence south 56° 43' 30" east, 124.34 feet; thence south 33° 58' 30" west, 399.69 feet to a point in the center line of said Santa Catalina Road; thence north 56° 43' 30" west along said center line, 127.79 feet, more or less, to the point of beginning, (more commonly known as 10501 Mills Road, Bell, California), and

WHEREAS, the lessee is willing to take and hold possession of the leased premises upon said terms and conditions and pay lessor the rentals and considerations hereinafter provided for;

NOW, THEREFORE, in consideration of the premises and the covenants of the parties each to the other herein made, the lessor hereby demises and leases to the lessee and the lessee takes and leases the property above referred to; and it is mutually agreed as follows:

1. TERM: That the term of this lease shall be for a period of ten (10) years, starting on April 1, 19____, and ending on March 31, 19____.

2. RENT: Lessee agrees to pay lessor as rental hereunder the total sum of $96,000.00, payable at the rate of Eight Hundred Dollars ($800.00) per month on the first day of each month during the lease term.

3. PURPOSE OF LEASE: It is expressly understood and agreed that lessee shall use the premises solely for the purposes of conducting a retail bicycle business therein, and things incidental and necessary thereto. Lessee shall conform the use of the leased premises according to all public laws, statutes, ordinances and regulations from time to time applicable and relating thereto.

4. REPAIRS: Lessee shall keep and maintain the entire leased premises, both interior and exterior, including plumbing, roof, electrical, parking area and plate glass in good order, condition and repair, and shall make any and all repairs of every kind and nature that might be required to said leased premises at lessee's own cost and expense and within a reasonable time and by exercising due diligence; and on the last day of said term or sooner termination of this lease, to surrender unto lessor said premises in the same condition as when received, reasonable use and wear thereof and damage by act of God or by the elements excepted, and to remove all of lessee's signs from the said premises.

5. PUBLIC LIABILITY INSURANCE: The lessee, at lessee's own cost and expense, shall procure and maintain in force and effect at all times during the term hereof, a policy or policies of public liability and property damage insurance issued by a good and reputable insurance company or companies, in which the lessor shall be named as the insured or one of the insured, covering the premises which are the subject of this lease.

6. DEFAULT: It is further expressly understood

and agreed in each and all of the provisions of this lease that conditions precedent are to be faithfully and fully performed and observed by lessee to entitle lessee to continue in possession of said premises hereunder, and that if any default be made, either in the payment of rent, and if the same continues after three (3) days' written notice from lessor to lessee, or in the observance, payment or performance of any of the other provisions, terms or conditions hereof, and if the same continues after fifteen (15) days' written notice thereof from lessor to lessee, then this lease shall, at the option of the lessor, immediately terminate and be at an end, and lessee shall be deemed to have forfeited all rights herein, and lessor, its successors and/or assigns, may thereupon reenter the said premises and take possession of the whole thereof by giving the notices required by law. A waiver by lessor of any default upon the part of lessee in the performance of any part of the covenants and conditions hereof shall not be construed or treated as a waiver of any subsequent or other default as to the same or any other matter.

7. TERMINATION: At the expiration of the term herein provided for, or any extension or renewal thereof, lessee covenants and agrees to quit and surrender possession of said premises in as good order and condition as reasonable use and wear will permit, damage by the elements excepted.

8. BINDING EFFECT: This lease and all of the terms and conditions hereof shall inure to and be binding upon the parties and their respective successors and assigns.

9. COSTS AND ATTORNEY'S FEES: In the event that lessor employs an attorney or other agent to enforce any of the terms, covenants and conditions of this lease, lessee agrees to pay to lessor a reasonable fee for such attorney or agent, whether such action is prosecuted to judgment or not, together with costs and expenses incurred by lessor in each instance.

10. TIME: Time is hereby declared to be of the essence in all particulars concerning this lease.

11. ASSIGNMENT: The lessee covenants not to assign this lease, or any extension thereof, and not to sublet the leased premises or any portion thereof without first obtaining the written consent of lessor thereto.

12. LIENS: Lessee shall indemnify and hold lessor harmless from any and all claims, demands, liens or causes of action arising out of lessee's use and occupancy of the premises.

13. NOTICES: All notices to lessee shall be mailed, postage prepaid, to lessee at the address of the leased premises. All notices to lessor shall be given to lessor at such address as shall from time to time be designated by lessor.

14. TAXES: Lessee shall pay before delinquency any and all taxes, assessments, license fees and public charges levied, assessed or imposed, and which become payable during the lease term.

15. OPTION TO EXTEND: At the expiration of the initial term, if this lease shall then be in full force and effect and the lessee shall have fully performed all of its terms and conditions, the lessee shall have an

option to extend this lease for a further term of ten years from and after April 1, 19____, upon the same terms, covenants and conditions hereof, except that the rental for said extended period shall be the sum of Nine Hundred Fifty Dollars ($950.00) per month.

IN WITNESS WHEREOF, each of the parties hereto have executed this lease on this _____ day of _____, 19____.

STATE COMPANY dba
GREAT STATE COMPANY

By _____   _____
                President   JOHN DOE

_____   _____
                Secretary   JANE SMITH DOE

Lessee   Lessor

EXECUTED IN DUPLICATE

STATE OF CALIFORNIA   )
) ss.
COUNTY OF LOS ANGELES   )

On this _____ day of _____, 19____, before me, a notary public, personally appeared JOHN DOE and JANE SMITH DOE, known to me to be the persons whose names are subscribed to the within instrument, and acknowledged that they executed the same.

_____
Notary public in and for said
county and state

STATE OF CALIFORNIA   )
) ss.
COUNTY OF LOS ANGELES)

On this _____ day of _____, 19___, before me, a notary public, personally appeared _____, known to me to be the president, and _____, known to me to be the secretary, of the corporation that executed the within instrument, and acknowledged to me that such corporation executed the same.

_____
Notary public in and for said
county and state

THREE–DAY NOTICE
TO PAY RENT OR QUIT

TO: HENRY JONES
        200 South Early Drive
        City, State

        And any and all other tenants in possession at
        200 South Early Drive
        City, State

NOTICE IS HEREBY GIVEN that within three (3) days after the service on you of this notice you are hereby required to pay the rent on the premises commonly known as 200 South Early Drive, City, County, State, of which you now hold possession (said rent amounting to $200.00, being the total of $100.00 due on June 1, 19___, and $100.00 due on July 1, 19____), or you are hereby required to deliver up possession of said premises within three (3) days after service upon you of this notice to the undersigned, as attorney for JOHN JONES, owner of said premises.

THIS IS A NOTICE TO PAY SAID RENT totaling $200.00 or quit and deliver up said premises within three (3) days from and after the date of service of this notice on you or the undersigned will institute legal proceeding on behalf of the owner against you to recover possession of the premises, together with treble said rent and damages for the unlawful detainer thereof by you, pursuant to Section 0000 of the Civil Code of the State of California and all other applicable sections of the laws of the state of California.

DATED: July 7, 19____, at City, State.

_____
JOHN BROWN, attorney for
JOHN JONES, owner of premises

STOCK PLEDGE AGREEMENT

THIS PLEDGE is made by the undersigned, RICHARD ROE, this 21st day of May, 19____, at Redwood City, California.

The undersigned hereby assigns, transfers to and pledges with GOTHIC, INC., a California corporation, two hundred (200) shares of the capital stock of XYZ CORPORATION, represented by certificate No. 01234 of said corporation, issued to and endorsed in blank by RICHARD ROE and delivered herewith, as collateral security for the payment of a promissory note in favor of GOTHIC, INC., in the principal amount of Two Thousand Dollars ($2,000.00), dated April 21, 19____ (and any renewals or extensions thereof), a copy of which is attached hereto and by this reference incorporated herein.

The undersigned does hereby constitute and appoint JOHN JONES, JR., his true and lawful attorney, irrevocable for the undersigned and in the name and stead of the undersigned, to sell, assign and transfer unto GOTHIC, INC., or its nominee, all or any part of the said 200 shares of stock pledged herein in accordance with the provisions hereof; and for that purpose to make all necessary assignments or transfers and to substitute one or more persons with like power, hereby confirming and ratifying all that said attorney or its substitute shall lawfully do by virtue hereof.

The undersigned hereby instructs his said attorney that in the event any amounts due on said promissory note in favor of GOTHIC, INC., shall not be paid when due, then the holder of said note may require the sale of the stock pledged hereby; and such sale may be made without advertisement or notice to the undersigned except by mail addressed to the undersigned at least four (4) days prior to such sale.

The undersigned pledgor further agrees that:

1. The pledgee or the holder of said promissory note may become the purchaser of the stock pledged hereby, or any portion thereof, at any sale authorized above;

2. Any stock rights, liquidating dividends, stock dividends, dividends paid in stock, new securities or other property to which the undersigned becomes entitled on account of the securities pledged hereby shall im-

mediately upon receipt be delivered to the pledgee and made subject to this agreement as collateral;

3. Without regard to who may be the registered owner at the time any part of the securities pledged hereby is released, the receipt of the undersigned shall be a complete and full acquittance for the collateral so delivered; and GOTHIC, INC., shall thereafter be discharged from any liability and responsibility hereunder.

_____

RICHARD ROE

Address: _____

_____

PROMISSORY NOTE

$2,000.00   Redwood City, California   May 21, 19____

ON DEMAND, and, if no demand is made, on May 21, 19____, I, RICHARD ROE, promise to pay to GOTHIC INC., or order, at Redwood City, California, the sum of Two Thousand Dollars, without interest.

Should default be made in the payment of said principal sum when due and suit be commenced or an attorney employed to enforce such payment, I agree to pay such additional sum as the court may adjudge reasonable as attorney's fees in said suit.

Principal amount of this note is payable in lawful money of the United States of America.

THIS NOTE IS SECURED BY A STOCK PLEDGE AGREEMENT of even date.

RICHARD ROE

LAST WILL AND TESTAMENT
OF
NATALIE DENO BROWN

I, NATALIE DENO BROWN, now residing in the county of San Diego, state of California, and being of lawful age and of sound and disposing mind and memory, and not acting under duress, menace, fraud or the undue influence of any person whomsoever, do hereby make, publish and declare this to be my last will and testament, and hereby expressly revoke any and all former wills and codicils to wills heretofore made by me.

FIRST: I declare that I am married and that my husband's name is WILLIAM JOHN BROWN. I further declare that I have one child, a daughter, whose name is RELVA LENA BROWN.

SECOND: I hereby direct my executor hereinafter named to pay all of my just, unsecured debts and the expenses of my last illness and funeral as soon as may be lawfully and conveniently done after my demise.

THIRD: All of my property, both real and personal, of whatsoever kind and character and wheresoever situated, I hereby give, devise and bequeath to my husband, WILLIAM JOHN BROWN.

FOURTH: In the event that my husband, WILLIAM JOHN BROWN, predeceases me, then all of my property, both real and personal, of whatsoever kind and character and wheresoever situated, I hereby give, devise and bequeath to my daughter, RELVA LENA BROWN, or her issue by right of representation.

FIFTH: I hereby nominate and appoint my husband, WILLIAM JOHN BROWN, as executor of this my last will and testament and authorize him to act as such executor without bond. In the event of his failure to qualify or to complete his duties as such executor, then I nominate and appoint my daughter, RELVA LENA BROWN, as executrix hereof without bond.

IN WITNESS WHEREOF, I have hereunto set my hand and seal at San Diego, California, this _____ day of _____, 19____.

_____
NATALIE DENO BROWN

The foregoing instrument, consisting of two (2) pages, including this page signed by the witnesses, was on the date hereof by the said NATALIE DENO BROWN subscribed, published and declared to be her last will and testament, in the presence of us, and each of us, who, at her request, and in her presence, and in the presence of each other, have signed the same as witnesses thereto.

_____ Address _____

_____

_____ Address _____

_____

POWER OF ATTORNEY (Special)

KNOW ALL MEN BY THESE PRESENTS:

    I, WILLIAM SMITH, have appointed and do hereby appoint MARY SMITH attorney-in-fact, for me in my name, to execute any and all documents, deeds and papers necessary to effect the sale of that certain real property commonly known as 1234 Allen Way, City, State;

    GIVING AND GRANTING unto said attorney full power and authority to do whatever is necessary to be done in and about the aforesaid business as fully as I could do if personally present, hereby ratifying all that my said attorney shall do or cause to be done by virtue of these presents.

    IN WITNESS WHEREOF I have hereunto set my hand and seal this _____ day of _____ 19__.

                                  _____

                                    WILLIAM SMITH

(Attach an acknowledgment.)

Appendix C

Correspondence

The letters in this section have been selected to include various legal problems from collections to probate matters. Multipage letters have not been included for reasons of space. However, such lengthy letters are usual in legal correspondence.

As you read this section, be alert to observe the following:

- Subject line in each letter.
- A letter with several inside addresses.
- A letter with *cc* (carbon copy) and *bcc* (blind carbon copy) notations. If the copies are photocopies, the notations should read *copy* instead of *cc* and *bc* instead of *bcc*. The *copy* or *cc* notation will appear on the original and all copies of the letter. The *bc* or *bcc* notation will appear on all copies but *not* on the original of the letter.
- A letter including in the body a complete address, which has been set in inside address style. This style of letter writing permits quick recognition of the address.

NOTE: The sample correspondence is included solely for purposes of illustrating letter style and the use of legal rhetoric in correspondence. See Chapter 8 for more detailed specifications for typing letters.

                              Date

Mr. John Doe
39624 Road Avenue
Torrance, California 00000

                              Re: Broker's Commission—Hale

Dear Mr. Doe:

My client, Harry Hale, real estate broker, has called to
my attention your failure to carry out an agreement to
sell your acreage on Highway 90 and to pay a commission
therefor pursuant to the listing agreement and deposit
receipt signed by you and Mrs. Jane Doe. Such failure on
your part has continued notwithstanding the fact that a
buyer has been obtained and stands ready to consummate
a purchase in accordance with the terms of said agreement
and receipt.

Under California law, a broker's commission is earned
under such a listing agreement and deposit receipt when
the broker has procured a buyer pursuant to the terms
thereof, and the right of the broker to his commission
is not affected by the failure of the seller to carry out
the agreement of sale. It is therefore incumbent upon you
to pay the agreed commission in the amount of $200.00,
whether you complete the sale or otherwise. The commission has been earned and is now due and payable.

Unless satisfactory arrangements have been made by Tuesday, April 14, 19____, at 5 p.m., I have been instructed
by my client to institute legal proceedings against you.

I trust that the time, court costs, and legal fees attendant upon such action can be avoided by your carrying
out the agreement of sale and payment of the stipulated
commission.

                              Yours very truly,

                              Richard Roe
                              Attorney at Law
RR:aa

bcc Mr. Harry Hale [This notation will appear on all copies
                   but will not show on the original let-
                   ter.]

Date

WWW Printing Company
100 Market Place
San Francisco, California 00000

> Re: Clear Ace Builders vs.
> Warren Word
> DCA 5 Civil No. 499
> (Respondent's Brief)

Gentlemen:

Enclosed is a copy of Respondent's Brief to be filed in the above entitled matter. It is due January 14, 19____, unless you are able to obtain an extension of time.

Please print, serve, and file the brief in accordance with the rules of the District Courts of Appeal for the state of California.

The attorney for the appellant is:

> Mr. William Abbel
> Attorney at Law
> 2177 North Maria Street
> Modena, California 00000

It is my understanding that you will do a compilation of table of cases, etc.; but if you have any questions about the brief's printing, please telephone me collect at once. Under the circumstances, no advance proof sheets need be sent for examination.

We have already received the Clerk's notice requiring this brief to be filed on or before January 14, 19____, and I will appeciate all you can do to expedite the work and filing.

Please acknowledge receipt of this order and, if possible, advise me of the date you believe the brief will be ready.

> Yours very truly,
>
> Richard Roe
> Attorney at Law

RR:aa
Enclosure

Date

Mr. Richard Roe
Attorney at Law
21031 Corner Boulevard
Lynwood, California 00000

                                    Re: Jane Smith Doe v.
                                        John Henry Doe
                                        No. 11111

Dear Mr. Roe:

Your letter of November 13, together with its enclosures,
is acknowledged.

It is noted from the file that the respondent has previously proceeded by way of affidavit, which resulted in a
dismissal on January 16, 19____ .

From a study of the file, it appears that this is not a
proper order for enforcement. The periodic interruptions
of support payments, occasioned by the change of custody,
places an undue burden on the Court Trustee and constitutes an unwarranted and unnecessary expenditure of funds
in processing the paper. Under such circumstances, we
are going to request the petitioner and respondent to
appear in court on the designated date and move the court
for a suspension of the enforcement proceedings.

Unless such order is modified through your office prior
to such date, we shall therefore expect your client to
appear as ordered.

                                    Yours very truly,

                                    HENLEY HANSON
                                    District Attorney

                            By_____
                                        CHARLES VICTOR
                                    Deputy District Attorney

CV:aan

cc: Mrs. Jane Smith Doe
    1000 Garden Avenue
    Blythe, California 00000

    Mr. John Henry Doe
    2987 Chicago Street
    Lynwood, California 00000

Date

Mrs. Jane Smith Doe
1000 Garden Avenue
Blythe, California 00000

Re: Doe versus Doe

Dear Mrs. Doe:

On December 20 we mailed a stipulation to you at your sister's address, 7105 Arden Avenue, Phoenix, Arizona 00000, which was to be signed and returned to us.

Inasmuch as the stipulation has not been returned, we are wondering if it may have been lost in the mail. We will appreciate your letting us know whether you received it.

If you still have the stipulation, it should be signed and returned.

Sincerely yours,

JONES and JONES

Henry L. Jones

HLJ:bb

Date

CLY Insurance Company
316 West Olive Avenue
City, State 00000

Attention: Mr. George M. Moot

Re: Robert Smith Account

Gentlemen:

Enclosed is trustee's check made payable to you in the sum of $100.10 for Robert Smith's insurance with the Raetter Program.

Please have the payment date changed from the first of the month to the tenth of the month. As you know, in the past whenever a payment was not made promptly on the first of the month, we received an overdue statement, plus additional charges.

The funds that are made available are usually mailed on the first of the month and do not get to me until later. Would you please take care of this matter so that we do not have these additional charges.

Very truly yours,

Richard Roe
Attorney at Law

RR:aa
Enclosure

Date

Mr. Richard Roe
Attorney at Law
21031 Corner Boulevard
Lynwood, California 00000

Re: John T. Smith
Case No. 11111-WW

Dear Mr. Roe:

Settlement terms acceptable to my client, Mr. Henry W. Wright, are as follows:

1) Four months' rent is due, but he will accept payment for two months and will waive payment for the other two months.

2) Smith must vacate the premises and the building must be left and remain on the premises as is.

Please advise as promptly as possible whether the above

can be concluded on the stated terms. Another month's rent will be due the first of June.

Thank you.

Sincerely yours,

SMITH and SMITH

Johnson Wylie Smith

JWS:an

bcc: Mr. Henry W. Wright [This notation will appear on all copies but not on the original letter.]

Date

Mr. John Henry Jones
Associate Counsel
Broad Title Insurance Company
1000 Mailon Building
Los Angeles, California 00000

> Re: Claim File No. 012345
> Johnson vs. Bree
> Superior Court Case
> No. 020202

Dear Mr. Jones:

Thank you for your letter of June 30, 19____. I concur that basing the second affirmative defense on imputed knowledge is incorrect. I will be able to correct this by properly framing the issues in the pretrial order.

I remain convinced that by forwarding several interrogatories and requests for admissions we should be able to clear the way for motion for summary judgment.

I will keep you informed.

Very truly yours,

Richard Roe

RR:aa

Date

Mr. Joseph Johnson
Attorney at Law
71509 Center Boulevard
Denver, Colorado

                              Re: King—Brasson Insurance
                                  Company Lease

Dear Mr. Johnson:

Enclosed herewith are the original and two copies of new
pages 2 and 3 of the Agreement of Sale. These should be
substituted for the old pages 2 and 3. The two new pages
incorporate changes requested by Mr. King.

If there are no changes desired by you, I would appreciate
your forwarding the agreement to Mr. King for execution.

                         Sincerely yours,

                         ALLEN, BELL, CLAY, DAWSON
                         and ELLENDER

                         By_____
                              Cyrus Dawson

CD:fls
Enclosure

Date

Mr. Fred G. Hall
Dean of the School of Law
University of California
Los Angeles, California 00000

Mr. Isaac J. Keln
Attorney at Law
750 Wellen Building
Fresno, California 00000

Mr. Walter X. Zolle
Attorney at Law
950 Battle Building
San Francisco, California 00000

Re: Study Session CEB
November 11, 19____

Gentlemen:

Enclosed with the copy of this letter addressed to each of you is a study outline for the testamentary trust film we plan to show on November 11.

This study outline will be given each person attending the forum. I believe it will be of some assistance to you in deciding what should be covered in your comments.

I look forward to seeing you on the eleventh.

Sincerely,

Richard Roe

RR:el
Enclosure

[Names are alphabetized. Copies of this letter must be prepared for the three addressees.]

Date

Mr. Parry A. Stein
Attorney at Law
222 Washington Square
Los Angeles, California 00000

                            Re: John Jenson—
                            Case No. 31000

Dear Mr. Stein:

I have received a letter from Mr. Charles A. Bree, who is
representing Mr. Wence Walters, owner of the property at
Star Avenue and Cardwell Street, Bay Meadows, California,
claiming reimbursement in the sum of $1,010.00 for street
improvements.

Please check this out in accordance with Mr. Jenson's
lease and advise whether or not said amount should be paid.

                            Very truly yours,

                            Roy S. Thomas
                            Attorney at Law

RST:aa

cc Mr. Charles A. Bree
   Bree, Bree and Jones
   975 Waters Building
   Long Beach, California 00000

bcc Len B. Brockman

[The cc notation will appear on the original and all
copies of the letter. The bcc notation will appear on
all copies but not on the original letter.]

Appendix D

Court Documents

The court documents in this section are to be typed in accordance with the instructions in Chapter 11. The legal instruments included are the following pleadings and other court documents:

Pleadings

- Complaint
- Complaint
- Plaintiff's Original Petition
- Defendant's Answer
- Answer to Complaint

Other Court Documents

- Assignment of Judgment
- Notice of Trial
- Notice of Sustaining of Demurrer to Complaint

- Waiver and Entry of Appearance
- Stipulation

NOTE: If these documents are to be typed for purposes of studying legal style and vocabulary, it is suggested that the local jurisdiction and venue be obtained and that the caption style preferred in the area be used. This information is available from the court clerk's office, the law library, or an attorney's office. Geographic place names should be changed to fit the area.

These documents are included in the volume to acquaint readers with legal style and vocabulary. They are not to be construed as being complete and exact legal documents.

PLEADINGS

COMPLAINT

IN THE CIRCUIT COURT OF THE FIRST CIRCUIT

STATE OF HAWAII

ANDREW B. CALDWELL, INC., Plaintiff, vs. DANIEL E. FARRELL, GEORGE H. IRELAND and JASPER K. LITTLE, Defendants, No. _____, COMPLAINT

COMES NOW plaintiff above named, by and through its attorney, RICHARD ROE, and complaining against defendants, alleges as follows:

I

Plaintiff is a corporation organized and existing under the laws of the state of Hawaii whose principal place of business is in Honolulu, city and county of Honolulu, state of Hawaii. Defendants, DANIEL E. FARRELL, GEORGE H. IRELAND and JASPER K. LITTLE, are residents of Honolulu aforesaid.

II

That on or about February 26, 19____, plaintiff and defendants, DANIEL E. FARRELL, GEORGE H. IRELAND and

JASPER K. LITTLE, executed a lease, plaintiff as lessor and defendants as lessees, of certain property described in said lease, a copy of which is attached hereto, marked Exhibit A, and made a part hereof by reference.

III

That thereafter plaintiff consented to the assignment of said lease by defendants to MAYBERRY CORPORATION, a Hawaii corporation. Plaintiff is without sufficient knowledge or information to form a belief as to whether said lease was, in fact, assigned by defendants to MAYBERRY CORPORATION.

IV

That defendants owe to plaintiff the sum of Five Thousand Two Hundred Twenty-One and 63/100 Dollars ($5,221.63) for additional percentage rent provided to be paid in said lease, and which defendants refused to pay, although the same was demanded by plaintiff in writing on May 21, 19____; and said amount still remains unpaid, to plaintiff's damage in the amount of $5,221.63.

V

That in accordance with the provisions of the lease, defendants were required to submit a monthly statement of their gross receipts, gross receipts being defined in the lease as "the gross selling price...of all merchandise sold in, on, through or from the demised premises by the lessees or anyone on behalf of the lessees or by concessionaire or other persons whether for cash or credit, whether or not payments be actually made; and charges made by lessees or by anyone on behalf of lessees or by or on behalf of any subtenant, concessionaire or other persons for the rendition of any service of any kind whatsoever to the lessees' customers and any other persons in, on, through or from the demised premises, including repair work and charges made by or on behalf of the lessees, lessees' subtenants, concessionaires or other persons in the course of any other business done, in, on, through or from the demised premises and...."

That defendants intentionally reported to plaintiff gross receipts of $211,434.77 received by them in 19____, when, in fact, defendants had gross receipts in the sum of $301,291.04 for 19____. That defendants paid rent for 19____ in the sum of $10,000.00 when required to pay the sum of $15,221.63 under the terms of said lease.

VI

That defendants have also failed and refused to pay plaintiff their prorated share of charges for utilities used at the premises, contrary to the terms of the lease, and all to the plaintiff's damage in the sum of $808.00.

WHEREFORE, plaintiff prays judgment as follows:

1. That plaintiff have judgment against the defendants in the sum of $6,029.63;

2. For costs of suit and reasonable attorney's fees;

3. For such other and further relief as the court may deem proper in the premises.

RICHARD ROE
591 Smith-Thomas Building
Honolulu, Hawaii

IN THE CIRCUIT COURT OF THE FIRST CIRCUIT
STATE OF HAWAII
ALICE BELOW CORDNER, Plaintiff, versus EDNA FARRELL, Defendant, Civil No. _____, COMPLAINT

I

Plaintiff and defendant are residents of Honolulu, city and county of Honolulu, state of Hawaii.

II

That on or about the 22nd day of October, 19____, on Puuloa Road, defendant so negligently and carelessly operated her motor vehicle so as to cause it to crash into and collide with plaintiff's motor vehicle, causing serious injuries to plaintiff as more specifically hereinafter set forth.

III

That as a result plaintiff sustained serious injuries to her body, neck, back and spine, in addition to great physical pain, suffering and mental agony, and claims general damages in the sum of $50,000.00.

IV

That by reason of the premises plaintiff has and will require medical care and attention, has and will suffer loss of earnings and earning capacity and property damage, for which she alleges special damages in a presently unascertainable amount, and begs leave of court to insert the same herein at the time of trial.

WHEREFORE, plaintiff prays judgment against defendant in damages as follows:

1. General damages in the sum of $50,000.00;

2. Special damages as alleged herein; and

3. Costs of suit.

Dated at Honolulu, Hawaii, this _____ day of

_____, 19____.

ALICE BELOW CORDNER,
Plaintiff
By JONES and JONES,
Her Attorneys

By_____
Harry I. Jones

PETITION (COMPLAINT)

IN THE _____ JUDICIAL DISTRICT COURT OF
DALLAS COUNTY, TEXAS
XYZ NATIONAL BANK versus LELAND KARY BONHAM, No. _____,
PLAINTIFF'S ORIGINAL PETITION

TO THE HONORABLE JUDGE OF SAID COURT:

Comes now XYZ NATIONAL BANK, hereinafter called plaintiff, complaining of LELAND KARY BONHAM, hereinafter called defendant, and for cause of action would show unto the court:

I

That plaintiff is a Texas banking corporation with its place of business in Dallas, Dallas County, Texas. The defendant is a resident of Dallas, Dallas County, Texas, where service of process may be had upon him at 202 North Hall Street.

II

On or about the 15th day of August, 19___, the

defendant executed and delivered to the plaintiff a promissory note, due and payable ninety (90) days after date, in the principal sum of $4,014.26, with interest at the rate of eight per cent per annum from date until maturity and ten per cent per annum thereafter until paid. Said note further provided for an additional sum of ten per cent of the principal and interest due if placed in the hands of an attorney for collection. A true and correct copy of said note is attached hereto and made a part hereof for all purposes.

III

The aforesaid note matured and became due on or about the 16th day of November, 19____, but, although the plaintiff has made repeated demands upon the defendant for payment thereof, the defendant has failed and refused, and still fails and refuses, to pay said note or any part thereof, and there is now due and owing from the defendant to the plaintiff the sum of $4,014.26, with interest thereon as provided in said note.

IV

By reason of the defendant's failure to pay said note as set forth hereinabove, the plaintiff, being at all times the owner and holder of said note, has placed the same in the hands of the undersigned attorneys for collection, agreeing to pay them the attorneys' fees provided in said note; and there is, therefore, an additional sum due in the amount of $431.66.

WHEREFORE, premises considered, the plaintiff prays that the defendant be cited to appear and answer herein; and that upon final hearing hereof, the plaintiff do have and recover judgment against the defendant in the sum of $4,014.26, together with interest and attorneys' fees as alleged hereinabove; and all costs herein incurred; and for such other and further relief, at law or in equity, to which the plaintiff may show itself justly entitled.

Respectfully submitted,

RUBY, SMITH, & THOMAS

By_____
Raymond T. Thomas
Attorneys for Plaintiff
1001 Western Building
Dallas, Texas 00000

ANSWER

IN THE DISTRICT COURT OF HARRIS COUNTY, TEXAS
G-127TH JUDICIAL DISTRICT
PATRICK QUENTIN ROBINSON versus SOLTER TRUITT, ULLY VICTOR WATSON, and YOUNG COMPANY, a corporation
DEFENDANT'S ANSWER

NOW COMES ULLY VICTOR WATSON and YOUNG COMPANY, defendants in this case, and in response to the complaint filed against them would make known to the court and jury as follows:

I

It is true that an automobile collision occurred at the approximate time and place stated in the complaint, involving the parties named in this suit. The charges of negligence against ULLY VICTOR WATSON and YOUNG COMPANY are denied as false. The allegations of the complaint are generally denied, and defendants ask that plaintiff be required to make strict proof by a preponderance of credible evidence as required by law.

II

At the time and on the occasion in question plaintiff, PATRICK QUENTIN ROBINSON, was a gratuitous guest in the vehicle being driven by ULLY VICTOR WATSON, without payment for such transportation.

III

Defendant, ULLY VICTOR WATSON, entered the intersection on a green light and defendant, SOLTER TRUITT, ran a red light. The collision in question was solely caused by the failure of SOLTER TRUITT to observe and obey the red traffic signal facing him.

WHEREFORE, premises considered, defendants pray that plaintiff take nothing by reason of this suit; that the defendants be discharged; and that they go hence with their costs without day; and for all such other and further relief, both general and special, at law and in equity, to which they may show themselves justly entitled, for which they will in duty bound forever pray.

ALLON, ALLON & XERES

By_____
            Attorneys for Defendants

0000 Middle Building
Houston, Texas 00000
Telephone 222-0000

IN THE MUNICIPAL COURT, FRESNO JUDICIAL DISTRICT
COUNTY OF FRESNO, STATE OF CALIFORNIA
EPHRAIM FRANKS, Plaintiff, versus BROWNTON COMPANY, INC.,
a California corporation, et al., Defendants
No. 12345
ANSWER TO COMPLAINT

Defendant, BROWNTON COMPANY, INC., a California
corporation, answers the complaint as follows:
ANSWER TO FIRST CAUSE OF ACTION

I

In answer to the allegations of paragraphs II
and III, this answering defendant denies that any obligation was incurred by this defendant at the place alleged
by plaintiff or on the date stated or on any other date;
and further specifically denies that this defendant became indebted to plaintiff on an open book account, or on
any other account, for lumber; and further specifically
denies that there is a balance due of $480.23, or any other
sum, from this defendant to plaintiff.

II

In answer to the allegations of paragraph IV, this
answering defendant admits that plaintiff demanded payment of said sum alleged due and that this defendant refused to pay it, but denies there is any sum due and
owing from defendant to plaintiff.

ANSWER TO SECOND CAUSE OF ACTION

I

In answer to the allegations incorporated by reference in paragraph I, defendant incorporates herein by reference paragraphs I and II of its answer to the alleged first cause of action, realleging each and every denial therein contained.

II

In answer to the allegations of paragraph II, this answering defendant specifically denies that on the date stated, or on any other date, there was an account stated upon which the sum of $480.23, or any other sum, was agreed upon as the balance due from this defendant to plaintiff.

ANSWER TO THIRD CAUSE OF ACTION

I

In answer to the allegations incorporated by reference in paragraph I, this answering defendant incorporates herein by reference paragraphs I and II of its answer to the alleged first cause of action.

II

In answer to the allegations of paragraph II, this answering defendant admits that plaintiff furnished to this defendant lumber, but specifically denies that the lumber sold to this defendant by plaintiff had a reasonable value in excess of that which defendant paid plaintiff, for the reason that the lumber was of inferior grade.

WHEREFORE, this defendant prays that plaintiff take nothing by his action; that defendant be awarded its costs of suit; and for such other relief as the court deems proper.

DATED: October 19, 19____.

_____

RICHARD ROE, Attorney for
Defendant, BROWNTON COM-
PANY, INC., a California
corporation.

OTHER COURT DOCUMENTS

ASSIGNMENT

IN THE MUNICIPAL COURT, FRESNO JUDICIAL DISTRICT
COUNTY OF FRESNO, STATE OF CALIFORNIA
BALDWIN FURNITURE CO., a corporation, Plaintiff, versus
LENIS M. NORRIS, also known as L. M. NORRIS, Defendant.
No. 12345
ASSIGNMENT OF JUDGMENT

FOR VALUABLE CONSIDERATION, plaintiff, BALDWIN
FURNITURE CO., a corporation, has transferred and assigned unto WENDELL WALDRON, INC., a corporation, and
its assigns, that certain judgment recovered by BALDWIN
FURNITURE CO., in the above entitled matter and against
LENIS M. NORRIS, defendant in the above entitled matter.
Said judgment was entered by the clerk of the above court
on April 30, 19____, in Minute Book 200A, page 76, for a
total amount of $2,100.03, together with all sums of money
that may be had or obtained by means of the judgment or
on any proceedings to be had thereupon.
DATED: December ____, 19____.

BALDWIN FURNITURE COMPANY,
a corporation

By_____
         President

SUPERIOR COURT OF THE STATE OF CALIFORNIA

FOR THE COUNTY OF FRESNO

JERRY KALOONIAN, plaintiff, versus LAWRENCE MOORE, JR.,

Defendant

No. 23456

NOTICE OF TRIAL

TO: DEFENDANT, LAWRENCE MOORE, JR., AND HIS ATTORNEY,

RICHARD R. ROE:

YOU, AND EACH OF YOU, PLEASE TAKE NOTICE that the trial of the above entitled matter has been set for June 22, 19____, at 10:00 a.m., in the Department of the Presiding Judge, Fresno County Courthouse, Fresno, California.

DATED: December 12, 19____.

_____

Attorney for Plaintiff

SUPERIOR COURT OF THE STATE OF CALIFORNIA

FOR THE COUNTY OF FRESNO

ALEN BART CARR and DELBERT EVERETT FARLEY, Plaintiffs,

versus GEOFFREY HARRY IBBETT, Defendant

No. 98765

NOTICE OF SUSTAINING OF DEMURRER TO COMPLAINT

TO: ALEN BART CARR AND DELBERT EVERETT FARLEY, PLAIN-

TIFFS, AND RICHARD C. ROE, THEIR ATTORNEY:

PLEASE TAKE NOTICE that the demurrer of the defendant to the complaint herein was, on November 1, 19____, sustained on the ground that it cannot be ascertained whether the contract upon which the action is founded is written or oral. You have ten (10) days in which to amend.

DATED: November 5, 19____.

_____
Attorney for Defendant

WAIVER AND ENTRY OF APPEARANCE

JURISDICTION AND VENUE

FANA GERTRUDE HIX, Plaintiff, versus ISADORE JOHN HIX, Defendant

No. 23-23232

WAIVER AND ENTRY OF APPEARANCE

BEFORE ME, the undersigned authority, on this day personally appeared ISADORE JOHN HIX, who, being first duly sworn, upon his oath states:

My name is ISADORE JOHN HIX, and I am the defendant in the above numbered and styled cause. I have received a copy of the plaintiff's first amended original petition filed herein. I have read said petition and understand the allegations contained therein, and I do not wish to contest the cause of action asserted by the plaintiff. I hereby enter my appearance in said cause for all purposes and agree that the same may be taken up and considered by the court without further notice to me at any time after the expiration of sixty days from the date of the filing of the plaintiff's original petition.

My mailing address is 2100 Westfeldt Road, City, State.

_____

ISADORE JOHN HIX

SUBSCRIBED AND SWORN TO BEFORE ME by the said ISADORE JOHN HIX on this _____ day of May, 19____, and to certify which, witness my hand and seal of office.

_____

Notary public in and for
Blank County, State

STIPULATION

SUPERIOR COURT OF THE STATE OF CALIFORNIA

FOR THE COUNTY OF LOS ANGELES

HAROLD I. JONES, Plaintiff, versus DONALD E. FOGER, Defendant

No. 123456, STIPULATION

IT IS HEREBY STIPULATED by and between the undersigned that the time for defendant, DONALD E. FOGER, to answer or otherwise plead to the Complaint for Damages filed herein on the 12th day of December, 19____, be and the same is hereby extended to and including the 20th day of January, 19____.

Dated this _____ day of December, 19____.

_____

Attorney for Defendant

_____

Attorney for Plaintiff

Appendix E

Forms or Law Blanks

Legal forms, whether they are obtained commercially, from a business firm, from a government agency, or from the courts, are of ever-increasing importance to the law firm. Chapter 10 discusses the preparation and use of law blanks.

Forms similar in function to those included in this section of the Appendix are available and used in many jurisdictions. These sample forms are only a few of the great number of forms used in law offices.

BUSINESS FORMS

- Individual Grant Deed
- Corporation Grant Deed

GOVERNMENT FORMS

- Marital Property Declaration
- Inheritance Tax Declaration
- United States Estate Tax Return (3 pages of a multipage form)

COURT FORMS

- Summons
- Subpena (*subpoena* in most states)

COURT FORMS – SELECTED PROBATE FORMS

- Petition (See pages 226-227.)
- Proof of Subscribing Witness
- Order for Probate (See page 230.)
- Order Appointing Inheritance Tax Referee
- Letters
- Creditor's Claim
- Inventory and Appraisement
- Attachment (for use with Inventory and Appraisement)

COURT FORMS – SELECTED DISSOLUTION FORMS

- Summons (Family Law)
- Petition (Family Law)
- Confidential Counseling Statement (Marriage)
- Request to Enter Default (Family Law)
- Interlocutory Judgment of Dissolution of Marriage (Family Law)
- Final Judgment (Family Law)
- Notice of Entry of Judgment (Family Law)

SPACE ABOVE THIS LINE FOR RECORDER'S USE

Individual Grant Deed

THIS FORM FURNISHED BY TICOR TITLE INSURERS

TO 1923 CA (12-74)

A. P. N.

The undersigned grantor(s) declare(s):

Documentary transfer tax is $_____

( ) computed on full value of property conveyed, or

( ) computed on full value less value of liens and encumbrances remaining at time of sale.

( ) Unincorporated area: ( ) City of _____, and

FOR A VALUABLE CONSIDERATION, receipt of which is hereby acknowledged,

hereby GRANT(S) to

the following described real property in the

County of _____, State of California:

Dated _____

STATE OF CALIFORNIA
COUNTY OF _____ } SS.

On _____ before me, the under-
signed, a Notary Public in and for said State, personally appeared

_____ known to me
to be the person_____whose name_____ subscribed to the within
instrument and acknowledged that_____executed the same.
WITNESS my hand and official seal.

Signature _____

(This area for official notarial seal)

Title Order No._____ Escrow or Loan No._____

MAIL TAX STATEMENTS AS DIRECTED ABOVE

SOURCE: Title Insurance and Trust, Los Angeles, California.
Printed by permission.

**Individual
Grant Deed**

TITLE INSURANCE
AND TRUST

A TICOR COMPANY

COMPLETE STATEWIDE TITLE SERVICE
WITH ONE LOCAL CALL

SOURCE: Title Insurance and Trust, Los Angeles, California.
Printed by permission.

RECORDING REQUESTED BY

AND WHEN RECORDED MAIL TO

Name
Street
Address
City &
State

MAIL TAX STATEMENTS TO

Name
Street
Address
City &
State

——————————————————— SPACE ABOVE THIS LINE FOR RECORDER'S USE ———————

Corporation Grant Deed

TO 1921 CA (12-74) THIS FORM FURNISHED BY TICOR TITLE INSURERS   A.P.N._____

The undersigned grantor(s) declare(s):
Documentary transfer tax is $_____ .
( ) computed on full value of property conveyed, or
( ) computed on full value less value of liens and encumbrances remaining at time of sale.
( ) Unincorporated area: ( ) City of _____ , and
FOR A VALUABLE CONSIDERATION, receipt of which is hereby acknowledged,

a corporation organized under the laws of the State of   hereby GRANTS to

the following described real property in the
County of   , State of California:

In Witness Whereof, said corporation has caused its corporate name and seal to be affixed hereto and this instrument to be executed by its_____President and_____Secretary
thereunto duly authorized.
Dated : _____

STATE OF CALIFORNIA
                                    } SS.
COUNTY OF_____
On _____ before me, the under-
signed, a Notary Public in and for said State, personally appeared
_____ known
to me to be the_____President, and
_____ known to me to be
_____Secretary of the Corporation that executed the
within Instrument, known to me to be the persons who executed the
within Instrument on behalf of the Corporation therein named, and
acknowledged to me that such Corporation executed the within Instru
ment pursuant to its by-laws or a resolution of its board of directors.

WITNESS my hand and official seal.

Signature_____

By_____
                                    President
By_____
                                    Secretary

(This area for official notarial seal)

Title Order No._____Escrow or Loan No._____

MAIL TAX STATEMENTS AS DIRECTED ABOVE

SOURCE: Title Insurance and Trust, Los Angeles, California.
Printed by permission.

MARITAL PROPERTY DECLARATION, FORM IT-3

ANSWER ALL QUESTIONS. If space insufficient, attach sheets of same size showing decedent's name, social security number and question number.

Full Name of Decedent	Social Security No.	Date of Death

1. DECEDENT AND SURVIVING SPOUSE WERE MARRIED ON	Date	In City of	In State of

2. Did decedent own any real or personal property at date of marriage? ☐ Yes ☐ No If **yes**, list below. (Also attach real property tax bill for year of marriage, if available)

Item No.	General description of each asset (See Instruction 15)	Approximate market value at date of marriage (See Instr. 16)

3. Decedent's occupation at date of marriage	4. Decedent's net worth at date of marriage

5a. Did decedent receive any real or personal property **after** date of marriage by gift, bequest, devise, descent, proceeds of life insurance or joint tenancy survivorship? ☐ Yes ☐ No If **yes**, complete 5b, 5c and 5d.

5b. Item No.	General description of each asset (See Instruction 15)	Full name and relationship of person from whom received	Date received	Approx. value on date received (See Instr. 16)

5c. IF CALIFORNIA INHERITANCE TAX DETERMINATION WAS MADE	Name of estate	Court case No. (if any)	County

5d. IF RECEIVED BY GIFT	Item No.	State of residence of donor at date of gift

6. Are any assets listed under 2 or 5b now on inventory of decedent's estate or included in Inheritance Tax Declaration, Form IT-22? **(See Instruction 17)** ☐ Yes ☐ No If **yes**, specify where each such item is shown on inventory or Form IT-22.

7a. Were any assets listed under 2 or 5b **transferred** to anyone (including decedent's spouse) during decedent's lifetime? **(See Instruction 17)** ☐ Yes ☐ No If **yes**, complete 7b and 7c.

7b. ANY SUCH ASSETS SOLD	Item No.	Date of sale	Proceeds received	Subsequent disposition of proceeds

7c. ANY SUCH ASSETS TRANSFERRED WITHOUT FULL CONSIDERATION	Item No.	Date of transfer	Names & addresses of persons to whom transfers made	Consideration, if any

I DECLARE UNDER PENALTY OF PERJURY THAT THIS DECLARATION, INCLUDING ANY ATTACHMENTS, HAS BEEN EXAMINED BY ME AND TO THE BEST OF MY KNOWLEDGE AND BELIEF IS TRUE, CORRECT AND COMPLETE. IF PREPARED BY A PERSON OTHER THAN THE DECLARANT, HIS DECLARATION IS BASED ON ALL INFORMATION OF WHICH HE HAS ANY KNOWLEDGE.

Signature	Date	Relationship: ☐ Spouse of decedent ☐ Representative of spouse
		If not spouse, explain in attachment:
Address		a. Why spouse is not signing, b. Declarant's relationship or connection with decedent and c. Basis of knowledge required to provide necessary information.

Signature of person preparing this declaration	Date	Address

Send this form and all attachments to the **Inheritance Tax Referee,** if one has been appointed, otherwise to STATE CONTROLLER, Division of Inheritance and Gift Tax

P. O. Box 1019 Sacramento 95805	107 South Broadway Los Angeles 90012	785 Market Street San Francisco 94103

IT-3 (REV. 11-72)

8a. Did decedent and surviving spouse reside outside California during marriage? (See Instruction 18)	☐ Yes	☐ No	If yes, complete 8b, 8c and 8d.	

8b. States in which resided, including California, after marriage	Inclusive dates (month and year if known)		Combined net worth of spouses upon taking up residence in each state (include value of all assets, including cash)
	From	To	

8c. Does net worth at date of last arrival in California include any separate property of either spouse?	☐ Yes	☐ No	If yes, state source and value.

8d. Trace subsequent disposition of combined net worth of spouses after last arrival in California.

9. Brief history of **decedent's** business or occupational career from marriage to death, showing dates. (See Instruction 19)

10. Brief history of **surviving spouse's** business or occupational career from marriage to decedent's death, showing dates. (See Instruction 19)

11. Did either spouse receive damages or a settlement for a personal injury after September 11, 1957?	☐ Yes	☐ No	If yes, show dates, amounts received and subsequent disposition.

12. Did decedent and surviving spouse ever enter into any written or oral agreement concerning the status of their property as community or separate?	☐ Yes	☐ No	If yes, attach copy of agreement or affidavit proving oral agreement.

13. Did spouse ever obtain a legal separation (separate maintenance) or an interlocutory divorce?	☐ Yes	☐ No	If yes, attach copy of decree and any property settlement agreement.
			Date of reconciliation, if any.

14. Give on attachment any additional information bearing upon the separate or community status of decedent's property.

NOTE: *It is vital that all pertinent information be given. Under the inheritance tax law there is no presumption that property acquired after marriage is community property; the burden of proof is upon the person so claiming.* (Revenue and Taxation Code Sections 13556, 13556.5)

372

STATE OF CALIFORNIA

INHERITANCE TAX DECLARATION, FORM IT-22

ANSWER ALL QUESTIONS. If space insufficient, attach sheets of same size showing decedent's name, social security number and question number.

Full Name of Decedent. (Show all names ever used)		Date of Death	Social Security No.
			Date of Birth

Place of Death. (Last usual address)	Cause of Death	Length of Last Illness

Attorney for Estate	Address	Telephone No.

Type of Court Proceeding	Case No.	Name of Executor/Administrator, If Any, and Title	
☐ Probate ☐ 650 Petition ☐ Other ☐ None	County and State	Address	Telephone No.

1. RESIDENCE OF DECEDENT AT TIME OF DEATH   NOTE: If claimed that decedent was not a California resident, attach completed form IT-2, Declaration Concerning Residence.

County   State

2. Did decedent leave a will?   ☐ Yes ☐ No   **If yes,** attach copy of will and any codicils.

3a. Was decedent a tenant of a California safe deposit box?   ☐ Yes ☐ No   **If yes,** attach copy of Contents of Safe Deposit Box prepared by County Treasurer.

3b. Has box been opened by County Treasurer?   ☐ Yes ☐ No   **If yes,** give date inventoried.

3c. Are any assets in box on date of death not reported on this form or a probate inventory?   ☐ Yes ☐ No   **If yes,** explain in attachment.

4a. JOINT TENANCIES. Did decedent, at date of death, hold any assets in joint tenancy or joint tenancy form? To obtain a release of Inheritance Tax Lien for real estate, it is necessary to submit date of deed, date of recordation and book and page number of record.   ☐ Yes ☐ No   **If yes, list all** jointly held personal property (including stocks, bonds, mortgages, checking and savings accounts, etc.) wherever located, and California real estate. Full amount must be shown, although portion has been released or transferred after death, and all assets must be included even if tax release or consent is not required.

Item No.	Name of surviving joint tenant	Relationship to decedent (See Instr. 5)	Description of each asset (See Instruction 7)	Market value at date of death (See Instr. 8)	FOR STATE USE ONLY

4b. Does surviving joint tenant **claim** contribution to any of the joint tenancy assets?   ☐ Yes ☐ No   **If yes,** give full particulars tracing source of funds, values, dates, etc., in attachment. (See Instruction 9)

NOTE: **Survivor's burden of proof of claim of contribution:** All joint tenancies are presumed to have been created from assets originally belonging to the decedent and subject to tax in full to the surviving joint tenant, except to the extent that the survivor can prove that the assets, or a portion, originally belonged to the survivor or that the survivor furnished consideration which was never received from the decedent. (Revenue and Taxation Code Sec. 13671:

I DECLARE UNDER PENALTY OF PERJURY THAT THIS DECLARATION, INCLUDING ANY ATTACHMENTS, HAS BEEN EXAMINED BY ME AND TO THE BEST OF MY KNOWLEDGE AND BELIEF IS TRUE, CORRECT AND COMPLETE. IF PREPARED BY A PERSON OTHER THAN THE DECLARANT, HIS DECLARATION IS BASED ON ALL INFORMATION OF WHICH HE HAS ANY KNOWLEDGE.

Signature	Date	Address
Relationship to Decedent		
Signature of Person Preparing This Declaration	Date	Address

THE INHERITANCE TAX REFEREE MUST HAVE THIS FORM TO BEGIN DETERMINATION OF THE TAX. Send this form and all attachments to the **Inheritance Tax Referee,** if one has been appointed, otherwise to STATE CONTROLLER, Division of Inheritance and Gift Tax.

P. O. Box 1019 Sacramento 95805	107 South Broadway Los Angeles 90012	785 Market Street San Francisco 94103

IT-22 (REV 9-77)

5. ASSETS OUTSIDE CALIFORNIA. Excluding assets listed at item 4a, did decedent own tangible or intangible personal or real property outside of California? ☐ Yes ☐ No **If yes,** describe property and give estimated value. (If probate is pending in another state, also attach copy of inventory.)

TRUSTS, LIFE ESTATES, POWERS OF APPOINTMENT (See Instructions 7, 8, 11)

6a. Was decedent a trustee or beneficiary of a "trustee" bank or savings and loan or similar account? ☐ Yes ☐ No **If yes,** attach a list of accounts giving balances at date of death, sources of funds and exact title in which each was held. (See Instruction 9)

6b. Did decedent enter into a declaration of trust, written or oral, or join in a trust agreement during his life time? ☐ Yes ☐ No **If yes,** attach copy of trust document or proof of the oral agreement, and a list of trust assets at date of death with estimated market value of each.

6c. Was decedent beneficiary of a trust not created by him? ☐ Yes ☐ No **If yes,** attach copy of trust documents and a list of assets at date of death and estimated market value.

6d. Was decedent a donee of a power of appointment? ☐ Yes ☐ No **If yes,** attach a copy of document creating power of appointment and a list of assets at date of death and estimated market value.

7a. HEIRS, BENEFICIARIES, SURVIVING JOINT TENANTS AND TRANSFEREES. List all even if there is no court proceeding.

Item No.	Name	Date of Birth	Full Address	Relationship to decedent (See * below and Instr. 5)	Approximate value of interest or percentage of estate (See Instr. 10)

* **Relationship must be by blood,** except for surviving spouse, son-in-law, daughter-in-law, adopted or mutually acknowledged child or issue of adopted or mutually acknowledged child. List all others who are not blood relatives as "strangers".

* **Attach blood tracing** for niece, nephew, grandniece, grandnephew, great grandniece or great grandnephew.

* **Adoption or mutual acknowledgment of child.** Affidavit or other proof is required for transferee claiming through adoption or mutual acknowledgment. (Revenue and Taxation Code Sections 13307, 13310)

7b. Did any beneficiaries named in will predecease decedent? ☐ Yes ☐ No **If yes,** list names, and if blood relatives list names of their children.

7c. Did decedent have any predeceased spouses? (Probate Code Sections 228, 229) ☐ Yes ☐ No **If yes,** give name, county of residence and date of death of each.

7d. Is any divorced spouse a creditor of decedent or his estate or claiming an interest in the estate? ☐ Yes ☐ No **If yes,** attach a copy of final decree and any property settlement agreement.

7e. Is California **previously taxed** property credit claimed? ☐ Yes ☐ No **If yes,** give name, county of residence and date of death of prior decedent. (See Instruction 6)

8. LIFE INSURANCE. Was there life and/or accident insurance in force on life of decedent? ☐ Yes ☐ No **If yes,** list below.

Item No.	Insurance Company	Face amount and type of policy (term, endowment, mortgage, etc.)	Owner of policy (See * below)	Beneficiary receiving proceeds and relationship to decedent (See Instruction 5)	Mode of payment and amount of proceeds received (See * below)

* **If owner was other than decedent or total proceeds exceed $50,000, or if decedent irrevocably selected mode of settlement, attach copy of IRS Form 712, obtainable from insurance company.**

ANNUITIES, SUPPLEMENTAL CONTRACTS AND DEATH BENEFITS

9a. Was decedent owner of annuity policies or supplemental contracts? ☐ Yes ☐ No   **If yes, list under 9c.**

9b. Did decedent have any interest in a "death benefit", "retirement plan", "profit sharing plan" or "stock purchase plan" or were any payments made under such plans by virtue of decedent's death? ☐ Yes ☐ No   **If yes, list under 9c.**

9c. Item No.	Company, or issuer of annuity, supplemental contract or death benefit	Type of policy or death benefit	Beneficiary and relationship to decedent (See Instruction 5)	Mode of payment	Lump sum or commuted value

9d. Is any item in 9c claimed to be nontaxable? ☐ Yes ☐ No   **If yes, explain below or in attachment.**

GIFTS AND TRANSFERS

10a. Did decedent transfer, **at any time during his life,** any real or personal property (stocks, bonds, notes, savings accounts, insurance policies, etc.) for other than money, for less than market value, or without any payment or consideration (including withdrawals or transfers from joint tenancy bank or savings and loan accounts)? ☐ Yes ☐ No   **If yes, list under 10b and answer 10c through 10g. (See Instruction 12)**

10b. Item No.	Name of transferee and relationship to decedent (See Instruction 5)	Date of transfer	Description of property and estimated market value at date of transfer (See Instructions 7, 8)	Market value at date of death (See Instr. 8)	FOR STATE USE ONLY

10c. Did decedent continue to receive all or part of the income after transfer, or continue to use property (including residing on real estate)? ☐ Yes ☐ No   **If yes to 10c, 10d or 10e, explain below or in attachment.**

10d. Was deed to any real property listed under 10b recorded after decedent's death? ☐ Yes ☐ No

10e. Was any restriction imposed by decedent on transfer of any property listed under 10b? ☐ Yes ☐ No

10f. Is it claimed that any property listed under 10b is not subject to inheritance tax? ☐ Yes ☐ No   **If yes, explain below or in attachment. ("Payment of gift tax" or "exemption under Gift Tax Law" is insufficient.)**

10g. Were California gift tax returns filed for any of the transfers listed under 10b? ☐ Yes ☐ No   **If yes, identify transfer and give amount of gift tax paid (including penalties and interest).**

11. Was decedent survived by a spouse? ☐ Yes ☐ No
If yes, attach completed form IT-3, Marital Property Declaration, if:
a. Date of death is prior to January 1, 1976, or,
b. Date of death is on or after January 1, 1976, and the total value of all property (including 100% of the community property) exceeds $100,000 in value, or if any of the property passes to someone other than the surviving spouse. **(See Instruction 14.)**

12. **ASSETS NOT OTHERWISE LISTED.** Assets standing in decedent's name alone, or in bearer form, including real property, stocks, bonds, mortgages, judgments, notes, accounts and loans receivable, cash, business or partnership interests, autos, farm equipment, interests in retirement funds, stock purchase plans or other employee benefits, furniture, furnishings, personal effects, insurance owned by decedent on life of any other persons, amounts due including tax or other refunds, and any other type of property. Also include assets in name of the surviving spouse which are community property. **(Probate cases.** If all property is listed in Inventory and Appraisement, do not list but make reference to Inventory and Appraisement.)

Item No.	Description of assets not otherwise listed (See Instruction 7)	Market value at date of death (See Instr. 8)	FOR STATE USE ONLY

13a. Was probate homestead granted or statutory homestead confirmed or exempt personal property set aside by probate court? ☐ Yes ☐ No **If yes, attach copy of court order.**

13b. Was a family allowance ordered by probate court? ☐ Yes ☐ No **If yes, attach copy of court order(s).**

13c. Has there been litigation affecting the estate as to distribution, entitlement or value? ☐ Yes ☐ No **If yes, attach copies of court orders. If litigation is pending, give case title, number, relevant issues and facts.**

14. Will Federal Estate Tax Return, Form 706, be filed? ☐ Yes ☐ No **If already filed, attach copy of page 1 of Form 706.**

Federal Estate Tax	$	☐ Estimated	☐ Paid
Maximum allowable credit for State death taxes	$	☐ Estimated	☐ Determined

ALLOWABLE DEDUCTIONS (See Instruction 13) Any deduction over $1,000 must be itemized.

15a. All Cases

Expenses of last illness (paid after death by transferee or estate, net after any insurance reimbursement) ....

Funeral expenses (net after burial insurance, social security or other reimbursement) ....

Debts of decedent (**if probate,** list only allowed claims) ....

Encumbrances on real property (state exact balance for each parcel); ....

Liens or security agreements on personal property (state exact balance for each asset) ....

Taxes a lien or due and unpaid at death: Income tax (net due at death)

Real property (state exact balance for each parcel) ....

Other taxes (itemize and explain) ....

Other deductions (itemize and explain) ....

15b. Probate Cases Only

Other debts (itemize and explain) ....

Ordinary executor's/administrator's commission ☐ Statutory ☐ Other ☐ Not claimed....................

Ordinary attorney's fees ☐ Statutory ☐ Other ☐ Not claimed....................

Costs of administration (filing fees, notices, etc.) ....

15c. Additional Professional Fees—Probate and Other Court Cases. (Show basis: tax work, joint tenancy, etc. Include only fees allowed under Revenue and Taxation Code Sections 13988.1)

Executor/Administrator ....

Attorney ....

Accountant ....

Itemization and detail of items under 15a, b, c.

Form **706**
(Rev. Jan. 1979)
Department of the Treasury
Internal Revenue Service

United States Estate Tax Return

Estate of citizen or resident of the United States (see separate instructions)

Decedent's first name and middle initial	Decedent's last name	Date of death

Domicile at time of death	Year domicile established	Decedent's social security number

Name of personal representative	Address (Number and street including apartment number or rural route, city, town or post office. State and ZIP code)

Name and location of court where will was probated or estate administered	Case number

If decedent died testate check here ▶ ⌞⌟ and attach a certified copy of the will.

Authorization to receive confidential tax information under 26 C.F.R. 601.502(c)(3)(ii) if return prepared by an attorney for the personal representative:

I declare that I am the attorney of record for the personal representative before the above court and prepared this return for the personal representative. I am not under suspension or disbarment from practice before the Internal Revenue Service and am qualified to practice in the State shown below—

Name of attorney	State	Address (Number and street, city, State and ZIP code)

Computation of Tax

1 Total gross estate (from Recapitulation, page 3, line 10)	**1**	
2 Total allowable deductions (from Recapitulation, page 3, line 29)	**2**	
3 Taxable estate (subtract the amount on line 2 from the amount on line 1)	**3**	
4 Adjusted taxable gifts (total amount of taxable gifts (within the meaning of section 2503) made by decedent after December 31, 1976, other than gifts which are includible in decedent's gross estate (section 2001(b))). See instructions	**4**	
5 Add the amount on line 3 and the amount on line 4	**5**	
6 Tentative tax on the amount on line 5 from Table A in the separate instructions	**6**	
7 Aggregate gift taxes payable with respect to gifts by decedent after December 31, 1976, including gift taxes paid by decedent's spouse for split gifts (section 2513) if decedent was the donor of such gifts and they are includible in decedent's gross estate. See instructions	**7**	
8 Gross estate tax. Subtract the amount on line 7 from the amount on line 6	**8**	
9 Unified credit against estate tax from Table B in the separate instructions . . **9**		
10 Adjustment to unified credit. See instructions **10**		
11 Allowable unified credit (subtract the amount on line 10 from the amount on line 9)	**11**	
12 Subtract the amount on line 11 from the amount on line 8 (but not less than zero)	**12**	
13 Credit for State death taxes not to exceed the amount on line 12; see Table C in the separate instructions and attach credit evidence	**13**	
14 Subtract the amount on line 13 from the amount on line 12	**14**	
15 Credit for Federal gift taxes (see section 2012 and attach computation) . . . **15**		
16 Credit for foreign death taxes (from Schedule P). (Form 706CE is required) . . **16**		
17 Credit for tax on prior transfers (from Schedule Q) **17**		
18 Total (add the amounts on lines 15, 16, and 17)	**18**	
19 Net estate tax. Subtract the amount on line 18 from the amount on line 14	**19**	
20 Prior payments. Explain in attached statement; see instruction 5 . . . . **20**		
21 United States Treasury bonds redeemed in payment of estate tax **21**		
22 Total (add the amount on line 20 and the amount on line 21)	**22**	
23 Balance due (subtract the amount on line 22 from the amount on line 19)	**23**	

Note: *Please attach the necessary supplemental documents; see instruction 6.*

Under penalties of perjury, I declare that I have examined this return, including accompanying schedules and statements, and to the best of my knowledge and belief, it is true, correct, and complete. Declaration of preparer other than the personal representative is based on all information of which preparer has any knowledge.

_____   _____
Signature of personal representative   Date

_____   _____

_____   _____   _____
Signature of preparer other than personal representative   Address (and ZIP code)   Date

Estate of:

General Information

1 Address of decedent at time of death (Number and street including apartment number or rural route, city, town or post office, State and ZIP code)

2 Place of death, if different than decedent's address (e.g., name of hospital)

3 Cause of death

4 Length of last illness

5 Decedent's physicians

Name	Address (Number and street, city, State, and ZIP code)

6 Date and place of birth

7 Decedent's business or occupation. If retired check here ▶ ☐ and state decedent's former business or occupation ▶ ....

8 Marital status of decedent at time of death

☐ Married—Date of marriage to surviving spouse ▶ ....

     —Domicile at time of marriage ▶ ....

☐ Widow or widower—Name and date of death of deceased spouse ▶ ....

☐ Single

☐ Legally separated—Name of legally separated spouse ▶ ....

☐ Divorced—Date divorce decree became final ▶

9 Did the personal representative make a diligent and careful search for property of every kind left by the decedent for whose estate this return is filed? . . . . . .

10 Do you elect the alternate valuation explained in instruction 12? . . . .

11 Do you elect the special valuation explained in instruction 13? . . . .

Please check the "Yes" or "No" box for each question

	Yes	No
9		
10		
11		

If "Yes," attach to this return a statement that includes the following information:

(i) The relevant qualified use;

(ii) The items of real property shown on the estate tax return to be specially valued pursuant to the election (identified by schedule and item number);

(iii) The fair market value of the real property to be specially valued under section 2032A and its value based on its qualified use (both values determined without regard to the adjustments provided by section 2032A(b)(3)(B));

(iv) The adjusted value (as defined in section 2032A(b)(3)(B)) of all real property which is used in a qualified use and which passes from the decedent to a qualified heir;

(v) The items of personal property shown on the estate tax return that pass from the decedent to a qualified heir and are used in a qualified use under section 2032A (identified by schedule and item number) and the total value of such personal property adjusted as provided under section 2032(A)(b)(3)(B);

(vi) The adjusted value of the gross estate, as defined in section 2032A(b)(3)(A);

(vii) The method used in determining the special value based on use;

(viii) Copies of written appraisals;

(ix) The date on which the decedent (or a member of his or her family who held the property before the decedent) acquired the property and on which he or she or a member of his or her family commenced the qualified use (if different from the date of acquisition);

(x) Any periods following commencement of the qualified use during which the decedent or a member of his or her family did not own the property, use it in a qualified use, or materially participate in the operation of the farm or other business within the meaning of section 2032A(e)(6); and

(xi) The name, address, taxpayer identification number, and relationship to the decedent of each person taking an interest in each item of specially valued property, and the value of the property interests passing to each such person based on both fair market value and qualified use.

Also attach to this return an agreement to express consent to personal liability under section 2032A(c) in the event of certain early dispositions of the property or early cessation of the qualified use. The agreement must be executed by all parties receiving any interest in the property being valued based on its qualified use. The agreement is to be in a form that is binding on all parties under applicable local law. It must designate an agent for the parties for all dealings with the Internal Revenue Service on matters arising under section 2032A.

Include below, the name, identifying number, relationship, and address of all parties receiving any interest in the specially valued property. For "Privacy Act" notice, see the Form 1040 instructions.

Name	Identifying number	Relationship	Address

Estate of:

Recapitulation

Item number	Gross estate	Alternate value	Value at date of death
1	Schedule A—Real Estate		
2	Schedule B—Stocks and Bonds		
3	Schedule C—Mortgages, Notes, and Cash		
4	Schedule D—Insurance on Decedent's Life		
5	Schedule E—Jointly Owned Property		
6	Schedule F—Other Miscellaneous Property		
7	Schedule G—Transfers During Decedent's Life		
8	Schedule H—Powers of Appointment		
9	Schedule I—Annuities		

10 Total gross estate (add lines 1 through 9). Enter here and on page 1, line 1 . . . .

Item number	Deductions	Amount
11	Schedule J—Funeral Expenses and Expenses Incurred in Administering Property Subject to Claims	
12	Schedule K—Debts of Decedent	
13	Schedule K—Mortgages and Liens	
14	Total of Items 11 through 13	
15	Allowable amount of deductions from item 14 (see note ¹) . . .	
16	Schedule L—Net Losses During Administration	
17	Schedule L—Expenses Incurred in Administering Property Not Subject to Claims .	
18	Total of items 15 through 17	
19	Schedule M—Bequests, etc., to Surviving Spouse	
20	Adjusted gross estate (see note ²)	
21	Greater of (i) $250,000 or (ii) one-half of amount on line 20 (see note ²) . . .	
22	Aggregate of gift tax marital deduction allowed to decedent with respect to gifts made after December 31, 1976 (exclude any gift which is includible in the gross estate of the donor by reason of section 2035 (certain gifts within 3 years of death))	
23	Aggregate of gift tax marital deduction which would have been allowable to decedent with respect to gifts required to be included in a gift tax return made after December 31, 1976, if the amount deductible with respect to any gift were 50 percent of its value (exclude any gift which is includible in the gross estate of the donor by reason of section 2035 (certain gifts within 3 years of death))	
24	Balance (subtract the amount on line 23 from the amount on line 22)	
25	Balance (subtract the amount on line 24 from the amount on line 21 (but not less than zero))	
26	Amount of marital deduction (smaller of (i) amount on line 19 or (ii) amount on line 25)	
27	Schedule N—Orphans' Deduction	
28	Schedule O—Charitable, Public, and Similar Gifts and Bequests	
29	Total allowable deductions (add amounts on lines 18, 26, 27, and 28). Enter here and on page 1, line 2 .	

¹ Note.—See paragraph 1 of the Instructions for the Recapitulation in the separate instructions.
² Note.—Enter at item 20 the excess of item 10, Total gross estate, over item 18, if the decedent and surviving spouse at no time held property as community property. If property was ever held as community property, compute item 20, Adjusted gross estate, and the reduced $250,000 limitation at item 21 in accordance with the separate Instructions for the Recapitulation and attach an additional sheet showing such computation.

Page 3

NAME AND ADDRESS OF ATTORNEY: TELEPHONE NO:

FOR COURT USE ONLY:

ATTORNEY FOR (Name)

SUPERIOR COURT OF CALIFORNIA, COUNTY OF FRESNO
1100 VAN NESS AVENUE
P.O. BOX 1628
FRESNO, CALIFORNIA 93717

CLK 0001.00 E07-70 R01-79

PLAINTIFF

DEFENDANT

SUMMONS

CASE NUMBER

NOTICE! You have been sued. The court may decide against you without your being heard unless you respond within 30 days. Read the information below.

If you wish to seek the advice of an attorney in this matter. you should do so promptly so that your written response. if any. may be filed on time.

¡AVISO! Usted ha sido demandado. El tribunal puede decidir contra Ud. sin audiencia a menos que Ud. responda dentro de 30 días. Lea la información que sigue.

Si Usted desea solicitar el consejo de un abogado en este asunto. debería hacerlo inmediatamente, de esta manera, su respuesta escrita, si hay alguna, puede ser registrada a tiempo.

1. TO THE DEFENDANT: A civil complaint has been filed by the plaintiff against you. If you wish to defend this lawsuit. you must. within **30** days after this summons is served on you. file with this court a written response to the complaint. Unless you do so. your default will be entered on application of the plaintiff, and this court may enter a judgment against you for the relief demanded in the complaint. which could result in garnishment of wages. taking of money or property or other relief requested in the complaint.

DATED: Clerk, By _____ , Deputy

(SEAL)

2. NOTICE TO THE PERSON SERVED: You are served
    a. ☐ As an individual defendant.
    b. ☐ As the person sued under the fictitious name of:

    c. ☐ On behalf of:

    Under: ☐ CCP 416.10 (Corporation)   ☐ CCP 416.60 (Minor)
            ☐ CCP 416.20 (Defunct Corporation)   ☐ CCP 416.70 (Incompetent)
            ☐ CCP 416.40 (Association or Partnership)   ☐ CCP 416.90 (Individual)
            ☐ Other:
    d. ☐ By personal delivery on (Date):

A written response must be in the form prescribed by the California Rules of Court. It must be filed in this court with the proper filing fee and proof of service of a copy on each plaintiff's attorney and on each plaintiff not represented by an attorney. The time when a summons is deemed served on a party may vary depending on the method of service. For example. see CCP 413.10 through 415.50. The word "complaint" includes cross-complaint. "plaintiff" includes cross-complainant. "defendant" includes cross-defendant. the singular includes the plural

Form Adopted by Rule 982
Judicial Council of California
Revised Effective January 1. 1979

(See reverse for Proof of Service)

SUMMONS

CCP 412.20, 412.30.
415.10

PROOF OF SERVICE
(Use separate proof of service for each person served)

1. I served the
   a. ☐ summons ☐ complaint ☐ amended summons ☐ amended complaint

   b. On defendant (Name):

   c. By serving (1) ☐ Defendant (2) ☐ Other (Name and title or relationship to person served):

   d. ☐ By delivery at ☐ home ☐ business (1) Date of:
      (2) Time of: (3) Address:

   e. ☐ By mailing (1) Date of: (2) Place of:

2. Manner of service: (Check proper box)
   a. ☐ **Personal service.** By personally delivering copies. (CCP 415.10)
   b. ☐ **Substituted service on corporation, unincorporated association (including partnership), or public entity.** By leaving, during usual office hours, copies in the office of the person served with the person who apparently was in charge and thereafter mailing (by first-class mail, postage prepaid) copies to the person served at the place where the copies were left. (CCP 415.20(a))
   c. ☐ **Substituted service on natural person, minor, incompetent, or candidate.** By leaving copies at the dwelling house, usual place of abode, or usual place of business of the person served in the presence of a competent member of the household or a person apparently in charge of the office or place of business, at least 18 years of age, who was informed of the general nature of the papers, and thereafter mailing (by first-class mail, postage prepaid) copies to the person served at the place where the copies were left. (CCP 415.20(b)) **(Attach separate declaration or affidavit stating acts relied on to establish reasonable diligence in first attempting personal service.)**
   d. ☐ **Mail and acknowledgment service.** By mailing (by first-class mail or airmail) copies to the person served, together with two copies of the form of notice and acknowledgment and a return envelope, postage prepaid, addressed to the sender. (CCP 415.30) **(Attach completed acknowledgment of receipt.)**
   e. ☐ **Certified or registered mail service.** By mailing to address outside California (by registered or certified airmail with return receipt requested) copies to the person served. (CCP 415.40) **(Attach signed return receipt or other evidence of actual delivery to the person served.)**
   f. ☐ Other (Specify code section):
      ☐ Additional page is attached.

3. The notice to the person served (Item 2 on the copy of the summons served) was completed as follows (CCP 412.30, 415.10, and 474):
   a. ☐ As an individual defendant.
   b. ☐ As the person sued under the fictitious name of:
   c. ☐ On behalf of:
      Under: ☐ CCP 416.10 (Corporation) ☐ CCP 416.60 (Minor) ☐ Other:
      ☐ CCP 416.20 (Defunct corporation) ☐ CCP 416.70 (Incompetent)
      ☐ CCP 416.40 (Association or partnership) ☐ CCP 416.90 (Individual)
   d. ☐ By personal delivery on (Date):

4. At the time of service I was at least 18 years of age and not a party to this action.

5. Fee for service: $

6. Person serving
   a. ☐ Not a registered California process server.
   b. ☐ Registered California process server.
   c. ☐ Employee or independent contractor of a registered California process server.
   d. ☐ Exempt from registration under Bus. & Prof. Code 22350(b)

   e. ☐ California sheriff, marshal, or constable.
   f. Name, address and telephone number and if applicable, county of registration and number:

I declare under penalty of perjury that the foregoing is true and correct and that this declaration is executed on (Date): . . . . at (Place): . . . . , California.

(For California sheriff, marshal or constable use only)
I certify that the foregoing is true and correct and that this certificate is executed on (Date): . . . . at (Place): . . . . , California.

_____
(Signature)

_____
(Signature)

A declaration under penalty of perjury must be signed in California or in a state that authorizes use of a declaration in place of an affidavit, otherwise an affidavit is required.

ATTORNEY OR PARTY WITHOUT ATTORNEY (NAME AND ADDRESS)	TELEPHONE NO	FOR COURT USE ONLY
ATTORNEY FOR (Name)		

SUPERIOR COURT OF CALIFORNIA, COUNTY OF FRESNO
1100 VAN NESS AVENUE
P.O. BOX 1628
FRESNO, CALIFORNIA 93717

CLK 0009.00 E 11-69 R01-79

PLAINTIFF

DEFENDANT

SUBPENA ☐ DUCES TECUM ☐ COURT ☐ DEPOSITION | CASE NUMBER
☐ OTHER (Specify):

THE PEOPLE OF THE STATE OF CALIFORNIA. TO (Name):

1. Unless you make a special agreement with the person requesting this subpena (See item 5),
   YOU ARE ORDERED TO APPEAR in this action as follows

   a. Date: Time: ☐ Dept.:   ☐ Div.:   ☐ Room:
   b. Address:

   c. ☐ and you are ordered to produce the records described in the accompanying affidavit.

2. a. ☐ You are ordered to appear in person.
   b. ☐ You are not required to appear in person if you comply with Evidence Code sections 1560 and 1561.

3. ☐ The personal attendance of the custodian or other qualified witness and the production of the original records is required by this subpena. The procedure authorized pursuant to sections 1560(b), 1561 and 1562 of the Evidence Code will not be deemed sufficient compliance with this subpena.

4. ☐ You are ordered to appear in your capacity as a peace officer or other person described in Government Code section 68097.1. (Item 6 must be endorsed by the clerk of the court.)

5. **CONTACT THE ATTORNEY REQUESTING THIS SUBPENA, LISTED ABOVE, OR THE PERSON WHOSE NAME APPEARS BELOW, BEFORE THE DATE ON WHICH YOU ARE REQUIRED TO APPEAR, IF YOU HAVE ANY QUESTION ABOUT THE TIME OR DATE FOR YOU TO APPEAR, OR IF YOU WANT TO BE CERTAIN THAT YOUR PRESENCE IS REQUIRED.**

   a. Name: b. Telephone No.

DISOBEDIENCE OF THIS SUBPENA MAY BE PUNISHED AS CONTEMPT BY THIS COURT. YOU WILL ALSO BE LIABLE FOR THE SUM OF FIVE HUNDRED DOLLARS AND ALL DAMAGES RESULTING FROM YOUR FAILURE TO OBEY.

(SEAL)   Dated: *Galen Larson*   Galen Larson, County Clerk and
Clerk of the Superior Court

6. Endorsed for service in a civil matter on a peace officer or other person described in Government Code section 68097.1.

   Dated: Clerk, By _____ , Deputy

Form Adopted by Rule 982
Judicial Council of California
Revised effective January 1, 1979

(See reverse for proof of service)
SUBPENA

CCP 1985–1997; Evid C 1560–1566;
Gov C 68097–68097.10; PC 1326–1332

PROOF OF SERVICE OF SUBPENA

1. I served a copy of this ☐ subpena ☐ subpena duces tecum and affidavit in support thereof, personally upon each of the following persons:

   a. Person served (Name):
   (1) Address:
   (2) Date and time of delivery:
   (3) ☐ Fees paid $_____   ☐ Fees not demanded
   (4) Fees for service $_____

   b. Person served (Name):
   (1) Address:
   (2) Date and time of delivery:
   (3) ☐ Fees paid $_____   ☐ Fees not demanded
   (4) Fees for service $_____

   c. Person served (Name):
   (1) Address:
   (2) Date and time of delivery:
   (3) ☐ Fees paid $_____   ☐ Fees not demanded
   (4) Fees for service $_____

   d. Person served (Name):
   (1) Address:
   (2) Date and time of delivery:
   (3) ☐ Fees paid $_____   ☐ Fees not demanded
   (4) Fees for service $_____

2. I received this subpena on (Date):

3. Person serving

   a. ☐ Not a registered California process server.   e. Name, address and telephone number, and if appli-
   b. ☐ Registered California process server.   cable, county of registration and number.
   c. ☐ Exempt from registration under Bus. & Prof.
        Code 22350(b).
   d. ☐ California sheriff, marshal, or constable.

I declare under penalty of perjury that the foregoing is   (For California sheriff, marshal, or constable use only)
true and correct and that this declaration is executed on   I certify that the foregoing is true and correct and that
(Date): . . . .   this certificate is executed on (Date): . . . .
at (Place): . . . . ,   at (Place): . . . .
California.   California.

_____   _____
              (Signature)   (Signature)

A declaration under penalty of perjury must be signed in California or in a state that authorizes use of a declaration in place of an affidavit, otherwise an affidavit is required

NAME AND ADDRESS OF ATTORNEY	TELEPHONE NO.	FOR COURT USE ONLY

ATTORNEY FOR:

SUPERIOR COURT OF CALIFORNIA, COUNTY OF FRESNO
1100 Van Ness Avenue, P.O. Box 1628
Fresno, California 93717

CLK 4005.00 E08-70 R07-75

ESTATE OF:

DECEDENT

PROOF OF SUBSCRIBING WITNESS	Case Number:

I, the undersigned, state (See footnote* before completing)

1. I am one of the attesting witnesses to the instrument of which Attachment 1 is a photographic copy. I have examined Attachment 1 and my signature is at the end of it.

    a. The name of the decedent was subscribed at the end of the instrument in the presence of the attesting witnesses present at the same time by
        (1) ☐ The decedent personally.
        (2) ☐ Another person in the presence of, and by the direction, of the decedent.
    b. The decedent acknowledged in the presence of the attesting witnesses present at the same time that the decedent's name was subscribed at the end of the original instrument by
        (1) ☐ The decedent personally.
        (2) ☐ Another person in the presence of, and by the direction, of the decedent.

2. At the time of subscribing or acknowledging the instrument the decedent declared to the attesting witnesses that it was decedent's ☐ will ☐ codicil. Then at the decedent's request and in the decedent's presence, the other attesting witnesses and I, in the presence of each other, signed as witnesses at the end thereof.

3. At that time the decedent was over eighteen years of age and appeared to be of sound mind.

4. I have no knowledge of any facts indicating that the instrument, or any part of it, was procured by duress, menace, fraud, or undue influence.

I certify (or declare) under penalty of perjury that the foregoing is true and correct and that this declaration is executed on (Date): . . . ., at (Place): . . . ., California.

. . . .   _____
(Type or print name and address)   (Signature of witness)

. . . .

ATTORNEY'S CERTIFICATION
(Check local court rules for requirements for certifying copies of wills and codicils)

I am an active member of The State Bar of California. I certify (or declare) under penalty of perjury that Attachment 1 is a photographic copy of each and every page of the ☐ will ☐ codicil presented for probate and that this declaration is executed on (Date) . . . . at (Place) . . . . California.

. . . .   _____
(Type or print name)   (Signature of Attorney)

* The declaration must be signed in California (CCP 2015.5). Affidavit required when signed outside California. No attachment permitted less than on a full page (California Rule of Court 201(b)).

Form Approved by the
Judicial Council of California
Effective July 1, 1975   **PROOF OF SUBSCRIBING WITNESS**   Prob C 20, 50, 329

SUPERIOR COURT OF CALIFORNIA, COUNTY OF . . . .

ESTATE OF	FOR COURT USE ONLY

ATTORNEY'S NAME, ADDRESS & TELEPHONE	CLK-4004.00 E08-70 R03-73
	CASE NUMBER

ORDER APPOINTING INHERITANCE TAX REFEREE

IT IS ORDERED that (name):

a disinterested person, is appointed Referee to appraise the above entitled estate.

When an Inheritance Tax Referee is appointed, such referee is authorized to fix the

clear market value of the estate as of the date of death of the decedent, or as of

the date of appointment if a conservatorship or guardianship, and to appraise all

interests, inheritances, transfers, and property of the estate subject to the payment

of inheritance tax under the laws of the State of California.

Dated: _____

_____
Judge of the Superior Court

ORDER APPOINTING INHERITANCE TAX REFEREE   PROB C 605

385

NAME AND ADDRESS OF ATTORNEY	TELEPHONE NO	FOR COURT USE ONLY

ATTORNEY FOR:

SUPERIOR COURT OF CALIFORNIA, COUNTY OF FRESNO
1100 Van Ness Avenue, P.O. Box 1628
Fresno, California 93717

CLK 4003.00 E02-62 R07 75

ESTATE OF:

DECEDENT

LETTERS

☐ TESTAMENTARY   ☐ OF ADMINISTRATION

☐ OF ADMINISTRATION WITH WILL ANNEXED   ☐ OF SPECIAL ADMINISTRATION

Case Number:

STATE OF CALIFORNIA, COUNTY OF . . . .

1. ☐ The last will of the above-named decedent having been proved, the court appoints (Name):

     a. ☐ Executor.
     b. ☐ Administrator with will annexed.

2. The court appoints (Name):

     a. ☐ Administrator of the decedent's estate.
     b. ☐ Special administrator of decedent's estate
        (1) ☐ with the special powers specified in the Order for Probate
        (2) ☐ with the powers of a general administrator.

3. The personal representative ☐ is ☐ is not authorized to administer the estate under The Independent Administration of Estates Act.

WITNESS, the clerk of the above-entitled court, with seal of the court affixed.

Dated:. . . . .

Clerk, by _____ , Deputy

[S E A L]

4.   **AFFIRMATION**

I solemnly affirm that I will perform the duties of personal representative according to law.

Executed on (Date): . . . . , at
(Place): . . . . California.

_____
(Personal Representative)

5.   **CERTIFICATION**

I certify that this document is a correct copy of the original on file in my office, and that the letters issued the above-appointed person have not been revoked, annulled, or set aside, and are still in full force and effect.

Dated:. . . . .

Clerk, by _____ , Deputy

[S E A L]

Form Approved by the
Judicial Council of California
Effective July 1, 1975

LETTERS

Prob C 463, 465, 501, 502, 540
CCP 2015.6

NAME AND ADDRESS OF ATTORNEY	TELEPHONE NO	FOR COURT USE ONLY

ATTORNEY FOR

SUPERIOR COURT OF CALIFORNIA, COUNTY OF FRESNO
1100 Van Ness Avenue, P.O. Box 1628
Fresno, California 93717

ESTATE OF

DECEDENT

CREDITOR'S CLAIM*

FOR COURT USE ONLY

Filed for approval . . . .
(Date)   (Deputy)

Duplicate mailed . . . . .
(Date)   (Deputy)

Presented to court for approval

. . . . .
(Date)   (Deputy)

CLK 4014.00 E11-68 R01-76

CASE NUMBER

THIS CLAIM MUST BE PRESENTED TO THE PERSONAL REPRESENTATIVE OR FILED IN THE OFFICE
OF THE CLERK OF THE COURT IN DUPLICATE WITHIN FOUR MONTHS AFTER THE DAY NOTICE
TO CREDITORS WAS FIRST PUBLISHED

DECLARATION OF CLAIMANT

1 Total amount of the claim is $

2 Claimant (Name):
   a [ ] An individual
   b [ ] An individual doing business under the fictitious name of:

   c [ ] A partnership
   d [ ] A corporation

3 The claimant's address is:

4 I am authorized to make the claim which is justly due or may become due. To my knowledge there are no offsets
or payments which have not been credited. I certify (declare) under penalty of perjury that this creditor's claim,
including any attachments, is true and correct and that this declaration is executed on (Date):
   at (Place) . . . . . , California

5

      (Type name and title)   (Signature)

(Items 6-9 to be completed by the personal representative)

6 a Date of first publication of notice to creditors: b. Date of death:
7 This claim was presented on (Date)
8 Claim is [ ] allowed for: $ [ ] Rejected for: $
9 Estimated value of estate:

   (Type or print name of personal representative)   (Signature of personal representative)

10 [ ] Approved for: $ [ ] Rejected for: $

Dated:

         (Type or print name)   (Signature of [ ] Judge [ ] Commissioner)

11 Total number of pages attached

(Continued on Reverse Side)

* See reverse side for instructions before completing. The declaration must be signed in California (CCP 2015 5), affidavit required when signed outside
California. No attachment permitted less than on a full page (California Rule of Court 201 (b))

Form Approved by the
Judicial Council of California
Effective January 1 1976   **CREDITOR'S CLAIM**   Prob C 705-708, 710
712-714, 717

Claims must be itemized showing the date the service was rendered, or the debt incurred. The item or service should be described in detail, and the amount claimed for each item indicated. If any debt was incurred after the date of death, except funeral claims, it must not be included as an item on this claim form.

If the claim is based upon a note or other written instrument, a copy of such note or instrument must be attached. If secured by mortgage, deed of trust or other lien on property that is of record, it is sufficient to state the date, book and page and county where recorded.

DESCRIPTION OF CREDITOR'S CLAIM

Date of Item	Item	Amount Claimed
		TOTAL $. . . . . . .

CREDITOR'S CLAIM

CLK 4014.00 E11-68 R01-76

NAME AND ADDRESS OF ATTORNEY	TELEPHONE NO	FOR COURT USE ONLY

ATTORNEY FOR:

SUPERIOR COURT OF CALIFORNIA, COUNTY OF FRESNO
1100 Van Ness Avenue, P.O. Box 1628
Fresno, California 93717

ESTATE OF:

CLK 4011.00 E08-70 R01-76

CASE NUMBER:

☐ DECEDENT ☐ CONSERVATEE ☐ WARD

INVENTORY AND APPRAISEMENT*	☐ FINAL ☐ PARTIAL NO.: ☐ SUPPLEMENTAL ☐ REAPPRAISAL FOR SALE	Date of Death or of Appointment of Guardian or Conservator:

APPRAISALS

1. Total appraisal by representative (Attachment 1) . . . . $
2. Total appraisal by referee (Attachment 2) . . . . $

TOTAL: $

DECLARATION OF REPRESENTATIVE

3. Attachment 1 & 2 together with all prior inventories filed herein contain a true statement of ☐ all ☐ a portion of the estate that has come to my knowledge or possession, including particularly all money and just claims against me. I have truly, honestly and impartially appraised each item as set forth in Attachment 1 to the best of my ability.

I certify (declare) under penalty of perjury that the foregoing is true and correct and that this declaration is executed
on (Date): at (Place): California.

. . . .
(Type or print name of representative including title of corporate officer)   (Signature of representative)

STATEMENT OF ATTORNEY REGARDING BOND
(Complete if required by local court rule)

4. ☐ Bond is waived
5. ☐ Bond filed in the amount of: $ ☐ Sufficient   ☐ Insufficient

Date:
_____
(Signature of attorney for estate)

DECLARATION OF INHERITANCE TAX REFEREE

6. I have truly, honestly, and impartially appraised to the best of my ability each item set forth in Attachment 2.
7. A true account of my commission and expenses actually and necessarily incurred pursuant to my appointment is
   Statutory commission: $
   Expenses (Specify): $
   _____

   Total: $
8. I certify (or declare) under penalty of perjury that the foregoing is true and correct and that this declaration was
   executed on (Date): at (Place): California.

. . . .
(Type or print name of referee)   (Signature of referee)

(Continued on Reverse Side)

* See reverse side for instructions before completing. The declaration must be signed in California (CCP 2015.5); affidavit required when signed outside California. No attachment permitted less than on a full page (California Rule of Court 201 (b)).

Form Approved by the
Judicial Council of California   **INVENTORY & APPRAISEMENT**   Prob C 481, 600-611, 784, 1550, 1901
Effective January 1, 1976

See Prob. C. 601, 604, 608, 609, 611, 1550, 1606, 1702, and 1901 for additional instructions.

Furnish extra copy for clerk to transmit to assessor. (Prob. C. 600, 1550, 1901)

See Prob. C. 600–602 for items to be included.

If ward or conservatee is or has been confined in a state hospital during the guardianship or conservatorship, mail a copy to Director of State Department of Health at Sacramento. (Prob C. 1550, 1554.1, 1901)

The representative shall list on Attachment 1 and appraise as of the date of death or date of appointment of guardian or conservator at fair market value moneys, currency, cash items, bank accounts and amounts on deposit with any financial institution (as defined in Probate Code Section 605), and the proceeds of life and accident insurance policies and retirement plans payable upon death in lump sum amounts to the estate, excepting therefrom such items whose fair market value is, in the opinion of the representative, an amount different from the ostensible value or specified amount.

The representative shall list on Attachment 2 all other assets of the estate which shall be appraised by the Referee.

If joint tenancy and other assets are listed for appraisal purposes only and not as part of the probate estate, they must be separately listed on additional attachments and their value excluded from the total valuation of Attachments 1 and 2.

Each attachment should conform to the format approved by the Judicial Council.

CLK 4011.01 E07-71 R01-76

ESTATE OF:

CASE NUMBER

ATTACHMENT NO:

(IN DECEDENTS' ESTATES, ATTACHMENTS MUST CONFORM TO PROBATE CODE 601
REGARDING COMMUNITY AND SEPARATE PROPERTY)

PAGE _____ OF _____ TOTAL PAGES
(ADD PAGES AS REQUIRED)

Item No.   Description   Appraised value
1. $

Form Approved by the
Judicial Council of California
Effective January 1 1976

INVENTORY AND APPRAISEMENT (ATTACHMENT)

Prob C 481
600-605 784
1550 1901

<table>
<tr><td>ATTORNEY OR PARTY WITHOUT ATTORNEY (NAME AND ADDRESS):</td><td>TELEPHONE NO.:</td><td>FOR COURT USE ONLY</td></tr>
</table>

ATTORNEY OR PARTY WITHOUT ATTORNEY (NAME AND ADDRESS):   TELEPHONE NO.: | FOR COURT USE ONLY

ATTORNEY FOR (NAME):

SUPERIOR COURT OF CALIFORNIA, COUNTY OF FRESNO
STREET ADDRESS: 1100 Van Ness Avenue
MAILING ADDRESS: P. O. Box 1628
CITY AND ZIP CODE: Fresno, California 93717
BRANCH NAME:

MARRIAGE OF
PETITIONER:

RESPONDENT:

CLK 0024.00 E07-70 R01-79

SUMMONS (FAMILY LAW)   CASE NUMBER:

<table>
<tr><th>NOTICE!</th><th>¡AVISO!</th></tr>
<tr><td>You have been sued. The court may decide against you without your being heard unless you respond within 30 days. Read the information below.</td><td>Usted ha sido demandado. El tribunal puede decidir contra Ud. sin audiencia a menos que Ud. responda dentro de 30 días. Lea la información que sigue.</td></tr>
<tr><td>If you wish to seek the advice of an attorney in this matter, you should do so promptly so that your response or pleading, if any, may be filed on time.</td><td>Si Usted desea solicitar el consejo de un abogado en este asunto, debería hacerlo inmediatamente, de esta manera, su respuesta o alegación, si hay alguna, puede ser registrada a tiempo.</td></tr>
</table>

1. TO THE RESPONDENT

The petitioner has filed a petition concerning your marriage. If you fail to file a response within 30 days of the date that this summons is served on you, your default may be entered and the court may enter a judgment containing injunctive or other orders concerning division of property, spousal support, child custody, child support, attorney fees, costs, and such other relief as may be granted by the court. The garnishment of wages, taking of money or property, or other court authorized proceedings may also result.

Dated: . . . .   Clerk, By _____, Deputy

(SEAL)

2. NOTICE TO THE PERSON SERVED. You are served
   a. ☐ As an individual
   b. ☐ On behalf of Respondent

     Under:
     ☐ CCP 416.60 (Minor)
     ☐ CCP 416.70 (Ward or Conservatee)
     ☐ CCP 416.90 (Individual)
     ☐ Other (specify):

   c. ☐ By personal delivery on (Date):

(See reverse for Proof of Service)

The response (printed form rule 1282) and other permitted papers must be in the form prescribed by the California Rules of Court. They must be filed in this court with the proper filing fee and proof of service of a copy of each on petitioner. The time when the 30 days to respond begins may vary depending on the method of service. For example, see CCP 413.10-415.50.

Form Adopted by Rule 1283
Judicial Council of California
Revised Effective January 1, 1980

**SUMMONS
(FAMILY LAW)**

CC 4503
CCP 412.20
CRC 1216

PROOF OF SERVICE

(Use separate proof of service for each person served)

1. I served the Summons (Family Law) and Petition (Family Law) on respondent (name):
   a. with (1) ☐ blank Confidential Counseling Statement   (5) ☐ completed and blank Property Declarations
        (2) ☐ Order to Show Cause and Application   (6) ☐ Other (specify):
        (3) ☐ blank Responsive Declaration
        (4) ☐ completed and blank Income and
            Expense Declarations
   b. ☐ By leaving copies with (name and title or relationship to person served):
   c. ☐ By delivery at ☐ home ☐ business
        (1) Date of: (3) Address:
        (2) Time of:
   d. ☐ By mailing
        (1) Date of: (2) Place of:

2. Manner of service: (Check proper box)
   a. ☐ **Personal service.** By personally delivering copies to the person served. (CCP 415.10)
   b. ☐ **Substituted service on natural person, minor, incompetent.** By leaving copies at the dwelling house, usual place of abode, or usual place of business of the person served in the presence of a competent member of the household or a person apparently in charge of the office or place of business, at least 18 years of age, who was informed of the general nature of the papers, and thereafter mailing (by first-class mail, postage prepaid) copies to the person served at the place where the copies were left. (CCP 415.20(b)) **(Attach separate declaration or affidavit stating acts relied on to establish reasonable diligence in first attempting personal service.)**
   c. ☐ **Mail and acknowledgment service.** By mailing (by first-class mail or airmail) copies to the person served, together with two copies of the form of notice and acknowledgment and a return envelope, postage prepaid, addressed to the sender. (CCP 415.30) **(Attach completed acknowledgment of receipt.)**
   d. ☐ **Certified or registered mail service.** By mailing to address outside California (by registered or certified airmail with return receipt requested) copies to the person served. (CCP 415.40) **(Attach signed return receipt or other evidence of actual delivery to the person served.)**
   e. ☐ Other (Specify code section):
        ☐ Additional page is attached.

3. The notice to the person served (Item 2 on the copy of the summons served) was completed as follows (CCP 412.30, 415.10, and 474):
   a. ☐ As an individual
   b. ☐ On behalf of Respondent
        Under: ☐ CCP 416.60 (Minor)   ☐ Other (specify):
            ☐ CCP 416.70 (Ward or Conservatee)
            ☐ CCP 416.90 (Individual)
   c. ☐ By personal delivery on (Date): . . . .
4. At the time of service I was at least 18 years of age and not a party to this action.
5. Fee for service: $ . . . .
6. Person serving
   a. ☐ Not a registered California process server.   e. ☐ California sheriff, marshal, or constable.
   b. ☐ Registered California process server.   f. Name, address and telephone number and
   c. ☐ Employee or independent contractor of a   if applicable, county of registration and number:
        registered California process server.
   d. ☐ Exempt from registration under Bus. & Prof.
        Code 22350(b)

I declare under penalty of perjury that the foregoing is true and correct and that this declaration is executed on (date): . . . . at (place): . . . . , California.

(For California sheriff, marshal or constable use only)
I certify that the foregoing is true and correct and that this certificate is executed on (date): . . . . at (place): . . . . at . . . . , California.

_____
(Signature)

_____
(Signature)

A declaration under penalty of perjury must be signed in California or in a state that authorizes use of a declaration in place of an affidavit; otherwise an affidavit is required.

ATTORNEY OR PARTY WITHOUT ATTORNEY (NAME AND ADDRESS):	TELEPHONE NO.:	FOR COURT USE ONLY
ATTORNEY FOR (NAME):		

SUPERIOR COURT OF CALIFORNIA, COUNTY OF
STREET ADDRESS:
MAILING ADDRESS:
CITY AND ZIP CODE:
BRANCH NAME:

MARRIAGE OF
PETITIONER:

RESPONDENT:

CLK 0025.00 E01-70 R01-79

PETITION FOR

☐ **Dissolution of Marriage**   ☐ **And Declaration Under Uniform Child**
☐ **Legal Separation**   **Custody Jurisdiction Act**
☐ **Nullity of Marriage**

CASE NUMBER:

1. RESIDENCE (Dissolution only)   ☐ Petitioner   ☐ Respondent
   has been a resident of this state for at least six months and of this county for at least three months immediately preceding the filing of this Petition for Dissolution.

2. STATISTICAL FACTS   a. Date of marriage: c. Period between marriage and separation
                                            b. Date of separation: Years: Months:

3. DECLARATION REGARDING MINOR CHILDREN OF THIS MARRIAGE
   a. ☐ There are no minor children.
   b. ☐ The minor children are:
      Name   Birthdate   Age   Sex

   c. IF THERE ARE MINOR CHILDREN, COMPLETE EITHER (1) or (2)
      (1) ☐ Each child named in 3b is presently living with ☐ Petitioner ☐ Respondent
              at (address):

          and during the last five years has lived in no state other than California and with no person other than petitioner or respondent or both.

          Petitioner has not participated in any capacity in any litigation or proceeding in any state concerning custody of any minor child of this marriage.

          Petitioner has no information of any pending custody proceeding or of any person not a party to this proceeding who has physical custody or claims to have custody or visitation rights concerning any minor child of this marriage.

      (2) ☐ A completed Declaration Under Uniform Custody of Minors Act is attached.

                               (Continued on reverse)

The declaration under penalty of perjury must be signed in California, or in a state that authorizes use of a declaration in place of an affidavit; otherwise an affidavit is required.

Form Adopted by Rule 1281
Judicial Council of California
Revised Effective January 1, 1980

**PETITION
(FAMILY LAW)**

CC 4503, 5158; CRC 1215

4. DECLARATION REGARDING COMMUNITY AND QUASI-COMMUNITY ASSETS AND OBLIGATIONS AS PRESENTLY KNOWN

   a. ☐ There are no such assets or obligations subject to disposition by the court in this proceeding.

   b. ☐ All such assets and obligations have been disposed of by written agreement.

   c. ☐ All such assets and obligations are listed in the property declaration to be filed with this petition.

   d. ☐ All such assets and obligations are listed below:

5. ☐ Petitioner requests confirmation of the following as separate assets and obligations:

ITEM   CONFIRM TO

6. Petitioner requests

   a. ☐ Dissolution of the marriage based on
      (1) ☐ irreconcilable differences. CC 4506(1)
      (2) ☐ incurable insanity. CC 4506(2)

   b. ☐ Legal separation of the parties based on
      (1) ☐ irreconcilable differences. CC 4506(1)
      (2) ☐ incurable insanity. CC 4506(2)

   c. ☐ Nullity of void marriage based on
      (1) ☐ incestuous marriage. CC 4400
      (2) ☐ bigamous marriage. CC 4401

   d. ☐ Nullity of voidable marriage based on
      (1) ☐ petitioner's age at time of marriage. CC 4425(a)
      (2) ☐ prior existing marriage. CC 4425(b)
      (3) ☐ unsound mind. CC 4425(c)
      (4) ☐ fraud. CC 4425(d)
      (5) ☐ force. CC 4425(e)
      (6) ☐ physical incapacity. CC 4425(f)

7. Petitioner requests that the court grant the relief or judgment specified in item 6, make injunctive and other orders as may be proper, and that

   a. ☐ Visitation rights be determined and child custody be awarded
      ☐ Petitioner ☐ Respondent ☐ Other (specify): . . . .

   b. ☐ Child support be awarded ☐ Petitioner ☐ Respondent

   c. ☐ Spousal support be awarded ☐ Petitioner ☐ Respondent

   d. ☐ Property rights be determined.

   e. ☐ Attorney's fees and costs be awarded ☐ Petitioner ☐ Respondent

   f. ☐ Wife's former name be restored (specify): . . . .

Petitioner declares under penalty of perjury that the foregoing, including any attachment, is true and correct and that this declaration is executed at (place): . . . . , California, on (date): . . . .

_____
(Signature of Petitioner)

. . . . (Type or print name of att'   y)   _____
(Signature   ttorney for Petitioner)

Space Below for Use of Court Clerk Only

Attorney(s) for . . . .

CLK 0027.00 E01-70 R01-75

SUPERIOR COURT OF CALIFORNIA, COUNTY OF . . . .

In re the marriage of

Petitioner:

and

Respondent:

CASE NUMBER

☐ **Petitioner's**　☐ **Respondent's**

**CONFIDENTIAL COUNSELING STATEMENT
(MARRIAGE)**

I understand that conciliation services are available to me through the court in this county.

☐ I would like marriage counseling.

☐ I would like to talk with a trained person about my present family situation.

☐ I do not desire counseling at this time.

Mailing address of requesting party:

Name:

Street:

City/State/Zip

Mailing address of other party:

Name:

Street:

City/State/Zip

Date:

_____

(Signature)

Form Adopted by Rule 1284 of
The Judicial Council of California
Effective January 1, 1975 **CONFIDENTIAL COUNSELING STATEMENT (MARRIAGE)**

ATTORNEY OR PARTY WITHOUT ATTORNEY (NAME AND ADDRESS):	TELEPHONE NO.:	FOR COURT USE ONLY

ATTORNEY FOR (NAME):

SUPERIOR COURT OF CALIFORNIA, COUNTY OF
STREET ADDRESS:

MAILING ADDRESS:

CITY AND ZIP CODE:

BRANCH NAME:

MARRIAGE OF

PETITIONER:

RESPONDENT:

CLK 0031.00 E01-70 R01-79

REQUEST TO ENTER DEFAULT	CASE NUMBER:

1. TO THE CLERK: Please enter the default of the respondent who has failed to respond to the petition.
2. A completed ☐ Income and Expense Declaration ☐ Property Declaration is attached.
3. A completed ☐ Income and Expense Declaration ☐ Property Declaration is *not* attached because (check at least one of the following)
   (1) ☐ There have been no changes since the previous filing.
   (2) ☐ The issues subject to disposition by the court in this proceeding are the subject of a written agreement.
   (3) ☐ There are no issues of child custody, child or spousal support, division of community property or attorney fees and costs subject to determination by this court.
   (4) ☐ The petition does not request money, property, costs or attorney fees.

Dated:

. . . .
(Type or print name)

_____
Signature of (Attorney for) Petitioner

3. DECLARATION
   a. ☐ No mailing is required because service was by publication and the address of respondent remains unknown.
   b. ☐ A copy of this Request to Enter Default including any attachments was mailed to the respondent's attorney of record or, if none, to respondent's last known address as follows
      (1) Date of mailing: (2) Addressed as follows:

   c. I declare under penalty of perjury that the foregoing is true and correct and that this declaration is executed on (date): . . . . at (place): . . . . , California.

. . . .
(Type or print name)

_____
(Signature of declarant)

FOR COURT USE ONLY
    Default entered as requested on (date):

                                              Clerk, by:

        Default NOT entered. Reason:

(See reverse for Memorandum of Costs and Declaration of Nonmilitary Status)

The declaration under penalty of perjury must be signed in California or in a state that authorizes use of a declaration in place of an affidavit; otherwise an affidavit is required. (CCP 2015.5)

Form Adopted by Rule 1286
Judicial Council of California
Revised Effective January 1, 1980

REQUEST TO ENTER DEFAULT
(FAMILY LAW)

CCP 585,587

4. MEMORANDUM OF COSTS

   a. ☐ Costs and disbursements are waived.
   b. Costs and disbursements are listed as follows

   (1) ☐ Clerk's fees . . . . $ . . . .

   (2) ☐ Process server's fees . . . . $ . . . .

   (3) ☐ Other (specify) . . . . $ . . . .

      . . . . $ . . . .

      . . . . $ . . . .

      . . . . $ . . . .

       TOTAL . . . . $ . . . .

I am the attorney, agent, or party who claims these costs. To the best of my knowledge and belief the foregoing items of cost are correct and have been necessarily incurred in this cause or proceeding.

I declare under penalty of perjury that the foregoing is true and correct and that this declaration is executed on (date): . . . . at (place): . . . . , California.

. . . .   _____
         (Type or print name)   (Signature of declarant)

5. DECLARATION OF NONMILITARY STATUS

Respondent is not in the military service or in the military service of the United States as defined in Section 101 of the Soldiers' and Sailors' Relief Act of 1940, as amended, and not entitled to the benefits of such act.

I declare under penalty of perjury that the foregoing is true and correct and that this declaration is executed on (date): . . . . at (place): . . . . , California.

. . . .   _____
         (Type or print name)   (Signature of declarant)

ATTORNEY OR PARTY WITHOUT ATTORNEY (NAME AND ADDRESS):	TELEPHONE NO.:	FOR COURT USE ONLY

ATTORNEY FOR (NAME):

SUPERIOR COURT OF CALIFORNIA, COUNTY OF
STREET ADDRESS:
MAILING ADDRESS:
CITY AND ZIP CODE:
BRANCH NAME:

MARRIAGE OF
PETITIONER:

RESPONDENT:

CLK 0032.00 E01-70 R01-79

INTERLOCUTORY JUDGMENT OF DISSOLUTION OF MARRIAGE	CASE NUMBER:

1. This proceeding came on for ☐ default or uncontested ☐ contested hearing as follows

   a. Date: ☐ Dept.: ☐ Div.: ☐ Room:

   b. Judge (name): ☐ Temporary judge

   c. ☐ Petitioner present in court ☐ Attorney present in court (name):

   d. ☐ Respondent present in court ☐ Attorney present in court (name):

   e. ☐ Claimant present in court ☐ Attorney present in court (name):

2. The court acquired jurisdiction of the respondent on (date):
   a. ☐ Respondent was served with process.
   b. ☐ Respondent appeared.

3. THE COURT ORDERS
   a. An interlocutory judgment be entered and the parties are entitled to have their marriage dissolved.

   b. After six months from the date the court acquired jurisdiction of the respondent a final judgment of dissolution may be entered upon proper application of either party or on the court's own motion, unless a dismissal signed by both parties is filed. The final judgment shall include such other and further relief as may be necessary to a complete disposition of this proceeding, but entry of the final judgment shall not deprive this court of its jurisdiction over any matter expressly reserved to it in this or the final judgment until a final disposition is made of each such matter.

   c. Jurisdiction is reserved to make such other and further orders as may be necessary to carry out the provisions of this judgment.

4. ☐ THE COURT FURTHER ORDERS
   a. ☐ Wife's former name be restored (specify):
   b. ☐ Other:

Dated: . . . . _____
                                         Judge of the Superior Court

5. Total number of pages attached: ☐ Signature follows last attachment

---

THIS INTERLOCUTORY JUDGMENT DOES NOT CONSTITUTE A FINAL DISSOLUTION OF MARRIAGE AND THE PARTIES ARE STILL MARRIED. ONE OF THE PARTIES MUST SUBMIT A REQUEST FOR FINAL JUDGMENT ON THE FORM PRESCRIBED BY RULE 1288. NEITHER PARTY MAY REMARRY UNTIL A FINAL JUDGMENT OF DISSOLUTION IS ENTERED.

No attachment permitted on less than a full page. Cal Rule of Ct 201(b)

Form Adopted by Rule 1287
Judicial Council of California
Revised Effective January 1, 1980

**INTERLOCUTORY JUDGMENT OF
DISSOLUTION OF MARRIAGE
(FAMILY LAW)**

CC 4512, 4514

ATTORNEY OR PARTY WITHOUT ATTORNEY (NAME AND ADDRESS):	TELEPHONE NO.:	FOR COURT USE ONLY
ATTORNEY FOR (NAME):		

SUPERIOR COURT OF CALIFORNIA, COUNTY OF
STREET ADDRESS:
MAILING ADDRESS:
CITY AND ZIP CODE:
BRANCH NAME:

MARRIAGE OF
PETITIONER:

RESPONDENT:

CLK 0034.00 E01-70 R01-79

FINAL JUDGMENT OF	☐ **DISSOLUTION OF MARRIAGE** ☐ **LEGAL SEPARATION** ☐ **NULLITY**	CASE NUMBER:

1. The court acquired jurisdiction of the respondent on (date):

2. THE COURT ORDERS

    a. ☐ A final judgment of dissolution be entered, and the parties are restored to the status of unmarried persons.

    b. ☐ A judgment of legal separation be entered.

    c. ☐ A judgment of nullity be entered on the ground of (specify):

       and the parties are declared to be unmarried persons.

3. ☐ THE COURT FURTHER ORDERS

    a. ☐ This judgment be entered nunc pro tunc as of (date):

    b. ☐ Wife's former name be restored (specify):

    c. ☐ Other:

Dated: . . . . _____

                                      Judge of the Superior Court

                        ☐ Signature follows last attachment.

4. Total number of pages attached:

No attachment permitted on less than a full page. Cal Rules of Ct 201(b)

Form Adopted by Rule 1289
Judicial Council of California
Revised January 1, 1980

FINAL JUDGMENT
(FAMILY LAW)

CC 4514, 4515

ATTORNEY OR PARTY WITHOUT ATTORNEY (NAME AND ADDRESS):	TELEPHONE NO.:	FOR COURT USE ONLY

ATTORNEY FOR (NAME):

SUPERIOR COURT OF CALIFORNIA, COUNTY OF
STREET ADDRESS:
MAILING ADDRESS:
CITY AND ZIP CODE:
BRANCH NAME:

MARRIAGE OF
PETITIONER:

RESPONDENT:

CLK 0035.00 E01-70 R01-79

NOTICE OF ENTRY OF JUDGMENT	CASE NUMBER:

You are notified that the following judgment was entered on (date):

1. ☐ Interlocutory Judgment of Dissolution of Marriage

> THE INTERLOCUTORY JUDGMENT TO WHICH THIS NOTICE REFERS DOES NOT CONSTITUTE A
> FINAL DISSOLUTION OF MARRIAGE AND THE PARTIES ARE STILL MARRIED. ONE OF THE PARTIES
> MUST SUBMIT A REQUEST FOR A FINAL JUDGMENT ON THE FORM PRESCRIBED BY RULE 1288.
> NEITHER PARTY MAY REMARRY UNTIL A FINAL JUDGMENT OF DISSOLUTION IS ENTERED.

2. ☐ Final Judgment of Dissolution of Marriage
3. ☐ Final Judgment of Legal Separation
4. ☐ Final Judgment of Nullity

Dated: . . . . Clerk, By _____ , Deputy

CLERK'S CERTIFICATE OF MAILING

I certify that I am not a party to this cause and that a copy of the foregoing was mailed first class, postage prepaid,
in a sealed envelope addressed as shown below, and that the mailing of the foregoing and execution of this certificate
occurred at (place): . . . . , California,

on (date): . . . . Clerk, By _____ , Deputy

Form Adopted by Rule 1290
Judicial Council of California
Revised Effective January 1, 1980

NOTICE OF ENTRY OF JUDGMENT
(FAMILY LAW)

Appendix F

Glossary

The glossary furnishes general legal meanings rather than the precise, documented meanings given in *Black's Law Dictionary* and other comparable legal dictionaries.

Acco fastener: A two-pronged fastener and bar used to fasten papers securely to a file folder.

Accounting: A report required in probate matters (unless it is waived) that accounts for all assets of the estate and all transactions during the period covered by the accounting.

Acknowledgment: Formal statement made before an authorized individual by which signer acknowledges that he signed the document freely and of his own will.

Action: Lawsuit; court proceeding. (*See* **civil action; criminal action**)

Action in personam: An action directed against a specific person.

Adjective law: (*See* **procedural law**)

Adjudge: To decide judicially.

Adjudication: Making or pronouncing a judgment or decree in a legal cause.

Ad litem: For the lawsuit; for that lawsuit only.

Administrative law: The laws brought into existence by each administrative agency (when empowered to make such laws) to permit the agency to gain those objectives for which it was created.

Administrator: (*fem.* **administratrix**) One appointed by the court to administer the estate of a decedent who left no will.

Administrator cta: (*See* administrator with will annexed)

Administrator cum testamento annexo: (*See* administrator with will annexed)

Administrator with will annexed: One appointed by the court to carry out the provisions of a will when either there is no named executor or the named executor cannot or will not act in that capacity. (*Also called* **administrator cum testamento annexo** *and* **administrator cta**)

Administratrix: (*See* administrator)

Admiralty court: Court with jurisdiction in maritime matters.

Admit: Agree — i.e., "admits paragraphs I and II" means agrees with the statements and facts contained in those paragraphs; to give possession.

Adoption: Legally making one who is of no prior relation a child of the family with all rights and privileges of other children in the family.

Affiant: One who makes and signs an affidavit.

Affidavit: A written statement of fact made voluntarily and sworn or affirmed to before a notary public or other qualified officer.

Affidavit of service: An affidavit certifying that service of a document has taken place.

Affidavit of service by mail: An affidavit showing the date and place of mailing of a document for service.

Affirmative defense: New matter used as a defense against a complaint.

Affix: Attach; place upon; sign.

Aforesaid: Stated before; stated earlier in the document.

Aggregate: Total; entire amount; complete whole.

Agreement: Written document that serves as evidence of an agreement; a meeting of the minds to a proposition between two or more persons.

Alimony: The support (usually money) paid by one ex-spouse to the other following a divorce or marriage dissolution.

Alimony pendente lite: An allowance for support to a spouse pending (during) a suit for divorce.

Allegation: A statement or assertion in a pleading expected to be proved.

Alternate executor: One named in a will to act as executor if the first named executor is unable or unwilling to act.

American Bar Association: The professional association that represents attorneys in the United States and to which most attorneys belong.

American Digest System: Major index to case law in the United States of America.

American Jurisprudence: A multivolume legal encyclopedia.

Ancillary proceeding: A legal proceeding that is a second or supplementary proceeding. In probate, an ancillary proceeding may be begun in another state to administer decedent's property located outside the state of his domicile.

Answer: A pleading that answers the allegations of a complaint; a written defense to allegations in complaint or petition.

Answer and cross-complaint: A pleading answering plaintiff's complaint or petition and including defendant's own complaint, which is called a cross-complaint.

Appeal: (*Noun*) A review by a higher (appeal) court of the action of a lower (trial) court; (*verb*) to take a case to a higher court for review.

Appearance: The filing with the court clerk of the first court document on behalf of a party to a lawsuit or other legal matter, together with payment of the filing fee if required.

Appellant: The party to the suit who appeals one court's decision to another court.

Appellee: The party in a lawsuit against whom an appeal is taken.

Appointment calendar: Desk calendar for the attorney and the legal secretary on which should be recorded scheduled court appearances, client appointments, and other such matters. A diary may also be used in this capacity.

Appraiser: One appointed by the court to appraise the assets of an estate.

Arraignment: Taking of a prisoner before the court to answer to a criminal charge.

Arrest: To take an individual into custody.

Articles of incorporation: The legal document by which a corporation is organized under state corporation laws.

Assign: To make over to another; to transfer.

Assignee: The one who receives the benefits of an assignment.

Assignor: The one who makes an assignment of a right or interest.

At law and in equity: According to law and according to the doctrines of equity.

Attestation clause: Clause in a will that is signed by the witnesses and that states that the witnesses and testator were all present at the time each signed the will.

Attesting witness: One who, upon request, signs his name to an instrument for the purpose of identifying or witnessing it.

Attorney: One who substitutes for another in managing a legal problem; one who acts as agent for another in managing a legal problem; also, one who has passed the bar and is licensed to practice law.

Attorney of record: The attorney on record with the court as representing a particular client.

Attorneys reference service (*also* **lawyers reference service**): A service, usually listed in the Yellow Pages of the telephone directory, through which one may receive guidance in selecting an attorney.

Bailment: Delivery of personal property from one party to another to be held in trust until a special condition has been fulfilled, whereupon the goods will be delivered as agreed.

Bankrupt: One who is the subject of bankruptcy proceedings.

Bankruptcy: The proceedings followed under bankruptcy law to legally relieve an insolvent person of debts.

Barrister: In England, the lawyer who conducts the trial before the bar.

Being duly sworn: Having properly taken an oath to tell the truth.

Beneficiary: One named in a will to receive all or part of the testator's property; one named to receive or benefit under the terms of an insurance policy; one named to benefit from a trust estate.

Bequeath: To make a gift of personal property by will.

Bequest: Gift of personal property by will.

Bill: *See* **complaint**; also, a formal written statement.

Bona fide: In good faith; openly; without fraud.

Bond: A money guarantee paid to a bondsman who will assure a person's attendance in court (*See also* **fidelity bond**)

Breach of contract suit: A lawsuit based on the legal doctrine that the terms of a contract were broken by one of the parties and that this may be the basis of a lawsuit.

Brief: A condensed statement, prepared by counsel, that will serve as basis for argument on a cause before an appellate court.

Business office forms: Those forms that business firms make available, free of charge, to law offices and others.

Calendar (*Noun*) *See* **appointment calendar**; (*verb*) to set a hearing date on the court calendar.

Canons: The canons of the Code of Professional Responsibility of the American Bar Association, which are statements of axiomatic norms, expressing in general terms the standards of professional conduct expected of lawyers in their relationships with the public, with the legal system, and with the legal profession.

Caption: A term used to include the following data required on all court documents: jurisdiction, venue, case title, court number, and title of court document.

Case law: The reported cases that together form a body of law or precedence upon which decisions in later cases may be based.

Case title: The names of the parties to the suit; the name of the owner of property or the decedent in a probate matter.

Causa: (Latin) Cause.

Cause: The origin or reason for a lawsuit; reason.

Cause of action: The event or act or series of events or acts upon which a lawsuit is based.

Certified copy: Copy of a legal document that has been signed and certified as being a true copy by the one who holds the original instrument.

Certify: To state or testify in writing; to establish as a fact.

Chain of title: All owners or part owners of a piece of real property to and including the present owner.

Citation: The abbreviation of the information necessary to identify a source of legal data; a source of legal data such as a reported case or a statute.

Citators: A series of law books that, when poperly used, inform the user whether the statutes referred to have been superseded or whether the cases cited have been modified or reversed.

Cite: To command a person to appear in a particular place at a particular time; to refer to a legal authority.

Civil action: An action whereby one party seeks redress from another party for a wrong committed or for the protection of a right.

Civil law: A branch of law adjusting differences between people or institutions. It includes all of the branches of law that involve business relationships, civil wrongs, and property ownership.

Claimant: One who claims or makes claim to a right; in bankruptcy, one who claims part of bankrupt's assets.

Client: Term used to designate those who make use of the legal services available in a law office.

Client documents: Those legal instruments prepared for the use of the client. One-party client documents are for the use of one individual. Two-party client documents are for the use of two individuals. Multiparty client documents are for the use of three or more individuals.

Code books: The law books containing the statutes passed by state and federal legislatures.

Codicil: An addendum to a will.

Collateral: (*Adj.*) Supplementary, additional; (*noun*) security for a loan.

Commercial forms: Those legal forms that may be purchased at a stationery store.

Commingle: Mix or mingle together, as monies.

Common law: The body of law that originated and developed in England following the Norman Conquest in 1066. The common law principle is used by our court system today.

Community property: Property owned in common by both husband and wife; property acquired during marriage that is not separate property.

Complaint: First pleading in a civil suit, which states the facts or allegations upon which plaintiff bases his action. (*Also sometimes called a* **declaration, petition, bill, narration**)

Concessionaire: One who has been granted or conceded special privileges.

Confidentiality: The quality of being secret or private in nature.

Confirm: To complete what was uncertain; to make assurance of truth.

Conform: To make like; to make the same; to add typed signatures and dates to copies of a document to make them identical in content with the original.

Consanguinity: Blood relationship.

Conservatee: The one who owns the property in a conservatorship, but who is incapable of managing the property.

Conservator: One appointed by the court to manage the property of a conservatee.

Conservatorship: Legal responsibility established to conserve or protect the property of those who, for reasons of age or infirmity, are unable to manage their property.

Consideration: Tangible or intangible benefits or goods.

Constitutional law: That branch of public law dealing with the establishment and interpretation of the constitutions, federal and state.

Contempt of court: Any act that willfully disobeys an order of the court; an act calculated to embarrass the court or delay the administration of justice.

Contest: To question.

Contract: Agreement between two or more persons to establish or remove a legal relationship.

Contract law: That branch of law concerned with the enforceability of agreements between people or institutions.

Conveyance: Transfer of legal title to land; the legal instrument transferring title to real property.

Corporation: A legal entity existing by authority of the laws of the state where the corporation was brought into existence.

Corpus Juris Secundum: A multivolume legal encyclopedia.

Costs of court: Those costs resulting from filing a lawsuit or other legal matter. Costs include filing fees.

Counsel: Attorney; advice.

Counterclaim: A claim presented by a defendant in opposition to or countering the claim of the plaintiff.

Court calendar: The schedule of cases to be heard in a court for any day, week, or other period of time.

Court clerk's office: The office serving a particular court, which office houses the court clerk and deputy court clerks employed to serve the court. Legal papers for the court are filed in the appropriate court clerk's office.

Court documents: Legal documents prepared for the use of the courts.

Court forms: Legal forms issued by a court clerk's office, usually free of charge.

Court number: The number, usually called the **docket number,** assigned to the case by the court clerk.

Court of appeal: A court that, on appeal of one party to the suit, reviews proceedings held in the lower court.

Court of original jurisdiction: Trial court that hears a lawsuit the first time it is in court.

Court of record: A court where written court documents must be filed and where all proceedings of the court are recorded for possible later reference.

Court reporter: One skilled in shorthand and certified to take verbatim testimony during court proceedings.

Courts: That part of the government established to apply the law and administer justice.

Covenant: An agreement; a pledge.

Credible evidence: Evidence that is worthy of belief.

Creditor's claim: A legal form that must be completed and presented in an estate matter before payment of the debt may be made.

Creditors' meeting: A meeting of all creditors of a bankrupt.

Criminal action: Lawsuit in which the government prosecutes an individual or institution for the alleged commission of a crime.

Criminal law: That branch of law dealing with crimes and punishment. The government is plaintiff and the individual or institution is the defendant who has allegedly violated a law.

Cross action: A legal action brought by the defendant named in a suit against the party who is the plaintiff in the suit.

Cross-complainant: The defendant in a civil suit who files a cross action against the plaintiff in the suit.

Cross-complaint: Pleading filed by defendant in a civil suit stating cause of action against original plaintiff.

Cross-defendant: The plaintiff in a civil suit in which a cross-complaint or a cross action has been filed.

Date line: The line of a legal instrument that furnishes the date of the document.

Debtor's petition: In bankruptcy proceeding, the initial petition filed and signed by the debtor.

Deceased: (*Adj.*) Having died recently.

Decedent: (*Noun*) One who has recently died.

Declaration: (*See* complaint)

Decree: (*Noun*) The judgment of the court; (*verb*) to issue an order or judgment.

Decree of distribution: In a probate matter, the decree that makes distribution of the assets of the estate.

Deed: (*Noun*) A conveyance; an instrument containing a contract; (*verb*) to give; to sign over.

Deems: Considers; determines.

Default: The failure of a party to a suit or contract to take the steps required of him.

Defendant: Party against whom a lawsuit is brought.

Defense attorney: Attorney representing a defendant.

Demise: (*Noun*) Death; (*verb*) to lease.

Demised premises: Leased property.

Demur: To question the sufficiency of the law in a pleading or set of facts that were alleged.

Demurrer: A pleading questioning that the pleading of the other side states facts of sufficient legal consequence to require further answer or proceeding.

Deponent: One who makes and signs a deposition.

Depose: To make a deposition; to make a statement.

Depositary: Person who receives a deposit.

Deposition: The testimony of a witness taken under oath and pursuant to law, which, when reduced to writing and authenticated, may be used at the trial.

Depository: Place where deposit is left.

Descriptive law: (*See* procedural law)

Devise: (*Noun*) A gift of real property made by will; (*verb*) to make a gift of real property by will.

Devisee: One who receives a gift of real property by provision of a will.

Diary: (*See* appointment calendar)

Digests: Series of books that serve as indexes to the reported cases comprising case law.

Discharge: A document filed when bankrupt is relieved of the burden of debts; a document filed when a conservator, guardian, executor, administrator, or administrator with will annexed is relieved of duties following distribution of the estate.

Disciplinary rules: The disciplinary rules of the Code of Professional Responsibility of the American Bar Association, which state the minimum level of conduct below which no lawyer can fall without being subject to disciplinary action. They are mandatory in character.

Dismissal: An order or judgment disposing of a lawsuit or action by dismissing it from court.

Dissolution of marriage: Legal separation of a man and wife by judgment of the court; termination of marriage by dissolution.

Divorce: Legal separation of a man and wife by judgment of the court.

Docket: (*Noun*) The book containing records of court actions; (*verb*) to enter a record in the docket book.

Docket number: (*See* **court number**)

Domicile: Residence.

Duress: Unlawfully forcing one to do or not to do something.

Encumber: (*also* **incumber**) To make real property subject to a charge or other liability.

Encumbrance: (*also* **incumbrance**) A charge or lien or fee against real property.

Encyclopedia, legal: Series of books containing legal doctrines or legal principles.

Endorsement: (*also* **indorsement**) Identifying information placed on the outside of the legal back; it includes document title, parties, and date.

Enjoin: To require, or to command a person to perform or to cease performing an act.

Ensue: To follow.

Equity: Very broadly, the rule of fairness, justness, and fair dealing among all persons.

Escalator clause: A clause, usually a part of a lease or contract, allowing for increased rental during the term of the agreement.

Esquire: A title used in England, which is comparable to "Mr." in the United States. Abbreviation: **Esq.**

Et al.: (Latin) And others.

Et ux.: (Latin) And wife.

Ethical considerations: The considerations of the Code of Professional Responsibility of the American Bar Association, which represent the objectives toward which every member of the profession should strive. They are aspirational in character.

Ex contractu: (Latin) From a contract.

Ex delicto: (Latin) From the crime or tort.

Ex parte: On one side only; for one side, by one side.

Execute: Sign; complete; make. A contract is executed when it has been signed, sealed, and delivered.

Executor: (*fem.* **executrix**) One named by the testator in his will to carry out the provisions of the will.

Extraordinary fees: The fees, in addition to statutory fees, that may be requested and ordered paid from estate funds. Such extraordinary fees are in payment of services provided by the attorney and/or the executor or administrator that are beyond the services usually required in such probate matter.

Federal estate tax form: A federal estate tax return, which is required by the Internal Revenue Service in an estate with assets over a specified amount at date of death.

Fee simple: Clear title to real property.

Felony: Serious crime. Punishment for a felony may be death or imprisonment in a state or federal penitentiary.

Fidelity bond: Good-faith bond, which assures protection of the money or goods covered. (*See also* **bond**)

Fiduciary relationship: A trust or good-faith relationship between the attorney and the client.

File: (*Noun*) Folder for legal or business papers; (*verb*) to place papers in a file folder; to deposit legal papers with a court clerk's office.

File number: The office-assigned number given each new matter to be handled by the firm.

Filing fee: A fee paid to the court clerk's office each time a new matter is filed with that office and a new appearance made.

Findings: That which has been learned and determined.

First cause of action: The first of two or more causes of action in a single pleading.

Foregoing: What precedes; has gone before.

Form file: An assemblage of copies of various legal documents prepared by the legal secretary and used as guides in the preparation of later similar documents.

Formal will: A will drawn and witnessed in accordance with state law.

Franchise: A special privilege conferred by government that does not apply to all citizens generally. Two franchises are: the right to be a corporation; the right of an insurance company to issue insurance policies.

General practice: A law office that handles a great variety of legal problems.

Good cause: Good or substantial reason.

Government forms: Those forms provided attorneys and others, usually free of charge, by various government agencies.

Grounds for suit: Basis for a lawsuit; the legal points relied upon.

Guardian: One legally responsible for the care of the person and/or property of a minor or incompetent who, because of age, incompetency, or other condition, is unable to administer his own affairs. Guardian of the person is responsible only for the welfare of the individual; guardian of the estate is responsible only for the estate (assets).

Guardian ad litem: Guardian during the suit; guardian for that suit only.

Guardian of the estate: (*See* guardian)

Guardian of the person: (*See* guardian)

Guardianship: Legal responsibility established to protect the property of minors and others who, for various legal reasons, are unable to administer their affairs.

Habeas corpus, writ of: A writ releasing a person from unlawful imprisonment.

Hand and seal: Signature and seal.

Hearing: Proceeding in a court of law.

Hearing date: The date a legal proceeding is held in a court of law.

Heirs: (*also called* heirs at law) Those named by law to succeed to an intestate estate.

Hereafter: After this point in time.

Hereby: By this; by this document.

Hereditaments: (her-e-DIT-a-ments) Things that may be inherited.

Hereinabove: Within this document but prior to this point in the document.

Hereinafter: Within this document but following this point in the document.

Hereof: Of this.

Hereto: To this.

Heretofore: Before now; prior to this point.

Hereunder: Under the conditions in this document; following this point in the document.

Hereunto: To this.

Holdover: The condition existing when tenant retains possession of the leased property following the term of a lease.

Holographic will: A will written entirely in the handwriting of the testator or testatrix.

Hypothecate: To pledge a thing without actually delivering possession of it.

In lieu of: Instead of; in place of.

In personam: (Latin) In person; directed against a specific person.

Inasmuch as: Since; in view of the fact that.

Incompetent: One who is incapable of managing his own affairs because of insanity, feeblemindedness, or similar condition.

Incumber: (*See* encumber)

Incumbrance: (*See* encumbrance)

Indorsement: (*See* endorsement)

Inferior court: Any court subordinate to the highest appellate court; a court where written court documents are usually not required as part of the procedure nor is a written record kept of the proceedings.

Insofar as: To the degree that.

Institute: To begin; to commence.

Instrument: A formal document; a written legal document.

Intangible personal property: Property having no value itself but representing value, such as a stock certificate or promissory note.

Interlocutory decree: An order of the court that precedes the final order or decree; a temporary decree.

Interrogatory: A list of questions drawn up to obtain testimony from a party or witness in a lawsuit; a series of questions used in the examination of a witness or party to the suit. Answers to an interrogatory are reduced to writing.

Intestate: Having died without leaving a will.

Intestate succession: Distribution of an estate in accordance with the laws of succession of the state.

Introductory paragraph: The first paragraph, unnumbered, of some court documents. Its purpose is to explain or introduce the subject of the document.

Inventory: An itemized list of assets or property; in probate, a list of all assets of an estate; in bankruptcy, a list of all assets of debtor.

Inventory and appraisement: A court form that includes a listing of all assets of an estate and, when completed, will show an appraisal of each item, together with the total appraised value of the estate.

Involuntary bankruptcy: Bankruptcy that one is forced into by a certain number of creditors.

Issuance of summons: Summons signed by a court officer or court clerk and ready for service on the defendant.

Issue: (*Noun*) Blood descendants of a common ancestor as against adopted children; outcome; a material point in a pleading; a fact; (*verb*) to emit; to send forth; to send out.

Joint tenants: Two or more persons having equal interest in property.

Jointly and severally: Separately or all together, as one or more of the parties to a matter.

Judgment: Official decision of the court.

Judgment by default: A judgment given as a result of the nonappearance of the defendant.

Jurisdiction: The authority of the court to act on or hear a particular legal matter.

Juror: A member of a jury.

Jury: A certain number of persons selected according to law and sworn to hear matters of fact and decide the truth of the evidence presented before them.

Landlord: An owner of leased or rented real property.

Last will and testament: An expression of the disposition one wishes made of property upon death.

Law: That set of rules or methods established to permit coexistence in a society.

Lawyers reference service: (*See* **attorneys reference service**)

Lease: A legal instrument by which the owner of property conveys to another a portion of his interest in and to that property.

Legacy: Gift by will of money or other personal property.

Legal assistant: Nonlawyer who is delegated a higher level of responsibility than that delegated the legal secretary.

Legal back (*or* **legal cover**): A cover, white or any of several colors, into which a legal document may be stapled, and on the back of which the endorsement may be made.

Legal newspapers: Those newspapers of general circulation whose principal service is the publication of legal notices and announcements.

Legal notepads: Yellow lined notepads 8½ by 13 inches in size, also available in 8½- by 11-inch length.

Legal procedure: Those steps necessary under the law to commence, continue, and conclude a particular legal problem.

Legal property description: (*See* real property description)

Legal secretarial trainee: A person, usually skilled in typing and shorthand, who is newly employed in a law office to perform secretarial or stenographic duties, and who is in training to become a legal secretary.

Legal Secretaries Association: A local association affiliated with the National Association of Legal Secretaries (International).

Legal secretary: A secretarial employee of a law office or legal department who, as a result of training and experience, performs tasks necessary to the smooth functioning of the office and the procedural aspects of legal matters.

Legatee: One named in a will to receive personal property; one named in a will to receive a gift of money.

Lessee: Tenant; renter; one who receives a portion of the owner's interest in and to property.

Lessor: Owner; landlord; one who lets a portion of his interest in property to another.

Let: To lease; to demise.

Letters: The legal paper issued to the petitioner by the court, which paper authorizes petitioner to act for another in a probate matter.

Letters of administration: The legal paper issued by the court to the duly appointed administrator of an estate, granting authority to administer decedent's estate according to law.

Letters of administration with will annexed: The legal paper issued by the court to the duly appointed administrator with will annexed, granting authority to administer decedent's estate in accordance with the will.

Letters of conservatorship: The legal paper issued by the court to the duly appointed conservator, granting authority to manage the property in a conservatorship.

Letters of guardianship: The legal paper issued by the court to the duly appointed guardian, granting authority to care for and administer the property and/or person of a minor or incompetent person.

Letters testamentary: The legal paper issued by the court to the duly appointed executor, granting authority to administer the estate of the testator according to the terms of the will.

Levy: To place upon (as taxes).

Lien: A charge or encumbrance placed upon property.

Liquidate: To pay; to settle; to adjust.

Liquidating dividends: Dividends resulting from a holding in a company whose assets have been converted to cash.

Litigant: Party to a lawsuit.

Litigation: A lawsuit; a contest in a court of law.

Living trust: A trust that functions while the trustor is living.

Martindale-Hubbell Law Directory: A multivolume directory listing names of lawyers and law firms and the branches of law in which they specialize, as well as other data.

Matter of record: A case filed with a court clerk and assigned a court (docket) number; a legal document so filed.

Meet and proper: Suitable and appropriate; suitable and correct.

Messenger: One whose chief occupation is delivering papers between the court and the law office and between law offices.

Metes and bounds description: A statement of the exact measurements and boundaries of a parcel of real estate.

Minor: One who is under the age of legal competence.

Minutes: Brief descriptive report of a meeting and action taken by those present at the meeting.

Misdemeanor: Crime less serious than a felony. Punishment may be a fine and/or imprisonment in a city or county jail.

Mnemonics: Method or technique for improving the memory.

Modification: Change; alteration.

Mortgage: A lien against property; a pledge of certain property against a debt.

Motion: A request or application for a rule or order; a court document requesting a rule or order.

Municipal court: A court whose jurisdiction covers city or local matters and small causes.

Napoleonic Code: A unified system of law adopted in France during Napoleon's tenure. Many Louisiana laws are based on this code.

Narration: (*See* complaint)

National Association of Legal Secretaries (International): The professional association organized by legal secretaries. Local associations of NALS may be found throughout the nation.

National Reporter System: A privately published series of law books that includes case reports of federal courts and all state appellate courts.

Negligence: Omitting to do something a reasonable man would do, or doing something a reasonable man would not do.

Nonlawyer: Anyone who is not licensed to practice law.

Notary public: A bonded public officer who administers oaths or certifies to the authenticity of certain documents.

Notice: A legal document notifying opposing party or interested persons of certain action, pending action, information, or knowledge.

Notice of appeal: A legal document filed with the court giving notice that a matter will be appealed.

Notice of appearance: A written notice (court document) given by defendant to plaintiff stating that he is appearing in the action by person or through his attorney.

Notice to creditors: A notice published in a legal newspaper, legally notifying creditors of the time to file their claims.

Notwithstanding: Regardless; however.

Numbered paragraph: Any paragraph that is numbered in a legal document, whether Arabic or Roman numbers are used.

Nunc pro tunc: Now for then; made now but effective on and dated an earlier time.

Nuncupative will: An oral will.

Offset: Deduction; counterclaim.

Omnibus clause: A clause usually added to the prayer of a pleading to permit granting of relief not specifically set forth in the prayer. It may read: *For such further order as the court deems proper.*

One-party court document: A document containing a case title with only one party named, as in: *Estate of JOHN JONES, Deceased.*

Opinion: A statement prepared by an attorney for a client including understanding of the law as it applies to the facts given; the statement by a judge of the decision reached in a particular cause.

Option: In a contract, an offer by owner that another shall have the right to continue the contract for a fixed charge or rental.

Order: A mandate; a command; a rule; a written direction of the court that is not a judgment.

Order to show cause (osc): A court order instructing the one addressed to give reason why he cannot or will not do a named thing.

Orphans' court: (*See* **probate court**)

Osc: (*See* **order to show cause**)

Partnership: A voluntary contract between two or more competent persons to place some or all of their skills and property in a joint project with a proportional sharing of profits and losses.

Party: A person or institution that is part of a lawsuit, whether plaintiff or defendant; a person who is part of a lease or other contract.

Party of the first part: Party named first in an agreement or contract; usually comparable to lessor or seller.

Party of the second part: Party named second in an agreement or contract; usually comparable to lessee or buyer.

Penalty of perjury statement: A statement used in some jurisdictions in lieu of requiring a signature before a notary public or other authorized person. Example: *I declare under penalty of perjury that the foregoing is true and correct.*

Pendente lite: (Latin) Pending litigation, during the suit.

Per annum: (Latin) For a year.

Per stirpes: By representation; distribution of an estate where heirs divide an inheritance that would have gone to one now deceased.

Personal property: Movable property; chattels.

Petition: A court document that makes application to a court for the exercise of certain judicial powers. (*See also* **complaint**)

Petition for probate of will: In a testate matter, the initial court document requesting that the will be admitted to probate.

Petitioner: One who makes or presents a petition.

Plaintiff: Party bringing or beginning the lawsuit.

Plat: (*Noun*) A map showing subdivisions of a piece of land into lots; (*verb*) to map; to plot.

Pleadings: Court documents that either present or answer contentions in a legal matter.

Pledge: Bailment of goods as security for a debt.

Pledgee: The party to whom goods are pledged.

Pledgor: The one making delivery of goods in pledge.

Pocket parts: (*See* pocket supplements)

Pocket supplements: (*also called* pocket parts) Paperbound editions of recent court decisions or recently enacted legislation, assembled for attachment to particular law books; a device for keeping law books current.

Points and authorities: A list of cases that the attorney believes support the case.

Power of attorney: A legal instrument authorizing another to act for one as agent.

Pray: Ask; seek.

Prayer: The closing paragraph of a pleading in which is stated the relief or remedy requested or prayed for.

Preliminary examination: (*See* preliminary hearing)

Preliminary hearing: (*also called* preliminary examination and pretrial) Hearing given the accused person by a judge to determine if evidence warrants holding the person for trial.

Premises: Real property; that which precedes; the foregoing statements or conditions.

Premises considered: All things preceding considered.

Prenuptial agreement: An agreement between two persons prior to their marriage, usually as regards their separate property.

Preponderance of evidence: Greater weight of evidence.

Presents: (PREZ-ents) The present document or instrument.

Pretrial: (*See* preliminary hearing)

Principal: Source of authority; a chief actor or doer.

Private law: That body of law having to do with relationships between or among people, i.e., real estate law, domestic relations, law of contracts.

Privileged information: Secret or confidential information.

Pro tem: Short for *pro tempore*, Latin for *for the time;* temporarily.

Probate: Proving of a will; the determination of a court establishing the validity of a will; a general term to include all matters handled in probate court.

Probate court: (*also called* orphans' court or surrogate's court) A court with jurisdiction over probate of wills and administration and distribution of decedents' estates and estates of minors and incompetent persons.

Procedural law: (*also sometimes called* adjective *or* descriptive law) Law that describes the procedure for preparing a case for court, continuing it through the court, and bringing the case to a conclusion.

Process servers: Individuals whose business it is to serve legal papers upon those named in the legal document.

Professional Legal Secretary (PLS): One who has successfully passed the six-part test of the National Association of Legal Secretaries (International).

Public law: That body of law directly involving the government, i.e., criminal law, maritime law, international law.

Public relations: Creation and maintenance of goodwill between an individual and his publics or between a firm and its publics.

Publication: Printing of a legal notice, as required by law, in a newspaper of general circulation, usually in a paper specializing in the publication of legal notices.

Publics: The many individuals or groups of people with whom the legal secretary comes into contact; individuals or groups of people with whom one associates or works.

Quitclaim deed: A deed of conveyance releasing all possible title or claim to real property.

Ratify: To approve; to confirm.

Real estate: (*See* **real property**)

Real property: Land and usually whatever is erected, affixed, or growing upon it.

Real property description: An exact identification of a parcel of real property; identification of a parcel of real property by boundaries and measurements, using terminal points and angles. (*See* **metes and bounds descriptions**)

Realty: Real property.

Receiver: One appointed to take charge of a bankrupt's property; one appointed by the court to receive and preserve property.

Receptionist: An office employee whose main responsibility is to greet clients, answer the telephone, and handle miscellaneous typing assignments.

Recordation: The act or process of recording a document; specifically, placing a copy of a legal document on file with an official records office.

Redress: Remedy; compensation or satisfaction for a wrong or injury sustained.

Referee in bankruptcy: An officer appointed by the bankruptcy courts to handle administrative matters in a bankruptcy proceeding.

Remise: To give up; to quitclaim.

Reporters: The various series of law books that are primary legal authority. The cases reported in the series have been heard in an appellate court. The Reporter series may be for a state, a geographical section that includes several states, or for the federal court system (National Reporter System).

Res: (Latin) Thing; object.

Residuary beneficiary: One named in a will to receive the residuary (remaining) estate not otherwise disposed of under the will.

Residuary clause: Clause in a will disposing of all property not otherwise disposed of in the will.

Respondent: Person against whom relief is sought or prayed when action is begun by petition.

Restraining order: An order of the court preventing the one named from doing a certain thing.

Return date: (*See* **return day**)

Return day: Day by which a summons must be answered or default action may be taken; day for return of writs of summons or subpoenas.

Ruled-and-numbered paper: Legal paper with double ruled line one and one-quarter inches from the left edge of the paper and a single ruled line three-eighths of an inch from the right edge of the paper. Numbers 1 through 32 (legal size) or 1 through 28 (letter size) are printed just left of the double ruled line. The ruled lines extend the full length of the paper.

Ruled paper: Ruled as **ruled-and-numbered paper** but containing no numbers.

Said: (*adj.*) The (but in a more specific sense).

Scilicet: (ss) (Latin) Namely.

Seize: To own; to possess.

Separate property: The individually owned property of a person or persons as against jointly owned property.

Serve: To make service of a legal paper on the one specified by delivering a copy and showing the original.

Service by mail: Serving of legal papers by placing the document in the United States mail in an evelope addressed to the person to be served.

Service of process: (*See* **serve**)

Signature clause: Statement immediately preceding the signature line of a legal document. Example: *IN WITNESS WHEREOF, I*

have hereunto set my hand and seal this ——————— *day of* ———————,
19———.

Situate: A form of *situated*, meaning *located*, which is frequently used in legal writing immediately preceding a real property description.

Solicitor: Attorney.

Special notice: Notice filed with the court by an attorney on behalf of the client, requesting notice of all action taken in a probate matter.

Specific bequest: Special bequest; definite bequest made in a will.

SS: (*See* scilicet)

Stare decisis: (STAR-rē-dē-SĪ-sis) (Latin) To stand by a decision. Refers to policy of courts to stand by precedent.

State inheritance tax forms: Forms issued by a state tax office, which forms must be completed and submitted in an estate matter so that state inheritance taxes may be computed.

Statute: Law passed by the lawmaking body of the nation or a state.

Statute of frauds: Statute providing that certain contracts must be in writing. Included among such contracts are those having to do with the transfer of title to real property.

Statute of limitations: Statute setting forth the time limits within which legal action must be commenced by plaintiff or petitioner. Time periods vary with the states and with the kind of civil or criminal cause.

Statutory law: That law originating with the legislatures and found in the general laws of each state or of the nation.

Stipulate: To specify; to arrange; to make an agreement.

Stipulation: An item or article in an agreement; a condition; a court document setting forth a condition or agreement.

Stranger: A designation for anyone receiving property under a will who is not a blood relative or surviving spouse of decedent.

Subpena (*or* **subpoena**): A legal form commanding the witness served to appear in court at a specific time. Failure to appear results in penalty.

Subpena (*or* **subpoena**) **duces tecum:** (Latin) Under penalty you shall bring with you; a legal form commanding the one served to appear in court with certain items. Failure to appear results in penalty.

Subscribe: Sign; write.

Substantive law: The great body of law that states the rights and obligations of all persons.

Subtenant: One renting or leasing from the original tenant.

Successor: One who follows or succeeds; one who takes the place of another who has left.

Summons: A legal form that, when served upon the person named therein, notifies the party that an action has been commenced against him in the court shown on the form.

Support: Furnishing of money or means for maintenance.

Surety: One who promises or undertakes to make payment or do some other act if the principal fails to pay or perform.

Surrogate court: (*See* **probate court**)

Surviving spouse: Spouse (husband or wife) remaining alive following the death of the other spouse.

Take nothing: Receive no benefit.

Tangible personal property: Personal property that may be touched, as against intangible personal property.

Tenant: One who holds land of another; one who has temporary use of another's real property.

Tenants in common: Tenants who hold the same land together.

Tenement: Anything that may be held or possessed; a building.

Testamentary trust: A trust created under the terms of a will.

Testate: Having died and left a will.

Testator: (*fem.* **testatrix**) One who by will makes disposition of property at death.

Thenceforth: Following that time or condition.

Thereafter: After that time or condition.

Therefor: For it; for them.

Therefrom: From that.

Thereof: Of that.

Thereon: On it; on that.

Thereto: To that.

Time runs (*or* time has run): Time begins to run when a summons has been served on defendant. Summons specifies the number of days allowed defendant to answer or appear in the matter.

Title of court document: The title of the particular legal document — e.g., petition, complaint, response, answer.

Title page: The first page of a court or client document.

To wit: Namely.

Tort law: That body of law concerned with the rights of individuals to be free from interference by others with regard to their persons, property, or reputations.

Transfer agent: A bank or other institution named by a corporation to handle transfers of ownership of the company's stock.

Trial: A judicial examination, criminal or civil, in accordance with the law.

Trust: An arrangement whereby property is held by one party for the benefit of another.

Trust estate: An estate or portion of an estate that has been placed in trust for the benefit of certain beneficiaries.

Trust provisions: The conditions and provisions set out in a trust agreement.

Trustee: Person or institution appointed to execute or manage a trust.

Trustor: One who creates a trust.

Unanimous: In complete agreement.

Undersigned: One who signed at the end of the document.

Unilateral: One-sided; ex parte.

Unimproved parcel of real estate: A portion of land with no buildings or other improvements.

United States Code: A series of law books containing the federal statutes.

Unlawful detainer: Unlawful or unjustified occupancy or possession of real property by one whose original occupancy was lawful, as, a tenant who refuses to leave the property upon termination of a lease, despite a demand for possession by the landlord.

Unliquidated damages: Unsettled damages; undetermined damages.

Vacate: To set aside; to supersede; to annul.

Venue: Geographical location.

Verdict: Formal decision or finding of a jury.

Verification: A sworn statement confirming the truth of the contents of an attached document.

Verify: To confirm; to prove to be true.

Verily: In truth; in fact.

Versus: (Latin) Against. (Abbreviations: v., vs.)

Voluntary bankruptcy: Bankruptcy proceedings initiated by the debtor.

Warrant: (*Noun*) A writ issued by a competent authority to an officer requiring the arrest of a person; an order authorizing one person to pay a certain sum of money; (*verb*) to assure that title to real property is good; to promise that certain facts are true.

Whatsoever: Whatever; what.

Whereas: When in fact; considering.

Wherefore: For that reason; for these reasons.

Wheresoever: Where it is; place.

Wherewithal: Money; means; resources.

Whomsoever: Whomever.

Whosoever: Whoever.

Will: A legal document by which one may arrange for disposal of property after death.

Without day: With no time fixed for subsequent meeting.

Witness: One who witnesses the signing of a will or other legal paper; one who personally sees a thing or a happening.

Writ of attachment: A legal document used to command a sheriff to attach or hold certain property of a named party.

Z-mark: Mark designed to fill an unused area of a legal document. The first line of the Z begins at the end of the line of type immediately preceding the blank space; the bottom line of the Z extends across the bottom of the blank space; the diagonal line joins the upper and lower lines to form a Z. A ruler is used.

Appendix G

Bibliography

Bate, Marjorie Dunlap, and Mary C. Casey, *Legal Office Procedures.* New York: McGraw-Hill Book Co., 1975.

Black, Henry Campbell, *Black's Law Dictionary*, Revised Fifth Edition by The Publisher's Editorial Staff. St. Paul, Minn.: West Publishing Co., 1979.

Brady, Patricia S., Editor for Legal Secretaries, Incorporated, *Legal Secretary's Handbook (California)*, eleventh edition. Los Angeles: Parker & Son Publications, Inc., 1977.

Clark, James L., and Lyn R. Clark, *HOW 2, A Handbook for Office Workers*, second edition, Belmont, Ca.: Wadsworth Publishing Co., 1979.

Hemphill, Charles F., Jr., and Phyllis Hemphill, *The Dictionary of Practical Law.* Englewood Cliffs, N.J.: Prentice-Hall, Inc., 1979.

Hemphill, P. D., *Business Communications With Writing Improvement Exercises.* Englewood Cliffs, N.J.: Prentice-Hall, Inc., 1976.

Himstreet, William C., and Wayne Murlin Baty, *Business Communications Principles and Methods*, fifth edition. Belmont, Ca.: Wadsworth Publishing Co., 1977.

Krogfoss, Robert B., editor, *Manual for the Legal Secretarial Profession*, second edition. St. Paul, Minn.: West Publishing Company, 1974.

Legal Secretary's Encyclopedic Dictionary. Englewood Cliffs, N.J.: Prentice-Hall, Inc., 1974.

Miller, Besse May, *Legal Secretary's Complete Handbook*, second edition. Englewood Cliffs, N.J.: Prentice-Hall, Inc., 1970.

Morton, Joyce, *Legal Secretarial Procedures.* Englewood Cliffs, N.J.: Prentice-Hall, Inc., 1979.

Sabin, William A., *The Gregg Reference Manual*, fifth edition. New York: McGraw-Hill Book Co., 1977.

Whalen, Doris H., *The Secretary's Handbook*, third edition. New York: Harcourt Brace Jovanovich, Inc., 1978.

Index